이 책을 먼저 학습한 독자들의 한 마디

한국어와 영어의 간극을 메워주는 가장 이상적인 책

토익 900을 넘겼지만 여전히 영자신문이나 영문잡지를 읽기에는 실력이 달림을 절감해 왔다. 영어를 읽다보면 기존 영문법 책으로 해결되지 않는 요상한 부분에 번번이 막혔기 때문이다. 한국어와 영어는 어순이나 구조가 달라 피치 못할 간극이 존재하는데, 이 책은 이러한 간극을 메워주는 데 있어 가장 이상적인 책이다. 기존의 내 문법지식으로는 도저히 이해되지 않았던 부분도 이 책을 보고서는 문맥에 맞추어 독자가 의미를 포착해내야 한다는 것을 알 수 있었다. 또한 영자신문이나 잡지에서 엄선된 문장들은 영어교재로도 아주 훌륭하지만 그 내용 또한 우수하여 일석이조의 효과를 얻을 수 있다. - oppi (온라인서점 Yes24) -

진정한 영어실력 향상을 위한 책

지루한 문법교재나 시험만을 위한 교재가 아닌 진정한 영어실력 향상에 도움이 되는 책이라고 생각합니다. 다양하고 풍부한 표현과 독해지문이 무엇보다 마음에 듭니다. 난이도가 낮은 책은 아니지만, 지루하지 않고 재미있게 공부할 수 있도록 쓰여져 있습니다.
- 김영빈 (온라인서점 인터파크) -

감히 '필독서'라고 말하고 싶은 책

과장광고가 판을 치는 요즘 필독서라는 말을 들으면 거부감부터 생기지만, 나는 이 책을 감히 '필독서'라고 말한다. 비록 내 영어가 아직 부족한 수준이지만, 분명히 말할 수 있는 건 『영어순해』가 말하는 것이 '진짜 영어'라는 점이다. 안타깝게도 그걸 깨닫는 데 10년이 걸렸다. 영문 컨텐츠를 자주 접하는 독자라면 다른 책은 다 제쳐두고 이 책을 먼저 숙독하기 바란다.
- 이영애 (온라인서점 인터파크) -

늘 곁에 두고 싶은 책

대학시절에는 다소 어렵다고 느꼈던 책인데 외국인회사에 근무하면서 살아있는 영어를 어느 정도 접하고 난 후 다시 보니 역시 좋은 책임을 실감합니다. 참으로 영어다운 주옥같은 문장들을 접할 수 있습니다. 돌이켜보면 중·고등학교 시절에 영어를 잘못 배운 탓에 대학시절에는 당연히 이 책이 어렵게 느껴졌던 것 같습니다. 늘 곁에 두고 함께하면 좋은 책이라 생각됩니다.
- 이기형 (온라인서점 인터파크) -

독해를 잘하려면, 무조건 이 책을 봐야 합니다~!

영어독해의 진정한 해법을 제시해주는 책이고, 중·고등학생들이 외국어영역 독해실력을 기르기에는 정말 탁월한 교재입니다. 영어독해의 정석이라고 할 수 있지요.
영어독해를 잘하시려는 분이나 모든 영어를 잘하고 싶으신 분들은 꼭 보세요~!

- 최인섭 (온라인서점 알라딘) -

영어 순해

4th Edition

영어순해 4th Edition

지은이 김영로
펴낸이 임상진
펴낸곳 (주)넥서스

초판   1쇄 발행 1999년 10월 5일
초판 14쇄 발행 2003년 9월 5일

2판   3쇄 발행 2004년 12월 1일
3판 23쇄 발행 2010년 10월 10일

4판   1쇄 발행 2011년 1월 25일
4판 39쇄 발행 2025년 11월 15일

출판신고 1992년 4월 3일 제311-2002-2호
주소 10880 경기도 파주시 지목로 5
전화 (02)330-5500 팩스 (02)330-5555

ISBN 978-89-5797-464-3 13740

저자와 출판사의 허락 없이 내용의 일부를
인용하거나 발췌하는 것을 금합니다.
저자와의 협의에 따라서 인지는 붙이지 않습니다.

가격은 뒤표지에 있습니다.
잘못 만들어진 책은 구입처에서 바꾸어 드립니다.

www.nexusbook.com

4th Edition

영문독해 능력 향상의 핵심은 바로 직독직해

영어 순해

김영로 지음

넥서스

| 머리말 |

조용히 외치고 싶은 말
한국 영어학도들에게 알림

당신은 자신의 거의 전부를 썩히고 있다!

과학자들의 조사에 의하면, 보통 사람은 자신이 갖고 있는 잠재능력 가운데 겨우 1/100 정도를 발휘하다가 이 세상을 떠난다고 합니다. 만일 이것이 사실이라면, 사람은 만물의 영장이라고 자랑스러워할 것이 아니라, 자신을 부끄럽게 여기고, 자기가 썩혀온 엄청난 잠재력을 조금이라도 더 개발하기 위해 노력해야 할 것입니다.

자, 오늘부터 노력해서 당신이 갖고 있는 잠재능력의 3/100 정도만이라도 발휘해야겠다고 생각해 보세요. 그렇게 되면, 분명히 당신 앞에는 새로운 세계가 펼쳐지고, 끝날 것 같아 보이지 않던 영어공부도 1년이면 충분히 끝날 수 있을 것입니다. 문제는 잠재능력을 개발하는 방법입니다. 과연 무엇이 가장 효과적인 방법일까요?

精神一到何事不成! — 그렇습니다. 정신을 한 곳에 기울이면 무엇이 이루어지지 않겠습니까? 위대한 사람들을 위대하게 만든 비결은 이들이 갖고 있던 뛰어난 집중력이었습니다. Einstein은 이러한 집중력을 이용해 잠재능력의 거의 1/3을 발휘했다고 합니다. 그러고 보니, 여기에 또 중요한 의문이 생기는군요. 어떻게 하면 이토록 귀중한 집중력을 기를 수 있을까요?

단순한 생활 — 위대한 사람들의 뛰어난 집중력은 바로 단순한 생활에서 나온 것입니다. 목욕할 때와 면도할 때에 각각 다른 비누를 사용하는 것조차 복잡하다고 해서 Einstein은 한 가지 비누를 사용했다고 합니다. 생활을 단순하게 했을 뿐만 아니라, 머릿속에도 불필요한 잡다한 것들을 집어넣지 않았다고 합니다. 차비를 내고 얼마를 거슬러 받아야 하는지조차 계산을 잘 하지 못했다고 하니 어느 정도인지 짐작할 수 있지 않습니까? 불필요한 곳에 들어가는 에너지를 최소한도로 줄여놓았으니, 자신이 하고 싶은 일에 에너지를 최대한 집중할 수 있었던 것입니다.

여러분, 여러분의 머릿속을 자주 청소해서 늘 깨끗이 비워두세요. 그래야 중요한 것이 있을 때 쉽게 들어갈 수 있습니다. 마음의 청소를 위해서는 Mozart와 같은 고전음악가들의 음악을 자주 듣고 조용히 명상하는 버릇을 들이는 것이 좋습니다.

| 가장 효과적인 영어 학습법 |

1 영어는 말이다!

필자가 말 같지 않아 보이는 이 말을 제목으로 내세운 데에는 두 가지 이유가 있습니다. 첫째, 영어는 말이기 때문에, 상당한 두뇌가 요구되는 수학이나 물리학과는 달리 누구나 효과적인 방법으로 공부하면 영어를 모국어로 하는 사람들 못지않게 영어를 잘할 수 있다는 것을 강조하기 위한 것이고, 둘째로는 영국인이나 미국인들이 사용하지 않는 말을 우리가 영어라는 이름으로 마음대로 만들어 쓸 수는 없다는 점을 또한 강조하기 위한 것입니다. 예를 들어, 텔레비전 프로그램에 외국인이 나올 때 한국 사람들이 흔히 "How do you think of Korea?"라고 물어보는데, 이것은 영어가 아닙니다. 이런 경우에 영어에서는 How를 사용하지 않고, What을 사용하기 때문입니다.

2 어느 것을 먼저 배워야 하는가, 말이냐 글이냐?

이 문제에 대해서는 아직도 의견이 일치하지 않는 것 같지만, 필자는 모국어를 배운 것처럼 외국어를 배우는 것이 가장 이상적인 방법이라고 생각합니다. 왜냐하면 말을 먼저 배우고 나면 그만큼 쉽게 글을 읽고 쓸 수 있지만, 글을 먼저 배우고 나서 말을 배우는 경우에는 말을 자연스럽게 하는 것이 일반적으로 어렵기 때문입니다. 예를 들어, 필자는 대학재학시에 영어로 글은 자유자재로 쓸 수 있었지만, 말하는 것은 그렇지 않았습니다.

3 가장 이상적인 방법 ─ 표현 중심의 학습

우리가 영어를 공부하는 목적이 네 가지 기술, 즉 듣기와 말하기, 읽기와 쓰기를 익히는 데에 있는 경우에 필자는 표현 중심으로 공부하는 것이 가장 효과적인 방법이라고 믿고 있습니다. 어떤 경우에 어떤 단어를 이용해서 말하거나 글로 표현한다는 것을 다 알고 있는 것 ─ 이것이 곧 영어를 완전히 습득한 상태인 것입니다. 여러분이 영어를 처음 배우기 시작했을 때부터 이런 식으로 표현을 익혀왔다고 생각해 보십시오. 중학교 1학년 때부터 시작했다 해도, 3년 뒤에는 거의 웬만한 말은 알아듣고 또 그렇게 말할 수 있었을 것입니다.

표현 중심으로 공부한다는 것은 이런 방법을 말합니다. 어느 날 공부를 하다가 다음과 같은 문장을 만났다고 가정해 봅시다.

Reports have it that the prisoner has escaped.
보도에 의하면 죄수는 탈출했다고 한다.

그런데, 여러분이 '보도에 의하면…라고 한다'라는 말을 표현하는 세 가지 방법을 이미 알고 있다고 가정해 봅시다. 그렇다면 여러분은 위의 예문을 적어도 네 가지로 나타내는 방법을 알고 있는 셈입니다.

> *Reports have it that* the prisoner has escaped.
= *It is reported that* the prisoner has escaped.
= *According to reports,* the prisoner has escaped.
= The prisoner has *reportedly* escaped.

이탤릭체로 되어 있는 부분들이 중요한 표현의 틀이라고 볼 수 있습니다.
그 다음날 또 다음 문장을 만나게 되었다고 가정해 봅시다.

Legend has it that the king was born a beggar.
전설에 의하면, 그 왕은 거지로 태어났다고 한다.

인간에게는 귀납 또는 연역할 수 있는 추리능력이 있으므로, 이런 결론을 내릴 수 있을 것입니다.

'…에 의하면, ~라고 한다' 는 뜻은 '…have[has] it that~.' 으로 나타낼 수 있구나. 그렇다면 다음과 같은 말을 할 수 있겠구나.

1) Rumor has it that~. 소문에 의하면, ~라고 한다.
2) A Korean proverb has it that~. 한국의 속담에 ~라는 말이 있다.
3) A political theory had it in those days that~. 그 당시 한 정치 이론에 의하면, ~라고 했다.

여러분이 지금까지 보아온 모든 영어 문장에서 이런 식으로 중요한 표현들을 익혀왔다고 생각해 보십시오. 그랬다면 이미 오래 전에 영어를 정복하셨겠죠. 제가 공부해온 방법이 바로 이것입니다. 이런 방법 덕분에, 저는 남들보다 훨씬 더 빨리 영어를 정복할 수 있었습니다. 이런 식으로 이 책을 끝까지 공부하세요. 그것으로 영어공부는 충분합니다. 그 다음에는 여러분이 좋아하거나 필요로 하는 책을 마음껏 즐기면서 읽을 수 있을 것입니다.

참고로, 다음에 주어져 있는 우리말을 이용해서 여러분의 구어영어(Spoken English) 표현능력을 시험해 보십시오. 20개 가운데 반 정도 맞았다면 비교적 괜찮다고 볼 수 있습니다.

1 저녁식사가 준비되었다. 가서 아빠를 모시고 오너라.
2 나는 이미 배가 부르다. 너 밥 더 먹을래?
3 가서 탁자 위에 있는 신문을 갖고 오너라.
4 탐은 텔레비전을 너무 많이 보는 것 같다.
5 걱정 말아요. 그 애는 학교에서 공부를 잘 해나가고 있지 않아요?
6 (전화벨이 울릴 때) 제가 받을게요.
7 (전화를 바꾸어 주면서) 이거 너한테 온 거야.
8 (문간에 초인종이 울릴 때) 나가 보아라.
9 바깥까지 바래다 주겠다.

10 학교까지 저를 태워다 주실 수 있습니까?
11 너는 여기서 기다리기만 하면 된다.
12 내가 돌아올 때까지 꼼짝하지 말고 여기에 있어라.
13 네가 대학을 나오도록 내가 도와주겠다.
14 난 네가 그를 나무라는 데 너무 심했다고 생각한다.
15 너 그런 짓을 하고 어떻게 무사할 수 있겠니?
16 도대체 너 내 방에서 무엇을 찾는 거니?
17 도대체 네가 뭐길래, 나보고 이래라 저래라 하니?
18 그는 뭐든지 자기 손에 넣을 수 있는 것은 갖고 싶어한다.
19 그는 점심식사하러 나가고 없다.
20 그 분이 언제 돌아오리라 예상하세요?

같은 내용을 반드시 한 가지로만 나타낼 수 있는 것은 아니지만, 위에 한글로 주어져 있는 내용을 영어를 모국어로 사용하는 사람들이 가장 흔히 쓰는 말로 옮겨 보면 다음과 같습니다.

1 Dinner is ready. Go get Dad.
2 I'm already full. (Do you) Care for more rice?
3 Go get me the paper on the table.
4 Tom seems to watch too much television
   (or I'm afraid Tom watches television too much).
5 Don't worry. He's doing well in school, isn't he?
6 I'll get it.
7 This is for you.
8 Answer the door.
9 I'll see you out.
10 Can you give me a ride to school?
11 All you have to do is just wait here.
12 Stay put here till I come back.
13 I'll help you through college.
14 I'm afraid you went too far in scolding him.
15 How can you get away with such a thing?
16 What the hell are you looking for in my room?
17 Who do you think you are, telling me to do this and that?
18 He wants to keep everything he can get his hands on.
19 He's out to lunch.
20 When do you expect him back?

여러분, 걱정하지 마세요. 앞에서 제가 말씀드린 방법으로 이 책을 끝까지 공부하시면, 이런 정도의 말은 저절로 술술 흘러나올 테니까요. 이 책의 하단에 이탤릭체로 되어 있는 글은 현대 구어영어를 익히는 데 더할 나위 없이 좋은 자료입니다. 이것을 완전히 소화하면 상당한 구어 영어실력을 얻을 수 있으리라고 필자는 확신합니다.

4 문법 중독자가 되지 말아라

우리나라 학생들 중에는 영어 문법 실력이 없어서 영어를 잘할 수 없다고 생각하고 있는 사람들이 많이 있는 것 같은데, 이것은 참으로 불행한 일입니다. 왜냐하면 문법은 이미 단어들이 주어져 있을 때 그것을 일정한 순서로 배열해서 의미가 통하게 만드는 방법을 일러줄 뿐이지, 대부분의 경우에 주어진 내용을 표현하는 데 필요한 단어들 자체를 가르쳐주는 것은 아니기 때문입니다. 예를 들어, "당신의 국적은 어딥니까?"라는 정보를 영어로 나타내는 과정을 생각해 봅시다. 물론 문법에서는 문법적으로 중요한 단어들(이를테면, What, is, your 따위)은 취급하지만, nationality라는 단어는 가르쳐주지 않습니다. 그렇다면 아무리 영어 문법 실력이 뛰어난 사람이라도, 이 단어를 모른다면 What is your nationality?라는 말은 할 수가 없을 것입니다. 반면에 이 표현을 익혀놓은 사람은 필요할 때에는 언제나 그것을 자동적으로 사용할 수 있을 것이며, 또 이 질문에 대해서는 (I'm) Korean.처럼 대답한다는 것도 아마 알고 있을 겁니다. 이런 식으로 영어에서 자주 사용되는 표현을 익혀나가다 보면, 어느 단계에 가서는 거의 모든 의사표현을 영어로 할 수 있는 능력이 생기는 것입니다. 왜냐하면 바로 이것이 사람이 언어를 습득하는 가장 보편적이고 자연스러운 방법이기 때문입니다.

혁명의 필요성 — 지금 미국의 일부 대학에서는 한국 학생들의 TOEFL 성적을 믿지 않으려는 경향이 일어나고 있다고 합니다. 높은 점수와는 달리, 한국 유학생들 가운데 많은 사람들이 교실에서 벙어리 노릇을 하거나 영어로 paper조차 제대로 작성하지 못하기 때문이라고 합니다. 이런 것을 보더라도, 이제 우리의 영어교육은 표현능력을 길러주는 방향으로 하루빨리 전환되어야 합니다. 사실, 표현능력이 생기면 이해능력은 저절로 생길 뿐만 아니라, 이해의 정도도 더욱 깊어지고 이해의 속도 또한 훨씬 더 빨라집니다.

5 영영사전을 사용하라

고등학교에 들어가면서부터 영영사전을 사용하고 될 수 있으면 영한사전을 멀리하는 것이 좋습니다. 왜냐하면, 영한사전은 영어식 표현방식에 친숙해질 수 있는 귀중한 기회를 빼앗아가지만, 영영사전은 그런 기회를 아낌없이 제공해 주기 때문입니다. 그러므로 영영사전을 사용하면 영어다운 영어를 훨씬 더 빨리 사용할 수 있는 능력이 생깁니다.

영어를 공부하는 우리나라 학생들을 위해 필자가 가장 먼저 추천하고 싶은 사전은 Longman Advanced Amarican Dictionary입니다. 용법 학습이라는 관점에서 이것은 지금까지 세상에 나온 모든 영어사전들 중에서 단연코 최고라는 칭찬을 받을 만합니다. 그리고 이 책을 보충해 줄 수 있는 좋은 사전으로 Collins Cobuild Advanced Learner's English Dictionary가 있습니다. 용법 공부를 위해서는 이 두 사전으로 충분하지만, 단어를 기억하고 어휘력을 넓히기 위해서는 어원과 동의어를 아는 것이 중요합니다. 이런 목적을 위해 필자는 Webster's New World College Dictionary를 추천합니다. 아무리 좋은 사전이라고 하더라도 하나만으로는 충분하지 않습니다. 영어를 제대로 하려면 이 세 사전은 반드시 갖추어야 합니다.

6 적어도 영어잡지 하나 정도는 읽어라

현대 사회가 과거 사회와 가장 두드러지게 다른 점은 엄청나게 빠른 발전(또는 변화)의 속도라고 볼 수 있습니다. 요사이 한 해 동안에 쏟아져 나오는 새로운 지식의 분량은 과거 몇 세기에 걸쳐서 나온 지식의 분량보다도 더 많습니다. 그래서 현대를 흔히 '지식 폭발의 시대'(the age of knowledge explosion)라고 부릅니다. 홍수처럼 쏟아져 나오는 정보를 기존 어휘만으로 나타낼 수 없는 경우가 많으므로 새로운 단어나 어구가 만들어져 나오는 것은 당연한 일입니다. 그러므로 시대에 뒤떨어지지 않으려면, 영어로 된 자기 전공분야의 학술지 한 가지와 일반 교양지 한 가지는 반드시 읽어야 합니다.

한국에서 쉽게 구할 수 있는 교양지로 필자는 <Reader's Digest>와 <TIME>, <Newsweek>를 추천하고 싶습니다. 그리고 작문에 관심이 많은 분들은 영자신문 하나를 읽는 것이 좋습니다.

참고로 현대영어에 대한 여러분의 실력이 어느 정도인지 다음 어휘나 어구로 측정해 보세요. 만일 다음 가운데 여러분이 알고 있는 것이 거의 없다면 여러분은 현대영어에 상당히 뒤떨어져 있다고 볼 수 있습니다. 반면에 주어진 말들 가운데 반 이상을 알고 있다면, 여러분의 현대영어 어휘실력은 상당히 우수하다고 볼 수 있습니다.

1 to clone
2 gene splicing
3 savvy [adj.]
4 zero-g environment
5 glut
6 to hype
7 laid-back
8 clout

9 strung out
10 to recycle
11 heady
12 bioclean
13 to bite the bullet
14 to bottom out
15 to level off
16 childproof
17 knee-jerk
18 press kit
19 CPI
20 R and D, R & D

| 해설 |

1 to produce a genetically identical duplicate of an organism by replacing the nucleus of an unfertilized ovum with the nucleus of a body cell from the organism(수정이 안 된 난자의 핵을 어떤 생물체로부터 떼어낸 체세포의 핵과 대치해서 그 생물체와 유전적으로 동일한 생물체를 만들어내다)

2 유전자 결합. 이것은 흔히 genetic engineering(유전공학) 또는 recombinant DNA(핵산 재결합)와 동의어로 사용되고 있다.

3 shrewd or discerning(영리하거나 분별력이 있는)

4 weightlessness(무중력 상태)   < zero-gravity environment>

5 oversupply(공급초과)

6 ① to deceive(속이다, 현혹시키다) ② to rouse or stimulate(자극하다) ③ to promote or publicize in a sensational way(선정적으로 홍보·광고하다)

7 relaxed; easygoing; unhurried(태평스러운, 느긋한)

8 power or influence(힘 또는 영향력)

9 ① addicted to a drug(마약에 중독되어 있는) ② physically debilitated from or as if from long-term drug addiction(장기적인 마약중독이나 마치 장기적으로 중독되어 온 것처럼 신체적으로 쇠약해져 있는)

10 to process (as liquid body waste, glass, or cans) in order to regain material for human use(사람이 이용할 재료를 다시 얻기 위해 액체 신체 배설물, 유리, 깡통 따위를 처리하다)

11 intoxicating; exciting; exhilarating; thrilling(취하게 하는, 신나게 하는, 신나는)

12 free or almost free of harmful or potentially harmful organisms (as bacteria)(박테리아와 같은 해롭거나 잠재적으로 해로운 생물체들이 없거나 거의 없는)   < a bioclean room >

13 to confront a painful situation with fortitude(고통스러운 상황을 꿋꿋하게 감수하다)

14 to decline to a point where demand begins to exceed supply and a rise in prices is imminent(수요가 공급을 초과하기 시작해서 가격이 곧 오를 점으로 하락하다)

15 to stop climbing higher or falling lower, and continue at a fixed height(더 올라가거나 내려가지 않고 고정된 상태가 계속되다)

16 designed to prevent tampering by children(어린이들이 손대지 못하도록 설계해 놓은)   <a childproof door lock>
17 readily predictable(쉽게 예측할 수 있는); automatic(자동의)   <a knee-jerk reaction>
18 a collection of promotional materials for distribution to the press(신문사에 나누어주기 위한 홍보자료들)
19 consumer price index(소비자 물가 지수)
20 research and development(연구와 개발)

이들 단어나 어구는 〈TIME〉에 자주 나오는 것들입니다.

| 이 책의 특징 |

1 비교언어학적인 접근방법

지금까지 우리나라에서 나온 영어독해에 관한 책들은 아무런 체계없이 예문을 나열만 해놓았거나, 분류를 했다고 하더라도 전통 문법의 분류방법을 이용해서 예문들을 분류해 놓은 것들이었습니다. 이 책은 그런 분류방법을 버리고, 영어와 한국어 사이의 비교언어학적인 접근방법으로 우리나라 사람들이 영어를 배우는 데 가장 중요한 면과 가장 어려운 면들을 모아서 체계적으로 다루고 있습니다. 아무튼, 이 책은 우리나라 사람들을 위해서 영어독해를 과학적인 방법으로 다루려고 시도했다는 데 가장 커다란 특징이 있다고 볼 수 있습니다.(목차를 자세히 살펴보면, 이 책의 특징을 쉽게 엿볼 수 있을 것입니다.)

2 논리적인 사고능력

대학생들이 많이 본다는 어떤 책에 영어의 구절을 옮겨놓은 말 중에 다음 문장이 있습니다 :

『규모가 큼에도 불구하고 분침은 길이가 14피트 이상이며, 각각 무게는 정확히 100파운드 이상이 나간다.』

여러분, 잘 생각해보십시오. 도대체 이게 무슨 말입니까? 필자는 이런 것을 궤변이라고 부릅니다. 이런 궤변과 비논리는 건전한 사고능력을 해칠 뿐만 아니라, 공부하는 분들의 귀중한 시간과 정력을 낭비하므로 하루빨리 교육에서 추방되어야 합니다.

필자는 이 책에 사용할 예문을 고를 때 반드시 두 가지 면을 고려했습니다. 첫째, 주어진 예문의 내용이 교육적인 가치가 있는가? 둘째, 그것이 영어를 가르치는 데 얼마나 가치있는 것인가? 물론 이 책에 실린 유머 중에는 교육적으로 좀 지나치다고 생각되는 것들도 더러 있기는 하지만 현대사회의 개방성에 비추어 볼 때 별로 큰 문제가 되지 않을 거라고 생각합니다. 그러나 논리적인 관점에서 볼 때 말이 되지 않는 예문은 이 책에 하나도 들어올 수 없도록 철저히 경계를 했습니다.

어쨌거나 일반적으로 우리나라 교육에서 가장 부족한 점이 논리적 사고에 대한 훈련의 부족이라고 생각해 왔기 때문에, 이 책에서 필자는 논리적인 면에 상당한 노력을 기울였습니다.

3 번역에 대한 새로운 시도

한국 학생들이 영어를 대할 때에 갖고 있는 가장 나쁜 습관 가운데 하나는 주어진 영문을 다 읽은 다음에 거꾸로 거슬러 올라가면서 번역을 해서 의미를 파악하려고 한다는 점입니다. 물론 이것은 영어에서 얘기를 엮어나가는 순서가 한국어와 다르기 때문에 생긴 버릇이겠지만, 이것은 원어민들의 얘기를 들으면서 바로 이해하지 못하게 만들고 있을 뿐만 아니라, 주어진 영문을 올바르게 이해하지 못하게 만드는 데 가장 커다란 요인으로 작용하고 있습니다.

여러분, 상식적으로 생각해 보십시오. 상대방이 어떤 언어를 사용하든지 간에, 그 사람의 말이나 글을 듣거나 읽어나가면서 한 마디 한 마디를 바로 이해해 나가는 것이 가장 빠른 방법이 아니겠습니까? 그래서 이런 버릇을 고치는 데 도움을 주기 위해서 이 책에서는 다소 우리말로의 어색함을 무릅쓰면서까지 영문을 우리말로 옮길 때 될 수 있는 대로 앞에서 뒤로 내려오면서 번역하려고 시도했습니다.

여러분, 만일 이런 버릇을 갖고 있다면 하루빨리 버리세요. 그리하면 영어의 의미가 더 잘 파악될 뿐만 아니라 영어의 어순에 더 빨리 친숙해질 수 있습니다.

4 현대영어와 구어체 영어

이 책에서는 전통적인 영어와 현대영어, 문어체 영어와 구어체 영어를 적절히 배합해서 영어의 모든 면에 친숙해질 수 있도록 만들어 놓았습니다. 일반적인 영어학습에서 이런 면까지 고려해 놓은 것은 아마 이 책이 우리나라에서는 처음 시도한 일일 것입니다.

현대영어의 가장 두드러진 특징 가운데 하나는 구어체 표현들이 문어체 속으로 밀고 들어오는 것이라고 볼 수 있습니다. 예를 들어, 과거에는 lay one's hands on이라고 했는데, 요즈음은 get이 lay라는 동사를 몰아내고 있어서 get one's hands on이라는 말이 많이 사용되고 있습니다.

이런 현상은 문법적인 면이나 구문에서도 나타나고 있습니다. 예를 들어, 과거에는 What I'm trying to do is to prove my innocence.라고 했으나, 현대영어에서는 구어체의 영향으로 What I'm trying to do is prove my innocence.라는 형태가 압도적으로 더 많이 사용되고 있습니다.

5 영양가도 높고 맛도 좋은 음식물

아무리 영양가가 높은 음식이라도 맛이 없다면, 그것은 훌륭한 음식이라고 볼 수 없습니다. 이 책에서는 주식에 대한 입맛도 돋구어주고, 또 주식에서 부족한 2차적인 영양분을 충분히 공급하려는 목적에서 공부하는 분들이 다소 피로를 느낄 만한 곳마다 재미있는 유머를 마련해 놓았습니다.

이들 유머는 청량제 구실을 해줄 뿐만 아니라 현대영어나 구어체 영어에 대한 영양분을 공급해주고, 영·미인들의 해학을 이해하는 데 도움을 주며, 또 여러분의 상상력을 넓혀주어서 앞으로 여러분이 인생을 살아가는 데 적지 않은 도움이 되리라 믿습니다. 아무쪼록 많이 웃으시고, 또 다른 분들에게도 많은 웃음을 전해주십시오.

| 이 책의 활용법 |

1 철저히 소화하라!

우리가 먹는 음식물이 우리에게 보탬이 되려면, 우선 소화가 되어야 합니다. 우리가 하는 공부도 마찬가지입니다. 이 책에 주어진 내용을 철저히 소화해서 그것이 여러분의 영어에 피와 살이 되도록 만들어야 합니다. 그렇지 않으면, 아무리 이 책이 좋다고 하더라도 당신에게는 그것이 별로 소용이 없다는 사실을 명심하십시오.

2 처음에 소화할 자신이 없는 문제는 지나가라!

연습문제 가운데 당신의 현재 실력으로는 도저히 이해할 수 없는 문제는 지나가고, 이 책을 끝까지 공부한 뒤에 그런 문제들만 다시 보십시오. 그래도 이해가 안 가는 문제는 일단 제쳐놓았다가 다음에 다시 한번 보십시오. 이렇게 계속해서 노력하면, 언젠가는 틀림없이 빛이 비치고, 잔잔한 기쁨을 맛볼 수 있을 것입니다.

3 모든 예문을 영작을 위한 자료로 생각하라!

이 책에 나오는 예문뿐만 아니라 앞으로 여러분이 듣는 말이나 읽는 글을 모두 영어로 말하고 글쓰는 능력을 기르기 위한 자료로 생각해 보십시오. 남들이 영어로 하는 말이나 써놓은 글이 새로운 각도에서 들리고 보일 것입니다. 사실, 이것이 가장 좋은 외국어 학습방법입니다. 일년 정도만 이렇게 하시면 거의 모든 의사표현을 영어로 할 수 있을 것입니다.

그리고 이 책 뒷부분에 나오는 번역문도 영작을 위한 자료로 이용할 수 있을 것입니다. 영어 원문을 공부하고나서 일정한 시간이 지난 뒤에 비교적 간단하고 쉬운 것을 골라서 거꾸로 영어로 옮겨보십시오. 일정한 기간 동안 이렇게 해나가면 틀림없이 영어를 보는 안목도 달라지고 영작에도 자신이 생길 것입니다.

감사합니다. 성공을 빕니다!

김영로

TABLE OF CONTENTS

머리말 **5**
가장 효과적인 영어 학습법 **6**
이 책의 특징 **13**
이 책의 활용법 **15**
차례 **16**

1장 영어 구조의 파악

STRUCTURE

1 기본구조 파악
자동사 (기본) **22**
자동사 (수동의 의미) **23** | EXERCISE 1 **24**
자동사의 타동사화 **26** | EXERCISE 2 **27**
자동사＋보어 (기본) **29**
자동사＋전치사구 (기본표현의 확산) **30** | EXERCISE 3 **31**
자동사＋보어 (의미) **34** | EXERCISE 4 **35**
보어의 형태 (영어의 구조적 특징) **37** | EXERCISE 5 **38**
보어와 영어식 사고 **40** | EXERCISE 6 **41**
상태와 동작 (자동-타동) **44** | EXERCISE 7 **48**
뼈대와 수식 **52** | EXERCISE 8 **55**
문장 구성요소의 이동 **59** | EXERCISE 9 **61**

2 정보의 결합
논리전개순서: 영어를 거꾸로 이해하려고 하지 말라 **63** | EXERCISE 10 **64**
정보결합장치: 동격 **71** | EXERCISE 11 **72**
정보결합장치: 부연설명 **74** | EXERCISE 12 **75**
정보결합장치: 관계사 **78** | EXERCISE 13 **79**
관계사절 → 형용사구 **83** | EXERCISE 14 **84**
정보결합장치: 분사구 **86** | EXERCISE 15 **87**

3 구조의 발전
접속전치사 - 절에서 구로 **90**
접속전치사 - 논리적인 관련 (구조와 정보) **91** | EXERCISE 16 **92**
That-clause의 진화 **95** | EXERCISE 17 **96**
접속전치사 with **99** | EXERCISE 18 **100**
접속전치사 at, on, in **105** | EXERCISE 19 **106**
문장부사 **110** | EXERCISE 20 **111**

2장 문맥파악을 위한 기초작업

STYLE

1 주어 전환
무생물 주어 **114** | EXERCISE 21 **115**

2 품사 전환
동사 → 명사 → 형용사 **117** | EXERCISE 22 **118**

3 반복 피하기
대명사로 바꾸어 쓰기 **122** | EXERCISE 23 **123**
명사 대리어(구) **126** | EXERCISE 24 **127**
대동사와 그밖의 대리어(구) **131** | EXERCISE 25 **132**
같은 뜻의 다른 말로 바꾸어 쓰기 **134** | EXERCISE 26 **135**
문체 바꾸어 쓰기 **138** | EXERCISE 27 **139**

3장 문맥의 파악

CONTEXT

1 글의 뼈대
Thesis Sentence **144**
Topic Sentence **145** | EXERCISE 28 **148**
Key Words **152** | EXERCISE 29 **153**

2 추려 읽기
뼈대와 예시 **159** | EXERCISE 30 **161**

3 논리 읽기
논리적인 관계를 보여주는 장치 **163** | EXERCISE 31 **167**

4 문맥과 의미
문맥이란 무엇인가? **179**
의미를 문맥 속에서 찾아야 하는 근본적인 이유 **179**
진정한 문맥의 파악이 의미하는 것 **180**
상상력의 필요성 **183** | EXERCISE 32 **184**

4장 영어식 사고방식

ENGLISH WAY OF THINKING

1 주의해야 할 전치사
전치사와 이동식 사고 **192**
전치사와 생략 **193** | EXERCISE 33 **194**

2 한국어와 다른 어순
주의해야 할 수동표현 **200** | EXERCISE 34 **201**

3 경제적인 동사
'비교' 타동사 **205** | EXERCISE 35 **206**

4 부정의 논리
간접부정 (완곡부정) **209**
부정+부정 **210**
한국어와 다른 부정의 논리 **211** | EXERCISE 36 **212**

5 한국어와 다른 수식
영어는 형용사를 좋아한다 **216**
수식어와 피수식어 사이의 관계 **217** | EXERCISE 37 **219**
하이픈-형용사 **222** | EXERCISE 38 **224**

5장 표현의 미학

EXPRESSION

1 표현의 범위
의미의 발전 **228** | EXERCISE 39 **229**

2 핵표현의 발견
표현의 색채화 **231** | EXERCISE 40 **233**

3 말의 유희
Pun **242** | EXERCISE 41 **243**

APPENDIX 1　　　　　　　　　　　　　모범 시험 문제

주제의 파악 **248**
논리적인 관계의 파악 **261**

APPENDIX 2　　　　　　　　　　　　　READING SELECTIONS

01 Lost and Found **290**
02 What Makes Tycoons Tick? **292**
03 "They Hassle People at Whim" **295**
04 "The Pole of Cold and Cruelty" **297**
05 The Man in the Water **301**
06 Fall Leads Man 'Inward' **304**
07 "Dig Into the World" **308**
08 Unforgettable Albert Einstein **312**
09 Jean-Paul Sartre (1905-1980) **318**
10 Bacon and the Experimental Method **321**

별책부록　　EXERCISE 뜻풀이
　　　　　　　여담 뜻풀이

〈일러두기〉 **부호 설명**

A: B	B는 A와 같은 뜻의 표현이다.
A = B	B는 A와 같은 뜻의 표현으로서, A 대신 문장에서 사용할 수 있다.
문맥 A = B	A와 B는 사전적으로는 같은 뜻이 아니지만, 문맥상 같은 의미로 쓰인 것으로서, 그 문장 안에서 A 대신 B를 사용할 수 있다.
A < B	B는 A의 기본이 되는 표현이다. 즉 A는 B에서 파생된 표현이다.

What Is Life?

Life is a challenge	—	meet it
Life is a song	—	sing it
Life is a gift	—	accept it
Life is an opportunity	—	take it
Life is an adventure	—	dare it
Life is a journey	—	complete it
Life is a sorrow	—	overcome it
Life is a promise	—	fulfill it
Life is a tragedy	—	face it
Life is a beauty	—	praise it
Life is a duty	—	perform it
Life is a struggle	—	fight it
Life is a game	—	play it
Life is a goal	—	achieve it
Life is a mystery	—	unfold it
Life is a puzzle	—	solve it

영어 구조의 파악
1 STRUCTURE

1 기본구조 파악

2 정보의 결합

3 구조의 발전

| 기본구조 파악 | **자동사 (기본)** |

자동사에는 주어진 동작을 받는 목적어가 없다. 다음 예문들은 영어의 자동사가 어떤 것인지를 잘 보여준다. 특히 우리말과 다른 점에 주목하라.

1 This knife **cuts** well.

2 There's something the matter with this pen. It won't **write**.

3 These shoes **wear** well; they will **last** for at least two years.

4 a. This play **reads** better than it **acts**.
　　b. The script reads well but **plays badly**.

5 a. Her letters always **read well**.
　　b. His novels always **read interesting**.
　　c. His scientific papers **read like novels**.
　　d. Her letters always **read as if she copied them from books**.

의미
1. 이 칼은 잘 든다.
2. 이 펜은 뭔가 이상이 있다. 써지지 않는다.
3. 이 신발은 질기다. 이것은 적어도 2년은 갈 것이다.
4. 이 희곡은 상연하는 것보다 읽는 것이 더 낫다.
5. a. 그녀의 편지는 언제나 읽기 쉽다.
　b. 그의 소설은 언제나 읽어보면 흥미롭다.
　c. 그의 과학 논문은 읽으면 마치 소설 같다.
　d. 그녀의 편지는 언제나 읽어보면 책에서 베낀 것 같다.

---

*The stores are **doing so badly** this year,*
yesterday I saw a shoplifter sneak up
to a counter and leave something.

| 기본구조 파악 | **자동사 (수동의 의미)** |

영어의 자동사 중에는 우리말로 옮겨보면 수동의 의미를 지닌 것들이 많다.

1. This book **sells** like hot cakes.
2. These clothes don't **wash** easily.
3. This material doesn't **dye** well.
4. The book will not **translate** well.
5. The door **locks** automatically.
6. The box **broke** open when it fell.
   cf. a. They **broke open** the box.
        = They **broke** the box **open**.
      b. They **popped open** bottles of champagne to celebrate.
      c. He went to the refrigerator and **pulled open** the door.
      d. One hand in his pocket, he **eased** the door **open**.

의미
1. 이 책은 불티나게 팔린다.
2. 이 옷은 세탁하기가 쉽지 않다.
3. 이 재료는 염색이 잘 되지 않는다.
4. 그 책은 번역이 잘 되지 않는다.
5. 그 문은 자동으로 잠긴다.
6. 그 상자는 떨어지자 깨져서 열렸다.
   cf. a. 그들은 그 상자를 깨뜨려서 열었다.
      b. 그들은 축하하기 위해 샴페인 병을 터뜨려서 열었다.
      c. 그는 냉장고로 가서 문을 당겨서 열었다.
      d. 한 손은 호주머니에 넣은 채, 그는 천천히 조심해서 문을 열었다.

---

*Sometimes a child **does poorly** because of anxiety over tests.*
Anxiety and trying to will remember
end up completely blocking memory during the exam.

EXERCISE 1

진한 글자 부분을 주목하면서 전체의 뜻을 파악하라.

1
   a. Democracy **reads well**, but it doesn't **act well**.

   b. This sounds **fine in theory**, but I am **not** sure I see it as a **working reality**.

2
   a. He's **doing well** at school.

   b. I'm sure I **did well** on the test.

   c. Most children **do quite well** on remarkably poor diets.

   d. Several types of forget-me-not plants grow best in cool, damp places, but others **do well** in dry soil.

   e. An 11-year-old girl in India gave birth to a son and both were reported **doing well** at their home.

   f. Helen **did well** during her growing years. Yet, in her senior year at college, her letters home began to be irregular. On the phone she sounded preoccupied.

   g. "You mean you stopped drinking just because she asked you to?"
"Yes."
"And you gave up cigarettes for the same reason?"
"That's right."
"And you stopped gambling just for her?"
"I did."
"Then, after all that, why didn't you marry her?"
"Well, I figured that since I had become such a clean-cut, desirable fellow, I could **do better**."

NOTE

1b. 문맥 = This sounds fine in theory, but it may not work in reality.
2c. **poor** = not good < good → well　　remarkably = quite.
2d. places = soil.　do well = grow well
2g. **give up cigarettes** = give up smoking = quit smoking = stop smoking
　　figure (that)~ = think~
　　just because she asked you to = for the same reason = just for her.
　　　Yes = That's right = I did.　do better = marry better

3 a. I think I **fared well** in the examination.

b. The unions will **fare badly** if the government's plan becomes law.

c. In 1983, television advertising should grow by nine percent, after inflation, the industry's forecasters say.
   Waterson predicted that classified advertising in the press, which has not **fared so well** in the past year, will pick up shortly and the entire industry will then really take off.

4 a. This medicine **works** well if you have anything the matter with your breathing.

b. A woman found that her wristwatch wouldn't **work**, so she wrote to the manufacturer. When she got no answer, she sent the company a telegram reading: "I have one of your watches. What time is it?" That **worked** — they sent her a new watch.

5 a. Life gets so complicated at times. Still, things always seem to **work out** in the end.

b. "Don't worry, Tom. I'm trying to **work things out**."

c. "John has yet to receive any acceptances to graduate school."
   "I'm sure **things will work out** for him."

NOTE

3c. **after (adjustment for) inflation** = in real terms 물가 상승율을 제하고, 실질 가치로   **pick up** (힘이 나거나 속도가 빨라지다) = get better; improve (더 좋아지다, 향상되다)   **take off** (the ground) (땅에서 '떠나다' = 이륙하다) 갑자기 두드러지게 성장하다

4a. **have anything the matter with** = have any trouble with = have anyting wrong with

4b. 구문 **reading** (단축절) = that read (관계절)
    write (a letter) **to** ~에게 편지를 쓰다
    문맥 **the manufacturer** = the company = they

5a. **get complicated** (복잡하게 되다, 꼬이다) ≠ **work out** (풀리다)
    문맥 **Life = things** (인간사)

5c. The problem **has yet to** be solved. (긍정 중심의 진술)
    = The problem has **not** been solved yet. (부정 중심의 진술)
    The result **remains to be seen**.
    = The result is **not** known.

기본구조 파악: 자동사의 타동사화

대부분의 영어 동사들은 자동사와 타동사로 모두 사용된다. 즉, 우리가 흔히 자동사로만 알고 있는 동사들이 타동사로 사용되는 경우가 많이 있으므로 주의해야 한다.

1 a. I'll **walk** home. (intransitive)
    b. I'll **walk** you home. (transitive)

2 a. She **got** pregnant.
    b. He **got** her pregnant.

3 a. He **overworked** and became sick.
    b. He **overworked** himself sick.

4 a. She **talked** to him about starting a business.
    b. She **talked** him into starting a business.

5 a. She **argued** with him about the decision.
    b. She **argued** him out of the decision.

의미

1. a. 나는 걸어서 집에 가겠다.
   b. 나는 걸어서 너를 집까지 데려다 주겠다.
      cf. 1) I'll **drive** you home. (너를 집까지 태워다 주겠다.)
           2) I'll **see** you home. (너를 집까지 바래다 주겠다.)
2. a. 그녀는 임신했다.
   b. 그는 그녀를 임신하게 했다.
3. a. 그는 과로해서 병이 났다.
   b. 그는 자신을 혹사하여 병이 났다.
      cf. He **overworked** his horse sick. (그는 자기 말을 혹사하여 병이 나게 했다.)
4. a. 그녀는 그에게 사업을 시작하는 것에 대해서 얘기했다.
   b. 그녀는 그를 설득해서 사업을 시작하게 했다.
5. a. 그녀는 그와 그 결정에 대해서 논쟁했다.
   b. 그녀는 그를 설득해서 그 결정에서 벗어나게[포기하게] 했다.
      cf. She **argued** him **into** the decision. (그녀는 그를 설득해서 그 결정을 내리게 만들었다.)

EXERCISE 2

진한 글자 부분을 주목하면서 전체의 뜻을 파악하라.

1. a. He **walked** me **to** exhaustion.
   b. He **walked** himself **to** exhaustion.

2. a. He **starved to death**.
   b. He **starved** himself **to death**.

3. a. In yesterday's edition of *The New York Times*, there was a tragicomical piece of news that a very fat woman, whose sole wish was to lose weight, **dieted herself to death**.
   b. The merest titter of a sneeze will get you "God bless you's" by the score, but when you almost **cough yourself to death**, all you get are dirty looks.
   c. "Nathaniel told me I should **wish** him **dead**, so I did. And he died."
      "But that's not possible. You can't **wish** someone **to death**."

4. a. He **walked into** the meal as if he hadn't seen food for days.
   b. Every day I **walk** myself **into** a state of well-being and walk away from every illness. I have **walked** myself **into** my best thoughts.

NOTE

2b. **starve to death** (굶어 죽음으로 가다) → 굶어 죽다
   starve~to death ~를 굶겨 죽게 하다 < put~to death
   freeze to death 얼어 죽다
   freeze~to death ~를 얼어 죽게 하다
3a. **lose weight** (몸무게가 줄다) ≠ gain weight(= put on weight)
3b. 문법 **God bless you** [단수] 누가 재채기할 때 감기 들지 않기를 빈다는 뜻으로 하는 말
   God bless you's [복수]
3c. wish someone to death = wish someone dead
   → Sally was scared **out of her wits**(= witless).
   Tom was stunned **beyond speech**(= speechless).
   = Tom was so stunned he couldn't speak.
4a. walk into a meal (걸어서 음식 속으로 들어가다) → 허겁지겁 음식을 먹기 시작하다 < get into → dig into (+음식), dig in
   문법 meal = food
4b. 문법 walk away from(= walk myself out of) ≠ walk myself into

5 a. You'll **grow into** your brother's suits before long.

   b. She soon **grew into** the job, although she wasn't qualified for it at first.

6 a. Remember that we could **laugh** you **out of** politics.

   b. He had seriously considered suicide, but **reasoned** himself **out of** it.

   c. Never try to **reason** the prejudice **out of** a man. It was not reasoned into him, and cannot be reasoned out.

   d. When she couldn't **talk** him **out of** the hazardous performance, she asked Helen to intervene.

   e. Presumably he meant to say simply that he thought it would be easier to **negotiate** the Cubans **out of** Angola than to **negotiate** the white minority **out of** power in South Africa—but that's not what he said.

7 a. The bright young lad thought he could **talk** his way **out of** anything. Stumped by a tough midyear exam, he wrote this excuse across the cover: "Only *God* knows the answers. Merry Christmas!"

   　He got his paper back, marked: "*God* gets an A. *You* get an F. Happy New Year!"

   b. Never will I understand adult children who live off their parents. Equally puzzling are parents who are willing to allow this situation to occur. My failed marriage did not drive me home to Mama, but it did drive me to better my own life and **work** my way **out of** debt by holding two jobs. I only asked for love and support, which is all any adult child should ask of parents.

NOTE

6d. 문맥 intervene = talk him out of it
6e. Presumably (문장부사) = I presume (that)~.　**mean to** (do) = intend to (do)
　　put~out of power ~을 권력(권좌)에서 물러나게 하다
　　→negotiate~out of power
　　talk~out of power
7a. 구문 marked (단축절) = which was marked (관계절)
　　stump = puzzle; perplex (어쩔 줄 모르게 만들다).　tough: very difficult
　　문맥 paper = exam paper
7b. 문맥 Equally puzzling are parents~ = Nor will I understand parents~
　　live off ~에 의지하여 살다.　make one's way 가다.　find one's way 찾아가다.　shoot one's way 총을 쏘며 가다.　work one's way 일(노력)하며 가다

| 기본구조 파악 | **자동사 + 보어 (기본)** |

보어가 될 수 있는 것은 명사(대명사, 명사구, 명사절 포함)나 형용사(형용사구 포함)다. 보어는 문장의 필수요소지만, 준보어는 추가적인 요소다.

1 a. He was **a millionaire**. [보어] < He was. (×)
　　b. He died **a millionaire**. [준보어] < He died. (○)
　　　 (He died + He was a millionaire)

2 a. He was **broke**. [보어]
　　b. He returned home **broke**. [준보어]

3 a. The day **was** cloudy.
　　b. The day **broke** cloudy. (The day broke + It was cloudy)

4 a. The box **was** open.
　　b. The box **broke** open.

5 a. You don't **look your age**; you look a lot younger.
　　b. You're a big boy now. **Act your age**.

6 a. You **look** tired.
　　b. You **sound** tired.

의미
1. a. 그는 백만장자였다.
   b. 그는 죽을 때 백만장자였다.
2. a. 그는 빈털터리였다.
   b. 그는 집에 돌아왔을 때 빈털터리였다.
3. a. 그날은 흐렸다.
   b. 그날이 샐 때에 날씨는 흐렸다.
4. a. 그 상자는 열려 있었다.
   b. 그 상자는 깨어져서 열렸다.
5. a. 너는 네 나이처럼 보이지 않는다. 훨씬 더 젊어 보인다.
   b. 넌 이제 다 컸다. 네 나이에 맞게 행동해라.
6. a. 너 피곤해 보인다.
   b. 네 목소리를 들으니 피곤한 것 같다.

| 기본구조 파악 | **자동사 + 전치사구 (기본표현의 확산)** |

말에도 생물체의 조직처럼 기본 구조가 있다. 이런 기본적인 구조를 파악하면 비슷하지만 다양한 표현을 만들어낼 수 있다.

기본 He **is like** his father in character.

파생
a. He **looks like** his mother.
b. It **seems like** ages since we went to the theater.
c. Sometimes I **feel like** an orphan.
d. You **sound like** a different person on the phone.
e. This meat **tastes like** mutton.
f. This flower **smells like** roses.
g. His scientific papers **read like** novels.

의미 그는 성격이 자기 아버지와 비슷하다.
a. 그는 외모가 자기 어머니와 비슷하다.
b. 우리가 극장에 갔다 온 지 아주 오래된 것 같다.
c. 때때로 나는 고아와 같다는 느낌이 든다.
d. 전화로 네 목소리를 들으면 마치 네가 다른 사람 같다.
e. 이 고기는 맛이 양고기와 비슷하다.
f. 이 꽃은 냄새가 장미와 비슷하다.
g. 그의 과학 논문은 읽어보면 마치 소설 같다.

One morning when it looked as if my husband was going to miss his commuter train, the family dashed around madly laying out his clothes, assembling his briefcase, helping in every manner possible. Billy, age two, wanted to do his bit, but kept getting in the way. Finally he discovered the one remaining job — and promptly sat down and devoured Daddy's breakfast.

EXERCISE 3

진한 글자 부분을 주목하면서 전체의 뜻을 파악하라.

1. Alain Delon said, he **stayed youthful** by "making love a lot and drinking a lot of water."

2. An honest politician is one who, when he **is bought, stays bought**.

3. As adults, some of us **held on to the belief** that anger is an unattractive and unacceptable emotion; we **stayed convinced** that if we expressed it, people would punish us with disapproval.

4. We need good humor to **stay sane** in this **crazy** world.

5. The realistic words of Springsteen's best songs are about the hurt of unemployed workers; about reconciliation with estranged parents through understanding *their* lives; about **staying hopeful** even though experience falls short of the American dream.

6. I was in misery about my physical shortcomings. I was too skinny. My hair wouldn't **stay combed**. I couldn't dance. If a girl smiled at me I blushed and turned away, pretending not to notice her, powerless to smile back, incapable of speaking a single word.

NOTE
1. **make love a lot** = make a lot of love. **drink a lot of water** = drink water a lot
3. **stayed convinced** = kept holding on to the belief (=kept believing) < believe that~ = be convinced that~
   문맥 held on to the belief = were convinced
4. 문맥 sane ≠ crazy (= insane)
5. 문맥 experience (= the reality) ≠ the American dream (= the ideal)
6. **in misery** = miserable
   문맥 couldn't (= wasn't able to) → powerless (= not able) → incapable of speaking (= powerless to speak)

7
a. He says he**'s off** cocaine.

b. Many experts in the field of addiction say it is more difficult to **get off** cigarettes, if you are truly hooked, than off cocaine.

c. If you **stay off** cocaine for a year, you probably won't relapse.

8
a. Many new businesses find it difficult to make a profit at all in their first year. They do well just to **break even** and stay in business.

b. The very best such consultants could make well over $100,000 a year. But most that he knows are scrambling—and ruining their family lives—just to **stay even**.

c. I was born around 4 a.m. on Oct 22, 1921, in Hartford City, Ind. When my father asked the doctor, "How much do I owe you?" the doctor replied, "I drove over here on a flat; if you'll change my tire, we'll **call it even**."

9
a. What can a person who **tests positive** and feels well do to help himself stay well, even though he has been exposed to the AIDS virus? There can be no guarantees, but it makes sense to try to stay healthy.

b. The water **was pure**.
  → The water **tested pure**.
  = The water proved pure on a test.
  = A test showed that the water was pure.

c. He **tested high** in comprehension.

d. The car **tested better** on the highway than in city traffic.

NOTE

7b. 문맥 hooked = addicted
7c. 문맥 relapse (다시 떨어지다 → 이전의 나쁜 습관으로 다시 돌아가다) = get back on it
8a. the **break-even** point = the point at which income equals expenditure
8b. **well** 상당히, 많이. **scramble** = struggle (고전하다)
    break even 이윤도 적자도 없는 상태에 도달하다
    stay even 이윤도 적자도 없는 상태에 머무르다
8c. **on a flat** 공기가 빠진 타이어로
    be even 빚진 것이 없다.   **call even** 빚진 것이 없다고 말하다
9a. **test positive** 테스트 결과 양성으로 판명되다.   **be exposed to** ~에 노출되다.   **make sense** (= be sensible) 합당하다
    문맥 **stay well = stay healthy** (건강을 유지하다)

e. It is currently estimated that only one of three people who **test positive** for the AIDS virus will come down with the disease.

f. A study found that preschool children whose parents read to them in an active, involving way **tested six to eight months ahead of other children.**

10 a. The eclipse day **was cloudy**.

b. The eclipse day **dawned cloudy**, but a slow clearing set in and astronomers took hope.

11 a. His career **read like** an advertisement for the rewards of hard work.

b. My life has not always **read as if** you might like to trade places with me instantly.

---

*If you want to **be enthusiastic**,*
act enthusiastic.

NOTE

9e. **It is currently estimated that~** 현재 추산에 의하면 = Current estimates have it that~ = According to current estimates, ~
be down with ~에 걸려 있다(상태 표현)　**come down with** ~에 걸리다(동작 표현)
　the disease = AIDS
9f. **in an active, involving way** 적극적으로 참여하는 방식으로
10b. a slow clearing <u>set in</u> = it <u>began</u> to clear up slowly
11b. **trade places with** = change places with ~와 자리를 바꾸다

기본구조 파악: 자동사 + 보어 (의미)

이 구문의 동사의 기본은 be 또는 become이라고 볼 수 있다. 그리고 일부 '상태'를 나타내는 제2형식 동사는 be보다는 remain에 더 가깝다(후자에는 '계속'의 의미가 들어 있음에 주의하라).

1 a. His warning **went** unheeded. (= remained)
   b. Because of the oil crisis many banks **went** broke. (= became)

2 a. Inflation still **runs** high in that country. (= remains)
   b. The well has **run** dry. (= become)

3 One day suddenly he **fell** gravely ill. (= became)

4 At these words her heart **grew** light. (= became)

5 Their patience has **worn** thin. (= become)

6 This contract still **holds** good. (= is or remains)

7 He **stands** fast in his resolve. (= is or remains)

의미
1. a. 그의 경고에 사람들은 계속해서 주의를 기울이지 않았다.
     (= People went on not heeding his warning.)
   cf. His warning **was** unheeded. (= People didn't heed his warning.)
   b. 석유위기 때문에 많은 은행들이 파산했다.
2. a. 그 나라에서는 인플레이션이 여전히 높다. b. 그 우물은 말라버렸다.
3. 어느 날 갑자기 그는 위중한 병에 걸리게 되었다.
4. 이런 말을 듣자 그녀의 마음은 가벼워졌다.
5. 그들의 인내심은 닳아서 얇아졌다. (= 그들은 더 이상 참을 수 없는 지경에 이르렀다.)
6. 이 계약은 아직도 계속해서 유효하다.
7. 그는 계속해서 결심이 확고하다.

NOTE
1a. **heed**: to pay attention to ~에 주의를 기울이다
1b. **broke**: bankrupt 파산한
7. **fast** = firm 확고한

EXERCISE 4

진한 글자 부분을 주목하면서 전체의 뜻을 파악하라.

1.
   a. Love of church **runs strong** in the family.
   b. Male chauvinism still **runs rampant** in many German businesses.
   c. We were **running late**, and tempers were **running high**.

2.
   a. We are **running low** on coffee and sugar.
   b. Today's world is **running low** on serenity but high on strains and stresses.

3.
   a. You **are average**.
   b. You **are about average**.
   c. If at first you don't succeed, you're **running about average**.

4.
   a. His words **ring false** to me.
   b. This argument **has a familiar ring**(= rings familiar).
   c. Though the scenario **has the ring of fiction**, it could become fact.

5.
   a. They **held firm** about their demands.
   b. She is **holding firm** in her conviction that this is a national tragedy.

6.
   a. My spine **went icy** at the horrible sight.
   b. The thought seems as absurd as worrying that an ocean may **go dry**.
   c. Darn it! What's the matter with this TV? Every time there's something I particularly want to see, the picture **goes foggy**.

NOTE

1. **rampant** = widespread; very common
4c. **have the ring of fiction** = ring fictitious = ring unreal ≠ ring true
    become fact = become a reality = come true
5b. **be holding firm in one's conviction that~** = be firmly convinced that~ (= firmly believe that~)

7
a. As a boy he often **went hungry**.
b. They often **went** for months **without meat**.
c. Strikes are a constant menace because workers may **go** months **without pay**.
d. He took what blue-collar job he could find, often **going** for long stretches **without work**.

8
a. Koreans **go barefoot** indoors.
b. Nature's way in fashion is exactly opposite to mankind's. In summer she wears heaviest clothing, but in winter she **goes naked**.
c. He told me you hadn't worn a bra in twenty years. He said most of the women in Clanton **go braless**.

We are always getting ready to live but never living.
- Ralph Waldo Emerson

Man is born to live and not to prepare to live.
- Boris Pasternak

Life is what happens while you're making other plans.
- John Lennon

NOTE
8b. go naked = wear no clothing
8c. go braless = don't wear bras

| 기본구조 파악 | **보어의 형태 (영어의 구조적 특징)** |

다음 예문들에는 영어의 기본적인 구조의 특징이 잘 나타나 있다. 보어 또는 준보어 노릇을 하는 말들의 형태에 주목하라.

1
a. Though friends for many years, they finally ended up **enemies**.
b. We drank to feel heavenly and ended up **feeling like hell**.
c. We drank to feel exhilaration and ended up **depressed**.
d. We drank to get calmed down and ended up **with the shakes**.
   (= shaken)
e. You'll end up **in hospital** if you drive so fast.
   (= hospitalized)

2
a. He died **a millionaire**.
b. He died **penniless and friendless**.
c. He died **believing that he had found the Far East**.
d. He died **without knowing that he had made a great discovery**.
   (He died + He didn't know that he had made a great discovery)

의미
1. a. 비록 여러 해 동안 친구였으나, 그들은 마침내 끝에 가서는 적이 되었다.
   b. 우리는 천국과 같은 기분을 맛보려고 술을 마셨으나 끝에 가서는 지옥과 같은 기분이었다.
   c. 우리는 즐겁기 위해 술을 마셨으나 끝에 가서는 침울해졌다.
   d. 우리는 진정하려고 술을 마셨으나 끝에 가서는 동요되었다.
   e. 그렇게 빨리 차를 몰면 병원신세를 지게 될 것이다.

2. a. 그는 죽을 때 백만장자였다.
   b. 그는 죽을 때 돈도 없고 친구도 없었다.
   c. 그는 죽을 때 자기가 극동을 발견했다고 믿었다.
   d. 그는 죽을 때 자기가 위대한 발견을 했다는 사실을 몰랐다.

NOTE
1b. 문맥 feel heavenly (= feel like heaven) ≠ feel like hell (= feel hellish)
1c. 문맥 exhilaration ≠ depression
1d. 문맥 calmed down ≠ with the shakes (= shaken)

EXERCISE 5

진한 글자 부분을 주목하면서 전체의 뜻을 파악하라.

1. a. During these times of economic hardship, we can barely **keep** our family **clothed** and **fed**.

   b. It's all we can do to **keep** our family **in food** and **clothing**; vacations are out of the question.
   = We can barely **keep** our family **fed** and **clothed**; we can't take a vacation.

2. a. **Keeping** Steve **in sandwitches** is going to be a full-time occupation tonight!

   b. "Did you make any money on your tobacco crop this year?"
   "Yes, I made just enough to **keep** Josh **in cigarettes** for another year."

3. a. Before **digging into** their food, they bowed their heads in prayer.

   b. The food arrived and as I **dug in**, I noticed that Nana wasn't eating.

NOTE

1b. get into food (음식 속으로 들어가다) → 먹다 (동작)
be in food (음식 속에 있다) → 먹고 있다 (상태)
get into one's clothes (자기 옷 속으로 들어가다) → 옷을 입다 (동작)
be in one's clothes (자기 옷 속에 있다) → 옷을 입고 있다 (상태)
get out of one's clothes (자기 옷 밖으로 나오다) → 옷을 벗다 (동작)
be out of one's clothes (옷 밖으로 나와 있다) → 옷을 벗고 있다 (상태)

2b. 여기 전치사 on은 '수단' 관계를 보여준다. make money의 수단이 your tobacco crop이다.
→ return on investment(ROI) "투자라는 수단으로 되돌아 오는 것" (투자 수익).
Profits have picked up this year but the return on capital remains tiny(수익이 금년에 향상되었으나 자본 수익은 아주 적다).

3a. bow one's head / in prayer (머리 숙여 기도하다) < bow one's head <u>and</u> pray
(첫째 동작)   (둘째 동작)
drop to one's knees in prayer 무릎 꿇고 기도하다
bow one's head in respect 머리 숙여 경의를 표하다

4. undress = take off all one's clothes. divest oneself of = take off. naked = without anything on (아무것도 입은 것이 없는)

4 In order to swim one **takes off** all one's clothes—in order to aspire to the truth one must **undress** in a far more inward sense, **divest oneself of** all one's inward clothes, of thoughts, conceptions, selfishness, etc., before one is sufficiently **naked**.
– Sören Kierkegaard

5 There are persons who shape their lives by the fear of death, and persons who shape their lives by the joy of life. The former **live dying**; the latter **die living**. Whenever I die, I intend to die living.
– Horace Kallen

6 If I stop one heart from breaking,
I shall not **live in vain;**
If I can ease one life the aching,
Or cool one pain,
Or help one fainting robin
Unto his nest again,
I shall not **live in vain.**
– Emily Dickenson

One of my favorite teachers at university was known for his droll sense of humor. Explaining his ground rules to one first-year class, he said,
  "Now I know my lectures can often be dry and boring, so I don't mind if you look at your watches during class. I do, however, object to your pounding them on the desk to make sure they're still running!"

---

1. 기본구조 파악

기본구조 파악 — 보어와 영어식 사고

보어의 임무는 명사나 대명사를 수식하는 것이므로 (보어는 동사를 도와서 주어진 문장의 의미를 완성할 뿐이지, 결코 동사를 수식하는 것이 아니다) 부사는 보어가 될 수 없다. 영어에는 다음과 같은 구조가 매우 발달되어 있는데, 다음 예문들에서 보어의 수식을 받는 말이 무엇인지 생각해 보라.

1　a. I have it **safe** at home.
　　　(I have it at home + It is **safe**)
　　b. Set your goals **high**.

2　a. You are **wrong**.
　　b. You got me **wrong**.

3　a. I can't **get** this door **open**. 〔동작 표현〕
　　b. Can't I **have** the door **open**? 〔상태 표현〕

4　a. I **have** everything **ready**.
　　b. I think I **have** this poem **memorized**.

5　a. I **have** his name **on the tip of my tongue**.
　　b. You'll **have** the car **in the ditch** if you are not careful.

의미
1. a. 그것은 안전하게 집에 보관되어 있다.
　b. 너의 목표를 높게 세워라.
2. a. 네 생각은 잘못되어 있다.
　b. 너는 내 말을 잘못 이해했다.
3. a. 난 이 문을 열 수가 없다.
　　(= I can't open this door.)
　b. 문을 열어둘 수 없을까?
4. a. 나에게는 모든 것이 준비되어 있다.
　b. 나는 이 시를 외웠다고 생각한다.
　　(= I think I have memorized this poem.)
5. a. 그의 이름이 혀끝에서 맴돈다(떠오를락 말락한다).
　b. 주의하지 않으면 차를 도랑에 처박겠다.

주의 이런 식의 표현은 특히 구어체 영어에서 많이 사용되므로 잘 익혀 두어야 한다.

EXERCISE 6

진한 글자 부분을 주목하면서 전체의 뜻을 파악하라.

1. a. I **have** a term paper **due** next week.
    (= I have to hand in a term paper next week.)

   b. I'm **having** some friends **over** for drinks this evening.
    (= Some friends are coming over (to my place) for drinks this evening.)

2. a. A Saturday-night toothache **had** me **at** the dentist early Monday morning.
    (= On account of a Saturday-night toothache I was at the dentist~)

   b. Although 33 states and the District of Columbia **have** seat belt laws **in effect**, many people still don't bother to buckle up.

   c. With a trade balance in the black and inflation under control, we now **have** conditions **in place** for sustained stability for our currency.

3. a. He insisted on **having** the agreement **down** in black and white.
    (= He insisted that we **write down** the agreement.)

   b. Once you've defined your goal, **write** it **down**. High achievers trace their accomplishments to the time they **committed** their goals **to paper**.

4. a. The pram **turned over**.

   b. You'll **have** that pram **over** if you don't take more care.

5. a. The ball **crashed through** the window.

   b. Look out where you kick that ball, or you'll **have** it **through** the window.

NOTE

1a. due (제출, 지불 등의) 기한이 된 → overdue (기한이 지난)

2b. be in effect 시행하고 있다
   문맥 buckle up = buckle one's seatbelt

2c. in the black (흑자를 내고 있는) ≠ in the red
   구문 With a trade balance in the black (구) = As we have our trade balance in the black (절)

3b. committed~to paper = wrote~down 문맥 accomplishments = achievements

6 a. He will **be back** soon.

  b. When do you **expect** him **back**?

7 a. You **are on** my team.

  b. I **want** you **on** my team.

8 a. He **is in** this house.

  b. I don't **want** him **in** this house.

9 a. I felt he was trying to control me, and I wanted to **break free**.

  b. If Jessica ever ends up getting into any trouble, she always manages to **wriggle free** unscathed.

10 a. The horse **is loose**.

  b. The animals **broke loose** and ran away.

  c. This pole is **coming loose** and will soon fall over.

  d. The chain **went loose** in his hands.

  e. My hair **works loose** when I run.

11 a. I simply couldn't **shake myself loose** from the temptation.

  b. All night the men on the rig had been pushing the drilling pipe deeper into the soil below Louisiana's Lake Peigneur. At about 1,240 feet the pipe, a 39-ton string of steel, got stuck and they couldn't **work** it **loose**.

  c. Oxidation is, of course, vital to life itself; our bodies add oxygen to food in a kind of flameless combustion to extract vital energy. But oxidation is not always beneficial, according to the latest scientific theory. When oxygen combines with an atom, it sometimes **jars loose** an electron. An electron-poor atom, known as a "free radical," automatically seeks another electron, and starts a chain reaction that can lead to cell damage.

NOTE

9a. 문맥 **break free** = break out of his control < get out of his control
9b. 문맥 **wriggle free** = wriggle out of it < get out of it
11c. 손해 Our bodies <u>add</u> oxygen to food / in a kind of flameless <u>combustion</u> / to <u>extract</u> vital energy (우리의 신체는 산소를 음식물에 가해서 말하자면 불꽃 없이 연소시켜서 필요한 에너지를 얻는다)

12
a. They **caught** him **red-handed**.

b. She was **caught shoplifting** in a department store.
(= They **caught** her **shoplifting** in a department store.)

c. I **saw** Tom **in the act of** snatching a gun.

d. As it turned out, I had **caught** Jordan **in training**.

e. I've **caught** her **in several lies** and lost respect for her.

f. Children are unpredictable. You never know **what inconsistency** they're going to **catch** you **in** next.

g. "Hey, I'm naked, Marcie!"
"What is that supposed to mean?"
"You **caught** me **in the shower**!"
"Shall I call you back?"

h. My husband, who is in his 40s, has a new hobby. He makes obscene phone calls. He dials numbers at random, and he has an "affair" with her on the phone. I have **caught** him **at it** several times. He says he isn't really doing anything wrong, it's just a harmless pastime. Then he begs me to forgive him.

13
a. We **have** demand **growing** by about 12% a year and supply **growing** by about 2% a year, which yields 10% inflation.

b. Heart disease, the nation's No.1 health problem, is down 20% since 1967. According to the American Heart Association, strokes have dropped by one-third. Life expectancy has risen to a record 73 years. The cholesterol controversy **has** Americans **eating** 6 1bs. less beef than a decade ago. They also drink 4% less alcohol. Though smoking figures among the young, especially females, are rising slightly, 1.8 million older smokers have given up cigarettes. In a country so lately thought to be dedicated to pleasure and self-expression that will be no small achievement.

NOTE **13b.** 수식어의 첨가에 따른 부정관사의 첨가
Bush → **an angry** Bush (화가난 Bush)
73 years → **a record** 73 years (기록적인 73세)
The cholesterol controversy **has** Americans **eating** 6 1bs. less beef~
= Because of the cholesterol controversy Americans eat 6 1bs. less beef~

be down = drop ≠ rise. by one-third = 33%

| 기본구조 파악 | **상태와 동작 (자동 – 타동)** |

영어의 동사 표현은 '상태'와 '동작'으로 나누어지는데, 동작 표현은 '자동사'와 '타동사'로 나누어진다. 그런데 상태에는 자체 안에 '계속'의 의미가 들어 있으므로 상태 동사는 진행형 시제를 사용하지 않는다.

1 a. He **has** a lot of money. (= possesses) [상태]
 b. He **is having** breakfast. (= is eating) [동작]

2 a. The bank **is** open.
 b. The bank **is opening** now.

3 a. She **is** polite.
 b. She **is being** polite. (= She is behaving politely now.)

4 a. He **is** dead.
 b. He **is dying**.

[의미]
1. a. 그는 돈이 많다.
   b. 그는 아침을 먹고 있다.
2. a. 은행이 개점되어 있다.
   b. 은행이 개점을 하고 있다.
3. a. 그녀는 예의바르다.
   b. 그녀는 예의를 차리고 있다.
4. a. 그는 죽었다.
   b. 그는 죽어가고 있다.

5 a. be married (to) ~와 결혼해서 살고 있다
 b. get married (to) ~와 결혼하다

6 1) a. be up 일어나 있다 [상태]
   b. get up 일어나다 [자동사]
   c. get someone up 일어나게 하다 [타동사]

2) a. be pregnant 임신 중이다
   b. get pregnant 임신하게 되다
   c. get someone pregnant 임신하게 만들다

3) a. be involved (in) 참여하고 있다
   b. get involved (in) 참여하게 되다
   c. get someone involved (in) 참여하게 만들다

7 1) a. be at an end 끝이 나 있다
      = be over
   b. come to an end 끝이 나다
   c. bring~to an end ~을 끝내다
      = put an end to~

2) a. be in existence 존재하고 있다
      = exist
   b. come into existence/being 태어나다
   c. bring~into existence/being 태어나게 하다

3) a. be in contact with ~와 접촉하고 있다
   b. come into contact with ~와 접촉하게 되다
   c. bring~into contact with ~와 접촉하게 만들다

4) a. be in power 권력을 잡고 있다
   b. come to power 권력을 잡게 되다
   c. bring~to power ~로 하여금 권력을 잡게 하다

5) a. be in use 쓰여지고 있다
   b. come into use 쓰여지게 되다 *cf.* fall into disuse
   c. bring~into use ~을 쓰여지게 만들다 *cf.* put ~ to use (~을 이용하다)

6) a. be in play 작용하고 있다
   b. come into play 작용하게 되다
   c. bring~into play ~을 작용하게 만들다

7) a. be on one's feet 일어서 있다
   b. get to one's feet 일어서다
   c. bring~to one's feet ~를 일어서게 만들다

8) a. be on one's knees 무릎을 꿇고 있다
   b. drop/fall to one's knees 무릎을 꿇다
      = kneel
   c. bring~to one's knees ~로 하여금 무릎을 꿇게 만들다

9) a. be off to a start 출발해 있다
   b. get off to a start 출발하다
   c. bring~off to a start ~을 출발하게 만들다

8 1) a. be of age 성년이 되어 있다
   b. come of age 성년에 이르다

2) a. be down with a cold
   b. come down with a cold

9 1) a. come about 발생하다
      = come to pass
   b. bring about 발생하게 만들다
      = bring to pass

2) a. come home to ~에게 명백해지다
   b. bring~home to ~을 …에게 명백하게 만들다

3) a. come to light 밝혀지게 되다
   b. bring~to light ~을 밝혀주다

10 1) a. be broke 돈이 떨어져 있다, 파산 상태에 있다
   b. go broke 파산하게 되다

2) a. be in effect 효력을 발휘하고 있다
   b. go into effect 효력을 발휘하게 되다
   c. put~into effect ~의 효력을 발휘하게 하다

3) a. be on a diet 다이어트 중에 있다
   b. go on a diet 다이어트에 들어가다
   c. put~on a diet ~로 하여금 다이어트를 하게 만들다

11 a. be apart 분리되어 있다
   b. come apart 분리되다   *cf.* fall apart
   c. take~apart 분리하다   *cf.* put together 조립하다

12 a. be in charge of ~에 대한 책임을 맡고 있다
   b. take charge of ~에 대한 책임을 떠맡다
   c put~in charge of ~로 하여금 …에 대한 책임을 지게 만들다

13 a. be on fire 불타고 있다
   b. catch fire 불이 붙다
   c. set~on fire ~에 불을 지르다
      = set fire to~

14 a. wear a beard 수염을 길러서 달고 다니다
   b. grow a beard 수염을 기르다

A missionary found himself face-to-face with a raging lion in a jungle.
"I'm going to eat you," roared the lion. "Prepare for death."
At that, the missionary dropped to his knees and prayed more fervently than he ever had before. Then cautiously peeking through his fingers, he saw the lion also kneeling, with front paws covering his eye. Looking toward heaven, the missionary exclaimed,
"Isn't it wonderful... to think that my words can soften a wild beast's heart."
Whereupon the lion dropped his paws and snarled. "Hold your tongue! I'm saying grace."

EXERCISE 7

진한 글자 부분을 주목하면서 전체의 뜻을 파악하라.

1
a. Alice is **in good condition**. She works hard to keep **healthy**.
b. I'm not **healthy**. I have to try to **get into shape**.

2
a. Don't act so foolishly. **Come to your senses**!
b. You must **be out of your senses** to think to marry such a girl. I'll do everything I can do just to **bring** you back **to your senses**.

3
a. Nothing **occurs** again as it **came about** before.
b. I expected a miracle to **happen**, then and there, and a miracle did **take place**. But, as so often happens with a major change, it **came about** over a period of time.

4
a. What you expect to **happen**, with deep conviction and emotion, can surely **come to pass**.
b. Most of the things people worry about never **come to pass**. The French essayist Montaigne made this point eloquently when he said, "My life has been a series of catastrophes — most of which never **happened**."

NOTE

1a. 문맥 healthy = in good condition (≠ in bad condition = out of condition)
1b. 문맥 get into shape = get healthy
　　　be in (good) shape (= be healthy) (≠ be in bad shape = be out of shape)
　　　get in(to) shape (= become healthy)
2a. 문맥 come to your senses (= act sensibly) ≠ act foolishly
3a. 문맥 come about (자동 표현) = occur
　　　bring about (타동 표현)
3b. 문맥 come about = take place = happen
4a. 문맥 come to pass (자동 표현) = happen
　　　bring~to pass (타동 표현)
4b. 문맥 happen = come to pass

5 a. As the smaller things **come into being**, you can make the major things **occur**.

    b. All human minds have inherent **creative capability**, even though they differ in their level of **creative power** and in the degree of usefulness of the things they **bring into being**.

6 a. Once a new idea **springs into existence**, it cannot **be unthought**.

    b. Physicists are now talking about the 'self-creating universe': a cosmos that **erupts into existence** spontaneously, much as a subnuclear particle sometimes **pops out of nowhere** in certain high-energy processes.

7 a. Keep an eye on the kids while I **put** lunch **together**.

    b. I'll **throw together** a couple of sandwiches for you.

    c. They all retired to the dining room, where a fabulous feast had been **assembled** as if by magic.

    d. If she spends half an hour **preparing** a meal, she will think that's gourmet food. Haven't you noticed how fast she **puts** a meal **together**?

8 a. In **putting** this book **together** I learned many things(= writing).

    b. "Try as I may, I can't get this thing **put together** right(= assembled)." "Did you read the instructions?"

9 a. They began to **pull together** instant rescue teams(= form).

    b. Please **get** a task force **together** to get this moving(= form).

NOTE

5a. 문맥   occur = come into being.   major (= greater) ≠ smaller
5b. 문맥   creative power = creative capability (power= capability).   bring into being = create
6a. 문맥   spring into existence = be thought ≠ be unthought = be put out of existence
          be in existence ≠ be out of existence
          come into existence ≠ go out of existence
          bring~into existence ≠ put~out of existence
6b. 문맥   pop out of nowhere = erup into existence.   cosmos = universe
    구문   Physicists are now **talking** <u>about</u> the 'self-creating universe.' (단문)
         = Physicists are now **saying** <u>that</u> the unvierse 'creates itself.' (복문)
7d. 문맥   put together = prepare
8b.   **try as one may** = no matter how hard one tries

10 a. He was trying hard to **put together** the financing for a picture (= arrange).

   b. Filmmakers can often **patch together** their financing from advance sales to videocassette distributors, cable-TV channels and foreign exhibitors.

11 a. A person who works hard every day to **scrape together** a living has no time to puzzle over bothersome philosophical questions(= scratch out; eke out).

   b. When Jobs and Wozniak **scraped together** thirteen hundred dollars by selling a van and two calculators and opened Apple Commputer, Inc., in Job's garage, the odds against their smashing success seemed awfully long.

12 a. We have to **get our act together** — we have to **organize ourselves**.

   b. The ritual of revival has many names : "born again" and "healing" or simply "**getting our act together**." Whatever the name, however large or small the act, the urge to **reassemble** the fragments of our lives into a whole is the same.

13 a. Healthy people **have** their heads **together**.

   b. Friends were saying that she was happier, more **together**, than she had been before (= integrated; mentally and emotionally stable).

   c. She reassured him that they were going to come out of this **together** and unscathed.

   d. "At first I was confused," she said. "Hysterical. I needed a few minutes to **get myself together**."

   e. Stop crying and **compose yourself** before he comes back(= get yourself together).

NOTE
- **10a.** put together the financing = raise the money
- **11b.** the odds against their smashing success seemed awfully long = it seemed extremely unlikely that they would succeed wonderfully
- **12a.** 圜訳 get our act together = organize ourselves
- **13a.** dementia (분리+정신) 치매

50 1장 STRUCTURE

14 a. I can't afford to **go to pieces**. Gotta **pull myself together**.

  b. The words *wholeness* and *health* are derived from the same Old English word, *hal,* meaning "sound," "complete." We know intuitively just by the way we use language that we don't like feeling **split**. When we feel **heartbroken**, disappointed, or hurt, we say things like "I've got to **pull myself together**," "I'm **coming apart at the seams**," or my relationship is "**splitting up**." We speak of **breakdowns** and **cracking up**. When we are feeling good about ourselves and our lives are running smoothly, we say, "I feel **complete**," "My life is **coming together**," or " Finally, I'm **of one mind** about the issue."

As a passenger boarded the Los Angeles-to-New York plane,
*he told the flight attendant to wake him and make sure he **got off** in Dallas.*
The passenger awoke just as the plane was landing in New York.
Furious, he called the flight attendant and demanded an explanation.
*The fellow mumbled an apology and, in a rage, the passenger **stomped off** the plane.*
"Boy, was he ever mad!" another crew member observed to her errant colleague.
"If you think he was mad," replied the flight attendant,
*"you should have seen the guy I **put off** the plane in Dallas!"*

| 기본구조 파악 | **뼈대와 수식** |

1 수식상의 원칙

대개 한 단어로 된 수식어는 피수식어 앞에 오지만, 구나 절로 된 수식어는 피수식어 뒤에 온다.

1) He has failed **chiefly for lack of funds**.

2) He is my **uncle on my mother's side**.

3) He read **everything (that) he could lay his hands on**.

의미
1) 그가 실패한 것은 주로 자금부족 때문이었다.
2) 그는 나의 외삼촌이다.
3) 그는 자기가 손댈 수 있는 것은 모두 읽었다.

2 수식어의 위치와 의미

1) a. She tried **not** to go.
   b. She did **not** try to go.

2) a. **Only** I hit him in the eye yesterday (Nobody else hit him in the eye yesterday).
   b. I **only** hit him in the eye yesterday (I didn't do anything else to him).
   c. I hit **only** him in the eye yesterday (I didn't hit anybody else in the eye).
   d. I hit him **only** in the eye yesterday (and I didn't hit anywhere else).
   e. I hit him in the **only** eye yesterday (He has only one eye and I hit him in it).
   f. I hit him in the eye **only** yesterday (It happened that recently).
   g. I hit him in the eye yesterday **only** (I haven't done it but that one time).

| 의미 | 1) a. 그녀는 안 가려고 애썼다.
b. 그녀는 가려고 애쓰지 않았다.
2) a. 나만이 어제 그의 눈을 때렸다.
b. 나는 어제 그의 눈을 때리기만 했을 뿐이다.
c. 나는 어제 다만 그의 ― 다른 사람이 아니라 ― 눈을 때렸을 뿐이다.
d. 나는 어제 그의 눈만 때렸을 뿐이다.
e. 나는 어제 그의 하나뿐인 눈을 때렸다.
f. 나는 불과 어제 ― 오래 전이 아니라 ― 그의 눈을 때렸다.
g. 나는 어제만 그의 눈을 때렸을 뿐이다.

3 수식어와 피수식어의 분리

영어에서는 문장의 뼈대 요소들을 될 수 있는 대로 문장의 앞 부분에 제시하려는 경향이 있다. (영어에 '가주어'와 '가목적어'가 발달되어 있는 것은 바로 이런 경향 때문이다) 따라서 비교적 길거나 매우 긴 수식어는 문장의 뒷부분으로 밀려나게 된다.

1) The **time** seems to have come / when we should pay more attention to the needs of the needy.

2) As President, Lincoln appointed **men** to his cabinet / whom he considered most capable for the job.

| 의미 | 1) 가난한 사람들에게 필요한 것들에 더 많은 관심을 기울여야 할 때가 온 것 같다.
주의 사선 이하의 수식을 받는 말은 time이다.
2) 대통령으로 있을 때, 링컨은 주어진 직책에 가장 유능하다고 생각한 사람들을 각료로 임명했다.

4 한국어와 다른 수식방법

1) a. a wave
   b. **a mountain of** a wave

2) a. a girl
   b. **an angel of** a girl

3.1) a. stability
   b. **a semblance of** stability

3.2) a. normality
   b. **a semblance of** normality

4) a. Life is based on carbon chemistry.
   b. Life, **as we know it on earth**, is based on carbon chemistry.

5) a. English is an international language.
   b. English is an international language, **as they call it**.
   = English is **what they call** an international language.

6) a. Times became "hard."
   b. Times became **what my father called** "hard."

7) a. He seldom goes to church.
   b. He seldom, **if ever**, goes to church.

8) a. Religion played little part in their lives.
   b. Religion played little, **if any**, part in their lives.

9) a. The economy of the country boasts a steady annual growth rate of 3%.
   b. The economy of the country boasts a steady **if unspectacular** annual growth rate of 3%.

10) a. Such a decision will bring about harmful results.
    b. Such a decision will bring about harmful **if not fatal** results.

의미

1) b. 산더미 같은 파도

2) b. 천사 같은 소녀

3.1) b. 안정 비슷한 것

3.2) b. 정상 비슷한 것

4) a. 생명이란 탄소의 화학작용에 기초한다.
   b. 생명이란, 지구상에 알려진 대로, 탄소의 화학작용에 기초한다.

5) a. 영어는 국제 언어이다.
   b. 영어는, 사람들이 말하듯이, 국제 언어이다.

6) a. 시대가 '어려워졌다.'
   b. 시대가 우리 아버지가 말하는 것처럼 '어려워졌다.'

7) a. 그는 교회에 거의 가지 않는다.
   b. 그는, 어쩌다 간다고 해도, 교회에 거의 가지 않는다.

8) a. 종교는 그들의 삶에 별 영향을 주지 못했다.
   b. 종교는, 얼마간의 영향을 주었다고 해도, 그들의 삶에 별 영향을 주지 못했다.

9) a. 그 나라의 경제는 지속적인 연 3% 성장률을 자랑한다.
   b. 그 나라의 경제는, 평장하지는 않지만 지속적인 연 3% 성장률을 자랑한다.

10) a. 이런 결정은 안 좋은 결과를 초래할 수 있다.
    b. 이런 결정은 치명적이는 않을지라도 안 좋은 결과를 초래할 수 있다.

EXERCISE 8

진한 글자 부분을 주목하면서 전체의 뜻을 파악하라.

1
  a. She **entirely** failed to understand the problem.
  b. She failed to **entirely** understand the problem.

2
  a. He shaved off his beard.
  b. He shaved off his **two-day growth of** beard.

3
  a. I don't want your company.
  b. I don't want **another minute of** your company.
    (= I don't want your company for another minute.)

4
  a. I don't even have clothes.
  b. I don't even have **a change of** clothes.
    (= I don't even have clothes to change into once.)

5
  a. Sanity is very rare; every man almost, and every woman, has **a dash of** madness.
  b. Although apparently rigid, bones exhibit **a degree of** elasticity that enables the skeleton to withstand **considerable** impact.

6
  a. He's become **something of** an expert on meditation(= quite).
  b. Trying to be all things to all people usually results in **not** being **much of** anything to anyone.

NOTE
2b. 구문 his **two-day growth of** beard (명사구) = his beard **that** had grown for two days (명사구+관계절)
4b. a change of clothes → two changes of clothes
                                 a few changes of clothes
5a. 문맥 sanity ≠ madness(= insanity)
5b. 문맥 a degree of = considerable.   elastic(≠ not rigid) ≠ rigid

7   a. With all his egoism he is without **an atom of affectation** and it is this complete naturalness that makes him endurable.

   b. You haven't got **a ghost of a chance** of winning the game(= even the slightest chance).

8   a. I had **a devil of a time** getting home through the snow(= a very difficult time).

   b. "I'm having **a devil of time** with calculus. I think I should drop the course."
   "Keep trying. Don't give up the ship."

9   a. At home again, I tried to get back into some kind of routine and **semblance of** normalcy.

   b. But in the capital city the new government is hard pressed to maintain even **a semblance of** order.

   c. The restaurant serves **a close approximation of** French cuisine.

10 a. Gangs roamed the streets, robbing and mugging with **something approaching** impunity.

   b. They regarded each other with **something very near to** affection.

   c. The new car doesn't have **anywhere near** the power our last one had.

   d. He didn't look like a private investigator.
   → He didn't look **anything** like a private investigator.
   → He didn't look **anything like her conception of** a private investigator.

NOTE
7a.   complete naturalness = being without an atom of affectation
       With all his egoism (구) = Although he is egoistic (절)
7b.   stand/have a chance of ~ing (~을 할 가능성이 있다)
8a.   a hell of 대단한/히 (아주 좋은/나쁜/큰) = one hell of = a heck of = a devil of
8b.   have a difficult time ~ing (~을 하는 데에 어려움을 겪다)
       have a difficult time ~with (~에 어려움을 겪다)
       → be busy ~ing
           be busy with~
       calculus = the course = the ship.   drop = give up
9b.   be hard pressed/put/pushed to do ~을 하는 데에 어려움을 겪다 = have difficulty doing~

※ 진한 글자 부분에 주의하여 다음 두 귀절의 번역이 옳은지 따져 보라.

11
a. From **a chaos of superstitions** and narrow ideas of a warlike tribal God, there emerged a monotheistic creed, inconsistent with dualism.
   미신의 혼돈과 호전적인 종족신의 편협한 사상으로부터, 이원론과는 부합되지 않는 일신론적인 교리가 생겼다.

b. The life and death of **any body of water** depend mainly upon its ability to maintain a certain amount of dissolved oxygen. This dissolved oxygen is what fish breathe. Without it they suffocate.
   물에 사는 생물의 생사는 용해된 산소가 일정한 양을 유지할 수 있는 능력 여하에 주로 달려 있다. 이 용해된 산소를 물고기가 호흡한다. 그것이 없으면 그들은 질식해서 죽는다.

12
a. Every successful man I have heard of has done the best he could with conditions **as he found them**, and not waited until the next year for better.

b. Poets are concerned with people and with life, and they use the medium of poetry to communicate their understandings and the truths of life **as they see them**. They try to give us the "feel of the idea" and the "experience beneath the idea." They interpret the innermost spirit of a people, of a country, of a civilization; for poetry is a revelation or an interpretation of life in some of its aspects. The poetic material is life **as it is known to the emotions**, and the emotions are universal and enduring. Moreover, the poet senses the eternal rhythm that runs through all of life.

13
a. With money we can buy / whatever it is / we believe / will take us towards greater happiness.

b. While the medical profession has conquered most of childhood diseases, boys and girls seem to be afflicted, as much as ever, with / whatever it is / that prevents them from being sleepy at bedtime.

14
a. He was beaming at her with **what she knew was** a phony smile.

b. Many governments intervene in the foreign exchange market to prevent the exchange rate from going too far in **what they consider to be** the wrong direction.

NOTE
13b. be afflicted with ~에 걸려 있다
14a. 문법 smile = beam

15 a. The party went on for **I don't know how** long.

b. She was born in the year of **Our Lord only knows**.

c. In an effort to conform to the sought-after female image, I starved my body and ingested **heaven-knows-what** chemical drugs.

One Sunday morning a few years ago, my dad and I went to move some cows out of a swampy paddock. We sent the dogs around and slowly all the cows headed for the gate — except one.

A black cow remained on the other side of the swamp. She stood staring at us, constantly mooing and not moving at all. The dogs ran at her, barking and jumping, yet she still didn't flinch. Finally Dad got impatient and we drove around the swamp towards the cow.

*We reached her wondering why she hadn't moved. She mooed again and, to our amazement, leaned her head towards something in the swamp. Looking towards the swamp, we saw a sheep trapped neck high in mud. We began digging and pulling hard at it, and after some time it **came free**. Only then did the cow stop mooing and begin trotting around the side of the swamp and out the gate. Every time I enter that paddock, I flash back to that day and think about the courage and intellingence that cow showed —all to help a farm friend.*

기본구조 파악 — 문장 구성요소의 이동

본래의 자리로부터 문장을 구성하는 요소들(주어, 동사, 목적어, 보어)이 위치를 옮기는 것은 두 가지 이유에서이다. 첫째, 문장의 균형 유지 또는 시적인 효과를 얻기 위해서이거나 의미상의 혼란을 피하기 위해서. 둘째, 강조를 위해서.

1 균형을 위한 이동

문장을 구성하는 어느 요소가 상대적으로 다른 요소보다 길 때에는 긴 요소는 뒤로 이동하고 뒤에 있던 요소가 앞 자리로 이동한다.

1) 주어와 보어의 자리 바꿈

   a. **He who loves reading** is happy.
   b. Happy is **he who loves reading**.

2) 목적어와 보어의 자리 바꿈

   a. His contribution **made** the expansion of the library *possible*.
   b. His contribution **made** *possible* the expansion of the library.

3) 목적어와 부사 (부사구, 부사절 포함)의 자리 바꿈

   a. Don't put off **what you can do today** *till tomorrow*.
   b. Don't put off *till tomorrow* **what you can do today**.

의미
1) 독서를 사랑하는 사람은 행복하다.
   - **비교** Be동사로 이루어진 문장에서의 자리 바꿈은 Be동사 앞에 있는 요소와 뒤에 있는 요소 사이에 일어난다.
     A is B. → B is A.
2) 그의 기부로 도서관을 확장할 수 있게 되었다.
   - **주의** 예문 a가 비문법적이라고 볼 수는 없으나, 목적어가 매우 길 때에는 possible이라는 단어가 어디에 연결되는지 잘 알 수 없으므로 사람들은 대개 b의 어순을 택한다. 그리고 영어에서는 될 수 있는 대로 문장의 앞 부분에 주어진 문장의 뼈대를 제시하려는 경향이 있다는 얘기가 여기에도 적용된다.
3) 오늘 할 수 있는 일을 내일로 미루지 마라.
   - **주의** 예문 a에서는 till tomorrow가 what-clause에 포함되어 있는 것으로 오해하게 만들 가능성이 있어서 이런 어순은 바람직하지 않다.

2 강조를 위한 이동

강조되는 말은 문두로 이동하는데, 이런 경우에는 그 부분이 강조되고 있다는 것을 보여주는 말(필자는 이것을 '강조장치'라고 부른다)이 있다는 점이 특징이다.

1) 보어의 강조

    a. Laughter is **so** *characteristic of our species* that man has been defined as the laughing animal.
    b. **So** *characteristic of our species* is laughter that man has been defined as the laughing animal.

2) 부사의 강조

    a. I *little* dreamed that I would meet her again.
    b. *Little* did I dream that I would meet her again.

의미

1) 인간이란 종에게 웃음은 너무도 독특하므로 사람은 웃는 동물이라 규정되어 왔다.
    주의 So는 강조장치이다.

2) 나는 그녀를 다시 만나리라고는 거의 생각하지 못했다.
    주의 부사의 이동에 따라 조동사 did가 들어갔다는 점에 주의하라. 주어진 문장 안에 be동사나 조동사가 있는 경우에는 조동사 do가 들어가지 않는다.
      1) He **was** never so happy!
        → Never **was** he so happy!
      2) I **have** never seen such a beautiful girl before.
        → Never before **have** I seen such a beautiful girl.

    A couple were returning to their seats after a trip to the movie theatre snack bar.
    "Did I step on your toes on the way out?"
    The guy asked the man at the end of the row.
    "You certainly did," the man responded angrily.
    "All right," the husband said to his wife.
    "This is our row."

EXERCISE 9

진한 글자 부분을 주목하면서 전체의 뜻을 파악하라.

1. a. You can **laugh** many worries you can't get rid of otherwise **to death**.(×)
   b. You can **laugh to death** many worries you can't get rid of otherwise.(○)

2. A good poem **resists to the death** its reduction to a flat statement.

3. The real art of conversation is not only to say the right thing in the right place but to **leave unsaid** the wrong thing at the tempting moment.

4. People who practice totemism, the worship of plants, animals, or objects as gods, usually **select for worship** objects that are important to the community.

5. Seeing is an activity not only of our eyes but of the brain, which works as a sort of selecting machine. Out of all the images presented to it, it **chooses for recognition** those that fit most neatly with the world learned by past experience.

6. X-rays are able to pass through objects and thus **make visible** details that are otherwise impossible to observe.

NOTE

1a. 문맥 laugh to death (웃어서 없애다) = get rid of by laughing. otherwise = by other means
    put~to death ~을 죽이다, 없애다. burn~to death 태워서 죽이다. starve~to death 굶겨서 죽이다
2. to the death (죽을 때까지) 시의 생명이 끝날 때까지, reduction to a flat statement (무미건조한 진술로 옮기는 것) 산문으로 바꾸어 쓰는 것 → flat = prosaic < prose (산문)
3. 문맥 to leave unsaid = not to say.
    at the tempting moment (= in the wrong place) ≠ in the right place
4. 문맥 practice totemism = worship plants, animals, or objects as gods
    순해 select for worship < select and worship (선택해서 숭배하다)
5. 문맥 choose = select
    순해 choose for recognition < choose and recognize (선택해서 인식하다)
6. otherwise (달리) X-ray를 이용하지 않고
    문맥 impossible to observe = invisible ≠ visible

7 I thought that I ought to **reject as downright false** all opinions which I could imagine to be in the least degree open to doubt—my purpose being to—discover whether, after so doing, there might not remain, as still calling for belief, something entirely indubitable.

8 A great deal of talent is lost in the world for want of a little courage. Every day **sends to their graves** obscure men whom timidity prevented from making a first effort; who, if they could have been induced to begin, would in all probability have gone great lengths.

Be bold and courageous. When you look back on your life,
you'll regret the things you didn't do more than the ones you did.

Be bold — and mighty forces will come to your aid.

NOTE	7.	문맥 open to doubt (= dubitable) ≠ indubitable (= not open to doubt)
		구문 my purpose being to discover~ (구) = for my purpose was to discover~ (절)
	8.	문맥 timidity = want of courage.　make a first effort = begin
		go great lengths (크게 성공하다) = achieve great success

| 정보의 결합 | **논리전개순서:** 영어를 거꾸로 이해하려고 하지 말라 |

어떤 사람이 영어로 얘기하고 있는데, 그의 얘기를 이해하기 위해 그가 얘기를 엮어나가는 순서와는 반대로 듣는다면 어떻게 될까? 그의 얘기가 순서대로 들어올 리가 없을 것이다. 불행하게도 번역 중심이라는 원시적인 교육 방법 때문에 우리는 이런 식으로 영어를 이해하려고 해 왔다. 이젠 그런 방법을 버리고 영어의 논리 전개 순서를 그대로 따라가면서 이해하려고 해야 할 때가 왔다.

1 He tried again / **only to fail.**

    a. He tried again
    b. He only failed

2 She called me this morning / **to say** that she couldn't come.

    a. She called me this morning
    b. She said that she couldn't come

3 You should not stress the one / **to the exclusion of** the other.

    a. You should not stress the one
    b. and exclude the other

4 They wrangled for eleven hours / **before** voting / **to accept** the pact.

    a. They wrangled for eleven hours
    b. They voted
    c. They accepted the pact

의미
1. 그는 또 다시 시도했으나 실패했을 뿐이었다.
2. 그녀는 나에게 오늘 오전에 전화해서 올 수 없다고 말했다.
3. 어느 하나를 강조하고 나머지 하나를 제외해서는 안 된다.
4. 그들은 11시간 동안 논쟁한 뒤에 투표를 해서 그 협정을 받아들였다.

EXERCISE 10

순서대로 읽어나가면서 뜻을 파악하라.

1
a. In the three centuries since 1650, the human inhabitants of the globe have **increased** fivefold / <u>to</u> **reach** a total of about 2.5 billions in 1950.

b. He made a capital gain of about 3.7% from holding stocks from 1995 to 1996 / plus a divident yield of 3.6%, / <u>for</u> a total return of 7.3%.

c. Americans shut their wallets in March and sent retail sales down 1% / <u>for</u> the steepest decline in more than two years.

2
a. Two atoms of hydrogen **combine** with one atom of oxygen / <u>to</u> **form** water.

b. Carbon and hydrogen **combine** wih oxygen / <u>to</u> **produce** light and heat.

c. Make money and the whole world **conspire** / <u>to</u> **call** you a gentleman.

d. The quiet mind, the youthful heart, the racing blood — these converge / <u>to</u> **produce** wonder.

e. When two forces work together, they add up / <u>to</u> **form** a single larger force. But when two forces oppose each other directly, their strengths subtract.

f. Calcium, the most abundant mineral in the body, **works** with phosphorus / <u>in</u> **maintaining** bones and teeth.

g. There is evidence to show that interferons **work** with immune cells / <u>in</u> **combatting** various forms of disease, not excluding cancer.

h. The local police are **cooperating** with the FBI / <u>in</u> the **search** for the criminals.

NOTE

1b. 　문맥　 gain = yield = return

1c. 　구문　 for the steepest decline in more than two years (구)
　　　　= , which is the steepest decline in more than two years (관계절)
　　　　= , the steepest decline in more than two years (동격구)

2e. 　문맥　 they add up to form a single larger force = their strengths increase ≠ their strengths subtract (subtract = decrease ≠ increase)

3. a. This book contains a totally new outlook which **combines** the wisdom of the past with scientific knowledge / <u>to</u> **solve** the problems of the present.

   b. Psycholinguistics **uses** the theoretical and empirical resources of both psychology and linguistics / <u>to</u> **examine** the mental processes underlying the use of language.

   c. Behavioral medicine **brings together** the wisdom of psychology and medical science / <u>in</u> **understanding** how to assess and diagnose illness, how to treat it, and particularly how to prevent it, as well as rehabilitation.

4. a. Empiricists **rely on** observation and experimentation <u>in</u> **deciding** what is true.

   b. Philosophers commonly **rely on** argument <u>to</u> **support** their own theories and <u>to</u> **refute** the theories of others.

5. a. Green plants **use** sunlight <u>to</u> **convert** carbon dioxide and water into sugar and oxygen.

   b. Muscles **rely on** magnesium <u>to</u> convert carbohydrates to usable energy.

   c. He **draws on** communist philosophy <u>in</u> support of his views concerning the origin of life.

6. a. Bats **rely on** their hearing / <u>to</u> **navigate** <u>to</u> **find** food at night.

   b. The artist **drew on** childhood memories / <u>in</u> **creating** his paintings.

   c. We **took advantage of** the dry weather / <u>to</u> **paint** the house.

   d. We **look to** gravity / <u>to</u> explain the structure of star clusters and galaxies, as well as the global motion of the expanding cosmos.

7. a. The microscopic plants that form the basis of the ecology of the sea **depend on** light as the source of energy / <u>to</u> **synthesize** starches.

NOTE 4b. support (= prove to be true) ≠ refute (= prove to be false)

b. They are **looking to** their parents / for financial aid.

c. The brain **depends on** the blood / for a continuous supply of oxygen and glucose.

d. An animal is bound to **depend on** other living creatures, ultimately plants, for its food supply; it must also **depend on** the activities of plants for a continued oxygen supply for its respiration.

8
a. When a question is complicated, don't give the first answer that comes to mind. **Take** time / for **reflection**.

b. A female toad / listening to male love calls / **scorns** the tenors / in favor of the basses.

c. In their day the primitivist hippies, who were always bad-mouthing modern civilization, **denounced** doing and saying / **in favor of** just being.

9
a. "I've been thinking about my mother a lot today."
"Why not go over / for a visit?"

b. After a short pause / for a sip of water, the speaker went on / to discuss the habits of lions in the wild.

10
a. Consequently, after World War I increasing numbers of spectators **deserted** the theater / for the movies.

b. At the last moment Bob **edged out** Henry / for first place in the contest.

NOTE		
	7d.	is bound to = must (이 단어 뒤의 also가 이를 보여준다.)
		depend on the activities of plants / for a continuous oxygen supply / for its respiration
		식물의 활동에 의존하여/ 계속해서 산소를 공급 받아 / 호흡한다
	8a.	Take time <u>for</u> reflection = take time **and** reflect(on it)
	8b.	scorn A <u>in</u> favor of B = scorn A **and** favor B
		listening to male love calls (분사구)
		= **that listens** to male love calls
		= **, when she listens** to male love calls (부사절)
		scorn (= dislike) ≠ favor (= like)
	9a.	go over **for** a visit = go over and visit her
	9b.	for a sip of water = and taking a sip of water (= and sipping water)
	10a.	desert A for B = desert A **and** go to B
	10b.	edged out Henry for first place = edged out Henry **and won** first place (근소한 차이로 Henry를 밀어내고 일등을 차지했다)

11 a. At an alarming rate, West European high school students have been **dropping** German / **in favor of** English, mainly because they believe English is easier to learn.

b. Schools in Wandsworth in South London have **abandoned** the long summer holiday, originally designed to allow pupils to help with the harvest, / **in favor of** five eight-week terms.

c. Maturity is patience. It is the willingness to **pass up** immediate pleasure / **in favor of** long-term gain.

d. The Democrats **rejects** Reagan's three-year, across-the-board slash in income tax rates / **in favor of** a much narrower one-year-reduction.

12 a. The operator **broke in** / say**ing**. "You need another 75¢ to continue the call."

b. Life in this electronic age is tough on kids. Two six-graders felt the call of the fishing pole one afternoon, and took along their walkie-talkies. Word of this got to the teacher, who borrowed a walkie-talkie from another student. The teacher tuned in and, sure enough, heard the truants, whereupon he promptly **cut in** / **to** suggest that they appear in the classroom posthaste, which they did.

13 a. Knowledge is **gained** / at the **cost** of innocence.
(= When one **gains** knowledge, one **loses** one's innocence.)

b. People usually become famous / **at the cost of** their privacy.
(= When people become famous, they usually lose their privacy.)

NOTE

11a. 문맥 drop (= give up) ≠ favor (= take up)
11b. 문맥 abandon (= give up) ≠ favor (= adopt)
   구문 originally designed~ (분사구 = 단축절) = **which was** originally designed~ (관계절)
   help (someone) with~ (어떤 사람이) ~(하는 것)을 돕다 → help (someone) to do~ (어떤 사람이) ~을 하는 것을 돕다
11c. 문맥 pass up (= refuse) ≠ favor (= seek)
11d. 문맥 slash = wide reduction (뒤에 나오는 narrower... reduction으로 보아)
12b. tough = very difficult.   felt the call of the fishing pole = felt like going fishing.
   sure enough 틀림없이, 아니나 다를까.   posthaste (말 타고 '우편물 운송하는 사람처럼 빨리') 가능한 빨리
   문법 suggest라는 단어에 들어있는 '해야 한다' 라는 개념 때문에 appear 앞에 should가 생략되므로 동사원형이 사용되었다.

14 a. Civilization today depends on wood, **at great cost to** the world's natural resources.

b. Protectionism may provide short-term benefits to special interests but / **at much greater cost** to the rest of society.

15 a. We cannot afford to make new friends **at the expense of** old ones.

b. In general, "speed reading" **emphasizes** coverage **at the expense of** understanding.

c. Amusements cannot be cultivated **at the expense of** the serious business of life. Man must put work before play.

d. In countless ways man **exploits** the environment / for immediate **gain** / at the expense of ultimate **loss**.
(= In countless ways man **exploits** the environment, **gaining** immediately but **losing** ultimately.)

16 a. It is possible for order to **accumulate** in one place **at the price of** entropy generated elsewhere.

b. The concentration of order in one region of the universe **is** always **paid for** by increasing disorder somewhere else.

c. According to the Entropy Law, whenever order is created anywhere on Earth or in the universe, it is done **at the expense of** causing an even greater disorder in the surrounding environment.

17 a. Anyone / who breaks the law / **does** so / at their **peril**.
(= If anyone breaks the law, they will **be in peril**.)

b. He is a man / to whom you **say** no / **at your peril**.

NOTE

14. 구문 at great cost (전치사구) = causing great harm (분사구)
15a. 문맥 at the expense of = and lose
15b. 문맥 at the expense of = and sacrifices / neglects
15c. 문맥 Amusements cannot be cultivated at the expense of the serious~ = Man must not cultivate amusements, sacrificing the serious~.   amusements = play.   the serious business of life = work.   cannot = must not
16a. 문맥 entropy (= disorder) ≠ order.   generate = accumulate
16b. 문맥 The concentration of order = Increasing order
16c. 문맥 cause = create
17a. 문법 Anyone을 대명사로 받을 때에 전통적으로 he or she(his or her, him or her)로 받아왔는데, 이것이 거추장스럽다고 현대인들은 they(their, them)를 이용한다.

18 a. We **sold** the house / <u>at</u> a **loss**.

b. The steel mill now **operates** / <u>at</u> a handsome profit.

19 a. In 1902, the book was **published** / <u>to</u> critical **acclaim**.
(= In 1902, the book was **published** <u>and</u> **acclaimed** by the critics.)

b. Work and play are both necessary for our happiness. We should not **stress** the one / <u>to</u> **the exclusion of** the other.

c. I **woke** out of my deep sleep / **to a gradual recognition** that I was at home and not in the dormitory.

d. How many times have you **daydreamed** through several pages of a good book / only to wake **up** / **to the realization** that you have no idea of the ground you have gone over?

20 a. He **smoked** a lot, **to the detriment of** his health.

b. **To his detriment**, it must be said that he allowed the prisoners to be tortured.

21 a. Knowledge and the search for knowledge have **persisted** through the centuries **to the enormous benefit of** human beings.

b. We in the Western world have **encouraged** scientific discovery and its application intensively for 200 years **to our vast material benefits**.

22 a. In ordinary life we **use** a great many words / <u>with</u> a total **disregard** of logical precision.

b. Anyone / who helps others / <u>with</u> no **thought** to personal gain / is essentially an altruist.

NOTE		
19b.	순해	<u>to</u> the **exclusion** of = <u>and</u> **exclude**
19c.	순해	<u>to</u> a gradual **recognition** = <u>and</u> gradually recognized
19d.	순해	<u>to</u> the **realization** = <u>and</u> realize
	문맥	the ground you have gone over = what you have read
20a.	순해	**to the detriment of**~ (전치사구)
		= doing harm to~ (분사구) = which did harm to~ (관계절)
20b.	순해	**to his detriment** = Although it will do him harm
22a.	순해	**with** a total disregard of logical precision = **and** totally disregard logical~
22b.	순해	**with** no thought to personal gain = **and** does not think of personal~

23 I had been puzzling over the problem for over an hour / without any result, / when all at once the solution flashed across my mind.

24 The mark of a first-rate intelligence, as F. Scott Fitzgerald said, is the capacity to entertain two contradictory propositions in one mind simultaneously / without going crazy.

25 As we look back, we can indeed see the notion of individual rights broadening out / to include more and more of the people, / until it came at length to be extended to them all.

26 Each year thousands of books **are published**, many of them / to **attract** momentary attention / only to **disappear** gradually from the shelves and the minds of readers — a few / to **remain** / in **circulation** as long as books are read.

27 In all its changes, water **is never lost**, / **disappearing** / only to **appear** again in another form / in the constant **service** of nature and civilization.

28 According to Hegel, a thesis **is created** / that **is opposed** by its antithesis / to **create** a synthesis, / which then **becomes** a new thesis.

29 A heroin dealer can be fined $50,000 and sentenced to up to 30 years in prison / with a minimum confinement of six years / before becoming eligible for parole. The same person trafficking in methaqualone faces a maximum of ten years in prison, a $30,000 fine and four years before parole.

NOTE
23. flash across one's mind 섬광처럼 자기 머리 속에 떠오르다 < cross one's mind
25. 문맥 extend = broaden out
26. 순해 remain in circulation 남아 돌아다니다
27. 문맥 in the constant service of = , constantly serving
29. 문맥 The same person trafficking in methaqualone = A methaqualone dealer (traffic = deal)

정보결합장치: 동격

정보의 결합

동격은 주어진 명사 앞에 오는 전치동격과 뒤에 오는 후치동격으로 구분되고, 또한 두 명사 사이에 연결장치(comma, of, etc.)가 있는 것과 없는 것으로도 나누어진다.

1
a. **A congenial sort of person**, *my father* has not made an enemy in his life.
b. *My father*, (who is) **a congenial sort of person**, has not made an enemy in his life.

2
a. *Goethe* **the poet** is far better known than *Goethe* **the scientist**.
b. **To get ahead in the world**, *that* was extremely difficult in those days.
c. They have done a wonderful *job* **of restoration**.
d. Zoo animals feel safe because of the *conviction* **that their cages are solid**.

의미
1. 사람들과 잘 어울리시는 분이시기 때문에, 아버지께서는 일생 동안 적을 한 명도 만들지 않으셨다.
2. a. 괴테는 과학자로서보다는 시인으로서 훨씬 더 잘 알려져 있다.
   b. 출세하는 것, 그것이 그 시절에는 지극히 어려웠다.
   c. 그들은 복구 작업을 매우 잘 해놓았다.
   d. 동물원의 동물들이 안전하다고 느끼는 것은 자신들의 우리가 튼튼하다고 믿기 때문이다.

Once, at a story conference, Charlie Chaplin, an unpredictable eccentric, kept slapping at a fly buzzing around his head. Calling for a swatter, he swung several times but missed. At last, the offender settled down before him, and Chaplin lifted the swatter for the death blow. He paused, looked carefully at the fly and lowered the swatter.
"Why didn't you swat him?" he was asked.
Shrugging typically, Chaplin said, "It wasn't the same fly."

EXERCISE 11

진한 글자 부분을 주목하면서 전체의 뜻을 파악하라.

1. **A political and economic conservative**, he displayed a strong social conscience that showed itself in deeds rather than words.

2. **The author of a geology book for junior high school students**, Golden is currently writing one on astronomy for the same audience.

3. Russia sidestepped the issue **of diplomatic recognition for East Germany**.

4. She arrived in Korea some three years ago with the express purpose **of taking care of Korean War orphans**.

5. **An extremely important process**, photosynthesis is the ultimate source of food for almost all organisms on earth.

6. **A bundle of past struggles, future aspirations and present tensions**, she is never in true repose.

7. This new educational system emphasizes the fact **that there is nothing like seeing for oneself**. That is, knowledge gained by actual experience is understood the best and is remembered the longest.

8. Saroyan was a literary nonconformist who brought to his freewheeling "folk tales" an unruly vitality, a rosy optimism and an exuberant defiance of artistic and commercial conventions. **The son of Armenian immigrants**, he quit school to write at 15 and by 26 had declared himself a genius.

NOTE 2. 문맥 one = a book.   the same audience = junior high school students
4. **some** = about.   **express**(adj.) = special; specific

9 Agatha Chirstie, **the famous mystery writer,** was asked how she liked being married to an archaeologist.
  "An archaeologist is the best husband any woman can have," she replied. "The older she gets, the more interest he has in her."

People are always blaming their circumstances for what they are.
I do not believe in circumstances.
The people who get on in this world are the people who get up
and look for the circumstances they want,
and if they cannot find them, make them.
— *Bernard Shaw*

| 정보의 결합 | **정보결합장치: 부연설명** |

앞에 나온 말의 일부 또는 전부를 다른 말로 풀이해 주는 것을 '부연설명'(elaboration)이라고 부르기로 한다.

1 부분부연

a. There are two forms or **aspects** of science.
b. The genes, or **units of heredity**, are composed of nucleic acid.
c. Suddenly he feels free — **the freedom that rises out of total despair.**

2 전체부연

a. He completed the task in a week, (which was) **a remarkable achievement.**
b. He saved the little girl from drowning at the cost of his life — (which was) **a heroic act.**

의미
1. a. 과학에는 두 가지 형태 또는 양상이 있다.
   b. 유전인자, 즉 유전의 단위는 핵산으로 이루어져 있다.
      주해 여기에 사용된 접속사 or는 다음과는 다르다는 점에 주의하라.
      cf. Which do you like better, beer or wine?
   c. 갑자기 그는 자유를 느낀다 — 전면적인(완전한) 절망에서 일어나는 그런 자유를.
2. a. 그는 그 과제를 1주일만에 끝마쳤는데, 그것은 놀라운 성과였다.
   b. 그는 물에 빠져 죽을 뻔한 소녀를 구해주고 자신의 목숨을 잃었는데, 그것은 영웅적인 행동이었다.
      주해 부연장치로는 or, comma, dash, that is (to say), which-clause 또는 '생략 which-clause' 등이 있다.

A woman was doing her housework in the nude when the doorbell rang.
"Who's there?" She asked. "Blind man" was the reply.
As the woman opened the door, the man said,
"Where do you want me to hang these blinds, lady?"

EXERCISE 12

진한 글자 부분을 주목하면서 전체의 뜻을 파악하라.

1. Nearly all societies at nearly all times had **a leisure class, a class of persons who were exempt from toil.**

2. He is a storybook example of the typical American business man, **a man who is willing to take the big risk to get the big reward.**

3. Plants in the Alps are **moving** to higher ground because of global warming, a **march** that might eventually lead dozens of species to extinction.

4. This good-versus-evil view of the world is one of Greenberg's central and consistent themes, **a perspective** nurtured from childhood in a Houston, Texas ghetto.

5. Mary suffers from SAD, short for seasonal affective disorder, **a syndrome** characterized by severe seasonal mood swings.

6. Educators in Japan are alarmed at the rise of "school refusal syndrome" — a **psychological ailment** of kids too stressed out to face going to class.

7. Unlike fats and proteins, carbohydrates are stockpiled in the muscles and livers as glycogen, **a readily available energy source** our bodies can tap as needed.

NOTE
1. 문맥 leisure = exemption from toil
2. 문맥 storybook = typical
   순해 willing / to take the big risk / to get the big reward 기꺼이 / 크게 모험하여 / 큰 보상을 얻으려고 하는
3. 문맥 march = movement
5. 문맥 syndrome = disorder.   mood = affective
6. stressed out (스트레스를 받아 나간) 스트레스를 받아 의욕을 잃은 → burned-out
7. 문맥 tap = avail themselves of.   available = tappable

8 The artist must find the common denominator, **that which is similar among us**, and draw upon that to produce a work which not only unites us but also separates us.

9 Everybody is intuitive, but the tiny voice of intuition is inaudible to most people, **those** who are eccentric in their thinking. When their thinking becomes centered, the voice of intuition is more clearly "heard."

10 a. British companies spent record amounts on advertising last year, **a sign that** national economic revival is imminent.

b. His memory on little things blanked out, **a sign** of aging.

c. The scientists wanted their research to be useful, **an indication** of their desire to work for the benefit of humanity.

d. Perhaps the saddest dilemma facing South Florida is the plight of the refugees from Haiti. Law enforcement officials pick up about 500 Haitians a month on Florida's beaches, but probably as many slip in without getting caught. The 600-mile journey from Haiti is often arduous, **a measure** of how desperately Haitians want to leave their country.

11 The best-known and most controversial technique used by biotechnology is gene-splicing, **the insertion of foreign genes into plants, animals or microbes.** Scientists have, for example, introduced rat-growth-hormone genes into the DNA of mice, resulting in larger mice, and firefly genes into tobacco plants, which then glow in the dark. Genetic engineering cannot, however, "cross" a cow with a frog to produce a new species.

NOTE

8. similar = common.   unite ≠ separate
9. who are eccentric in their thinking = whose thinking are not centered (eccentric = not centered ≠ centered).   heard = audible (inaudible = not heard)
10b. (which is) a sign of aging = a sign that he was aging = which shows that~
10c. an indication of their desire to work~ = an indication that they wanted to work~ = which indicates that~
     desire = want
10d. a measure of = an indication of = which shows
11. introduce = insert.   result in = produce.   genetic engineering = gene-splicing

12 One Wall Street adage has it that if a person has not made his first million dollars by the time he is 30, he is never going to make it. In 1776 Adam Smith wrote that it was young people who had "the contempt of risk and the presumptuous hope of success," **precisely the skills needed to found new businesses**. Indeed, a large number of entrepreneurs have achieved success at a very early age. One of many examples: William Gates, 26, dropped out of Harvard in 1975 during sophomore year to form Microsoft, which makes software for personal computers. Its 1981 sales: $15 million.

13 Each year, thousands of Americans die from fires. In too many of the cases, death occurs because so much skin is burned away that vital body functions are disrupted. Essential fluids ooze out, and natural defenses are too weakened to fight off bacterial infection. To prevent these complications, doctors try to cover burn sites with skin grafts from undamaged portions of the patient's body, but often there is too little skin left and they have to resort to using skin from pigs or cadavers. Being foreign tissue, these grafts are usually rejected in three to 25 days. The ideal solution would be artificial skin, **a goal that has eluded scientists**. But last week a team of Boston researchers announced they had a successful skin substitute made from a startling mixture of ingredients: cowhide, shark cartilage and plastic.

14 An estimated 25 million Americans have dyslexia, **a condition that has been detectable for years by a battery of tests**. Dyslexics, who are often left-handed or ambidextrous, tend to reverse letters (b for d), twist words (was for saw), confuse word order (please up hurry), subtract from left to right, or have difficulty with sequential thinking. Despite these problems, they may be intellectually brilliant, with oral skills so keen they are able to bluff their way through early grades. Dyslexics can become high achievers like Edison, Einstein, General Patton, Nelson Rockefeller and Bruce Jenner. But they are often misdiagnosed as retarded or emotionally disturbed.

NOTE

12. **adage**: an old saying. **One Wall Street adage has it that**~ = According to one Wall Street adage, ~
    presumptuous: too bold or forward; overconfident
    문맥 form = found

13. **ooze out**: to flow or leak out slowly. **fight off**: 싸워서 물리치다. **resort to**: to turn to. **elude**: to escape from. *cf.* I remember his face very well, but his name eludes me for the moment(= ~but I can't remember his name).

14. **dyslexia**: impairment of the ability to read, often as the result of genetic defect or brain injury (읽기 장애)
    battery: set; series; array. **sequential thinking**: 계열사고(순서대로 따져나가는 사고). **bluff their way through early grades**: (속이면서) 저학년 생활을 헤쳐나아가다. **retarded** = mentally retarded (정신적으로 발육이 늦은)

정보의 결합 — 정보결합장치: 관계사

관계사는 종속절을 인도하는 일종의 특수한 접속사로 접속사 역할과 함께 대명사, 형용사 또는 부사 역할을 한다.

1
 a. Sailors **who are superstitious** will not embark on Friday. 〔제한적 용법〕
   = *Superstitious* sailors will not embark on Friday.
 b. Sailors, **who are superstitious**, will not embark on Friday. 〔서술적 용법〕
   = Sailors, *as they are superstitious*, will not embark on Friday.

2
 a. This is the house (**that**) he built.
 b. He changed his mind, **which** made me angry. 〔선행사 = 주절 전부〕

3
 a. I gave him **what** I had. (= that which)
 b. I gave him **what money** I had. (= the money that)

4
 a. He is a walking dictionary. 〔단정적인 진술〕
 b. He is **what you call** a walking dictionary. 〔객관적인 진술〕

의미

1. a. 미신을 믿는 선원들은 금요일에 배를 타려고 하지 않는다.
   b. 선원들은 미신을 믿기 때문에, 금요일에 배를 타려고 하지 않는다.
   순해 서술적 용법의 관계사절의 의미는 주절과의 논리적인 관련 속에서 찾아야 한다.

2. a. 이것이 그가 지은 집이다.
   b. 그는 자신의 생각을 바꾸었다. 그런데 그것이 나를 화나게 만들었다.
   순해 주절 전체를 받을 수 있는 관계사는 서술적 용법의 which뿐이다.

3. a. 나는 그에게 내가 가진 것을 주었다.
   b. 나는 그에게 내가 가진 돈을 주었다.

4. a. 그는 살아 있는 사전이다.
   b. 그는 사람들이 살아 있는 사전이라고 부르는 그런 사람이다.

....

> Charlie, I am warning you against your hours.
> The night before last, you came home yesterday.
> Last night, you came home today.
> This evening, if you come home tomorrow, I won't be here.

....

EXERCISE 13

진한 글자 부분을 주목하면서 전체의 뜻을 파악하라.

1. a. I said nothing **that** made him angry.
   b. I said nothing, **which** made him angry.

2. A man **who** can stick to nothing is sure to fail, no matter what he may undertake.

3. I am **that which** was, which is, and which shall be.
   cf. The sum of all my experiences adds up to the person I am today.

4. Effective knowledge is **that which** includes knowledge of the limitations of one's knowledge.

5. A woman with true charm is one **who** can make a youth feel mature, an old man youthful, and a middle-aged man completely sure of himself.

6. Robots are not a panacea for all the ills **that** industry is heir to.

7. Do not trust **such** men **as** praise you to your face.

8. Kant made a powerful and ineffaceable impression upon me, the like of **which** I never afterwards experienced in any of my philosophical reading.

9. One of the major embarrassments **to which** lecturers are submitted is the audience's looking at their watches. I once asked John Erskine if he found the ordeal particularly trying.
   "No," he replied, "not until they start shaking them!"

NOTE 9. **be submitted to** = be subject to. **trying**: that tries one's patience; annoying; exasperating; irksome

10 Love is creative, greatly enriching the lives of both the receiver and the giver. It is the only thing in the world **of which** one cannot give anyone too much. Genuine love has firmness and discipline **for which** there can be no substitute; it can never harm or inhibit or spoil; it can only benefit.

11 It is possible that science may in principle describe the structure and actions of man as a part of physical nature. It is clear, however, that man is not thus completely accounted for. Left wholly out of consideration is the realm of ideas and idealism, of understanding and emotion, **that** gives life its human significance.

12 The teachers at our Sunday school took turns giving the lesson. Usually they'd round it off with, "Now, children, the moral of this story is…"
   One day, Miss Brown, the teacher **whose** turn it was, made the story particularly exciting, and the youngsters were delighted. One boy asked if Miss Brown might not give the lesson more often. "We like her very much," he explained, "because she hasn't any morals."

13 Dean Rusk, former secretary of state and now professor of international law at the University of Georgia in Athens, is constantly called upon to give interviews, and is accordingly well prepared. One day last spring, arriving early at the university's studio, where a television show was to be taped, he took his place on the set and reviewed his notes while the crew completed preparations. The floor manager announced that they would begin in five minutes. Rusk produced a compact from his pocket, took out a powder puff and applied it to his bald head, **which** would otherwise reflect the TV lights. He then put the compact away and announced he was ready to begin.

14 Many parts of the U.S. are experiencing **what may become** the worst winter on record since 1870.

NOTE
10. You **cannot be too** careful of your health. = The more careful of your health, the better it is.
11. **physical nature**: physical world.   **realm**: area; sphere
    문맥 describe = account for = consider
12. **take turns -ing**: 차례로 (돌아가면서, 교대로) ~하다.   **round off**: to finish; end
13. **tape**: to record on magnetic tape (녹화하다).   **produce**: to take out (꺼내다)

80 1장 STRUCTURE

15 I liked him very much but I was not in any way **what the world calls** "in love" with him.

16 A new encyclopedia is designed to shrink as man learns more.
   Most encyclopedias require additions as new discoveries are made. But chapters will have to be deleted from *The Encyclopedia of Ignorance*, a compendium of **what** man does not know in the sciences, as discoveries are made — about how gravity works, for example, or how plants produce flowers, or why people become addicted to drugs and alcohol.
   The book, recently published by Pergamon Press of New York, contains contributions from 60 eminent scientists writing on what they do not understand in their fields.

17 Possibly for the first time, a soccer match has been delayed by laughter. Five thousand Athenian soccer fans, awaiting the start of an exhibition match between a Greek team and a Chinese team last year, rose and stood in respectful silence as **what they took to be** the Chinese national anthem reverberated from the stadium's loudspeakers. The Chinese team on the field, observing all those standing Greeks, also came to polite attention, assuming that the Greek anthem was being played.
   Then a lilting female voice rose above the unfamiliar music — to extol the virtues of a local toothpaste.

18 In spite of the injury to his leg, Clark, at six, had no reluctance to attend school. During his later preschool years he had been willing to spend more and more time away from his mother. His parents had talked enthusiastically of school, and Clark accepted it at their valuation. The teacher was for him an extension of his parents, armed with the same powers of conferring pleasure through approval and pain through criticism, and to Clark that pleasure or pain was important. Clark participated in **whatever** way the teacher suggested. If the group set out to make a big picture showing the fire department, Clark painted his section diligently. If

---

NOTE
16. 문맥 delete ≠ add. understand = know
17. 문맥 rose and stood in respectful silence = came to polite attention
    as what they took to be the Chinese national anthem reverberated from the stadium's loudspeakers =, assuming that the Chinese national anthem was being played (on the stadium's loudspeakers)

the group was talking about the visit to the firehouse, Clark was properly attentive. Clark had **what the teacher, Miss Baron, thought of as** good work habits. Left to himself, he kept busy for longer than the others, who were all too prone to forget their work for play or chatter.

19 There is a question about the extent **to which** any one of us can be free of a prejudiced view in the area of religion.

20 Behind the Polish military move loomed the shadow of the Kremlin. Indeed, if the government of General Jaruzelski had not imposed the crackdown, the Soviets certainly would have. The presence in Warsaw of high-ranking Soviet officers, including Marshal Viktor Kulikov, even suggested a direct Soviet role in planning **what amounted to** an invasion by proxy. For more than a year, the Kremlin had made it clear that it would not indefinitely tolerate the development of a union movement that could challenge a Communist government as directly as Solidarity had — a movement that was calling, in effect, for government by consent of the governed.

Napoleon was one day searching for a book in his library, and at last discovered it on a shelf somewhat above his reach. One of the tallest men in the staff stepped forward, saying:
"Permit me, sir. I am higher than Your Majesty."
"You are longer," said the Emperor with a frown.

| NOTE | 20. **loom**: to appear or come into sight indistinctly, especially in a large, portentous, or threatening form (특히 크거나 불길하거나 위험적인 모습으로 희미하게 나타나거나 시야에 들어오다).   **crackdown**: an action taken to stop an unlawful or disapproved activity (단속).   **amount to**: to be equal to (~와 다름없다).   **proxy**: 대리인   **make clear**: 분명히 밝히다.   **indefinitely**: 무기한으로.   **in effect**: actually; virtually (사실상 ~나 다름없이)   **government by consent of the governed**: 피지배자의 동의에 의한 정치(즉, 민주정치)
구문 what amounted to an invasion by proxy = the crackdown |

| 정보의 결합 | **관계사절 → 형용사구** |

'주격 관계대명사 + 동사'로 이루어져 있는 형용사절은 흔히 줄여져서 형용사구가 된다.

1 a. Many of them hold *opinions* (that are) **different from mine**.
　　b. The *man* (who is) **talking to the teacher** is John's father.
　　c. The *map* (that was) **made by them** was not entirely wrong.

2 a. He sent me a *telegram* **saying**(=which said) that he would be back soon.
　　cf. He went out, **saying** that he would be back soon.
　　b. Art is an *international language*, **appealing**(=which appeals) directly to the senses.

의미　1. a. 그들 중에 많은 사람들은 나의 의견과 다른 견해를 갖고 있다.
　　　　b. 선생님에게 얘기하시는 분이 쟌의 아버지이시다.
　　　　c. 그들에 의해 만들어진 지도가 전적으로 그릇된 것은 아니었다.
　　　　　주의 '주격 관계대명사+be동사+형용사(현재분사 또는 과거분사)'로 이루어져 있는 형용사절에서는 관계대명사와 be동사를 생략할 수 있다.
　　　2. a. 그는 나에게 전보 한 통을 보냈는데, 그것은 곧 돌아오겠다는 내용이었다.
　　　　　cf. 그는 밖으로 나가면서 곧 돌아오겠다고 말했다.
　　　　　주의 이 문장은 관계대명사로 바꾸어 쓸 수 없다는 점에 주의하라.
　　　　b. 예술은 하나의 국제어로서 우리의 감각에 직접적으로 호소한다.

Weak Heart

An Irish story tells of the young man with a weak heart who inherited a fortune in Ireland. The lawyer thought the priest would be the best bet to tell him. "Don't you worry your head about it," said the priest. "I'll look in on the lad and let him know."

*　At the cottage, the priest talked about one thing and another. "Pat, my boy, if you were ever to come into money, BIG money, what would you do with most of it?"*

*　"Sure, Father, it's hard to say. I suppose I'd give most of it to you for the church." Whereupon the priest fell dead.*

EXERCISE 14

진한 글자 부분을 주목하면서 전체의 뜻을 파악하라.

1. A shoplifter **caught stealing a ring in a jewelry store** pleaded, "Please don't call the police. I'll be glad to pay for it."
   When the cashier presented him with the bill, he said, "That's a little more than I'd planned to spend. Could you show me something less expensive?"

2. Behind aluminum's versatility lie properties **so diverse** that they almost seem to belong to several different metals.

3. One summer, in almost all store and restaurant windows on the Massachusetts island of Nantucket, large signs were posted **prohibiting** the entry of people with bare feet. There was, however, a noticeable exception. A small shop off the main street boldly displayed the message "Bare Feet Welcome." The shop: the local sandal maker.

4. Reading is not only a supplement to experience. Good reading is experience itself. The author who can write with power and insight and truth can make his perceptions a part of your awareness of the world around you. Thus the person who deprives himself of the wisdom and understanding of great writers deprives himself of an invaluable experience that can be gained in no other way.
   Through books, you can listen to the best minds of your own time and of all time, **speaking** on subjects of universal interest.

NOTE
1. **shoplifter**: a person who steals articles from a store during shopping hours.   **be caught -ing**: ~하다가 붙잡히다(들키다).   **plead**: to beg (간청하다)
2. **versatility**: adaptability to many uses (여러가지 용도에 사용될 수 있는 것)   **property**: attribute (속성); characteristic quality.   **diverse**: varied (다양한)
3. **post**: to put up (붙이다)
   문맥 displayed the message = posted the sign
4. **a supplement to**: ~을 보충해 주는 것.   **mind**: a person having intelligence or regarded as an intellect
   문맥 awareness = perceptions = wisdom and understanding

5. Darwin, after going round the world, spent the whole of the rest of his life in his own house. Marx, after stirring up a few revolutions, decided to spend the remainder of his days in the British Museum. Altogether it will be found that a quiet life is characteristic of great men and that their pleasures have not been of the sort that would look exciting to the outward eye. No great achievement is possible without persistent work, **so absorbing and so difficult** that little energy is left over for the more strenuous kinds of amusement.

6. Italians survive in spite of a vast gap between them and their increasingly weak and ineffective governments. They survive in spite of a welfare system that is out of control, schools and social services that are in disarray and, perhaps worst of all, a bureaucracy **so swollen and inept** that it is mocked as *lacci e laccioli*, shackles and snares. Last November a series of powerful earthquakes struck southern Italy, leveling and isolating entire villages, killing 3,000 people and leaving 300,000 homeless. Relief was rushed in, including $50 million in U.S. aid. So far, because of bureaucratic bungling, only $4.2 million of the U.S. funds have been spent to help the victims. That is scarcely surprising, considering that survivors of earthquakes that rocked the Sicilian province of Belice 13 years ago are still living in temporary housing.

A man I know got a promotion at work, and as a result enjoys a new status at home.
After a hard days' work, he goes home just as beat as before, but his family no longer calls him "grouchy." "Now they say I'm under 'executive tension,'" he reports.

NOTE
5. **stir up**: to incite or provoke (자극해서 일어나게 하다, 도발하다)
   characteristic: typical (전형적인)(뒤에 전치사 of가 온다는 점에 주의하라.)   **absorbing**: taking all one's attention; very interesting; engrossing
   문맥 the remainder = the rest (그 나머지).   **strenuous** = difficult
6. **disarray**: disorder; confusion.   **rock**: to shake; cause to tremble or vibrate.   **housing**: houses
   문맥 bungling = ineptness = ineffectiveness

| 정보의 결합 | **정보결합장치: 분사구** |

분사구는 크게 네 가지로 나누어진다. 보어(또는 준보어) 역할을 하는 것, 형용사절이 줄어서 이루어진 것, 부사절이 줄어서 이루어진 것, 두 번째 이후의 동작을 분사구로 나타낸 것.

1 **Feeling a little uncomfortable in a new suit,** I arrived at the Head Office in good time.
= I arrived at the Head Office in good time, **feeling a little uncomfortable in a new suit.**

2 She received the message **saying** that Bill was missing.
(= which said)

3 **Other things being equal,** the simplest explanation is the best.
(= If other things are equal)
= The simplest explanation is the best, **other things being equal.**

4 This train leaves here at 10, **arriving** at the next station at 10:30.
(= and arrives)

의미
1. 새 양복을 입어서 다소 불편한 기분으로, 나는 정해진 시간보다 상당히 일찍 본사에 도착했다.
   good: considerable (상당한) → in a *good* while (상당한 시간이 지난 뒤에)
2. 그녀는 전갈을 받았는데, 그것은 빌이 행방불명이라는 내용이었다.
3. 다른 조건들이 같다면, 가장 간단한 설명이 가장 좋은 것이다.
4. 이 기차는 이 곳을 10시에 떠나서, 10시 반에 다음 역에 도착한다.

주의 위의 네 가지 종류의 분사구 가운데에서 첫 번째와 세 번째 분사구는 위치를 이동할 수 있다.

Sign and Co-Sign

Every day at noontime I play video games at an arcade. This sign appeared one day on the machine: "A fool and his money are easily parted."
This hurt my ego, so I ripped off the offending notice and threw it away. There under the first sign was another: "The truth hurts, doesn't it?"

EXERCISE 15

진한 글자 부분을 주목하면서 전체의 뜻을 파악하라.

1. **Living as we do** in a money-oriented society, we naturally prize money too much.

2. a. **Given the opportunity**, they might be able to make something better of their lives.
   (= If they were given the opportunity)

   b. **Given their inexperience**, they've done a good job.
   (= Considering that they're inexperienced)

3. a. Who do you think you are, **ordering me to do this and that?**

   b. What do you think you're doing, **telling me to shut up?**

4. He lay with his eyes open, **gazing** at the morning light **streaming** in through the curtains.

5. While trying to locate an item in the meticulously kept files of a co-worker **known** for his high opinion of himself, I came upon a large folder **boldly labeled**: MISTAKES. **Consumed with curiosity**, I opened it. The file was empty.

NOTE

1. **Living as we do** = As we do live.　**money-oriented**: 금전본위의, 금전지향적인.　**prize**: to set a value upon; value highly
2. **do a good job**: 일을 잘 하다
4. **stream in**: 시냇물처럼 흘러들어오다 < get in
5. **locate** = find.　**come upon** = come across; discover by chance.　**consume**: to absorb completely (완전히 ～의 관심을 사로잡다); engross

6   A new ad posted in our apartment house by a young boy announced that he would wash a car for 50 cents. I promptly took advantage of his offer and, knowing that I was his first customer, gave him an extra quarter for a job well done. Upon passing his sign about ten minutes later, I was amused to see that it now read: "Car Wash 75 ¢ — Experienced."

7   Each day in our small town the siren at the fire station blows at 6 p.m. One evening it sounded at 7:15 p.m. **Concerned**, a group of us townspeople gathered to see which way the fire trucks would go.
   When they didn't leave the station, we asked what was going on. "There isn't any fire," we were told. "The firemen are having a meeting and not enough of them showed up."

8   One evening, my sister-in-law's family decided that they would fly the American flag every day instead of just on special days. The next morning they carried out that decision. Soon after the flag was placed in the bracket on the porch, there was a knock on the front door. When my sister-in-law answered it, she found the mailman standing there. **Pointing** to the flag, he asked, "Why is the flag flying today?"
   After listening to the explanation, the mailman walked away saying, "Thanks, I just wanted to make sure I wasn't working on my day off."

9   Throughout his long career as one of America's best-known novelists, Dos Passos has remained true to his belief that a writer is an architect of history. **Convinced** that tomorrow's problems can best be solved by searching the past, he has dedicated his life to accurately portraying the sights and sounds of the world around him for future generations to see and understand. As a portrait of 20th-century America, Dos Passos' novels are unsurpassed.

NOTE
6. **ad** = advertisement (광고).   **post**: to put up (세우다, 붙이다).   **take advantage of**: to make use of (이용하다)
   quarter: one fourth of a dollar; 25 cents
7. **Concerned**: Worried.   **go on**: to happen; take place.   **show up**: to come; arrive; appear
   문맥 sounded = blew
8. **answer the door**: (초인종이나 노크 소리를 듣고) 문간에 나가보다
   on one's day off: 자기가 근무하지 않는 날에(자신의 휴무일에)
9. **convince**: to persuade (설득하다, 확신시키다).   **dedicate**: to devote (바치다).   **portray**: to describe; depict; delineate.
   구문 **for future generations to see and understand** = so that future generations can see and understand them (미래 세대들이 그것들을 보고 이해할 수 있도록)

10 Vice President Hubert Humphrey, **addressing** a group of educators in Washington not long ago, outlined in some detail his own teaching experience, which includes a short stint as associate professor of political science at a Minnesota college. "I mention my teaching background," Humphrey said, "because, **considering** the precarious future of public office, I thought you might like to look me over."

11 As of all other things, one can have too much even of reading. **Indulged in to excess**, reading becomes a vice — a vice all the more dangerous for not being generally recognized as such. Yet excessive reading is the only form of self-indulgence which fails to get the blame it deserves. The fact is surprising; for it is obvious to anyone who candidly observes himself and other people that excessive reading can devour a man's time, dissipate his energies, vitiate his thinking and distract his attention from reality.

*Things are so tough in Miami
even the holdup men are taking IOUs.*

NOTE

10. **address**: to speak to.   **stint**: an assigned period of work (근무기간).   **precarious**: uncertain; insecure
    look over: to examine
11. **indulge oneself in**: ~에 탐닉하다.   **to excess**: excessively
    구문 **for not being** (구) = because it is not (절)   **dissipate**: to waste or squander (낭비하다).   **vitiate**: to corrupt; weaken morally; debase.   **distract**: to draw away; divert
    문맥 **to excess** = too much.   **such** = dangerous

| 구조의 발전 | **접속전치사 – 절에서 구로** |

대부분의 전치사구는 절이 발전해서 이루어진 표현 형태라고 볼 수 있다. 그러므로 이들 전치사구를 인도하는 전치사는 접속사가 발전해서 이루어진 품사라고 볼 수 있다. 일반 전치사와 구별해서, 이들 전치사를 필자는 '접속전치사' 라고 부른다.

1
  a. He failed again. I got disappointed.
  b. He failed again, **so** I *got disappointed*.
  c. He failed again, **to** *my disappointment*.

2
  a. The envelope was yellow. It was old.
  b. The envelope was yellow **because** *it was old*.
  c. The envelope was yellow **with** *age*.

3
  a. He is heavy. He is a small boy.
  b. He is heavy **though** *he is a small boy*.
  c. He is heavy **for** *a small boy*.

4
  a. He fell in love with her. He first saw her.
  b. He fell in love with her **when** *he first saw her*.
  c. He fell in love with her **at** *first sight*.

5
  a. He went there alone. I warned him not to.
  b. He went there alone **though** *I warned him not to*.
  c. He went there alone **despite** *my warning*.

의미
1. 그가 또다시 실패해서 나는 실망했다.
2. 그 봉투는 오래 묵어서 누렇게 변색되었다.
3. 그는 어린 아이지만 무겁다.
4. 그는 그녀를 처음 보았을 때에 그녀와 사랑에 빠졌다.
5. 그는 내가 그러지 말라고 경고했지만 혼자서 거기에 갔다.

| 구조의 발전 | **접속전치사 – 논리적인 관련(구조와 정보)** |

대부분의 접속사에는 논리적인 관련을 보여주는 '의미'가 나타나 있지만(예를 들어, because 에는 '이유'가 드러나 있다) 접속전치사에는 그런 의미가 나타나 있지 않으므로 문맥 속에서 찾아내어야 한다.

1   a. He is getting worse **for drinking**.
(He is getting worse + He drinks)
→ He is getting the worse **because he drinks**.

b. I felt none the better **for the medicine**.
(I felt none the better + I took the medicine)
→ I felt none the better **though I took the medicine**.

c. He is clever **for a child**.
(He is clever + He is a child)
→ He is clever **though he is a child**.

2   a. A wise man grows wiser **with age**.
(A wise man grows wiser + He grows older)
→ A wise man grows wiser **as he grows older**.

b. He came to see me **with a heavy rain falling**.
(He came to see me + A heavy rain was falling)
→ He came to see me **though a heavy rain was falling**.

c. What a lonely world it will be **with her away**!
(What a lonely world it will be + She goes away)
→ What a lonely world it will be **if she goes away**!

의미   1. a. 그는 술을 마시기 때문에 그만큼 더 악화되고 있다.
b. 나는 그 약을 먹었지만 조금도 더 나아진 느낌이 들지 않았다.
c. 그는 어린아이지만 현명하다.

2. a. 현명한 사람은 나이가 들어감에 따라서 더욱 현명해진다.
b. 그는 비가 많이 내리고 있었지만 나를 만나러 왔다.
c. 그녀가 떠나버린다면 세상은 얼마나 외로워질까!

EXERCISE 16

진한 글자 부분을 주목하면서 전체의 뜻을 파악하라.

1. He seemed a little surprised at the question, **which seemed to have nothing to do with the subject under discussion**.

2. **Diffident at first of my powers**, I learned in the end to have confidence.

3. You can't wait for symptoms to appear. **Undetected and untreated**, high blood pressure will get you. It's a sneaky, silent killer.

4. **With all his staunch individualism**, he was a man who knew how to cooperate.

5. Fires were not unusual in the old city of London, **with its labyrinth of narrow streets and tightly packed wooden houses.**

6. It is an extraordinary thing that the Greeks, **with their lively and penetrating minds**, never realized the possibilities of either microscope or telescope.

7. Even **with the impressive advance in language-teaching methodology made in the last three decades**, it is not difficult to find lessons that violate the principle of "sentence connectedness." In their emphasis on structure, the currently available audiolingual texts often fail to pay sufficient attention to vocabulary and meaning **with the result that** many pattern-practice drills contain sentences that are only tenuously connected, if at all.

NOTE
2. 문맥 diffident (= lacking confidence) ≠ confident
3. 구문 undetected and untreated (분사구) = If it is **not detected** and **treated** (부사절)
   문맥 get = kill
7. the principle of "sentence connectedness" = the principle that sentences must be logically well connected.   **In their emphasis on structure**: (그것들은) 구조를 강조하느라

8   In the field of politics women play an important part also. Not many women have been elected to the national Congress, and though there have been women governors of two states, there has never been a woman president. Yet women are so important as voters that no candidate for office can afford not to be aware of their attitudes. Women did not have the right to vote until 1920, but woman suffrage did not, as many men predicted, merely double the total number of votes cast on each side of a question, with the women voting the same as their husbands. Instead, women began to study the issues and candidates and make up their own minds.

9   **Between delicate sips of tea**, he said education was a wonderful thing.

10 **For its sermons to the contrary**, the world loves a big spender.

11 He went to see the football game **in spite of his doctor's advice to the contrary**.

12 Questions of education are frequently discussed as if they bore no relation to the social system **in which and for which the education is carried on**. This is one of the commonest reasons for the unsatisfactoriness of the answers.

13 Thus the evidence is accumulating that history may be about to repeat itself. Businessmen in various countries are today making money by selling arms to the communists, just as their predecessors did to aid Hitler up to the outbreak of World War II. Many people in the West who **should know better** are blindly assuming that the East will not risk a big war. The same kind of miscalculation was made in the late 1930's.

NOTE
8. suffrage = right to vote.   each side of a question: 주어진 문제의 양쪽
12. **bore no relation to** = were not related to
13. **be about to (do)** = be going to (do).   **the East**: 공산진영

14   a.   He went there alone **against my advice**.

b. A woman boarded an airliner after having obviously spent too much time in the bar at the terminal. The stewardess, **against her better judgment**, complied with the woman's request for a martini, but rejected a refill order minutes later. The incensed passenger demanded, "What's your name, girl? I'm gonna report you!"

"My name?" said the stewardess. "Of course, it's right here." She pointed to the nameplate on her uniform.

The passenger stared at the nameplate. She blinked. She stared again. Then she settled back in her seat in defeat. "Guess you're right," she muttered. "I can't read it."

"Give me all your money or you're geography!"
said the armed robber to the cashier.
"Don't you mean 'or you're history'?"
"Don't change the subject!" snapped the robber.

NOTE	
14a. 구문	**against my advice** (구)
	=, though I advised him against it (절)
	=, though I advised him not to (do so)
14b. 구문	**against her better judgement** (구)
	= though she judged it would be better not to (절)

구조의 발전 — That-clause의 진화

That-clause는 발전해서 명사 (또는 명사구) 또는 접속전치사구를 이룬다. 이 절이 구로 바뀔 때에 가장 많이 사용되는 전치사는 of라는 점에 주의하라.

1 Her tone implied **anger**.
→ Her tone implied **that she was angry**.

2 Her face betrayed no sign **of embarrassment**.
→ Her face betrayed no sign **that she was embarrassed**.

3 He insisted **on my having a try**.
→ He insisted **that I (should) have a try**.

4 The prospect is **for prices to continue rising faster than salaries**.
→ The prospect is **that prices will continue rising faster than salaries**.
= It is expected that prices will continue rising faster than salaries.
= Prices are expected to continue rising faster than salaries.

의미
1. 그녀의 목소리는 그녀가 화가 나 있다는 것을 암시해 주었다.
2. 그녀의 얼굴에는 당황하고 있다는 표시가 전혀 보이지 않았다.
   betray: to show; indicate; reveal
3. 그는 내가 한번 해봐야 한다고 주장했다.
4. 물가가 봉급보다 계속해서 더 빨리 올라갈 전망이다.

주의 That-clause가 구로 바뀔 때에 그 절 앞에 있는 관련된 단어에 따라서 구의 모습(특히 전치사)이 달라진다. 그러므로 다음과 같은 표현의 틀을 기억해야 한다.

1. a. a sign that~
   b. a sign of~
2. a. insist that~
   b. insist on~
3. a. The prospect is that~
   b. The prospect is for~

EXERCISE 17

진한 글자 부분을 주목하면서 전체의 뜻을 파악하라.

1. He **feigned ignorance** about the matter. (= pretended not to know)

2. "Who is that widow?" he asked, **feigning indifference**.

3. An undefinable something about the room seemed to suggest **masculine habitation**. (= that it was inhabited by a male)

4. Thus the idea **of the earth as the center of the universe** was destroyed.

5. NASA thought the project might run to $8 billion. Still, when offered some $3 billion less than that, the agency **faked optimism**, took the money and kicked off the work.

6. In the course of the meal, I remarked to the President that most of his advisers seemed to be putting the risk **of a soon-renewed Middle East war** at "somewhere between 60 and 70 percent."

7. American financial tycoon Carnegie **spoke of the disgrace of dying rich** and argued that the millionaire should "be but a trustee for the poor."

8. A teenage girl in Florida and a man of 30 in Utah killed themselves, leaving notes that **spoke of depression** over Lennon's death.

9. Carter rightly calls Reagan naive for thinking the Soviets can be intimidated into accepting deep cuts in their existing arsenal by the threat **of a future U.S. buildup**.

NOTE
5. **run to** < come to = to cost (비용이 들다).   **kick off**: to start
6. The damage **stands at** $5 million. (피해액은 5백만 달러다.)
   The police **put** the damage **at** $5 million. (경찰은 피해액을 5백만 달러로 보고 있다.)
9. **naive**: foolishly simple.   **arsenal** = weapons

10 There was not a line in her countenance, not a note in her soft and sleepy voice, but **spoke of an entire contentment with her life**. (=Every line in her countenance, every note in her soft and sleepy voice, said that she was entirely content with her life.)

11 The workers trust their bosses to make the right decisions because there is a pervasive sense that both labor and management are working together. In Japanese companies, as a general rule, managers rise from within the corporate ranks, adding to the feeling **of camaraderie and shared experience**. (= that they are comrades and share experience)

12 In this view, deep spending cuts and a one-year modest tax reduction could result in the worst of all possible economic worlds: an inflationary recession. Thus some economic advisers are telling the White House to fight to the end for its tax plan — at the very time that the Administration is having trouble countering Democratic troops in line. The outlook is not only **for a long argument in Congress,** but **for divided counsel within the Administration.**

13 To be sure, there is nothing in the state of East-West relations today that would make a Soviet attack likely. But Western strategists cannot afford to rule out the possibility **of a sudden change in Moscow's policy.** In case **of a sudden military threat**, NATO could not mount a credible deterrent — at present force levels and with the present economic and political weaknesses of many Western governments. In terms of numbers, the alliance today is outnumbered, outgunned, out-tanked and outplaned. This is primarily the result of the massive buildup of Soviet armed forces.

NOTE
10. **countenance**: face
11. **pervasive**: widespread
    share experience: (경험에는 고통스러운 것과 즐거운 것 두 가지가 있으니까) 동고동락하다
    문제 labor = workers.　management = managers = bosses.　feeling = sense
    camaraderie and shared experience = working together
12. **spending cuts**: (연방정부의) 지출삭감.　**result in**: to bring about; lead to; cause.　**the worst of all possible economic worlds**: 가능한 최악의 경제사태.　**Democratic troops in line**: (자기들의 방안을 통과시키려고) 대열을 가다듬고 투쟁하고 있는 민주당원들.　**outlook**: prospect. **counsel**: advice
13. **rule out**: to exclude (배제하다).　**mount a credible deterrent** = deter it credibly (믿을 만하게 그것을 저지하다)
    cf. **mount an attack on** = attack.　**in terms of**: regarding; concerning; with regard to

14 Most of the official indicators show Italy's economy to be in serious trouble. Inflation pushes along at nearly 21%. Industrial production has slumped by 5.4% since last August, and unemployment idles 1.5 million people. The battered lira continues to decline in value, and **projections are for a government deficit of at least $31.2 billion by year's end**. Milan's Borsa Valori, the country's principal stock exchange, shut down abruptly for three days last month to forestall a panic after a sharp sell-off sliced share prices by 20% in an hour. Nothing like that had happened since 1917, in the aftermath of Italy's humiliating World War I defeat at Caporetto.

15 Perhaps **the most encouraging forecast** by the members of the TIME Board of Economists **is for a slowdown in inflation**. They predict that it will end the year at around an 8.6% annual rate, vs. 13.2% for the last quarter of 1980. The small surplus in world petroleum markets is now keeping a tight grip on oil prices, and that will remove one of the key causes of recent inflation. Homeownership costs, which account for about one-fourth of the consumer price index, are up from a year ago, but the increases are tapering off because sales are slow. Good crops and heavy livestock production so far this year should moderate food price increases in the months ahead. Finally, a stronger U.S. dollar will make the costs of imported goods lower and keep pressure on domestic companies to hold down their prices. Walter Heller, President Kennedy's chief economic adviser, concludes that the U.S. is "virtually guaranteed a lull in inflation for most of the year."

16 An endless variety of laws, restrictions, customs and traditions affects the practice of abortion around the world, although **the general trend is toward liberalized laws.**

NOTE

14. **official indicators**: 공식적인 경제지표들.   **projection**: an advance estimate; forecast.   **stock exchange**: 증권거래소.   **forestall**: to prevent.   **panic**: a widespread fear of the collapse of the financial system, resulting in unreasoned attempts to turn property into cash, withdraw money, etc.

15. **taper off**: to diminish or stop gradually.
    moderate: to cause to become moderate; restrain.   **lull**: a short period of quiet or of comparative calm, lessened activity, etc.
    　　forecast = prediction.   **are up** = have increased

| 구조의 발전 | **접속전치사 with**

With는 형용사구나 부사구를 만든다. 우리 한국인에게 더 중요한 것은 부사구이므로 여기서는 부사구에 대해서 연구해 보기로 하자. 특히 with가 만드는 부사구의 구조에 주의하기 바란다.

1 WITH + NP

He is sure to succeed **with such knowledge and experience**.
(He is sure to succeed + He has such knowledge and experience)
→ He is sure to succeed **since he has such knowledge and experience**.

2 WITH + NP + -ING

With everybody insisting on going there, I don't know whom I should send.
(Everybody insists on going there + I don't know whom I should send)
→ **As everybody insists on going there**, I don't know whom I should send.

3 WITH + NP + P.P.

We are born **with our eyes closed**.
→ When we are born, our eyes are closed.

4 WITH + NP + ADJ. or ADV.

Don't speak **with your mouth full**.
→ Don't speak **when your mouth is full**.

| 의미 | 1. 그는 그런 지식과 경험이 있으므로 틀림없이 성공할 것이다.
2. 모두가 거기에 가겠다고 주장하고 있어서, 나는 누구를 보내야 할지 모르겠다.
3. 우리는 눈을 감고 태어난다.
4. 입 안에 음식이 가득 차 있을 때에는 말을 하지 마라.

EXERCISE 18

진한 글자 부분을 주목하면서 전체의 뜻을 파악하라.

1. We've had a pretty lean time these last few months, **with my husband out of work.**

2. Mrs. Smith had her hands full, **what with three children, an invalid husband and an aged mother to look after.**

3. The young couple already have a child between them, **with another on its way.**

4. I ascended the platform **with nothing ready in my mind.**

5. I can't read anything **with children around.**

6. They lived in the same house nearly a year and a half **without a single word spoken between them.**

7. **With the earth cut away from his feet,** Oliver resumed his aimless drift along the continent.

8. He sat, (with his) **head down,** thinking over the matter.

9. I stood straight as a needle, **my shoulders back, my head high, my eyes avoiding hers.**

10. **With fightings in Iraq and elsewhere in the world today going on incessantly,** that goal of a warless world seems remote to attain as ever.

NOTE **1. have a hard time:** 어려움을 겪다 (lean = hard)

11 **With Israel insisting on having direct talks with the Arab states on a Middle East settlement,** the possibility for a successful peace pact seems remote.

12 **With the Communist regime in the north still going to every length to slander South Korea,** Korea's reunification seems as far away as ever.

13 Meanwhile, it was reported that the most prospective sites for the conference are Seoul and Busan, **with the latter being a stronger possibility**.

14 Bernard Berenson, the art historian, loved life. When he was almost 90, he said, "I would willingly stand at street corners, **hat in hand**, asking passersby to drop their unused minutes into it."

15 **With nearly 60 percent of her entire population still dependent upon the land for a livelihood,** that country should direct more efforts toward the modernization of farming methods before anything else.

16 In Sweden, as you drive through certain intersections on a red traffic light, a photo is automatically taken. You receive in the mail a picture of your car going through the light, **with time and date printed on it**, and a summons. Conveniently, you may pay the 300-kronor fine at your local bank or post office.

17 A mother accompanied by two young sons was in a hurry to get a six-pack of beer checked out at the supermarket. In order to have the exact change, she borrowed three cents from one of her boys. "Then it happened," she relates. "There I stood, eight months pregnant, **with my four-year-old screaming,** 'Please don't buy beer with my pennies, Mommy!'"

NOTE
12. **go to every length** = do everything.   **go to any lengths** = do anything.
    Korean parents usually **go to great lengths** to send their children to best schools. (= take great pains)
15. **livelihood**: means of sustaining life; living (생계수단).   **direct/make efforts toward**: ~을 위해 노력을 기울이다
16. **in the mail**: 우편으로.   **summons**: an order or command to come, attend, appear, or perform some action (여기서는 '벌금을 내라는 명령서'라는 의미로 쓰였음).   **fine**: a sum required to be paid as punishment or penalty for an offense (벌금)
17. **check out**: 계산을 하고 나가다.   **relate**: to tell

18 It was six o'clock on a bitterly cold and drizzly morning, and a group of hunters waited in misery in the duck blind. At length one hunter, **his hands blue and ice forming on his eyebrows**, said aloud what all were thinking privately.

"Fellows," he said, **his teeth chattering**, "I don't believe I can stand much more of this pleasure."

19 One of the running jokes in the days of President Lyndon B. Johnson's Administration was the President's diet. Mrs. Johnson did everything she could to keep him on it, and he often went to great lengths to indulge himself in his favorite high-calorie treats.

One day, at a Washington Senators baseball game, someone in the large party in the President's box ordered hot dogs and began passing them around. The President was suddenly seen sitting doubled over, **his head between his knees**, wolfing down a hot dog. Off his diet again, he was afraid that Lady Bird might be watching the game on television and see him eating it.

20 As a rookie in the Atlantic City, N.J., police department, I was assigned a beat on the boardwalk. Hardly a day went by when I didn't come upon a child who had become separated from his parents.

One afternoon, I spotted a small boy standing alone, obviously lost. I tried first to gain his confidence — I took him to the nearest ice-cream stand and bought him a cone. Time passed **with no sign of the boy's parents**, so the next step was to call for a patrol car to take him to headquarters. I told the small fry to stay put while I went to the call box. When I returned, he was nowhere in sight.

Within minutes, the car arrived, and one of the patrolmen asked me where the child was. I felt stupid; it's humiliating to say you've lost a lost child. But I told the officers what had happened and gave a description of the boy.

"What did you treat him to?" asked one of the men.

"An ice-cream cone. Why?"

NOTE **18. blind**: a place of concealment, as for a hunter; ambush (매복장소). **at length**: at last. **stand**: to bear; put up with
19. running: continuous. **do everything one can**: to do one's best. **go to great lengths**: to take great pains (무척 애를 쓰다). **double up**: to double over; bend over (허리를 굽히다). **wolf down**: to gulp down (꿀꺽 삼키다)

"Because," answered the officer, "that kid lives only a few blocks from here, and you're about the fifth rookie he's conned for a treat!"

21 The gunman was almost a caricature of his violent breed — "a terrorist with a capital 'T,'" as one of his interrogators put it. Mehmet Ali Agca, a 23-year-old Turkish hit man **with at least one spectacular murder to his credit**, could have passed — and nearly did — for a Palestinian or a Latin American. His ideological underpinnings were loose; his slogans made him out to be anti-everything. He had sprouted from the far fringes of the Turkish right, but his two-year crusade against the Pope could just as easily have served the purposes of the anarchistic left. One of the world's most-wanted criminals, he had floated **with impunity** across Western Europe, arriving in Italy well dressed, well armed and well supplied with cash.

22 William Garcia was a successful California anaesthesiologist when his life began to disintegrate at 40. He had a serious automobile accident, then marital problems surfaced, leading him and his wife to separation and divorce. Feeling depressed and guilty, Garcia turned to drugs. He checked into a psychiatric hospital in Arizona but stayed only six weeks before returning to California — and to drugs. Although he managed to keep practicing medicine, his professional reputation suffered. At 42, totally strung out on narcotics and **with his career in ruins**, Garcia checked into a motel and deliberately overdosed on heroin.

Garcia's suicide attempt failed. But each year a disturbing number of physicians do manage to kill themselves. Accurate statistics are hard to come by because many suicides go unreported, but different experts estimate that from 36 to 77 of every 100,000 physicians die by their own hand every year, at least three times the rate for the population at large. Put another way, almost as many doctors commit suicide annually — upwards of 130 — as graduate from Harvard Medical School. Of all professionals, doctors may be the most self-destructive. Says Garcia, now on the staff of Los Angeles'

NOTE
20. **stay put**: 그 자리에 남아 있다. **about**: perhaps. **con**: to swindle; cheat
    문제 obviously lost = obviously separated from his parents. **fry** = child
21. **breed**: a kind; sort; type. **a terrorist with a capital "T"** (= a Terrorist): a great or special terrorist. **as one of his interrogators put it** = as one of his interrogators called him. **with at least one spectacular murder to his credit** = who was believed to be responsible for at least one spectacular murder. **pass for**: ~로 통하다. *cf.* take~ for.... **underpinning**: foundation. **with impunity**: without being punished

Suicide Prevention Center : "**With the statistics the way they are for physicians**, I feel very fortunate to have made it."

Although blessed with challenging work, social position and comparative wealth, doctors contend with long hours and the knowledge that a single mistake can maim, disable or even kill. These pressures often carry over into their personal lives. Says Los Angeles Psychiatrist Robert Litman: "By and large, doctors are not good, steady companions. They're good providers but lousy lovers.."

"What is the meaning of the insignia on your uniform?" asked the nosy woman.
"I'm a naval surgeon," he replied.
"Goodness," she exclaimed, "how you doctors specialize these days!"

| NOTE | 22. **disintegrate**: to break up.　**surface**: to come to the surface; become known.
strung out [slang]: suffering from the physical or mental effects of addiction to a narcotic drug
overdose on: to take an overdose of.　**come by**: to get; obtain.　**go unreported** = are not reported
the population at large = the entire population.　**upwards of** = over; more than.
With the statistics the way they are for physicians = As the statistics are the way they are for physicians (의사들의 자살 통계숫자가 현재와 같으므로).
to have made it = to have survived (자살하지 않고 살아남게 된 것).　**contend**: to fight; struggle
by and large: on the whole; in general; considering everything.　**lousy**: very bad
self-destruction = committing suicide = dying by one's own hand = killing by oneself = suicide |

| 구조의 발전 | **접속전치사 at, on, in** |

1 a. Many people fled to other lands **at the outbreak of the war**.
　　→ Many people fled to other lands **when the war broke out**.

　b. **At this rate** we will soon run out of money.
　　→ **If we go on spending at this rate**, we will soon run out of money.

2 a. **On investigation** some curious facts came to light.
　　→ **When an investigation was made**, some curious facts came to light.

　b. He will prove, **on a closer acquaintance**, a kindhearted man.
　　→ He will prove, **when you get acquainted with him more closely**, a kindhearted man.

3 a. His mother died **in childbirth**.
　　→ His mother died **while (she was) giving birth to a child**.

　b. One must be careful **in passing judgments on a person's character**.
　　→ One must be careful **when he passes judgments on a person's character**.

의미
1. a. 많은 사람들이 그 전쟁이 일어나자 다른 나라로 달아났다.
　b. 이런 비율로 나간다면 우리는 곧 돈이 떨어질 것이다.
2. a. 조사해 보니 몇 가지 재미있는 사실이 드러났다.
　b. 더 가까이 사귀어보면 그는 친절한 사람이라는 것이 드러날 것이다.
3. a. 그의 어머니는 출산 중에 돌아가셨다.
　b. 다른 사람의 인격에 대해 판단을 내릴 때는 주의해야 한다.

NOTE
1a. flee: to run away
2a. come to light: to become known
3a. give birth to: 낳다
3b. pass judgments on = judge

EXERCISE 19

진한 글자 부분을 주목하면서 전체의 뜻을 파악하라.

1. It would be an ill-bred person who did not feel his blood boil **at the infliction of such malignant cruelty**.

2. The rapid technological advances of the twentieth century have been bought **at the expense of** an alarming depletion of our natural resources.

3. Horowits delights in simple pleasures, with a few choice friends who visit him regularly and for whom he plays the piano **at the slightest encouragement**.

4. This visa can be renewed **upon a new application**.

5. There are many books of which you cannot get the full value **on a single reading**.

6. **On a closer look**, he found the dark object was a dead tree.

7. A good writer is wise **in his choice of subjects**, and exhaustive **in his accumulation of materials**.

8. Whatever the learned may say about a book, and however unanimous they are **in their praise of it**, it is of no use to you unless it interests you.

9. **In our admiration for greatness**, we tend to overlook errors that are often to be found in great work. Because of this tendency, I believe it necessary to examine for error those theories which are generally accepted.

NOTE
1. **malignant**: very malevolent or malicious
2. **depletion**: gradual using up or destruction
3. **delight in**: to rejoice in.   **choice** [adj.]: carefully chosen

10 If consumption goes on at present rate, world reserves of copper, lead, and tin will be exhausted by the turn of the century. And **at present rate of consumption**, world reserves of iron ore could run out in less than a hundred years.

11 One of the characteristics most puzzling to a foreign observer is the strong and imperishable dream the American carries. **On inspection**, it is found that the dream has little to do with reality in American life. Consider the dream of and the hunger for home. The very word can reduce nearly all of my countrymen to tears.

12 Language is an indispensable instrument of human society. It is the means by which individuals understand each other and are enabled to function together as a community. Indeed, it is unlikely that any human organization could either be formed or long maintained without language. Certainly, **in the absence of communication**, the complex structure of modern society would be utterly impossible.

13 When comedian Joey Bishop was host of the "Tonight Show," he was plagued with autograph seekers. One day, when someone stopped him on the street and asked if he was Joey Bishop, he smiled politely and replied, "No. I only look like Joey Bishop."

   Then, **on second thought**, he asked the woman if she was a fan of Joey Bishop's. She smiled politely and replied, "No. I only look like a fan of Joey Bishop's" — and walked away.

NOTE
10. run out = be exhausted
    문맥 at present rate of consumption = if consumption goes on at present rate
11. have little to do with: ~와 거의 관계가 없다
    reduce someone to tears: to make someone weep < bring ~ to tears
12. 문맥 in the absence of = without.   communication = language
13. plague: to vex; harass; trouble; torment

14 A doctor was in the bathroom of a lunatic asylum watching his mad patients bathe. Suddenly one of them cried, "It's time for the doctor to bathe." Then another cried, "Let's drown him!" **On his crying**, all in the bathroom gathered around the doctor, with their eyes fixed on him. They insisted on his being drowned.

 Seeing his danger, the doctor thought out a trick. "All right, my lads," he said. "But suppose now you give the doctor a good cheer before you drown him."

 This reasonable proposition being at once agreed to, a loud cheer resounded through the building. This unusual noise, needless to say, at once brought the keepers to the bathroom.

15 America's "Marxophobia" must be the single greatest obstacle to its efforts to promote democracy around the world. Washington's reluctance to give aid to Nicaragua will probably send that country right into the arms of the Soviets. America must stop getting jittery **at the mere mention of socialism**. It should also cast a wary eye on some of the governments it *does* back, such as Argentina and Chile.

 Dictatorships cannot be the friends and allies of a country that professes the highest regard for democracy and human rights. The United States must be understanding toward democratic experiments like that in Nicaragua.

16 Norway has one of the toughest drunk-driving laws in the Western world. Any driver who is found to have more than .05-percent alcohol in his blood automatically spends a minimum of three weeks confined in a special facility. There offenders make furniture, stud snow tires, do electrical work, or perform household chores. In addition to serving time, they lose their license for one year **on the first offense,** and permanently if convicted again within five years.

 Hardly anyone, no matter how influential he might be, beats the rap. Of some 20,000 Norwegians sentenced to such facilities in the past four years, several have been celebrities, including members of the parliament.

NOTE
14. **lunatic asylum**: a mental hospital
 They insisted on his being drowned = They insisted that he (should) be drowned
15. **Marxophobia**: fear of Marxism.   **jittery**: very uneasy or nervous.   **back**: to support or help
 regard: respect and affection; esteem
16. **confine**: to keep shut up; detain.   **serve time**: to be in prison.   **beat the rap** = escape the punishment

17 My husband and I first met while we were teachers in Idaho. We planned to be married during spring vacation in my hometown in New Mexico. Since we had such a long distance to drive, we wrote a letter to the superintendent of schools asking if we might be granted two days of personal leave in order to make the trip. The superintendent replied that the school board, **in determining valid reasons for personal leave**, did not include getting married. Since there was no such provision, he went on, he would grant us the two days as medical leave — on the premise that we were both clearly suffering from lovesickness!

> *When I asked my wife to wash my quilted coat, she looked at the laundry-instruction tag and said,*
> *"It says it should be washed alone. To save electricity and water, I'll wait till I have something else that has to be washed alone and do them both together."*

구조의 발전 — 문장부사

하나의 절이 발전해서 이루어진 부사나 부사구를 편의상 문장부사라고 부르기로 한다.

1 **Understandably,** he bitterly attacked Communism.
  → **It is understandable that** he bitterly attacked Communism.

2 **Conceivably,** the situation could get worse.
  → **It is conceivable that** the situation could get worse.

3 People thought that the prisoner was **deservedly** sentenced to death.
  → (People thought that the prisoner deserved death sentence + He was sentenced to death)

4 Much has been said, **and with reason**, against entrance examination.
  → Much has been said against entrance examination, **and there is reason for that.** (= and it is justifiable)

5 The criminal is **reportedly** still at large.
  → **According to reports,** the criminal is still at large.
  → **It is reported that** the criminal is still at large.
  → **Reports have it that** the criminal is still at large.

의미
1. 그가 공산주의를 신랄하게 공격한 것은 이해할 만하다.
2. 그 사태가 더욱 악화될 수 있다는 것은 생각할 수 있는 일이다.
3. 사람들은 그 죄수가 사형선고를 받은 것은 마땅하다고 생각했다.
4. 사람들이 입학시험을 반대하는 얘기를 많이 해왔는데, 거기에는 그럴 만한 이유가 있다.
5. 보도에 의하면 그 범인은 아직도 붙잡히지 않았다고 한다.

At a grand Christmas party, a young man asked an attractive elderly lady for a dance.
*"Sorry, I don't dance **with a baby**," refused the lady.*
*The young man challenged, "Sorry, I didn't know you are **pregnant**."*

EXERCISE 20

진한 글자 부분을 주목하면서 전체의 뜻을 파악하라.

1 To practice what one preaches is **admittedly** not so simple.

2 Such kind of conflict can be **properly** described as suicidal.

3 I think I could be **justly** blamed if I saw only people's faults and were blind to their virtues.

4 The Arabs argue, **with some justification**, that Israel so far has benefited most since the ceasefire.

5 There is nothing praiseworthy in sacrifice itself, and before a man does a self-sacrificing thing, he may **reasonably** ask himself if it is worthwhile.

6 In sum, all of us might **profitably** heed the advice of that Senate committee on nutrition — and reduce our sugar consumption.

7 To control the number of illegal aliens entering the U.S. in the future, the Administration is considering sanctions — **presumably** stiff fines — against employers who **knowingly** hire such immigrants.

8 Hua Kuo-feng presumably became premier with Mao's blessing, but there is no evidence that the chairman anointed him as his own successor. Thus the chances are that it may take weeks if not months before the divided leadership can agree on a new head of the party.

NOTE
3. 문맥 were blind to (= didn't see) ≠ saw. virtues ≠ faults
6. **heed**: to pay close attention to; take careful notice of
7. **alien**: foreigner. **sanction**: 제재조치. **stiff**: severe; high. **fine**: 벌금
8. **blessing**: approval. **anoint**: to appoint; designate
   The chances are that~ = It is likely or probable that~; Probably~. **leadership** = leaders

9   Five years later, the heads of all the nations in the European Community conferred on Monnet the title of Honorary Citizen of Europe — the only man ever to be so honored. **And for good reason.** His was a noble idea — to unite the nations of Europe in the service of peace and worldwide cooperation. And, to a remarkable degree, his vision has triumphed.

10 Mr. Jones lived for the most part, retired in the country, with one sister, for whom he had a very tender affection. This lady was now somewhat past the age of thirty, an era at which, in the opinion of the malicious, the title of old maid **with no impropriety** might be assumed. She was of that species of women whom you rather commend for good qualities than beauty.

11 At a trial in Detroit's Recorder's Court, a young woman who had accused the defendant of making an improper proposal was asked to state the question that **allegedly** had been asked. It embarrassed her to repeat it, so she was permitted to write it on a piece of paper. After the judge, prosecutor and defense counsel had read it, it was passed to the jury. Each juror read it, and gave it to the next juror.
   After an attractive female juror had read it, she attempted to pass it to the man on her right, but found him dozing. Without comment, she nudged him and gave him the slip of paper. The awakened juror read the note, smiled at her, nodded, and put the note in his pocket!

12 As soon as a stranger is introduced into any company, one of the first questions which all wish to have answered, is, how does that man get his living? And **with good reason**. He is no whole man until he knows how to earn a blameless livelihood.

NOTE
9. **His was a noble idea** = His idea was a noble one.   **in the service of** = for
10. **the malicious** = malicious people.   **with no impropriety** = with propriety = properly
    commend: to recommend; praise
    era = age
11. **recorder**: a judge who has the same criminal jurisdiction as a police judge
12. earn/get one's living/livelihood = earn/get a living/livelihood

문맥파악을 위한 기초작업
2 STYLE

1 주어 전환

2 품사 전환

3 반복 피하기

| 주어 전환 | **무생물 주어** |

일반적으로 우리말은 무생물 주어를 회피하는 경향이 있으나, 영어(문어체)는 무생물 주어를 많이 사용한다. 이것이 영어의 문체를 우리말 문체보다 더 다양하게 만드는 요인 중의 하나다.

1 Why do **you** think so?
→ **What** makes you think so?

2 **His father** died suddenly, and he had to give up school.
→ **His father's sudden death** forced him to give up school.

3 Compare them carefully, and **you** will see the difference.
→ **A careful comparison of them** will show you the difference.

4 The reporting was so real that nearly **everyone** was convinced that the "invasion" was really taking place.
→ **The realism of the reporting** convinced nearly everyone that the "invasion" was really taking place.

의미
1. 어째서 너는 그렇게 생각하느냐?
2. 아버지가 갑자기 돌아가시자 그는 학교를 그만두지 않을 수 없었다.
3. 그것들을 자세히 비교해 보면 그 차이를 알게 될 것이다.
4. 그 보도는 너무도 생생해서 거의 누구나 그 '침공'이 실제로 벌어지고 있는 것으로 믿었다.

Three **absent-minded** professors were sitting in a railroad station waiting for a train. They were so **absorbed** in thought that they failed to **notice** the arrival of the train. Suddenly one of them noticed it as it started to pull out, and they all rushed for it. Two of them caught the train. A bystander **consoled** the third who missed it.
  "You shouldn't feel bad," he said, "At least two of you made it."
  "Yes, I know," **replied** the professor, "but those two came to see me off."

EXERCISE 21

진한 글자 부분을 주목하면서 전체의 뜻을 파악하라.

1   His fatness renders him unable to touch his toes.

2   The flood left many people in the village homeless.

3   The introduction of labor-saving technology has cost many people their jobs.

4   The U.S.-led boycott of the Olympics cost the Soviets millions of dollars in lost revenues.

5   **Arson is suspected in a fire** that destroyed three downtown businesses over the weekend.

6   At 52, he was the chief hope of continuity for the Islamic revolution, **whose terrifying politics have split Iran into bitter and contending factions**.

7   Notice seen on the bulletin board of a Florida air base: "The following enlisted men will pick up their Good Conduct medals in the supply room this afternoon. **Failure to comply with this order will result in disciplinary action**."

8   He is secretive about his age: **published estimates put him in his early 70s**, but he has the look and vigor of a man much younger, turning out three novels a year with metronomic regularity.

NOTE
5. **business**: a commercial or industrial establishment; store, factory, etc.
6. **politics**: political methods, tactics, etc.; sometimes, specifically, crafty or unprincipled methods
7. **comply with**: to act in accordance with.   **result in**: to lead to.   **disciplinary action**: 징계조치
   주의 인용된 두 문장 중에 처음 것은 지시하는 말임. → Students entering the class late **will please** sit at the back of the room. (늦게 강의실에 들어오는 학생들은 강의실 뒷자리에 앉아주기 바랍니다.)

9   Precisely **what ails Brezhnev** is a closely guarded secret, known only to a handful of Kremlin insiders. **Speculation has included cancer of the jaw, emphysema, heart disease, gout, and leukemia.**

10 College students would be better prepared for independent thinking **if there were less emphasis on conformity in high school.**

11 **The next 25 years in science will see** the elimination of infectious disease as a cause of death, new sources of energy, solutions for the disposal of radioactive waste, and computers that will create as well as solve problems.

12 **Egypt's problems defy easy solution.** The per capita income is a meager $469 per year. Its middle class is beset by an acute lack of affordable housing. Industry is virtually stagnant, and productive foreign investment is anemic. The country now imports half of its food.

13 **In Egypt, a patina of superficial prosperity gilds a fragile economic core.** The revenues from new trade policies and foreign investment are flowing to an all too visible superclass of the very rich. But at the same time, the great mass of Egyptians are struggling with overcrowding, a breakdown of critical services and lack of productive jobs.

14 Most people have covered the windowpanes of their homes or apartments with thick black paper or tinfoil, in order to keep the lights on during the blackout. The reason is not so much the fear of air strikes as the noisy urging of young people and children who act as self-appointed civil defense wardens. **The briefest glimpse of light from a window starts a chorus of "Turn it off" from a dozen directions.**

NOTE
10. **conformity**: action in accordance with customs, rules, prevailing opinion, etc.; conventional behavior
11. **radioactive waste**: 방사능 폐기물
12. The beauty of the scene **defies** description = The beauty of the scene is beyond description = It is impossible to describe (in words) the beauty of the scene.   **meager**: small; inadequate.   **beset**: to trouble from all directions; harass; besiege.   **acute**: very serious; critical; crucial.   **housing** = houses.   **virtually**: in effect; practically; almost.   **anemic**: 빈혈증의
14. **patina**: a thin crust or film; appearance.   **gild**: to coat with a gold color.   **fragile**: easily broken, damaged, or destroyed; frail.   **all too visible**: (어딜 가나) 너무도 눈에 잘 띄는.   **critical**: very important; vital.   **services**: 상수도, 전기 따위의 시설

| 품사 전환 | **동사 → 명사 → 형용사** |

영어에서는 같은 내용을 ①절이나 구로, ②품사를 바꾸거나, 또는 ③행위나 행위자를 중심으로 나타낼 수 있다. 언제나 우리말과 다른 표현방식에 주의하기 바란다.

1 a. Disease frequently **accompanies** war.
   → Disease is a frequent **accompaniment** of war.
   b. He **succeeded** as a novelist.
   → He was a **success** as a novelist.
   → He was a **successful** novelist.

2 a. Power **tends** to corrupt.
   → Power has a **tendency** to corrupt.
   b. He **studied** the problem carefully.
   → He made a careful **study** of the problem.
   c. She **resembles** her mother closely.
   → She bears a close **resemblance** to her mother.

3 a. John **works** hard.
   → John is a hard **worker**.
   b. Younghee **speaks** English well.
   → Younghee is a good **speaker** of English.

의미
1. a. 질병은 흔히 전쟁에 수반된다.
   b. 그는 소설가로 성공했다.
2. a. 권력은 부패하는 경향이 있다.
   b. 그는 그 문제에 대해 주의깊게 연구했다.
   c. 그녀는 어머니를 많이 닮았다.
3. a. 쟌은 부지런히 일한다〔공부한다〕.
   b. 영희는 영어로 말을 잘 한다.

....

Good translations are like women:
If (they are) faithful they are not beautiful,
if beautiful they are not faithful.

....

EXERCISE 22

진한 글자 부분을 주목하면서 전체의 뜻을 파악하라.

1. The bill **had a rough passage** through the House of Lords.

2. a. Kennedy **had a fresh way of doing** things.
   b. Accidents **have a disconcerting way of making** new history.

3. He **had a surface acquaintance with** a number of ancient writers.

4. Her face had grown pale, and she **made a futile attempt at** a smile.

5. The Greeks **made no formal distinction between** philosophical thought and natural sciences.

6. She **made a late appearance at** the party.

7. For several years he **engaged in a casual practice of law** at his home.

8. Though defeated, our team **put up a plucky defense** against their taller and huskier opponents.

9. Questions of education are frequently discussed as if they **bore no relation to** the social system in which and for which the education is carried on.

10. Singing commercials are **a recent invention**.

11. No reasonable person would **take offense at** what you said.

12. Dancing as a performing art was **a relatively late development** in the United States.

13 The automobile was **a total wreck**, but the driver, luckily, escaped with minor cuts and abrasions.

14 Carl's sore arm is not **a new development** but the return of a chronic ailment.

15 Love is blind, but marriage is **an eye-opener**.

16 About this time, I **got hold of** a book on how to save energy. It was **a real eye-opener**.

17 Any presidential candidate whose appeal is mainly to partisans in his own party is **a sure loser** in 1980.

18 She has pursued life and love with fierce energy all of her 50 years. She is one of Germany's best-known actresses, **a performer in 54 films**, including "Silk Stockings" and "Decision Before Dawn" in Hollywood.

19 A: "May I please get this prescription refilled?"

B: "I'm sorry. We can't **give** you a **refill on** that, sir. You have to get a new prescription from your doctor."

20 I called the operator and asked her to **place a call** for me. She replied stiffly, "You can save time and money by dialing the number yourself."

"I know," I said, "but I've got the time and I'd like to spend some of it before it stacks up." She mumbled something and **gave** me **a disconnect**.

21 Business, now limping along, will start to improve as winter melts into spring, but recovery will be slow and painful. A tax cut to spur individual saving, consumer spending and business investment is almost **a certainty** before year-end.

NOTE
19. **get a prescription filled**: (의사의) 처방대로 약방에 가서 약을 구하다
21. **winter melts into spring**: 겨울이 녹아서 봄이 되다(즉, 겨울이 지나가고 봄이 오다).   **spur**: to stimulate
before year-end = before the year ends

22 Strange as it seems, the most common way of **gaining illegal entry into** residences is through unlocked doors. Burglars frequently stroll apartment hallways and residential streets looking for the door that opens with the turn of a knob. Even if you are home, your doors should be locked at all times, including those in your garage.

23 In a town near Amsterdam they had to erect a statue to somebody no Dutchman ever heard of — "Pieter." He's the brave little Dutch boy who stuck his finger in the dike and saved the area from flooding.

 The story of Pieter is entirely **an American invention**, but so many American visitors asked about him that the Dutch decided it was only sensible to erect a statue in his honor.

24 Art may be defined as skill on the part of man in the production of the beautiful, or in **giving embodiment** or **expression to** the ideal. The beauty of Nature is changing and transient. It **has its coming and going**. The storm may smite and darken it, or the rude hand of winter lay it low. Art captures it and represents it for us in permanent and ideal forms. The painter, the sculptor, the architect, and the musician or tone poet, seize the angels of beauty as they pass, and hold them fast that they may bless us.

25 Bing Crosby writes of an experience he had while traveling by train through the Southwest many years ago:

 Our train was stopped, and we were told **there'd be a wait**, so I walked up and down the track behind the train. The rear brakeman, a hard-bitten little Texan, was walking up and down, too, swinging his lantern. He came up to me and said, "They tell me that rascal Bim Crosland's aboard. **They say he's quite a singer**, but as far as I'm concerned, Larry Ross could run him in a gopher hole."

 I agreed with him and thought no more of it. In the morning, there came

---

NOTE

22. 문맥 the door that opens with the turn of a knob = the unlocked door
23. **only**: just; quite; really
24. **transient**: passing away with time; not permanent; temporary; transitory.   **smite**: to strike or attack with powerful or disastrous effect.   **lay low**: to cause to fall by hitting.   **fast**: firmly.   **that~may ...** = so that~may ...
25. **hard-bitten**: tough; stubborn; dogged.   **He's quite a singer**: 그는 대단한 가수다.   *cf.* I'm not much of a singer (= I don't sing well).   **run someone into a gopher hole**: ~를 쥐구멍에라도 들어가고 싶게 만들다   **hoax**: to deceive

a knock on our door. It was the brakeman. He eyed me with a twinkle and said, "You hoaxed me, didn't you? You're Bim Crosland yourself! Just for that, you've got to sign my book."
  So I signed it: "Bim Crosland."

26 Not long ago, dying at home was a fact of life for the terminally ill. Today that is no longer true. Enormous progress in medical technology makes it possible to **put up a strong fight** against a disease and to prolong life, but one consequence is that more and more terminal patients spend their final days in hospitals.

27 If you see a pelican standing with its flat feet on a sandy beach, you may not think that **he is much of a flier**. But he is. Watch him as he moves along at about twenty-six miles an hour, almost touching the tops of the waves. Often he flies with his companions in a long line of pelicans. They follow one another up, over and down the waves, move their wings together and stay the same distance from one another. This is a perfect group flying show.

Jim Bouton, sportscaster and author of "Ball Four",
on the reception to his book:
"Pete Rose would scream at me from the dugout
because I revealed too much.
Now he's posing in magazine ads in his underwear."

NOTE
26. the terminally ill = terminal patients (죽을병에 걸려 있는 사람들)
27. The bird **is** not **much of** a flier. = The bird is not a good flier. = The bird does not fly well.
   cf. He's quite a singer.

반복 피하기 — 대명사로 바꾸어 쓰기

영어는 반복을 싫어하는 언어다. 수사적인 목적을 위해서 같은 말을 되풀이하는 경우를 제외하고, 영어에서는 대부분 한번 나온 말은 다른 말로 바꾸어 쓴다.

1 후치 대명사

a. If you want **a true friend**, you will find **one** in him.
b. If I am **a fool**, you are **another**.
c. He is still **a mere child** and should be treated as **such**.

2 전치 대명사 (명사 앞에 오는 대명사)

a. **Ours** is still a developing **country**.
b. To some of **his** contemporaries **Socrates** looked like a sophist.
c. Reports have **it** that the criminal is still at large.

3 유사 대명사

a. You should read Shakespeare and other **immortals**.
 (= immortal writers)
b. From the classical philosophers I turned to the **moderns**, thinking that among them, perhaps, I should find what I wanted. (= modern philosophers)
c. The first circulating library was opened in London in 1740. **Rivals** quickly sprang up in London and in the provinces as well. (= Rival circulating libraries)

의미

1. a. 네가 진정한 친구를 원한다면, 그한테서 진정한 친구를 찾을 것이다.
   b. 내가 바보라면 너도 바보다.
   c. 그는 아직 어린 아이이므로, 아이로 대우받아야 한다.
2. a. 우리나라는 아직도 개발도상국이다.
   b. 일부 동시대인들에게 소크라테스는 궤변론자처럼 보였다.
   c. 보도에 의하면 그 범인은 아직도 붙잡히지 않았다고 한다.
3. a. 셰익스피어와 그밖의 불후의 작가들을 읽어야 한다.
   b. 고대 철학자들로부터 나는 현대 철학자들에게로 방향을 바꾸었는데, 그것은 어쩌면 그들에게서 내가 원하는 것을 찾게 될지도 모른다는 생각을 했기 때문이었다.
   c. 최초의 이동 도서관은 1740년 런던에서 개관했다. 경쟁 이동 도서관들이 런던과 다른 지방에서도 빠르게 생겨났다.

EXERCISE 23

진한 글자 부분을 주목하면서 전체의 뜻을 파악하라.

1. You must help them, and **that** at once.

2. They thought him shy, **which** he was, and dull, **which** he was not.

3. It is undeniable that Hitler was a genius, albeit the most evil **one** the modern world has known.

4. We are all equal in **this**, that we all have twenty-four hours a day.

5. In terms of **their** traditional functions, arts have lost their reason to exist.

6. Instead of getting rid of **his** prejudices, the average person whitewashes them and tries to pass them off as principles.

7. In spite of **its** aloofness and independent bearing, the domesticated cat has come to depend upon man for food and protection.

8. Like the infant whose birth **they** symbolize, stars, by living and dying, enable whole new worlds to be born.

9. Not because of **their** superior intelligence but because of the conditions under which **they** have had to do **their** work, anthropologists have developed ways of studying human groups which have been found to have certain advantages over the methods characteristic of the workers in other fields.

NOTE
3. **albeit**: although
5. **reason to exist**: 존재해야 할 이유, 존재이유
6. **whitewash**: to conceal the faults or defects of.   **pass off**: to be accepted
7. **aloof**: reserved and cool (주위에서 벌어지는 일에 초연한).   **bearing**: manner; way of behaving; mien
9. **have an advantage over~** : ~보다 한 가지 장점을 갖고 있다.   **characteristic of** = peculiar to (~에게 독특한)
   cf. It is **typical of** him to arrive late for an appointment (그는 전형적으로 약속시간에 늦게 도착한다).

10 **It is the bravest quality of all, this ability to look past dark times to brighter ones**, to believe that questions do have answers, that challenges can be met, that problems will be solved.

11 I saw Strictland not infrequently, and now and then played chess with him. He was of a severe temper. Sometimes he would sit silent and absent-minded, taking no notice of anyone; and at **others**, when he was in a good humour, he would talk in his own hesitating way. He never said a clever thing, but he always said exactly what he thought.

12 Sometimes I ask myself at night what I have done that day, what new thought or idea I have had, what particular emotion I have felt, what there has been to mark it off from **its fellows**; and more often than not it appears to me insignificant and useless.

13 A deep mistrust of science and technology is expressed by many in our society today. Were **it** to prevail, this sense of suspicion and frustration could result not only in our failure to solve our present crises, some of them the result of past misuses of technology, but also in our future inability to deal with problems we may not even be in a position to predict.

14 If looked at through the eyes of some of **its** greatest writers, the Victorian Age can be seen as an age of change and doubt. Yet in the eyes of very many Victorians it was an age of progress, confidence, and achievement; and those who came immediately afterwards looked back on the period as essentially one of stability.

NOTE

10. **do have answers**: do는 뒤의 동사를 강조하는 구실을 한다.   **meet**: to deal with; cope with (처리하다)
11. **not infrequently**: 드물지 않게(= frequently; often).   **now and then**: sometimes; occasionally; once in a while.   **He was of a severe temper** = He had a severe temper.   **humour**[humor]: mood
12. **mark~off from...** = distinguish~from....   **more often than not**: more than 50% of the time
    cf. **as likely as not**: probably
13. **Were it to prevail** = If it were to prevail.   **result in**: to lead to; cause; end in
    유의 inability = failure.   deal with = solve.   problems = crises

15 **Legend has it that** John F. Kennedy decided to enter politics one evening after a long conversation with his father. Joe, Sr. was supposed to have told Jack that since Joe, Jr. had given his life for his country during the war, it was now up to Jack to uphold the family's tradition of political public service. The entire family would support Jack, his father said. And, as the story goes, Jack heeded his father's urging, and decided to enter politics on the spot.

But the truth is somewhat different. Certainly there was a political tradition in the Kennedy family. To be sure, Joe, Sr. wanted to see this tradition carried on, and certainly he felt it should be carried by Jack since Joe had died. But this is all too simple — for it takes everything into account except the one most important thing — the remarkable personality of Jack Kennedy.

16 It is a peculiar sensation, this double-consciousness, this sense of always looking at one's self through the eyes of others, of measuring one's soul by the tape of a world that looks on in amused contempt and pity. One ever feels his twoness — an American, a Negro; two souls, two thoughts, two unreconciled strivings.

The history of the American Negro is the history of this strife, this longing to merge his double self into a better and true self. In this merging he wishes neither of the older selves to be lost. He would not Africanize America, for America has too much to teach the world and Africa. He would not bleach his Negro soul in a flood of white Americanism, for he knows that Negro blood has a message for the world. He simply wishes to make it possible for a man to be both a Negro and an American, without being cursed and spat upon by his fellows, without having the doors of opportunity closed roughly in his face.

NOTE

15. Legend has it that = The story goes that; It is said that; According to legend.   **enter politics**: 정계에 들어가다.   **up to:** the duty or responsibility of; dependent upon; incumbent upon: It's up to you whether you decide to take the job.   **heed**: to pay attention to.   **on the spot**: 1) at the place mentioned (즉석에서) 2) at once; immediately.   **take into account**: take into consideration

16. look on: 구경하다, 방관하다.   **in amused contempt and pity**: 재미있다는 듯이 경멸하고 동정하면서.   **One ever feels his twoness** = An American Negro always feels his doubleness.   **two unreconciled strivings**: 두 개의 화해되지 않은 투쟁.   **merge**: to unite.   **bleach**: to whiten (표백하다).   **spit upon**: ~에게 침뱉다.   **in one's face**: before one (자신의 면전에서)

문맥 bleach his Negro soul in a flood of white Americanism = Americanize his African soul.
for he knows that Negro blood has a message for the world = for his African soul has too much to teach the world and America

| 반복 피하기 | **명사 대리어(구)** |

1. **Democracy** in the true sense of **the word** is still unknown in that country.

2. **Khrushchev** first met Stalin in 1925, when **the younger man** was elected a delegate to the 14th Party Congress.

3. In 1950, one person out of 30 earned $10,000 or more a year. Today, one person out of three earns **that much**.

   cf. Ghana has twenty-three tribes, speaking **as many** different languages.

4. a. The American woman enjoys more leisure and freedom than **her Korean sister**.

   b. French students have far more homework than **their American counterparts**.

   c. The Japanese prime minister had a brief discussion over the matter with **his British opposite number**.

의미
1. 진정한 의미에서의 민주주의는 아직 그 나라에는 알려져 있지 않다.
2. 호루시초프는 1925년에 처음으로 스탈린을 만났는데, 그 해에 그는 제14차 공산당 전당대회에 대표로 선출되었다.
3. 1950년에는 30명 가운데 1명이 1년에 만 달러 또는 그 이상의 수입을 얻었는데, 오늘날에는 3명 가운데 1명이 그만한 수입을 얻는다.
   cf. 가나에는 23개 부족이 있는데, 이들이 사용하는 언어도 이들의 수만큼 된다.
4. a. 미국 여성은 한국 여성보다 더 많은 여가와 자유를 누리고 있다.
   b. 프랑스 학생들은 미국 학생들보다 숙제가 훨씬 더 많다.
   c. 일본 총리는 그 문제에 대해서 영국 총리와 간단히 협의했다.
      * opposite number = counterpart

The late actress Dame Madge Kendal was asked,
when well along in years, how she managed to look so well.
Her reply: "I try to fill up my wrinkles with intelligence."

EXERCISE 24

진한 글자 부분을 주목하면서 전체의 뜻을 파악하라.

1. The author of a geology book for junior high school students, Golden is currently writing one on astronomy for **the same audience**.

2. I will neither give a deadly drug to anybody, if asked for, nor will I make a suggestion **to this effect**.

3. The domestication of the wolf is by no means so difficult as is usually supposed, especially in the case of the American species. There is, however, one striking difference between the modern dog and **his wild cousins**.

4. We are all familiar with the distinction represented by the words "civilization" and "culture." Civilization, as I have already suggested, is usually thought of as in the main materialistic achievement, culture as religious, academic and artistic; and it is then assumed that not merely a parallelism but even a causal relationship exists between **the two phenomena**.

5. As he tells in the *Apology*, Socrates in his time defied both tyranny and democracy. He had no respect for either **the powerful few** or **the powerful many**. Although no voice has ever been raised more eloquently than his in defense of the individual, he was no democrat in the free and easy sense of **the term**. It was a democracy that killed Socrates — and that died in the process. Greek civilization never recovered from **this old man's** death.

NOTE

2. **deadly**: lethal. **if asked for** = even if I am asked for (one) = even if somebody asks me for one

4. **in the main**: mainly; on the whole; largely (주로, 대체로). **parallelism**: close resemblance; similarity
   a causal relationship: 인과관계

5. **defy**: to resist or oppose boldly or openly
   문맥 the powerful few = tyranny. the powerful many = democracy. this old man = Socrates

6 Most casual visitors to the zoo are convinced, as they stroll from cage to cage, that the funny gestures of the inmates are no more than a performance put on solely for their entertainment. Unfortunately, however, nothing could be farther from the truth than this view of the contented, playful caged animal. Recent research has amply demonstrated that many caged animals are in fact facing a survival problem as severe as that of **their cousins in the wild** — a struggle to survive, simply, against the monotony of their environment. Well fed, well housed, well cared for, and protected from its natural enemies, the zoo animal in its Super-Welfare State existence is bored, sometimes literally to death.

7 I did not know Nehru at all intimately; in fact, I did not even meet him many times. But his personality made an immediate impression at one's first meeting with him, and this impression did not change over the years. Nor was the effect he made just an impression; **the word** is weak and too cold. "Captivation" comes nearer to the truth. Here was a human being who could win one's heart and keep it.

   This would be something remarkable in anyone in any walk of life; but in someone whose position was humble and obscure it might not be so surprising as it was in a world-famous statesman who has left a deep mark, **and this** on the whole world and not just on his own country. In this great statesman, the lovable human being was not smothered by the eminent public figure; I should say that, in Nehru, there was not even the faintest touch of pomposity or self-importance or self-consciousness. He retained the spontaneity and the buoyancy of youth after he had been carrying for years an unusually heavy burden of office. It was not till his last years that the unforeseen breach between India and China began to bow him down under its weight.

8 It is my Aunt Grace's practice to travel by bus and to notice what most people miss. One Saturday morning the 144 bus passed a busy intersection often confused with the next. When Grace looked out the window, she saw

---

NOTE

6. **put on**: to stage (공연하다).   **care for**: to take care of; look after.   **existence** = life.   **to death**: to the extreme; extremely

7. **at one's first meeting with him** = when one first met him.   **win**: to gain.   **walk of life**: 사회의 신분이나 계층. → people from all walks of life.   **smother**: to stifle; suffocate; suppress.   **touch**: a trace; tinge (자취, 흔적).   **retain**: to continue to have; keep.   **breach**: a break in friendly relations (불화)

   문맥 **eminent** = famous ≠ **obscure**

two young girls outfitted for camping. They looked nervous. When her bus arrived at the next intersection, she saw two young men outfitted in the same manner standing by a car. They, too, obviously were waiting for an appointment.

Grace got off the bus (which meant she would have to wait an hour or so for the next) and approached the young men. They spoke to her in a foreign accent. Grace described the girls she had seen, and the young men left. When **the small happy band** returned to thank her, what she had supposed was confirmed. There had, indeed, been a mix-up!

Anxious to return good for good, **the chattering little group** insisted they be allowed to take her home. Grace refused. Grace is independent. And, from the soft telling of it, you can see that it matters, and you can understand why the young people agreed and crossed the avenue to a gift shop and returned with a little cotton elephant.

Now there is **a remembrance** in Grace's apartment, but there are also four young people who, whatever direction they take, are bound to remember a strange city where a lady took the trouble to be friendly to them.

9 Our era has also been widely known as the Age of Anxiety, especially since the publication of W. H. Auden's poem of **that title** in 1947. Not that the poet was responsible for generating **the feeling**. He merely captured it, gave it a name, and made us more aware of its pervasiveness. Thirty-two years later, the anxiety has not gone away; if anything it has been heightened. How much of it can be attributed to the accelerated acquisition of scientific knowledge and its widespread application? Plenty.

It would be an exaggeration to say that the Age of Anxiety was brought on by the Age of Science. There is no way to measure precisely how much of our anxiety is directly related to science and how much to other factors in our lives. But there seems little doubt that science has been a major producer of anxiety.

NOTE
8. **outfit**: to equip (필요한 장비를 갖추어 주다).　**a foreign accent**: 낯선 말투.　**the small happy band**: 만나기로 약속한 사람들을 만나서 즐거워하는 네 젊은이들.　**matter**: to be of importance; be significant
　문맥 outfitted in the same manner = outfitted for camping.　mix-up = confusion
9. **Not that** = I don't mean that.　**if anything** = if there is any difference (어떤 차이가 있다면)
　문맥 era = age.　the feeling = anxiety

10 Of the 1,139 students in Harvard class of 67, 90 students declared themselves "undecided" about their career plans; of this year's 1,000 or so, there are at least 250 **in that limbo.**

The English people in particular love to make jokes against themselves, to laugh at themselves. I believe this can only happen in a nation which is completely self-confident and spiritually healthy.
Here is a way the English laugh at themselves:
An English businessman went to the bank to ask for a loan, as his business, like some English businesses these days, was doing very badly. After making some notes about the man's requirements, the bank manager said,
"I should really refuse your request, but I'll give you a sporting chance. Now, one of my eyes is an artificial eye. If you can tell me which is the glass eye, I shall grant you the loan."
The customer looked carefully at the manager's eyes for a few moments, and then said,
"It's your left eye."
"That's absolutely correct," said the manager.
"You shall have your loan. But tell me, how on earth did you guess which is my glass eye? It's a perfect match for the other eye."
"Well," said the customer, "the glass eye appeared to me more sympathetic than the real eye."

NOTE
10. **class of 67**: 67년 졸업생
   문맥 there are at least 250 in that limbo = at least 250 declared themselves undecided about their career plans

| 반복 피하기 | **대동사와 그밖의 대리어(구)** |

1 a. Ideas are funny things — they never **work** unless you **do**.
   b. No man ever behaved more grandly when (he was) unjustly condemned to die than **did** Socrates.
   c. Computers spare men from making a lot of unnecessary conjectures. **So do** the bikinis.
   d. They don't believe in miracles and **neither do** we.

2 a. "Will this trick work?"
      "I hope **so**."
   b. "Will they be back in time for the meeting?"
      "I don't think **so**." (or I'm afraid **not**.)

3 a. Do as you are told, **or** you will be punished.
   b. Come at once; **otherwise** you'll be too late.

의미
1. a. 아이디어란 우스운 거다 — 우리가 이용하지 않으면 아무런 소용이 없으니 말이다.
   b. 지금까지 아무도 부당하게 사형선고를 받았을 때 소크라테스보다 더 위대하게 행동한 사람은 없었다.
   c. 컴퓨터는 사람들에게 많은 불필요한 추측을 하지 않게 해준다. 비키니도 마찬가지다.
   d. 그들은 기적을 믿지 않는데, 우리도 마찬가지다.
2. a. "이 계략이 효력을 발휘할까?"
      "난 그러길 바란다."
   b. "그들이 회의에 늦지 않게 돌아올까?"
      "난 그렇게 생각하지 않는다."
3. a. 지시받은 대로 해라, 그렇지 않으면 처벌을 받을 것이다.
   b. 당장 오너라, 그렇지 않으면 넌 너무 늦을 것이다.

To the Letter

Author James Thurber depended on words for entertainment.
He told me once about a trick he played on a nurse during one of his hospital stays.
He asked her what seven-letter word had three U's in it.
She thought and then said, "I don't know, but it must be unusual."

EXERCISE 25

진한 글자 부분을 주목하면서 전체의 뜻을 파악하라.

1. I have no patience with the college graduate who whines that his diploma doesn't help him get ahead in business. And less patience with the college graduate who tries to prove that it **does**.

2. A young accountant stayed late at the office day after day. Finally, the boss called him in and asked for an explanation.
   "Well, you see, sir," he stammered, "my wife works, too, and if I get home before she **does**, I have to fix dinner."

3. It always amazes me the way a real-estate agent's attitude changes when you're trying to sell instead of buy. I once called in an agent to sell my house.
   "It's a big house," I said. "It even has two wings."
   "Most turkeys **do**!" he said.

4. I do not deny that the feeling of success makes it easier to enjoy life. A painter, let us say, who has been obscure throughout his youth, is likely to become happier if his talent wins recognition. Nor do I deny that money, up to a certain point, is very capable of increasing happiness; beyond that point, I do not think it **does so**. What I do maintain is that success can only be one ingredient in happiness, and is too dearly purchased if all the other ingredients have been sacrificed to obtain it.

5. The cost of the internal transportation system in a big city is massive. Year by year the cost of oil and electricity consumed in the hauling of people has been accumulating, and **so has** the human cost, in physiological wear and tear.

NOTE

1. **have no patience with** = can't put up with. **whine**: to grumble; complain. **get ahead**: to rise; advance; succeed
2. **fix**: to prepare
3. **the way**: how
4. **let us say**: 이를테면. **win**: to gain. **maintain**: to assert; argue. **dearly**: at a high cost
   문맥 make it easier to enjoy life = makes one happier. his talent wins recognition = he becomes famous (famous ≠ obscure). purchase = obtain

6   As long as the term "art" is applied to a realm so vast and indefinite as to embrace literature, music and dance, theater and film, the visual and decorative arts, and other equally diverse activities, their classification — the way in which each is regarded as being either unique or like others — will remain a controversial but necessary undertaking. Classification is a useful approach to the organization of knowledge in any field: the classification of plants and animals in the 18th century led to the discovery of evolution in the 19th. In the arts, classification can be of immense help in understanding the interrelations between arts and in drawing attention to characteristics of each that might **otherwise** go unnoticed.

7   The growth of circulating libraries aided the expansion of literature. At a time when the prices of books were very high in relation to the purchasing power of the great majority of the population, circulating libraries were an important social invention. They furnished those who had acquired a taste for reading with access to books **otherwise** out of their reach. They helped to reduce the gap between interest in reading and purchasing power.

   The first circulating library was opened in London in 1740. Rivals quickly sprang up in London and in the provinces as well. By the end of the century, about 1,000 libraries dotted the country. Their rapid success testifies to the growing interest in reading.

8   The importance of the fast-moving stream of events in our modern world makes it imperative that we be well informed. Significant social, economic, and political issues, all demanding serious and open-minded investigation, require more than ever before a higher level of reader enlightenment.

   To advance in knowledge one must forever learn more, study more, reason more. Reading helps accomplish this; in college about eighty-five percent of all study involves reading. If, **as it certainly does**, progress comes through study, then reading is perhaps the student's chief means to academic progress.

NOTE
5. **wear and tear**: damage
    문맥 **hauling = transportation**
6. **embrace**: to include; contain.   **undertaking**: task
7. **furnish**: to provide; supply.   **otherwise out of their reach** = that might otherwise have been out of their reach.   **testify to**: to bear witness to; be evidence of; indicate
    문맥 **access = reach**
8. **imperative**: absolutely necessary; urgent.   **reason**: to think coherently and logically; draw inferences or conclusions from facts known or assumed.   **a means to** ~에 대한 수단
    문맥 **enlightenment = being well informed**

| 반복 피하기 | **같은 뜻의 다른 말로 바꾸어 쓰기** |

1 God certainly **looks after** the man who **takes care of** business first.

2 If Soviet women **cherish** golden trinkets, young Moscovites **go for** hand-me-down American-made clothing.

3 Civilization **has to do with** the environment in which we live. Culture **is concerned with** life itself and the way it is lived.

4 Modern civilization **rests upon** machinery and science as distinguished from one **founded on** agriculture and handicraft commerce.

5 Though the Europeans and Japanese are reluctant to revalue their **moneys**, the countries with strong **currencies** may have to make a joint upward movement of 5% to 10% within a year or two.

6 Meese will **oversee** the cabinet and domestic-policy staff. Baker will **direct all functions of** the White House staff. Both will sit on the National Security Council.

의미
1. 하느님께서는 할 일을 먼저 돌보는 사람을 보살펴주신다.
2. 소련의 여성들이 금으로 만든 장신구를 좋아한다면, 모스크바의 젊은이들은 값싼 미제 기성복을 좋아한다.
3. 문명은 우리의 생활환경과 관계가 있으나, 문화는 생활 자체와 생활양식과 관계가 있다.
4. 현대문명은 기계와 과학에 기반을 두고 있다, 농업과 수공상업에 기반을 둔 문명과는 달리.
5. 비록 유럽과 일본은 화폐를 재평가하기 꺼려하지만, 강력한 통화를 가진 국가들은 1년 또는 2년 이내에 함께 5~10% 평가절상하지 않을 수 없을지도 모른다.
6. 미즈는 내각과 국내정책 담당 직원들을 감독하게 되고, 베이커는 백악관 직원들을 감독하게 될 것이다. 두 사람은 모두 국가안보회의 임원이 될 것이다.

NOTE
1. 문맥 takes care of = looks after
2. hand-me-down: secondhand; ready-made and cheap.   문맥 go for = cherish
3. 문맥 is concerned with = has to do with
4. as distinguished from = unlike.   문맥 founded on = resting on (rest on = be founded on)
5. 문맥 currencies = moneys
6. 문맥 direct all functions of = oversee

EXERCISE 26

진한 글자 부분을 주목하면서 전체의 뜻을 파악하라.

1. Millions of French families live without the conveniences common to other industrial economies. One out of three French homes is officially considered to be "overpopulated," 28% have no hot water, 55% **are without** baths, and 77% **lack** telephones.

2. With regard to theory and practice there are two opinions. Some say that theory is one thing and practice another, so that they do not necessarily go together. Others **are of the opinion** that it is because of the inaccuracy of theory that the two do not **agree**.

3. The Koreans are a mainly rural people, but they are gradually becoming urbanized. In 1925, fewer than 5 percent of the population lived in cities. By 1970, more than 30 percent of South Koreans and probably almost **as high a percentage** of North Koreans **were city dwellers**.

4. In his study of historical change, McLuhan believes that the invention of a certain, crucially relevant tool or machine initiates huge changes in the environment which, in turn, **engineer transformations** in both man's social relations and his perception of experience.

NOTE

1. **convenience**: useful, handy or helpful device, article, service, etc.   **industrial economy**: an industrial economic state (산업경제국가)
   문맥 have no = are without = lack
2. **with regard to**: as to; concerning; about.   Theory is one thing and practice (is) another (thing) = Theory is different from practice; Theory and practice are two different things.   **not necessarily** = not always.
   문맥 go together = agree.   are of the opinion = say
3. 문맥 were city dwellers = lived in cities
4. **crucial**: of supreme importance; decisive; critical.   **relevant**: appropriate; pertinent.   **huge**: very large; immense; vast; enormous.   **perception of experience**: (경험에 대한 인식) 세계관 또는 가치관을 의미함
   문맥 engineer = initiate.   transformation = change

5   Inactivity is another myth. Surveys show that people over sixty spend much less time being entertained by radio and television than people in their twenties.

Another incorrect assumption is that old people are full of complaints. Some studies indicate that the old have at least one thing in common with the young: both seem to feel generally happier and more satisfied with themselves and their way of life than the middle-aged.

6   We know very little about Shakespeare, because, in his days, historical stories were devoted to the lives of kings. It was beyond imagining that a common actor would be of interest in the future. Similarly **in Scott Joplin's lifetime, it never occurred to anyone that history would want to know what a songwriter — especially a black one — was like.**

7   Man, Nietzsche thought, tugs himself in two opposite directions. The Greek god of wine, Dionysus, represents the feeling part of man: vital, creative, inspired but, if carried to excess, also deranged and destructive. Apollo, the sun god, **stands for** the reasoning part of man, drawn toward order, systems, and justice **with the risk, of course**, of deadening overorganization.

8   Even when a suspect is **apprehended**, the chances of his getting punished are mighty slim. In New York State each year there are some 130,000 felony arrests; approximately 8,000 people go to prison. There are 94,000 felony arrests in New York City; 5,000 to 6,000 **serve time**. A 1974 study of the District of Columbia came up with a similar picture. Of those arrested for armed robbery, less than one quarter went to prison. More than 6,000 aggravated assaults were reported; 116 people **were put away**. A 1977 study of such cities as Detroit, Indianapolis and New Orleans produced slightly better numbers, but nothing to counteract the exasperation of New York Police Commissioner Robert McGuire: "The criminal justice system almost creates incentives for street criminals."

NOTE

7. **tug**: to pull; drag.   **if (it) is) carried to excess** = if it is excessive.   **deranged**: disorderly; insane   **deaden**: 감정을 잃게 하다

8. **mighty** [colloq.]: very; extremely.   **felony**: a serious crime, such as murder or armed robbery.   **come up with** = produce.   **aggravated assault**: 가중폭행.   **exasperation**: great annoyance; anger.   **criminal justice system**: 형사사법제도.   **incentive**: stimulus; encouragement

   유의 **apprehend** = arrest.   **some** = approximately.   **get punished** = go to prison = serve time = be put away

9 For some, mention of automation calls up an image of a world of robots in which humans do not work. For others, automation **suggests** the intricate engineering problems of self-regulating system. To many, automation **is practically synonymous with** mechanization in industry. For most, however, the term is a vague one having something to do with electronics and automatic production. Just what it all **means** for the man in the street is not too clear.

10 The new unemployment rate: 8.9%. Everyone who hears that percentage will know it is fraught with troublesome forebodings. Yet the modern habit of mistaking statistics for reality makes it easy to overlook the fact that the rate stands for an indigestibly large number of individuals — 9.5 million. Each point in the unemployment rate also **represents**, as the President explained last month, roughly $19 billion in potential but lost federal revenues, plus some $6 billion in financial assistance that the Government disburses to the jobless. Such statistical elaborations usefully suggest the vast scope of unemployment and its staggering cost in both forfeited wealth and rescue efforts. Yet it is essential to remember that statistics tell nothing whatever about the reality of joblessness.

That reality is always personal and almost always lashed with a confusion of difficult emotions. Indeed, the psychological cost of joblessness is more hurtful to many victims than the strain of making financial ends meet. A few individuals, true enough, are so oddly disposed that they can take unemployment with upbeat nonchalance, making a lark of it or seizing the opportunity to switch careers. Still, Americans more typically take a cruel psychic bruising when they lose a job (Never mind the cause). And if joblessness goes on for long, men and women of all ages, occupations and economic classes tend to suffer a sharp loss of self-esteem, a diminished sense of identity, a certain murkiness of purpose, a sense of estrangement from their friends — a sort of feeling of exile from wherever they feel they really belong.

NOTE

9. **call up**: to make one remember; recall.　**intricate**: complex.　**be synonymous with**: to have the same or nearly the same meaning as.　**vague**: not clear.　**the man in the street** = most (people); the ordinary (or average) man.　**have to do with**: ~와 관계가 있다

10. **fraught with**: filled, charged, or loaded with.　**the Government** = the federal government(연방정부)　**disburse**: to pay out.　**forfeited** = lost.　**make ends meet**: to get just enough money for one's needs; manage to keep one's expenses within one's income(수지를 맞추다).　**are so oddly disposed** = have so odd a disposition(너무도 이상한 성격을 갖고 있어서).　**upbeat**: cheerful; optimistic.　**nonchalance**: calmness.　**make a lark of**: make fun of.　**take a cruel psychic bruising**: 잔인한 마음의 상처를 입다　**never mind the cause** = it doesn't matter what the cause is; regardless of the cause

문맥 **roughly** = some.　**joblessness** = unemployment.　**career** = job

| 반복 피하기 | **문체 바꾸어 쓰기** |

1 College graduates **with active interest in the arts** proved more creative than those **who had no interest in the arts**.
  (A→A'): *who had active interest in the arts*
  (A'→A): *without any interest in the arts*

2 At the beginning of this century, **a newborn could expect to live to the age of about 50;** today **the expectancy is about 70**.
  (A'→A): *a newborn can expect to live to the age of about 70*

3 A country **within which the divisions have gone too far** is a danger to itself; a country **which is too well united** is a menace to others.
  (A→B): *which is too badly divided*

4 It is often said that **in prosperity we have many friends**, but **we are usually neglected when things go badly**.
  (A→A'): *when things go well*
  (A'→A): *in adversity*
  (B'→B): *we usually don't have friends*

의미
1. 예술에 적극적인 관심을 갖고 있는 대학졸업자들이 예술에 관심이 없는 대학졸업자들보다 더 창의적이라는 것이 드러났다.
2. 이 세기 초에 새로 태어난 어린아이는 약 50세까지 살 수 있으리라 기대할 수 있었는데, 오늘날에는 기대수명이 약 70세다.
3. 너무 심하게 분열되어 있는 나라는 그 자체에 위험이 되며, 너무 잘 단결되어 있는 나라는 다른 나라들에 위협이 된다.
4. 일이 잘 될 때에는 친구가 많으나, 일이 잘 되지 않을 때에는 대개 친구가 거의 없다고, 사람들은 흔히 말한다.

NOTE 3. 문맥 menace = danger.   others = other countries

EXERCISE 27

진한 글자 부분을 주목하면서 전체의 뜻을 파악하라.

1. Today young men and women meet each other with much less difficulty **than was formerly the case.**

2. Geisel has a military appearance but a civilian mind. **With Medici it is the other way around.** Geisel is smarter and he seems to belong to no one. He stands a better chance of winning the presidential election.

3. A certain historian has said of history that "it devours the present." I do not quite understand what he means, but in science **it is surely the other way about**: the present devours the past. This does something to extenuate a scientist's misguided indifference to the history of ideas.

4. Birds are particularly sensitive to weather changes, and rooks especially so. When they build their nests higher than usual in the trees, it has often been noticed that a warm, fairly dry summer follows. **The same applies** when they fly high, and **the opposite is the case** if they are seen flying low.

5. A motor-vehicle survey has revealed that, in 1940, each car on the road contained an average of 3.2 persons. In 1950, **the occupancy had declined to 2.1 persons per car.** By 1960, **the average was down to 1.4 persons.** If we project the statistics to 1980, **every third car going by will have nobody in it.**

NOTE

1. **than was formerly the case** = than in the past (or than did their counterparts in the past)
2. **he seems to belong to no one**: 그는 아무에게도 속하지 않는 것처럼 보인다(즉, 그를 지지하는 사람들의 범위가 넓다는 뜻이다). **stand/have a good chance of ~** : ~할 가능성이 많다
3. **the other way about** = the other way around. **devour**: to eat up; swallow up; consume or destroy **extenuate**: to lessen the seriousness of (잘못이나 죄 따위의 무거움을 가볍게 해주다); forgive. **does something to extenuate** = somewhat extenuate. → The return of some market stability did nothing to calm fears of economic uncertainty to come. (어느 정도 시장이 안정을 되찾았지만 다가올 경제적인 불확실에 대한 두려움은 전혀 가라앉지 않았다). *cf.* His morning walks **did much for** his health. **be indifferent to**: ~에 무관심하다: She is indifferent to what others think of her(= She doesn't care what others think of her).
4. 문맥 **is the case** = applies

6   In his innocence, man held his own special planet to be the center of the starry universe until Copernicus, 431 years ago, dared to challenge this dogma. The earth moves around the sun, he said, not **vice versa**. It was a profound and troubling idea. Yet it was still far from the whole truth, for it kept the sun at the center of things. And that misconception persisted in the minds of most until the coming of photography and the large telescopes of the 20th century.

7   First, Americans were told to trim the fats and cholesterol from their diets. Then they were warned about the hazards of sugar. **The latest villain is the most common condiment of all — salt.** The National Academy of Sciences and the U.S. Food and Drug Administration have advised everyone to cut down on salt to prevent high blood pressure. Scary books like "Killer Salt" trumpet the danger lurking next to the pepper mill, and food manufacturers have joined the battle with low-sodium canned goods and salt substitutes like No-Salt. But many experts in hypertension are mounting a counterattack. The frantic campaign against salt, they warned last week, should be taken with more than a large grain of the same.

The experts agree that some of the nation's 40 million to 60 million hypertensives should reduce their salt intake. But they seriously doubt that this would do any good for the population at large. "We do not have the scientific data to recommend that the general population go on a low-salt diet," says Dr. John H. Laragh of New York Hospital-Cornell Medical Center. At a scientific symposium in Arlington, Va., Laragh and his colleagues noted that a low-salt diet is hard to follow, and may actually be harmful.

8   Let us suppose you are interested in buying a pair of contact lenses. Be prepared to pay $175.00 or more. Generally there are three main reasons why people want contact lenses. You may need them because your cornea is

---

NOTE

6. **In his innocence** = Because of his innocence (무지했기 때문에).   **innocence**: ignorance
    hold: to believe.   **vice versa**: in the opposite way from that just stated; conversely
    persist: to continue to exist or prevail; remain
    문맥 **things** = the universe

7. **trim**: to reduce.   **hazard**: danger.   **villain**: 악한, 범인.   **cut down on**: to reduce.   **scary**: causing alarm; frightening.   **hypertension** = high blood pressure.   **mount a counterattack**: 반격을 가하다
    hypertensive: a patient with high blood pressure.   **the population at large** = the general population; ordinary people

misshaped and ordinary glasses are not satisfactory. If so, **you'll be in the group that comprises 1 to 2 per cent of contact lens wearers**. But you may want them for a sport, avocation, or vocation. Perhaps you're a baseball player, a boxer, a swimmer, an aviator, an actor, or perhaps you're engaged in an industry where flying particles may endanger your eyes. If you get your contact lenses for one of these reasons, **you are in the same group with about 20 per cent of the users**. But if for some reasons you feel that spectacles are handicapping your appearance and you'd rather have invisible glasses, **you'll have lots of company. About 79 per cent of the users** hope to improve their looks.

9. When I was very young and the urge to be someplace else was on me, I was assured by mature people that maturity would cure this itch. **When years described me as mature, the remedy prescribed was middle age.** In middle age I was assured that greater age would calm my fever and now that I am fifty-eight perhaps senility will **do the job**. Nothing has worked. Four hoarse blasts of a ship's whistle still raise the hair on my neck and set my feet to tapping. The sound of a jet, an engine warming up, even the clopping of shod hooves on pavement brings on the ancient shudder, the dry mouth and vacant eye, the hot palms and the churn of stomach high up under the rib cage. In other words, **I don't improve**; in further words, once a bum always a bum. I fear the disease is incurable.

10. In my own experience of the appreciation of poetry I have always found that the less I knew about the poet and his work, before I began to read it, the better. A quotation, a critical remark, an enthusiastic essay, may well be the accident that sets one to reading a particular author; but an elaborate preparation of historical and biographical knowledge has always been a barrier to me. I am not defending poor scholarship; and I admit that such experience, solidified into a maxim, would be very difficult to apply in the study of Latin and Greek. But with authors of one's own speech, and even with some of those of other modern languages, the procedure is possible. At

---

NOTE
8. **comprise**: to make up; form; constitute. **avocation**: hobby. **company**: a group of people
9. **the urge to be someplace else**: 어딘지 딴 곳에 가고픈 충동. **was on me** = took possession of me
   now that = since. **do the job** = calm my fever. **I don't improve** = 나의 방랑벽은 낫지 않는다
   Once a bum always a bum: 한번 방랑자가 되면 내내 방랑자가 된다.

least, it is better to be spurred to acquire scholarship because you enjoy the poetry, than to suppose that you enjoy the poetry because you have acquired the scholarship. I was passionately fond of certain French poetry long before I could have translated two verses of it correctly. **With Dante the discrepancy between enjoyment and understanding was still wider.**

— T.S. Eliot, *Dante*

It was near Christmas and the 92-year-old man was looking forward to seeing his three sons. When the first arrived, he said,
"Merry Christmas, Dad. Sorry I couldn't buy you a present, but I just bought a snowmobile."
The father said that was all right.
The second son came in a few minutes later and said,
"Merry Christmas, Dad. Sorry I couldn't buy you something, but I just got a new car."
The father said he understood.
The third son walked in and said,
"Merry Christmas, Dad. Sorry I didn't bring you a present, but I had big losses at the card table."
The father nodded.
"Boys," he finally said, "there's something I want you to know before I leave this world. Your mother and I were never married."
"You mean we're…" they gasped in unison.
"Yep, you sure are," the old man said. "And cheap ones too."

NOTE 10. **accident**: chance. **set one to reading** = cause one to read. **elaborate**: painstaking **solidified into a maxim** = if it were solidified into a maxim (만일 그것이 굳어져서 금언이 된다면) **spur**: to stimulate. **discrepancy**: disagreement; difference
문맥 scholarship = knowledge

3 CONTEXT
문맥의 파악

1 글의 뼈대

2 추려 읽기

3 논리 읽기

4 문맥과 의미

| 글의 뼈대 | **Thesis Sentence** |

한 편의 논문(a paper)에서 요지가 들어 있는 문장을 '명제문장'(Thesis Sentence)이라고 하고, 한 문단(a paragraph)의 요지가 들어 있는 문장을 '주제문장'(Topic Sentence)이라고 하며, 한 문장(a sentence)에서 핵심이 되는 단어를 '핵심단어'(Key Words)라고 한다.

도시의 교외에 거주하는 사람들에 관한 한 편의 짧은 논문을 쓴다고 가정해 보자. 이 논문의 뼈대는 다음과 같은 모습일 수 있을 것이다.

TITLE:
제목
The Similarity of Suburbanites

INTRODUCTION:
서론
1. **(thesis sentence)** People who live in the suburbs are alike in age, race, and politics.

DISCUSSION:
본론
2. **(topic sentence)** Suburbanites are alike in age.

3. **(topic sentence)** Suburbanites are also alike in race

4. **(topic sentence)** A third similarity among people who live in the suburbs is their political orientation.

CONCLUSION:
결론
5. **(conclusion)** It is interesting that suburbanites are similar in age, race, and political views.

글의 뼈대 — Topic Sentence

Example 1

(topic sentence) **To get the most out of your textbooks, you should follow several steps very carefully.** (discussion) **First**, you should make a preliminary survey of each book to get a general idea of what the book contains. **Second**, you should read for deeper understanding and formulate questions as you read. **Next**, make notes of the major points of each chapter. **Then**, test yourself to be sure that you can answer questions likely to be raised in class and examinations. (conclusion) **Finally**, review your notes and reread any parts of the book that are unclear to you.

> **의미** (주제문장) 교재에서 최대한 많은 것을 얻기 위해서는, 몇 가지 단계를 매우 주의해서 따라야 한다. (본론) 첫째, 대충 각 교재를 훑어보고 그 책의 전반적인 윤곽을 파악해야 한다. 둘째, 보다 깊은 이해를 위해 읽어야 하며, 읽어나가면서 질문을 만들어야 한다. 다음에는, 각 장의 요지에 대한 노트를 만들라. 그리고 나서, 스스로 테스트해서 교실과 시험에서 제기될 가능성이 있는 질문에 답할 수 있도록 확실히 해두어야 한다. (결론) 마지막으로, 노트를 재검토하고 교재에서 분명히 이해되지 않은 부분은 다시 읽어보라.

Example 2

(topic sentence) **Thinking depends upon knowledge.** (discussion) **It is true that** the person who has much knowledge is not necessarily a good thinker. **But it is also true that** the person who is developing good techniques for thinking will do a better job with much knowledge than he would with little. (conclusion) **What is more**, improving your knowledge often tempts you to do more thinking by rousing your curiosity and by making you more aware of the areas where thought is necessary.

> **의미** (주제문장) 생각하는 것은 아는 것에 좌우된다. (본론) 많이 아는 사람이 반드시 훌륭하게 생각하는 것이 아니라는 것은 사실이다. 그러나 생각하기 위한 좋은 기술을 개발하는 사람은 많이 알고 있는 경우에는 거의 알지 못하는 경우보다 더 잘 생각하리라는 것 또한 사실이다. (결론) 더구나, 지식을 향상시키게 되면 흔히 자극을 받아서 더 많은 생각을 하게 되는데, 이것은 지식의 향상이 호기심을 불러일으켜주고 생각이 필요한 영역에 대해서 더 많이 의식하게 만들어주기 때문이다.

> **주의** 주제 문장이 반드시 문두에 오는 것은 아니다. 대개 연역적인 방법으로 글을 써나가는 사람들은 문두에 제시하지만, 귀납적인 방법을 택하는 경우에는 주제 문장은 구절 끝에 온다.

Example 3

I do not deny that the feeling of success makes it easier to enjoy life. A painter, let us say, who has been obscure throughout his youth, is likely to become happier if he wins recognition. **Nor do I deny that** money, up to a certain point, is very capable of increasing happiness; beyond that point, I do not think it does so. **(topic sentence) What I do maintain is that** success can only be one ingredient in happiness, and is too dearly purchased if all the other ingredients have been sacrificed to obtain it.

의미 나는 성공했다는 생각이 삶을 즐기는 것을 더 쉽게 만들어준다는 사실을 부정하지 않는다. (왜냐하면) 예를 들어, 젊은 시절에 줄곧 명성이 없던 화가가 자신의 재능을 인정받게 되면 더 행복해질 가능성이 있으니까. 또한 나는 돈이 어느 정도까지는 행복을 증가시켜줄 가능성이 매우 크다는 사실도 부정하지 않는다. 그러나 그런 정도를 넘으면 나는 그렇다고 생각하지 않는다. 내가 주장하는 것은 성공이란 행복의 한 요소에 불과하며, 만일 그것을 얻기 위해 모든 그밖의 다른 요소들이 희생되었다면 성공은 너무도 비싸게 산 것이라는 점이다.

주의 위의 예문에는 필자가 강조하는 부분이 뚜렷이 나타나 있다. 우선, I do not deny that...이라는 말로 보아서 이 부분은 필자가 다른 사람들의 견해를 인정해 주는 것이지 필자 자신의 강한 주장을 내세우는 곳은 아니라는 것을 알 수 있다. 이것은 Nor do I deny that...에 대해서도 적용된다. 그러나 What I do maintain...에서는 부정적인 말인 do not deny가 maintain(주장하다)이라는 긍정적인 말로 바뀌어져 있고, 또 그 앞에는 이 말을 강조하는 말이 있는 것으로 보아 이 부분에 주제가 들어있다는 것을 쉽게 알 수 있다.

모든 글이 이런 식으로 쓰여 있는 것은 아니지만, 글의 뼈대를 중심으로 읽는 습관을 기르는 것은 대단히 중요하다. 왜냐하면 그래야만 중요한 부분을 빨리 알아볼 수 있고, 또 전반적인 독서 속도도 높일 수 있기 때문이다.

Example 4

There are three common errors which help to account for the weaknesses of contemporary education.

The first is the mistaken idea that schools exist principally to train boys and girls to be sociable, "integrated with their group," "equipped with the skills of social living," "adjusted to family and community cooperation." Obviously that is one of the aims of schooling.

But another aim, even more important, is to train the individual mind as intensely and to encourage it as variously as possible, since much of our better and more essential life is lived by us as individuals and since, in the advancing age of mass culture, it is vital for us to maintain personal independence.

The second error is the belief that education is a process which stops completely as soon as adult life begins. Too many young graduates drop their languages, forget their science, abandon their economic and political thinking. It is like learning music and then never going to a concert or playing a single note.

The third error is the notion that learning and teaching always ought to have immediate results, show a profit, lead to success. It is true that education is intended to benefit the entire personality. But it is not possible, not even desirable, to show that many of the important subjects which are taught as part of education will make the learner rich, fit him for social life or find him a job.

주의 이 구절은 각 paragraph의 뼈대를 잘 보여준다. 특히 bold face로 되어 있는 부분에 주의하기 바란다.

의미 현대교육의 약점들을 설명해주는 데에 도움이 되는 세 가지 흔한 오류가 있다.

그 첫 번째 오류는 이런 그릇된 생각이다 — 즉, 학교의 주된 존재목적은 학생들을 다른 사람들과 어울리기를 좋아하고, "자기들의 무리와 통합되고," "사회생활의 기술을 갖추게 하며," "가정과 지역사회의 협조에 적응하도록" 훈련시키는 일이라는 것이다. 분명히 이것이 학교교육의 목표 가운데 하나이기는 하다.

그러나 또하나의 목표 — 이것은 더욱 중요한데 — 는 개별 학생들의 두뇌를 될 수 있는 대로 집중적으로 그리고 다양하게 훈련시키는 것이다. 왜냐하면, 우리의 보다 더 훌륭하고 본질적인 삶의 많은 부분은 개인으로서의 우리에 의해 영위되고, 대중문화가 발달되고 있는 시대에는 우리가 개인의 독자성을 유지하는 것이 매우 중요하기 때문이다.

두 번째 잘못은 교육이 성인생활이 시작되자마자 완전히 정지되는 과정이라고 믿는 것이다. 너무도 많은 학교를 졸업한 젊은이들이 언어에 대한 공부 (또는 관심)를 그만두고, 과학을 잊어버리며, 경제와 정치에 대한 생각을 버린다. 이것은 마치 음악을 배우고 나서 한번도 음악회에 가지 않거나 단 한 곡조도 연주하지 않는 것과 흡사하다.

세 번째 오류는 배우는 것과 가르치는 것이 언제나 당장 결과를 가져오며, 물질적인 혜택을 보여주며, 성공으로 이끌어주어야 한다고 생각하는 것이다. 사실 교육의 목적은 전체의 인격에 혜택을 주는 것이다. 그러나 교육의 일부로 학교에서 가르치고 있는 중요한 과목 가운데 많은 것들이 배우는 사람을 부유하게 만들거나 사회생활에 적합하게 만들어주거나 일자리를 얻게 해주리라는 것을 보여주는 것은 가능하지도 않고 바람직하지도 않다.

Tact

A WOMAN walked into the shoe store, tried on dozen pairs of shoes,
without finding a proper fit. Finally, the bored assistant told her,
"Madam, we can't fit you because one of your feet is larger than the other."
The woman walked out of the store without buying anything.
In the next store, the fitting proved equally difficult.
At last, the smiling assistant explained,
"Madam, do you know that one of your feet is smaller than the other?"
The woman left the store happily with two new pairs of shoes under her arm.

EXERCISE 28

각 지문의 주제문장(topic sentence)을 찾아보라.

1. Oysters like warm waters. They grow best in temperatures between 66° and 70° F. In southern waters they grow to full size in two or three years. In the north it takes about four years for them to grow.

2. The yak is an animal about the size of a small ox. It lives in Tibet, a province on a high plateau in China. The inhabitants use the yak for transportation. They also drink the yak's milk, eat its meat for food, and weave its fur into cloth. The yak is the most useful animal in Tibet.

3. Although Einstein felt no need for religious ritual and belonged to no formal religious group, he was the most deeply religious man I have known. He once said to me, "Ideas come from God," and one could hear the capital "G" in the reverence with which he pronounced the word. On the marble fireplace in the mathematics building at Princeton University is carved, in the original German, what one might call his scientific credo: "God is subtle, but he is not malicious." By this Einstein meant that scientists could expect to find their task difficult, but not hopeless: the Universe was a Universe of law, and God was not confusing us with deliberate paradoxes and contradictions.

4. Although most honey bees are industrious, some are like humans and take a lackadaisical attitude toward work. They leave the hive late and return early, making as few trips as possible. Some bees go to extremes to get out of work and even follow a life of crime by becoming "robber" bees. These honey "hoodlums" have all the cunning of the infamous Black Bart when they raid the honey stores of other hives. Usually the raids are foiled by alert guard

---

NOTE

2. **(of) about the size of** = about as large as. → **He is (of) about my age.** = He is about as old as I am.
   weave~into cloth: ~을 짜서 옷감으로 만들다

3. **ritual**: ceremony; rite (의식, 의례).　**capital**: 대문자.　**reverence**: feeling or attitude of deep respect, love, and awe, as for something sacred; veneration.　**credo**: 신조.　**malicious**: having ill will; spiteful
   deliberate: 의도적인, 고의적인

bees assigned to protect the rich stores of honey. But the successful robbers return to their hives to boast about their exploits. By unusual dances they communicate to others in the hive that they have found "The Soft Touch." Other bees, too lazy to work, are dazzled and go off to try their luck at stealing.

5 "Why should I study English?" objected a rebellious youth. "I know English. I am English."

But not everyone who is studying English really knows English, nor is knowing all of the same kind. A professional ball player may know how to pitch a curve. A physicist may know the same thing, but he will know it in quite a different way. His way of knowing will be better, for though he may not be able to pitch a curve as well, yet other things being equal, if he spent as much time in practice as the professional player, in all likelihood he could pitch a better curve. In other words, analytic knowledge is an aid and support to experimental knowledge.

6 **To a certain extent**, doubt is good for the mind. People who doubt are not in danger of being ruled by emotion. **But** a man who completely lacks any positive beliefs is often a useless man, and a life without a belief in something positive is unbearable. **Instead of** doubting everything, we should be ready to believe when there is sufficient evidence, and we should try not to judge a case while evidence is lacking. **In other words**, our mental attitudes should be "critical" but not "negative."

NOTE　**4. industrious**: hard-working; diligent.　**human**: a human being.　**lackadaisical**: lacking in interest or effort; listless.　**go to extremes** = go to extreme lengths (지극히 애를 쓰다).　**cunning**: skill in deception; slyness; craftiness (간교함).　**infamous**: having a very bad reputation; notorious.　**Black Bart**: 미국의 전설적인 강도의 이름.　**foil**: to keep from being successful; thwart; frustrate (좌절시키다).　**boast**: to brag (뽐내다. 자랑하다).　**exploit**: an act remarkable for brilliance or daring; bold deed; feat.　**dazzle**: to cause wonder to; captivate (매혹시키다).　**try one's luck at**: ~에 자신의 운을 시험해 보다

5. nor is knowing all of the same kind = and knowing is not all of the same kind, either (아는 것이 또한 모두 같은 종류에 속하는 것은 아니다).　**other things being equal** = if other things are equal (만일 다른 조건들이 같다면)　**in all likelihood**: most probably (십중팔구).　**experimental**: experiential; empirical (경험적인)

6. be in danger of: ~할 위험 속에 놓여 있다.　**positive**: affirmative (긍정적인).　**critical**: 비판적인.　**negative**: 부정적인

7   A few years ago I met a man who was running a freight elevator in one of the downtown office buildings in New York. I noticed that his left hand had been cut off at the wrist. I asked him if the loss of that hand bothered him. He said, "Oh, no. I hardly ever think about it. I am not married; and the only time I ever think about it is when I try to thread a needle." **It is astonishing** how quickly we can accept almost any situation — if we have to — and adjust ourselves to it and forget about it.

8   Investigators who have studied very young children in school overwhelmingly present a grim picture. The child too often stumbles insecurely through kindergarten and the early grades. His friends who were delayed a year or so quickly catch up and pass him — usually become most stable and highly motivated. His learning retention frequently remains lower than that of his later-starting peers, regardless of how bright he is. In other words, it is hard to escape **the conclusion** that early schooling is little short of crippling.

9   A work of literature **may** be studied in relation to its author, the culture from which it springs, and the text itself. One **may** study a writer's work for the information it gives about the character of the writer or his world view. A reader must be careful, however, in judging a man from his writings: the attitudes and values of the hero of a novel do not necessarily reflect those of the author. Because a literary work is a product of an age, a knowledge of the political and economic conditions and the philosophic and religious ideas of that age is useful. **But** however interesting and helpful, concern for the author or his background is essentially **secondary**. The study of the work itself is **primary**. If one is to get at the heart of a novel, a play, or a poem, he must focus on its content and structure. He must concern himself with the experience the author communicates and the form in which he communicates it.

NOTE   7. **run**: to operate (운행하다).   **bother**: to trouble; annoy
  8. **grim**: frightful; ghastly; horrible (무서운).   **stumble**: to proceed in a confused, blundering manner (갈피를 잡지 못하고 잘못을 저지르며 나아가다).   **highly motivated**: "높은 동기를 갖고 있는", 즉 무척 배우려고 하는(= very eager to learn).   **little short of** = almost.   **crippling**: disabling
  9. **in relation to**: ~와 관련해서.   **spring from**: ~로부터 나오다.   **world view**: 세계관.   **be careful in -ing**: ~하는 데에 주의하다.   **not necessarily** = not always.   **get at** = to grasp; understand.   **focus on** = concentrate on.   **concern oneself with**: ~에 관심을 갖다

10 As individuals, we find that our development depends upon the people whom we meet in the course of our lives. (These people include the authors whose books we read, and characters in works of fiction and history.) The benefit of these meetings is due as much to the differences as to the resemblances; to the conflict, as well as the sympathy, between persons. Fortunate the man who, at the right moment, meets the right friend; fortunate also the man who at the right moment meets the right enemy. I do not approve the extermination of the enemy: the policy of exterminating or, as is barbarously said, liquidating enemies, is one of the most alarming developments of modern war and peace, from the point of view of those who desire the survival of culture. One needs the enemy. So, within limits, the friction, not only between individuals but between groups, seems to me quite necessary for civilisation. The universality of irritation is the best assurance of peace. A country within which the divisions have gone too far is a danger to itself; a country which is too well united — whether by nature or by device, by honest purpose or by fraud and oppression — is a menace to others. In Italy and in Germany, we have seen that a unity with politico-economic aims, imposed violently and too rapidly, had unfortunate effects upon both nations. Their cultures had developed in the course of a history of extreme, and extremely sub-divided regionalism: the attempt to teach Germans to think of themselves as Germans first, and the attempt to teach Italians to think of themselves as Italians first, rather than as natives of a particular small principality or city, was to disturb the traditional culture from which alone any future culture could grow.

— T.S. Eliot, *Notes towards the Definition of Culture*

NOTE   **10. be due to** = result from.   **exterminate**: to destroy or get rid of entirely; wipe out; annihilate.   **liquidate**: to dispose of or get rid of, as by killing.   **friction**: disagreement or conflict because of differences of opinion, temperament, etc.   **irritation** = friction.   **device**: a plan; scheme; trick.   **fraud**: deceit; trickery; cheating.   **menace** = threat.   **regionalism**: devotion to one's own geographical region   **principality**: a country; a state

글의 뼈대 — Key Words

Example 1

I have but one **lamp** by which my feet are guided, and that is the **lamp of experience**. I know of no way of judging the future but by **the past**.

의미 나에게는 내 발길을 안내해주는 다만 하나의 등불이 있는데, 그것은 곧 경험이라는 등불이다. 나는 과거(경험)에 의존하지 않고 미래를 판단하는 길을 모른다.

문맥 the past = experience

Example 2

Men are **not equal** in physical strength, intelligence, attractiveness, or health. In these characteristics the law of nature is **diversity**.

의미 사람들은 체력이나 지능, 매력 또는 건강 면에서 동등하지 않다. 이들 특징에서 자연의 법칙은 다양성이다.

문맥 diversity = inequality

Example 3

Descartes insisted that, if we are to discover truth, it is necessary that we **question** everything at some time in our lives. To him the beginning of wisdom lay in **doubt**.

의미 데까르뜨의 주장에 의하면, 진리를 발견하려면, 우리의 인생에서 어느 때에 모든 것을 의심하는 것이 필요하다고 한다. 그에게 지혜의 시작은 곧 의심에 놓여 있었다.

문맥 doubt = questioning

Two London cockneys were drinking tea. One of them said,
"Alfie, I've known you for 55 years now, and I hate to tell you this — but you are pretentious. Everything you do from the time you get up in the morning until you go to bed at night is pretentious."
Alfie seemed a little hurt. He looked at his friend and said, "Pretentious... moi?"

EXERCISE 29

다음 각 구절에서 핵심단어(Key Words)를 찾아내고, 빈칸에 들어갈 적당한 말을 골라라.

1. We have no way to judge the future except by the past. Our vision into the future is dim but we have some light from the lamp of _____.

   (A) hope
   (B) truth
   (C) future
   (D) experience

2. The average person expresses himself differently in writing and in speaking. With proper practice the difference can be overcome, and one's writing will become more _____.

   (A) clear and precise
   (B) like his talk
   (C) interesting to read
   (D) widely known

3. Beethoven believed that music should be a medium for the expression of the composer's ideas and that all other considerations were of secondary importance. For him, the primary emphasis was upon _____.

   (A) style
   (B) form
   (C) content
   (D) popular appeal

4. Air resists the motion of objects passing through it. Airplanes and automobiles are streamlined so that they can pass through the air with _____.

   (A) no resistance
   (B) less resistance
   (C) less speed
   (D) full speed

5. It has always been dangerous to teach men new ideas contrary to those which are generally accepted. The first men who taught that the earth is round were _____.

   (A) persecuted
   (B) rewarded
   (C) right
   (D) conformists

NOTE
3. 문맥 emphasis = importance
5. persecute: to oppress cruelly (박해하다). conformist: 기존 체제나 전통, 관습 따위를 따르는 사람

6. We cannot assume that the educated persons of a community are its only clear-thinking inhabitants, for it has been shown that good judgment is not necessarily proportional to _____.

   (A) experience   (B) wisdom
   (C) heredity   (D) education

7. Rice requires a great deal of water in order to grow. In most rice-growing regions the rainfall does not provide sufficient moisture for the crop. The rice fields must be _____.

   (A) dug   (B) irrigated
   (C) cultivated   (D) fertilized

8. Mountain-climbing involves many risks, and the climber must be alert at all times. Reckless climbers soon meet with an accident. The job is really one for a man who is _____.

   (A) bold   (B) strong
   (C) frightened   (D) prudent

9. Books almost inevitably suffer in the process of being made into movies. There may be scenes in a book that seem to be made for filming, but the preliminary preparation that gives the scenes their significance is not readily transferable to _____.

   (A) mass production   (B) paper
   (C) celluloid   (D) the imagination

NOTE

6. **not necessarily** = not always. **proportional to**: ~에 비례하는
   문맥 good judgment = clear thinking
7. 문맥 moisture = water
8. **involve**: to include by necessity; entail; require. **alert**: on one's guard against danger; watchful and ready to meet danger. **reckless**: not caring about danger; careless; heedless; rash; too hasty. **meet with**: to experience; come upon; come across; encounter. **prudent**: cautious; discreet; circumspect; not rash
   문맥 The job = Mountain-climbing. alert = prudent ≠ reckless
9. **suffer**: to experience loss (피해를 보다). **preliminary**: introductory (도입하는, 예비적인). **readily**: without difficulty; easily. **celluloid**: film; movies

10. Man is one of the most formidable of all animals and the only one who persistently chooses to attack his own species. Throughout history, he has never, except for short periods of time, dispensed with _____.

(A) community   (B) vigorous outdoor sports
(C) biological perpetuation   (D) fierce warfare

11. The great incentive to learning a new skill or supporting discipline is an urgent need to use it. For this reason many scientists do not learn new skills or master new disciplines until the _____ is upon them to do so.

(A) evidence   (B) information
(C) opportunity   (D) pressure

12. It can be said that any scientist of any age who wants to make important discoveries must study important problems. Dull problems yield dull answers. It is not enough that a problem should be interesting. A problem must be such that it _____ what the answer is — whether to science generally or to mankind.

(A) chances   (B) happens
(C) matters   (D) seems

13. The view of a knowledge of physical science as a means of "getting on" is unquestionable. There is no occupation whose pursuer will not find some knowledge of science to be _____.

(A) absorbing   (B) acceptable
(C) profitable   (D) interesting

NOTE

10. **formidable**: fearful; dreadful; frightful.   **persistently**: continually; stubbornly.   **choose**: to decide; prefer.   **dispense with**: to get rid of; do away with; do without; manage without
11. **incentive**: stimulus; motive; encouragement.   **discipline**: a branch of learning (학문의 한 분야)
    urgent = pressing
12. **yield**: to produce
    dull(= uninteresting) ≠ interesting.   matter = be important
13. **physical science**: 자연과학.   **get on**: to succeed.   **absorbing**: very interesting; engrossing

14 Men require the opportunity to do challenging work. I don't include in this category the many tasks which are merely repetitive drudgery. I am not interested in _____.

(A) necessary work
(B) creative work
(C) monotonous work
(D) artistic work

15 A writer must be very careful to say only things that are true. He must not make any statements or implications which are false. He must be _____.

(A) imaginative
(B) clever
(C) educated
(D) accurate

16 The term "culture shock" has been coined to describe the effect that immersion in a strange culture has on the unprepared visitor. It is what happens when the familiar psychological clues that help an individual to function in society are suddenly replaced by _____.

(A) new ones that are alien and incomprehensible
(B) better ones that are hard to understand
(C) new ones with which he is very familiar
(D) inferior ones that he has already experienced

17 Love of truth is the core of this man's philosophy. He is always ready to revise his views when presented with adequate evidence of their lack of _____.

(A) validity
(B) interest
(C) importance
(D) popularity

NOTE

14. challenging: causing competitive interest, action, or thought, especially because new, unusual, or difficult. **category**: 범주. **drudgery**: uninteresting work. **monotonous**: 단조로운
　문맥 repetitive drudgery = monotonous work

15. 문맥 make any statements or implications which are false = say things that are not true
　accurate = true ≠ false

16. coin: to make up; devise; invent. **have an effect on**: ~에 영향을 미치다. **immersion**: 진입. **clue**: hint; suggestion (실마리, 암시). **function**: to act in a required or expected manner
　문맥 alien(= unfamiliar) ≠ familiar

17. core: 핵심. **revise**: to correct; change or amend. **when presented** → when he is presented **adequate**: enough; sufficient
　문맥 validity = truth

18 Modern criticism, through its exacting scrutiny of literary texts, has demonstrated with finality that in art beauty and truth are indivisible _____.

(A) and one
(B) and two
(C) and never expressed
(D) and forever separated

19 The self-made man tends to emphasize the worth of material success and to _____ seemingly nonproductive activities.

(A) support
(B) approve of
(C) eliminate
(D) disapprove of

20 Little Indian girls learned from their mothers to cook and to make clothing. Boys learned from their fathers how to fish, hunt, and fight. They did not have schools where they learned to read and write, but we cannot say that they had no _____.

(A) recreation
(B) religion
(C) books
(D) education

It's really amazing what you see on the beaches these days.
Thirty-year-old women, and they're still growing out of their bathing suits!

NOTE
18. **criticism**: 비평.   **exacting**: demanding great care, patience, effort, etc.; arduous; onerous (힘드는)
   scrutiny: a close examination (정밀한 조사).   **with finality**: conclusively (결정적으로, 결론적으로)
19. **self-made man**: 자수성가한 사람.   **seemingly**: 겉으로 보기에
   문맥 emphasize(= approve of) ≠ disapprove of

각 지문의 주제를 가장 잘 표현하는 제목을 골라라.

1 George Willard, the Ohio village boy, was fast growing into manhood, and new thoughts had been coming into his mind. All that day, amid the jam of people at the Fair, he had gone about feeling lonely. He was about to leave Winesburg to go away to some city where he hoped to get work on a city newspaper and he felt grown up. The mood that had taken possession of him was a thing known to men and unknown to boys. He felt old and a little tired. Memories awoke in him. To his mind his new sense of maturity set him apart, made of him a half-tragic figure.

(A) Boyhood
(B) Coming to Maturity
(C) Winesburg
(D) Tragedy of a Village Boy

2 The child whose parents are fond of him accepts their affection as a law of nature. He does not think very much about it, although it is of importance to his happiness. He thinks about the world, about the adventures that come his way and the more marvelous adventures that will come his way when he is grown up. But behind all these external interests there is the feeling that he will be protected from disaster by parental affection. On the other hand, the child from whom for any reason parental affection is withdrawn is likely to become timid and unadventurous, filled with fears and self-pity, and no longer able to meet the world in a mood of gay exploration.

(A) The Adventurous Child
(B) The Timid Child
(C) The Absence of Parental Affection
(D) The Importance of Parental Affection

NOTE

1. **growing into manhood** = grow into a man. *cf.* **come of age**: reach the age when one is qualified for full legal rights (성년에 이르다). **amid**: in the middle of; among. **jam**: crowd; crush. **fair**: 정기적으로 열리는 장, 자선시(bazaar). **go about**: to move from place to place. **take possession of** = to possess (사로잡다); seize; take hold of. **set him apart (from others)**: to separate him from others. He **made** a great statesman **of** his son. = He made his son a great statesman.
2. **disaster**: any serious or sudden misfortune; calamity; catastrophe. **withdraw**: to take back; remove **meet the world**: 세상일에 대처하다. **gay**: joyous; merry; happy
   문맥 **affection = fondness**

| 추려 읽기 | **뼈대와 예시** |

말에는, 내용으로 보아, 일반적인 진술(generalization) 또는 주장(argument)을 이루는 부분과 그것을 뒷받침해 주는 예시(illustration) 부분이 있다. 글을 읽을 때에 예시부분을 괄호로 묶으면 주어진 글의 뼈대를 더 쉽게 볼 수 있다.

Example 1

The Assiniboins were thrifty people who utilized all of their dead prey: (the meat was their food; their clothing came from the hides; their tools and weapons came from the bones and horns. Once the other parts had been disposed of, the children used the buffalo's ribs as sleds.)

의미 아시니보인족(미국 대평원에 거주했던 한 인디언 부족)은 알뜰한 사람들로 자기들이 잡은 동물(들소)의 모든 부분을 이용했다 : 즉, 고기는 식량으로, 가죽은 옷으로, 뼈와 뿔은 도구와 무기로 이용했다. 나머지 부분들을 처분하고 나면, 어린이들이 들소의 갈비뼈를 썰매로 사용했다.

요령 예시부분은 이미 앞에 한 번 나온 말에 대한 설명이므로 대부분의 경우에 속독(rapid reading)이 가능하다. 그러니, 평소에 이런 부분은 될 수 있는 대로 빨리 읽어나가도록 노력해야 한다.

A Good Example

Course listed in a bulletin of the Bristol Community College in Fall River, Mass.: "Decisions, Decisions, Decisions — This course is for people who have a tough time making decisions day in and day out. This is not a stuffy, stifling approach to problem-solving. So don't register if you think you have all of the answers. If you don't know whether you want to sign up for this course, you are eligible."

NOTE 문맥 utilize = dispose of = use

Example 2

Mark Twain was an angry prophet who saw his republic choked by the corporate state. But he never did arrive at a consistent view of his world. His feeling toward the technological society was widely ambivalent. (He admired technology; he despised it. The U.S. was corrupted; it was the hope of the world. Man was a splendid fellow; man was changelessly evil.) His own life reflected these inconsistences. (He delivered a fine speech lampooning accident insurance at a time when he himself was a director of an accident company.) The most consistent product of such inconsistency was humor.

의미 마크 트웨인은 성난 예언자로 자기의 공화국이 기업국가에 의해 질식되는 것으로 보았다. 그러나 그는 결코 자신의 세계에 대해서 일관성있는 견해를 갖지 못했다. 기술사회에 대한 그의 생각은 널리 모순적인 것이었다. 그는 한편으로 과학기술을 찬양했는가 하면 또 한편으로는 그것을 경멸했고, 미국이 썩었다고 여기면서도 그것은 세계의 희망이라고 생각했으며, 사람을 놀라운 존재로 생각하면서도 변함없이 나쁜 존재라고 생각했다. 그 자신의 삶이 곧 이러한 모순적인 생각들을 반영해 주었다. 그는 멋진 연설로 사고보험을 조롱했는데, 그때 그 자신이 사고보험회사의 이사였다. 이러한 일관성없는 생각에서 나온 가장 일관성있는 산물이 해학이었다.

....

An employer, interviewing an applicant, remarked,
"You ask high wages for a man with no experience."
"Well," the prospect replied,
"it's so much harder work when you don't know anything about it."

....

NOTE **choke**: to suffocate; stifle (질식시키다). **a corporate state**: 기업국가 (국가를 하나의 기업집단으로 보는 견해에서 나온 말임 — 따라서 '공화국이 기업국가에 의해서 질식된다'는 말은 국가의 정치적인 이상이 국가의 경제적인 면 때문에 죽어가고 있다는 뜻이다). **deliver/make a speech**: 연설하다. **lampoon**: to attack or ridicule by means of a piece of strongly satirical writing (강력하게 풍자적인 글로 공격하거나 조롱하다)

문맥 **ambivalent** = inconsistent. **despise** ≠ **admire**

EXERCISE 30

다음 각 구절에서 예시하는 부분을 괄호로 묶어라.

1. Eisenhower's major virtue, which appeared less important in 1962 than it does now, was a sense of proportion; he had an instinctive knowledge of what could be done and, **more important**, what could not be done. As far back as 1951, **for example**, when the French were fighting in Vietnam, he foresaw nothing but swamps. "I'm convinced that no military victory is possible in that kind of theater," he noted. In 1955 members of his Cabinet predicted imminent war with Red China in the Formosa Strait. **Ike knew better**: "I have so often been through these periods of strain that I have become accustomed to the fact that most of the calamities that we anticipate really never occur."

2. Admirals and generals do not win war. Presidents do. Consider: Washington (the nearest thing we had to a President during the Revolution), Lincoln, Wilson and Franklin Roosevelt.

   Admirals and generals do not lose wars. Presidents do, or at least they fail to win them. Consider: Truman in Korea and Lyndon Johnson in Viet Nam.

   In conflict, everything rests on grand strategy, a President's concept of how the threats, purposes and realities of power should be used. No vision, no victory. Washington wisely employed young America's guerrilla instincts, honed in skirmishes on the frontier, to beat the massed British armies.

> **NOTE**
> 1. **a sense of proportion**: 어떤 관련되어 있는 요소 사이의 관계에 대한 파악(여기서는 '할 수 있는 일이 무엇이고, 보다 중요한 것은, 할 수 없는 일이 무엇인지를 아는 것'이란 의미로 쓰였음).   **As far back as 1951**: 멀리 1951년으로까지 거슬러 올라가서, 그보다 훨씬 이전인 1951년에 이미.   **swamp**: marsh; bog; morass (늪).   **note**: to mention (언급하다).   **imminent**: impending (임박한).   **the Formosa Strait**: 대만 해협.   **Ike knew better**: 아이젠하워는 그들보다 더 잘 알고 있었다 (즉, 그는 전쟁이 일어나지 않으리라는 것을 알고 있었다).   **strain**: great tension (커다란 긴장).   **calamity**: disaster; catastrophe (재난).
> 2. **the nearest thing we had to a President during the Revolution**: 미국의 혁명 기간중에 대통령에 가장 가까운 존재 (그 당시에는 대통령이 없었으니까).   **conflict** = war.   **rest on**: to depend on.   **grand**: magnificent.   **strategy**: 전략.   **instinct**: talent; knack (재주).   **hone**: to sharpen (갈다, 연마하다).   **skirmish**: a brief fight or encounter between small groups; brush.   **beat**: to defeat.   **massed**: 한 곳에 많이 몰려 있는.   **best**: to outdo; surpass (능가하다).   **Confederacy**: (남북전쟁 때의) 남부동맹.   **firepower**: 화력.   **figure out**: to understand; reason out (생각해내다).
>   use = employ = turn to = marshal (여기서는 이들 네 단어는 같은 의미로 사용되었음)

Lincoln, whose first commanders were bested by field tacticians of the Confederacy, turned to big armies, superior firepower and generals like Grant, who knew how to use them. Wilson and Roosevelt marshaled American industrial capacity to win World Wars. Johnson and Truman never figured out what they wanted, so they never made up their minds how to fight.

3   Franklin's vision also was the source of many of the paradoxes of his character. He was deeply involved in numerous causes, yet remained strangely aloof. He was a revolutionary with a sense of humor. He was earnest because he knew that we really do make our own world, and so we must make it the best world we can. Yet he was skeptical because he realized that the result of human effort is often a sorry and ludicrous botch. Some of these paradoxes have passed from Franklin into the American character — that mixture of conviction and skepticism, zeal and humor, liberalism and conservatism.

4   Sincere people recognize the direction in which their lives are meant to go. When Albert Schweitzer, the great missionary doctor, was a boy, a friend proposed that they go up in the hills and kill birds. Albert was reluctant, but, afraid of being laughed at, he went along. They arrived at a tree in which a flock of birds were singing; the boys put stones in their catapults. Then the church bells began to ring, mingling music with the birdsong. For Albert, it was a voice from heaven. He shooed the birds away and went home. From that day on, reverence for life was more important than the fear of being laughed at. His priorities were clear.

NOTE

3. **be involved in**: ~에 관여하고 있다.   **cause**: any objective or movement, especially one involving social reform.   **aloof**: apart; detached; distant in sympathy, interest, etc.; reserved and cool (초연한).   **He was a revolutionary with a sense of humor** = He was a revolutionary but he had a sense of humor.   **skeptical**: incredulous; doubting; distrustful; not easily persuaded or convinced.   **sorry**: miserable; wretched.   **ludicrous**: ridiculous; laughably absurd; preposterous.   **botch**: a bungling or unskillful piece of work (엉망으로 해놓은 일).   **zeal**: intense enthusiasm; ardor; fervor

4. **mean to (do)** = intend to (do).   **reverence**: respect; veneration (존중)

| 논리 읽기 | **논리적인 관계를 보여주는 장치** |

잘 쓰여진 글에서는 하나의 문장이 그 앞이나 뒤에 있는 문장과 일정한 논리적인 관련을 갖는다. 여기서는 이러한 관계를 보여주는 몇 가지 장치에 대해서 살펴보기로 하자.

Example 1

One of the most difficult lessons to learn in painting is when to stop. In overworking, **not only** will your painting lose its spontaneity and freshness, **but** you may very well find that you _____ the painting altogether.

(A) lose (B) like
(C) begin (D) bring

요령 'not only x but (also) y' 구조에서 x와 y의 내용은 같거나 비슷해야 한다.

정답 A

의미 그림을 그릴 때 배워야 할 가장 어려운 일 가운데 하나는 언제 그만 그리느냐는 것이다. (왜냐하면) 지나치게 많이 그리게 되면, 그림이 자연스러움과 신선함을 잃을 뿐만 아니라, 그림을 통째로 잃게 될 가능성이 매우 높기 때문이다.

Example 2

The English Reformation was prompted less by religious than by economic motive — **that is**, by concern _____.

(A) more for peace than for war
(B) more for war than for peace
(C) less for money than for truth
(D) less for truth than for money

요령 that is (to say)라는 부연장치로 보아 by concern~ = less by religious than by economic motives라는 등식관계가 성립되어야 한다.

정답 D

의미 영국의 종교개혁을 재촉한 것은 종교적인 동기보다는 경제적인 동기였다 — 다시 말해서, 진리에 대한 관심보다는 돈에 대한 관심이었다.

※ 주요 '부연' 장치 : comma, colon, dash, or, i.e. [id est], that is (to say), in other words, put another way, etc.

Example 3

Emerson's faith was not in machinery but in man thinking, **whereas** we today are _____ machines that think, and suspicious of any man who tries to.

(A) aware of
(B) ashamed of
(C) independent of
(D) proud of

요령	whereas는 '대조'(contrast) 관계를 나타낸다.
정답	D
의미	에머슨의 믿음은 기계가 아니라 생각하는 인간에게 있었으나, 반면에 우리는 오늘날 생각하는 기계에 대해서 자랑스럽게 여기고, 생각하려는 사람에 대해서는 의심한다.

※ 주요 '대조' 장치 : but, although/though, while, whereas, meanwhile, on the other hand, on the contrary, conversely, rather than, not, instead of, as opposed to, in contrast with, as compared with, as against, etc.

Example 4

Much recent housing and city planning has been _____ **because** those who have undertaken the work have had no clear notion of the social functions of the city.

(A) improved
(B) bettered
(C) established
(D) handicapped

요령	because는 '이유'(reason) 또는 '원인'(cause)을 나타낸다.
정답	D
의미	많은 최근 주택과 도시 계획은 지장을 받아왔는데, 그 이유는 그런 일을 담당해온 사람들이 도시의 사회적인 기능에 대해서 전혀 분명하게 이해를 하지 못해왔기 때문이다.

Example 5

Many writers seem to believe that man is an exception to the order of nature, for they picture his actions as being determined only by himself. But they are in error, for man is a part of nature and **hence** must _____.

(A) determine his own actions (B) exist in a separate realm
(C) follow nature's laws (D) conquer nature's laws

> **요령** hence는 논리적인 '귀결'(corollary)을 나타낸다.
>
> **정답** C
>
> **의미** 많은 글쓰는 사람들은 사람이 자연의 질서에 예외적인 존재라고 믿고 있는 것 같다. 왜냐하면 그들은 사람의 행동이 오로지 자기자신에 의해서 결정되는 것으로 묘사하니까. 그러나 그들은 잘못 속에 빠져있다. 왜냐하면 사람은 자연의 일부이고, 따라서 자연의 법칙을 따라야 하기 때문이다.
>
> ※ '귀결' 또는 '결과'를 나타내는 말 : therefore, accordingly, consequently, as a result, etc.

Example 6

Corn is the most important of all American crops, and annually the corn crop is greater than the combined production of wheat, oats, barley, rye, rice and buckwheat. Used mainly as feed for livestock, corn is as basic to the American agricultural economy **as** iron is to _____.

(A) commerce (B) industry
(C) agriculture (D) production

> **요령** 윗 구절의 마지막 문장의 뼈대는 'A is to B as/what C is to D'로 '유추'(analogy) 관계를 나타낸다. 간단히 말해서, analogy는 두 사물 사이의 상대적으로 비슷한 점이다. 다음과 같은 비례관계가 하나의 좋은 예다.
>
> 2 : 5 :: 6 : 15
>
> **정답** B
>
> **의미** 옥수수는 모든 미국의 농작물 가운데서 가장 중요하며, 한 해의 옥수수 생산량은 밀, 귀리, 보리, 호밀, 벼, 메밀을 합친 생산량보다 더 많다. 주로 가축을 위한 먹이로 사용되는데, 옥수수는 미국의 농업경제에 필요불가결하다, 철이 공업에 필요불가결하듯이.
>
> ※ '유추' 관계를 보여주는 말 : like, as, similarly, likewise, etc.

Example 7

Wealth is not merely banknotes or even gold and silver and precious stones. Ultimately it is things — the food in the stores, the minerals from the ground, the ships on the oceans, etc. It is also having clever artists, musicians, writers, technicians, and so on. **In short**, a country's wealth lies in the richness of its soil and in the skill of its _____.

(A) people
(B) engineers
(C) statesmen
(D) leadership

요령	In short는 앞에 나온 말을 '요약' 해 준다.
정답	A
의미	부라는 것은 단순히 은행지폐나 심지어 금과 은과 보석만을 가리키는 것이 아니다. 궁극적으로 그것은 물건이다 — 가게에 있는 식품이라든지, 땅에서 파낸 광물, 바다 위의 배 따위와 같은. 그것은 또한 현명한 화가, 음악가, 문필가, 기술자 따위를 갖는 것이다. 요컨대, 부라는 것은 한 나라의 토양의 비옥함과 그 나라 국민의 기술에 놓여 있다.

※ 요약하는 데에 사용되는 말 : to sum up, to conclude, in conclusion, in brief, in a nutshell, etc.

"You will have exactly two hours,"
said the professor as he handed out examination papers to a roomful of students.
"Under no circumstances will I accept a paper given to me after the deadline has passed."
Two hours later he broke the silence.
"Time is up," he said. But one student continued to work furiously.
The professor was glaring out from behind the pile of exams
when the tardy student approached him, almost 15 minutes later,
with his exam clutched behind his back.
When the professor refused to accept it,
the student drew himself up to full stature and asked,
"Professor, do you know who I am?"
"No," said the professor.
"Terrific," replied the student, and he stuffed his paper into the middle of the pile.

EXERCISE 31

다음 빈칸에 가장 알맞은 말을 골라라.

1. As we shall see, the two subjects are closely connected, and might, indeed, be regarded as different aspects of a _____ topic.

   (A) double (B) dual
   (C) identical (D) single

2. The forces of socialization that lead the individual to accept social institutions in their present form are not easily broken and _____.

   (A) valued (B) emphasized
   (C) transformed (D) mended

3. Both content and style are essential to good poetry. A good subject does not insure a good poem, and an elaborate form is ridiculous in the absence of _____.

   (A) something to say (B) elaborate style
   (C) a complex purpose (D) insignificant content

4. Ideas can sometimes be communicated better by gestures than by words. It is much less effective to tell a person to leave the room than to _____.

   (A) ask him to go (B) point to the door
   (C) say nothing at all (D) get up and go out

5. It has been said that knowledge is power, but great power lies in the ability to utilize knowledge. A trained and powerful mind surely contains something, but its chief value consists in what it _____.

   (A) contains (B) retains
   (C) forgets (D) can do

NOTE
1. **dual**: double; twofold (이중적인)
3. **in the absence of** = without
   문맥 subject = content. form = style
5. **utilize**: to put to use or make practical use of. **consist in** = to lie in
   문맥 what it can do = its ability

6. The existence of evil is a proof of the existence of God. If the world consisted wholly and uniquely of goodness and righteousness, there would be no need for God, for the world itself would be God. God is, because _____ is.

(A) proof
(B) God
(C) goodness
(D) evil

7. In order to enjoy the detachment and to exercise the reason of a Hume or a Gibbon, two things, besides intelligence, are required: self-knowledge and a sense of humor. One must neither _____ oneself nor take oneself too seriously.

(A) receive
(B) expand
(C) deceive
(D) destroy

8. Any patient who participates in a medical experiment must sign an "informed consent" document. This form has two purposes: to ensure that human subjects fully understand the experimental nature of the treatment and to guarantee that their decision was made _____.

(A) deliberately
(B) accidentally
(C) altruistically
(D) without pressure

9. Though many of the teachings of Socrates are generally accepted today, in his time they disagreed with the prevalent ideas and were considered to be very _____.

(A) radical
(B) conventional
(C) conservative
(D) philosophical

NOTE

6. **uniquely**: only; solely.   **righteous**: morally right; fair and just; virtuous
7. **exercise the reason of a Hume or a Gibbon**: 흄과 같은 철학자나 기번과 같은 사학자의 이성을 구사하다.   **David Hume (1711-76)**: Scottish philosopher and historian.   **Edward Gibbon (1734-94)**: English historian
8. **"informed consent"**: 자기가 내용을 충분히 알고서 한 동의.   **altruistically**: 남들을 위해서
   문맥 **form** = document.   **guarantee** = ensure
9. **prevalent** = generally accepted.   **radical**: extreme; favoring fundamental or extreme change.   **conventional**: traditional.   **conservative**: 보수적인

10. As rational beings, we can, to some extent, control our surroundings. We may _____ of social or economic forces, but we, as citizens, can work to change our society.

(A) be at the mercy (B) be at the cost
(C) follow the lead (D) take the lead

11. At first, each star appears separated from all the others; but, as one looks a little longer, _____, pairings appear, and groupings emerge.

(A) many stars come into view (B) constellations dissolve
(C) clusters begin to take shape (D) every star becomes distinct

12. There are certain things that the world quite obviously needs: tentativeness, as opposed to dogmatism, in our beliefs; an expectation of cooperation, rather than _____, in social relations; a lessening of envy and collective hatred. These are things which education could produce without much difficulty.

(A) despair (B) rejection
(C) operation (D) competition

13. People who scorn the study of the past and its works usually assume that the past is entirely different from the present, and that hence we can learn _____.

(A) something worthwhile from the past
(B) something worthwhile from the present
(C) nothing worthwhile from the past
(D) nothing worthwhile from the present

14. During the Middle Ages, singers wandered from place to place. Wherever they went they were welcomed. They often narrated tales of happenings near and far in their songs. They were _____ of their time.

(A) preachers (B) news commentators
(C) minstrels (D) poets

NOTE

10. 문맥 **can control** ≠ may be at the mercy of (=cannot control)
11. 문맥 **take shape** = appear = emerge
12. **tentativeness**: 확실한 증거가 있을 때까지 판단이나 믿음을 정지하는 것. **dogmatism**: 독단적인 생각이나 주장
    as opposed to = rather than; instead of. **lessen**: to decrease. **collective**: 집단적인
13. **scorn**: to view or treat with contempt; despise. **assume**: to suppose; take for granted
14. **narrate**: to tell; give an account of. **preacher**: a person who preaches; especially, a clergyman (목사)
    minstrel: 중세의 유랑 시인 또는 가수

15 If we are to improve the quality of a piece of writing, we must do more than merely criticize it. We must explain why we criticize it. Inferior work is most effectively remedied when we know _____.

(A) exactly how poor it is (B) what good writing is
(C) why it is poor (D) who wrote it

16 Just why sleep is necessary still baffles researchers. It doesn't seem to be essential for health. Long periods of sleep deprivation may cause transient disorientation, but the effects aren't _____.

(A) permanent (B) mysterious
(C) apparent (D) abnormal

17 The male suicide rate is about four times as high as the female rate. But women attempt suicide nearly three times as often as men; they succeed less often because they use less _____ methods, such as taking pills, while men tend to favor guns.

(A) terrific (B) scientific
(C) lethal (D) mortal

18 To understand something thoroughly, we must know its parts. For example, we know a house when we are familiar with its rooms and with the various details of its construction. Words are built much like houses; we shall understand words better by familiarizing ourselves with _____.

(A) the best modern writers
(B) the laws of syntax
(C) available reference sources
(D) the elements of which they are made

NOTE

15. 문맥 inferior = poor
16. **baffle**: to confuse so as to keep from understanding or solving; puzzle; confound. **deprivation**: 박탈 < deprive (빼앗다). **disorientation**: confusion, especially with respect to time, place, and the identity of persons and objects
    문맥 permanent ≠ transient (= not permanent)
17. **lethal**: causing or capable of causing death; deadly; fatal. **mortal**: that must eventually die (죽게 마련인)

19 When recombinant DNA ignited the genetic revolution in 1973, scientists and businessmen were attracted by its near miraculous medical potential. But today, with impending food shortages and vanishing arable land, gene splicing is moving down to the _____.

(A) village (B) school
(C) church   (D) farm

20 Although the aim of a science is the acquisition of information, the information must of course be reliable. Hence there is a necessity in the sciences for a systematized way of amassing knowledge. It is this _____ that marks the essential difference between a science and any other discipline.

(A) reliability   (B) reliable information
(C) scientific exactitude (D) systematization

21 Contemporary composers have been showing a strong reaction to this kind of realism. In fact, _____ began as far back as the beginning of our century.

(A) the revolt (B) the show
(C) the ideal   (D) the realism

22 Americans have never been known for snobbishness. They are better characterized by their belief in equality of the individual and their _____, born out of frontier neighborliness and suspicion of putting on airs.

(A) incurable audacity
(B) impatience with pretense
(C) preference for authoritarianism
(D) inferiority complex

NOTE

19. **recombinant DNA**: DNA 재조합; 이 말은 '유전자 결합' (gene splicing) 또는 '유전공학' (genetic engineering)과 동의어로 사용된다. **medical potential**: 의학에 이용할 수 있는 가능성. **impending**: imminent (임박한). **vanish**: to pass gradually out of existence; come to an end. **arable**: 경작가능한

20. **acquisition**: 획득 < acquire (획득하다). **amass**: to collect; gather. **exactitude**: accuracy (정확성)
    문맥 information = knowledge. acquire = amass

21. 문맥 revolt = reaction

22. **snobbish**: 속물스런. **frontier neighborliness**: 개척시대의 친절. **audacity**: daring; shameless or brazen boldness; insolence; impudence. **inferiority complex**: 열등감
    문맥 putting on airs = pretense = snobbishness

23 Exile, says de Tocqueville, is the most cruel of all punishments, for while it inflicts suffering, it teaches _____. It crystalizes the minds of its victims, fixes in them the notions acquired in youth.

(A) something (B) nothing
(C) anything (D) much

24 Some writers are only of historical interest. Their message may have stirred men in their own time, but they do not move us today. Truly great authors are those whose message speaks not only to their contemporaries but also to _____.

(A) popular taste (B) succeeding generations
(C) various nationalities (D) literary critics

25 It is the characteristics of a good detective story that one vital clue should reveal the solution to the mystery, but that the clue and its significance should be far from _____.

(A) suggestive (B) obvious
(C) logical (D) constructive

26 Two basic and interrelated aims of Western civilization are to preserve human life and to provide economic security. There is a concurrent striving for health and for _____.

(A) happiness (B) art
(C) freedom (D) wealth

27 When she discovered a worthy cause, Mrs. Saunders contributed freely her time and talents, but her monetary gifts were of necessity _____.

(A) limited (B) generous
(C) charitable (D) wasted

NOTE

23. **exile**: 귀양, 유형. **Alexis de Tocqueville** (1805-59): French author and statesman. **crystalize**: 굳어지게 만들다

24. **contemporary**: 동시대인, 당대인
   문맥 **stir** = **move** = **speak to** (감동시키다)

25. **detective story**: 추리소설. **vital**: of crucial importance (결정적으로 중요한)

26. **interrelated**: 서로 관련되어 있는. **preserve**: 보존하다. **security**: 안정. **concurrent**: simultaneous (동시적인). **strive**: to make great efforts; try very hard. 문맥 **striving** = **aim**

27. **cause**: (사회적인 개혁을 위한) 운동이나 목적. **of necessity**: necessarily; inevitably (어쩔 수 없이)
   charitable: kind and generous in giving money or other help to those in need; lenient
   문맥 **gift** = **contribution** (기부)

28. Why is life worth living? What do you like most about it or want most from it? From what do you get your most thorough satisfactions? Are you substantially like others in your wants, or do your life desires add up to a _____ pattern?

(A) usual (B) common
(C) distinctive (D) universal

29. The anthropologist has become so _____ with the diversity of ways in which different people behave in similar situations that he is not apt to be surprised by even the most exotic customs.

(A) indifferent (B) varied
(C) unaware (D) familiar

30. Despite your imagined freedom, you are chained always by the laws of cause and effect. You may be free to leap from a skyscraper or to refrain from eating for a week, but you are not free to _____.

(A) commit murder (B) perform these actions twice
(C) escape the consequences (D) compel others to do likewise

31. The facts of metropolitan congestion are _____ ; they are visible in every phase of the city's life. One encounters congestion in the constant stopping of traffic, or in the even more tightly packed subway train.

(A) encouraging (B) imaginary
(C) negligent (D) undeniable

NOTE

28. **thorough**: complete.　**substantially**: really; actually.　**add up to**: 합쳐서 ~가 되다.　**do your life desires add up to a ___ pattern?** = are you ___ in your wants? (문체를 바꾸어 썼다는 점을 생각하라.)

29. **anthropologist**: 인류학자.　**diversity**: difference; variety.　**be apt to (do)**: be inclined or likely to (do); tend to (do).　**exotic**: strange.　**indifferent**: uninterested

30. **the laws of cause and effect**: 인과법칙.　**refrain from**: to hold oneself back from; avoid

31. **congestion**: 혼잡.　**phase**: aspect; side; part.　**encounter**: to meet with; face
    문맥 **packed = congested**

32 A central belief of the middle class in which I grew up was that the son of a ditchdigger could become a college president, whereas the careless son of the top family in town could easily make mistakes from which he would not recover. These twin beliefs were not _____; each year they were illustrated by specific lives in our community, and are still being illustrated.

(A) legendary (B) legitimate
(C) different (D) conspicuous

33 The heterodox opinions of one age frequently become the orthodox views of its successor. Flaws in existing views are pointed out, and eventually these views are altered or discarded. Dogmatisms are _____.

(A) unpopular (B) rational
(C) transitory (D) eternal

34 When I first read the book, I accepted its ideas only tentatively; but since then they have become so entrenched in my philosophy that I can no longer _____.

(A) think any other way   (B) read any other book
(C) believe them to be true (D) express them otherwise

35 Of professor Baker's latest book I can say only that his and my views remain worlds apart, and though I yield to no one in my admiration for his smooth-flowing literary style, my opinions of what he has to say are _____.

(A) quite another matter   (B) just the same
(C) different from each other   (D) far from being just

NOTE

32. ditchdigger: 도랑 파는 노동자. **specific**: particular; certain. **legendary**: 전설적인, 전설 속에 나타난 **legitimate**: lawful (합법적인). **conspicuous**: noticeable; striking; outstanding

33. orthodox: approved or conventional (공인된, 전통적인). **its successor** = its succeeding age (그 다음 시대) **flaw**: defect; fault; error. **eventually**: in the end. **alter**: to change. **discard**: to throw away; abandon. **dogmatism** = dogmatic view (독단적인 견해). **transitory**: not enduring or permanent; transient; ephemeral
  문법 heterodox = not orthodox ≠ orthodox. views = opinions

34. tentatively: not finally; provisionally (잠정적으로). **entrenched**: established; settled; rooted; embedded **otherwise**: in another way; differently

35. late: recent. **worlds apart**: 천지차이인. **yield**: 양보하다, 굽히다, 지다. **smooth-flowing literary style**: 유창한 문체. **what he has to say** = what he says (in the book). **another matter**: 별개의 문제(즉, 다른 문제)

36 Cancer of the pancreas has spread with baffling and deadly results: U.S. cases have doubled in two decades and the disease now kills 20,000 Americans annually. It is also one of the hardest cancers to treat: _____ of its victims survive more than three years.

(A) almost all (B) hardly any
(C) none (D) not all

37 Nothing in the characteristics of any of the standard dialects of English — British, Canadian, American, South African, and others — creates any serious difficulties in understanding. We have, among English-speaking people, _____.

(A) no difficulties at all in understanding each other
(B) not flat sameness, but unity in diversity
(C) difficulties in understanding each other
(D) complete unity without variety

38 Though faulty hypotheses are excusable on the grounds that they will be superseded in due course by acceptable ones, they can do grave harm to those who hold them because scientists who fall deeply in love with their hypotheses are proportionately _____ to take "no" as an experimental answer.

(A) indifferent (B) ready
(C) susceptible (D) unwilling

39 Until the accident in Pennsylvania, nuclear reactors had had a remarkable record of safety. Opposition to nuclear energy is, however, essentially based on the _____ that more serious accidents will occur at some unpredictable time in the future.

(A) anticipation (B) improbability
(C) inevitability (D) generalization

NOTE

36. **pancreas**: 췌장.　**baffle**: to confuse; puzzle; confound. (요령) 법풀가처럼 '엄격하게' 생각하라.
37. **flat**: complete; absolute.　**diversity**: difference; variety
38. **hypothesis**: 가설.　**on the grounds that they~**: ~라는 근거 위에서.　**supersede**: to replace (대치하다) **in due course**: 때가 되면.　**grave**: serious; ominous.　**proportionately**: 비례적으로 (즉, 자신의 가설을 깊이 사랑하게 되면 될수록).　**"no"**: 그 가설에 대한 부정.　**experimental**: for the sake of experiment; designed to test; tentative (잠정적인).　**susceptible to**: easily influenced by or affected with (~에 쉽게 영향을 받거나 걸리는)
39. **nuclear reactor**: 원자로.　**anticipation**: expectation; presentiment.　**inevitability**: 불가피함.　**generalization**: 일반화시켜서 하는 진술 (보기: "미국인은 실제적이다.")

40 Changes in a developing science are not to be compared to the tearing down of old buildings to make way for new ones, but rather to the gradual evolution of a zoological type. We must not believe that discarded theories have been _____.

(A) of any purpose in present research
(B) seriously considered
(C) used in molding new ideas
(D) either sterile or in vain

41 The function of "truth" drugs is to tear down inhibitions that keep the individual from expressing emotions freely. Put a stopper into the spout of a kettle, bring the water in the kettle to a boil, and the steam will force out the stopper. Similarly, inhibitions function as a stopper, and the drugs _____.

(A) alleviate painful symptoms   (B) tend to remove them
(C) jam down the stopper   (D) keep the patient tense

42 Thanks to the natural resources of the country, every American, until quite recently, could reasonably look forward to making more money than his father, so that, if he made less, the _____ must be his; he was either lazy or inefficient.

(A) wealth   (B) possession
(C) expense   (D) fault

43 A bottle-fed baby is often encouraged to finish off the last drop of his formula, whether he wants it or not. Mothers who bottle-feed also tend to switch their babies to solid foods, with their high calorie content, earlier than do breast-feeders. Such habits in infancy may set a later pattern of _____.

(A) overeating   (B) indulgence
(C) malnutrition   (D) sickness

NOTE

40. are not to = should not. **compare A to B**: regard A as similar to B; liken A to B. **tear down**: to demolish; raze (허물어 뜨리다). **gradual**: 점진적인. **evolution of a zoological type**: 동물의 진화와 같은 유형의 진화. **mold**: to shape (형성하다). **sterile**: unfruitful

41. inhibition: 억제해 주는 것. **stopper**: 병마개. **spout**: 주둥이. **bring~to a boil**: 끓게 만들다. **force out**: 힘으로 밀어내다. **alleviate**: to make less hard to bear; lighten or relieve. **symptom**: 증세. **jam down**: 꼭 눌러서 막다

42. thanks to: ~덕분에. **natural resources**: 자연자원. **look forward to**: to expect. **so that**: 그래서, 그러므로. **inefficient**: lacking the necessary ability; unskilled; incapable

43. bottle-feed: 우유를 먹이다. **formula**: 한 번에 먹이기로 정해놓은 우유의 분량. **solid food**: 단단한 음식(즉, 씹어서 먹는 음식). **with their high calorie content** = which has a high calorie content (or which contains high calorie). **in infancy** = in babyhood. **set**: to establish. **malnutrition**: 영양공급 불량, 영양실조

44 Research team scientists are products of this century. And the involvement of the entire citizenry of a country is a development of the past few decades. Every educated person nowadays is _____ some of the achievements and characteristics of science.

(A) beside himself with (B) familiar with
(C) friendly to (D) puzzled over

45 Most histories in totalitarian countries are nationalistic, patriotic, sentimental, and preoccupied with the national ego and the delusion of the particular country's complete _____.

(A) peacefulness (B) superiority
(C) prosperity (D) dependence

46 A research study revealed that the white-collar worker was extremely concerned about the impression his clothing made on his superiors. Although blue-collar workers were less aware that they might be judged by their clothing, they recognized that any deviation from the accepted pattern of dress would draw _____ from their fellow workers.

(A) indifference (B) indignation
(C) ridicule (D) sympathy

47 Humans, computers and animals could be said in some sense to think. Yet the thought processes of each of these would be _____ : each would have its own strengths and its own weaknesses. The merit of a particular combination of strengths and weaknesses would depend on the job to be done.

(A) complex (B) different
(C) mysterious (D) similar

NOTE
44. **is a development of the past few decades** = is a phenomenon that has developed in the past few decades. **beside oneself with**: ~ 때문에 제정신이 아닌
45. **the particular country's**: '특정 국의' 란 뜻이 아니라 '자기 나라의' 란 뜻이다.
46. **white-collar worker**: 정신(사무직) 노동자. **blue-collar worker**: manual(or physical) laborer. **concerned (about)**: worried; anxious. **superior**: 상관. **recognize** = be aware. **deviation**: 이탈, 벗어남 **indifference**: 무관심. **indignation**: anger
47. **in some sense**: 어떤 의미에서, 어떤 관점에서 볼 때. **the job to be done**: 처리해야 할 일

48. Efforts of the theorists to account for the universal appeal of music and to explain its effects have, since the 19th century, been various, contradictory and highly _____.

(A) in tune   (B) controversial
(C) harmonious   (D) uniform

49. Scientists have found both good and bad uses for nuclear energy. Our main source of power when oil is exhausted will probably be atomic power plants. There is, on the other hand, the danger of thermonuclear weapons almost certain to be used in future wars. There are a few people who blame scientists for the possibility of world destruction and who feel that the discovery of nuclear energy has been _____.

(A) morally wrong   (B) scientifically important
(C) understood by few   (D) subject to international control

50. Law gave birth to the concept of freedom. It is true that you can have no security in a situation in which every person and everything around you acts capriciously, unpredictably, or, in other words, lawlessly; but the point I wish to make is that while you would have no security in such an environment, it is more important that you would have no _____ in such an environment. The reason you could not be free in such a situation is that you could not get anywhere you wanted to go or successfully do anything you wanted to do.

(A) obligation   (B) freedom
(C) expectation   (D) prospect

NOTE

48. 문맥 account for = explain
49. **exhaust**: to use up; expend completely.   **power plant**: 발전소.   **on the other hand**: from the opposed point of view.   **thermonuclear weapon**: 핵무기.   **subject to**: ~의 지배 밑에 놓여있는
50. **give birth to**: to originate; create.   **concept**: 개념.   **capriciously**: whimsically (변덕스럽게)

| 문맥과 의미 | **문맥이란 무엇인가?** |

우리가 남의 얘기를 듣거나 글을 읽는 것은 그 사람이 얘기하려는 것을 올바르게 파악하려는 데에 일차적인 목적이 있다. 그런데 어떤 특정한 단어나 구절의 '구체적인 의미'는 주어진 문맥 속에서 결정되므로, 문맥의 파악은 의미의 파악에 선행조건이다.

<WEBSTER'S NEW WORLD DICTIONARY>는 문맥을 이렇게 규정하고 있다:

the parts of a sentence, paragraph, discourse, etc. immediately next to or surrounding a specific word or passage and determining its exact meaning
(어떤 특정한 단어나 구절 바로 가까이에 있거나 둘러싸고 있고 그것의 정확한 의미를 결정해 주는 문장, 문단, 얘기 따위의 일부)

간단히 말해서, 문맥이라는 것은 어떤 특정한 단어나 구절의 의미를 결정해 주는 언어의 환경(또는 배경)이라고 볼 수 있다.

다음 각 예문에서 볼드체 단어의 의미를 결정해주는 것이 무엇인지 생각해 보라.

1) Trees are large **plants**. (식물)
2) This is the largest power **plant** in the country. (시설, 공장)
3) In the spring he **plants** some flowers in the garden. (심다)

| 문맥과 의미 | **의미를 문맥 속에서 찾아야 하는 근본적인 이유** |

구체적인 사물을 가리키는 말은 사전의 풀이와 어떤 개인이 그 말에 대해서 갖고 있는 개념이 일치하지만, 추상적인 말은 '막연하기' 때문에 사전의 정의와 개인의 머릿속에 들어있는 개념이 반드시 일치하지는 않는다. 예를 들어, 학문의 한 분야로서 '철학'이라는 단어에 대해서 생각해 보자. 이 단어에 대해서 Aristotle이 갖고 있던 생각과 현대의 어떤 철학자의 생각과 이제 막 이 단어의 의미를 희미하게 깨닫기 시작한 한국의 어느 고등학생이 갖고 있는 생각은 일치하지 않을 것이다. 그렇다면 이들 세 사람이 의미하는 '철학'이라는 말의 뜻을 이해하려면 이들이 거기에 대해서 쓴 글이나 한 얘기 속에서 찾아내는 수밖에 다른 방법이 없을 것이다. 이런 관점에서 볼 때 사전은 '막연한 일반적인 의미의 안내자'에 불과하다.

| 문맥과 의미 | **진정한 문맥의 파악이 의미하는 것** |

분명히, 언어는 놀라운 도구이기는 하지만, 그것은 어디까지나 하나의 도구에 지나지 않기 때문에 '사물 자체'를 완벽하게 그려낼 수는 없다. 그러므로 자기가 나타내려고 하는 것을 언어로 '완벽하게' 나타낼 수 있는 사람은 이 세상에 아무도 없다. 그러므로 모든 얘기나 글은 필연적으로 '불완전하게' 마련이다. 이런 불완전한 글에서 표면상으로 드러나있는 의미만 붙잡고 늘어져 보았자 본래 그 글을 쓴 사람이 나타내려고 한 뜻을 제대로 파악할 수 없을 것이다. 바로 여기에 '줄 사이에 숨은 뜻을 읽으라'(Read between the lines)는 말의 진정한 뜻이 놓여 있다. 다시 말해서, 바로 여기에 진정한 문맥파악의 뜻이 있다.

구체적으로, 문맥을 파악한다는 것이 어떤 것인지 알아보기 위해서, 문맥을 제대로 파악하지 못한 데서 저질러진 잘못을 예를 들어 살펴보기로 하자.

Example 1

Real life is, to most men, a long second best, a perpetual compromise between the ideal and the possible.　　　　　　　　　　— Bertrand Russell

그릇된 풀이　대부분의 사람에게 실생활이란 기나긴 차선이며, 이상적인 것과 가능한 것 사이의 영구적인 타협이다.

비판　주어진 문장을 번역한 사람은 "a perpetual compromise between the ideal and the possible"이 "a long second best"와 다른 개념인 것처럼 알고 있으나, 문맥으로 보아 전자(the former)는 후자(the latter)를 달리 설명한 말이라는 것을 알 수 있다. 만일 이 둘이 별개의 개념이었다면 Russell은, 십중팔구, 그 둘을 comma 대신에 접속사 and로 연결했을 것이다.

올바른 풀이　실제 생활이라는 것은, 대부분의 사람에게, 하나의 긴 차선, 즉 이상적인 것과 가능한 것 사이의 기나긴 타협이다.

Party Line

The story goes that while at a cocktail party,
T.E. Lawrence was approached by a woman of uncertain age
who had a reputation for trying to add celebrities to her list of social acquaintances.
Using the heat wave as a means of engaging him in conversation,
she assailed Lawrence with: "Ninety-two, Colonel Lawrence! Imagine it! Ninety-two!"
"Many happy returns, madam," he replied.

Example 2

Embodying the bad as well as the good of America, Theodore Roosevelt was admired by his countrymen almost as much for his failings as for his "finer qualities." If he gave voice to the nobler aspirations of the nation, his defects were those of a majority of the people. Harry Thurston Peck noted that "the self-consciousness, the touch of the swagger, the love of applause and of publicity, the occasional lapse of official dignity, even the reckless speech, the unnecessary frankness, and the disregard of form" which characterized Roosevelt were in reality "traits that...were national."

그릇된 풀이 테오도르 루즈벨트는 미국의 선과 악을 구현하였기 때문에 국민들로부터 그의 보다 뛰어난 자질 못지 않게 그의 실수에 대해서도 찬미를 받았다. 그가 국민의 보다 숭고한 열망을 표명했을 때마다 그의 결점은 국민 대다수의 결점이었다. 헤리 터스턴 페크는, 루즈벨트의 특징이었던 '자의식, 허풍, 갈채와 평판에 대한 열망, 때때로의 공식적인 위엄의 쇠퇴, 심지어 무모한 언변, 불필요한 솔직성 및 형식의 무시'는 실제로는 국민적인 특성이라는 것을 주목했다.

비판 이 번역문에는 오류가 한두 가지가 아니다.

1) 옮긴이는 원문의 비중을 전혀 고려하지 않았다. 이 글에서는 루즈벨트의 좋은 점보다 '결점'에 비중이 있다는 점을 알아야 한다.
2) '그가 국민의 보다 숭고한 열망을 표명했을 때마다 그의 결점은 국민 대다수의 결점이었다.' 도대체 이것이 무슨 뜻인가? 이것은 문맥을 파악하지 못한 데서 나온 잘못이다.
3) '때때로의 공식적인 위엄의 쇠퇴'라는 말도 무슨 뜻인지 분명하지 않다.
4) 윗 구절에서 다음 단어들은 각각 같은 의미로 사용되었다는 사실을 알아야 한다.
   the bad = failings = defects
   the good = "finer qualities" = nobler aspirations
   America = his countrymen = the nation = a majority of the people
   embody = give voice to
5) 그리고 문맥(뒤에 나오는 주절)으로 보아 If he gave voice to the nobler aspirations of the nation이라는 말은 근본적으로 If his merits were those of the nation이라는 말을 문체상의 반복을 피하기 위해서 그렇게 나타낸 것이라는 점을 알아야 한다.

올바른 풀이 씨어도어 루스벨트는 미국인의 좋은 점뿐만 아니라 나쁜 점도 갖고 있었는데, 그는 그가 가진 '보다 더 훌륭한 자질'에 못지 않게 결점 때문에 미국인들로부터 찬양을 받았다. 그의 좋은 점이 미국인의 좋은 점을 대변해 주는 것이었다면, 그의 결점은 국민 대다수의 결점이었다. 헤리 서스턴 펙의 지적에 의하면, '다른 사람들 앞에서의 부자연스러운 행동이라든지, 다소 으스대는 점이라든지, 갈채와 평판에 대한 사랑, 가끔 관리로서 체신에 맞지 않는 행동을 하는 것, 심지어 함부로 얘기를 하는 것과 불필요할 정도의 솔직함과 격식을 무시한 것'은 루스벨트의 특징이었는데, 이것은 실제로 미국인의 특징이었다고 한다.

진단 이러한 오류는 앞의 보기에서와 마찬가지로 근본적으로 영어실력의 부족과 문맥에 대한 이해의 부족에서 그 원인을 찾을 수 있을 것이다. 문맥에 대한 이해의 부족이라는 말은, 바꾸어 말하면, 논리적인 사고의 부족이라는 말과 같다. 이런 잘못을 저지르지 않으려면 철저히 사고하는 버릇을 들여야 한다. 진리 탐구에는 '적당히 넘어가는 일'은 있을 수 없다.

Example 3

But democracy is usually a tumultuous and unseemly affair, especially when men feel strongly about vital issues. Probably since the first popular assembly convened there have been presiding officers who turned a deaf ear to delegates they did not like. Rival factions have always tried to pack the galleries and to shout down their opponents. **To take note of these historical facts is not to condone them.** An unending effort has to be made to create procedural safeguards strong enough to curb the ineradicable human impulse to unfairness. But critics should not pretend they were born yesterday and are innocent of any knowledge of pressure tactics in politics.

그릇된 풀이   민주주의는 특히 인간이 중대문제에 관해 큰 관심을 가질 때 떠들썩하고 보기 흉한 것이 된다. 아마도 최초의 민중집회가 소집되었을 때 싫은 대표들에게는 귀를 기울이지 않는 사회자들이 있었을 것이다. 서로 적대되는 파에서는 언제나 방청석을 꽉 채우고 소리를 질러 반대파의 발언을 봉쇄하려고 했다. 이러한 역사적인 사실을 상기시켜도 그들의 마음을 달래지는 못할 것이다. 부당성에 대한 인간의 뿌리깊은 충격을 억제할 만한 강력한 절차상의 안전책을 마련하려는 끊임없는 노력이 있어야만 한다. 그러나 비평가들은 자기네들이 신진들이기 때문에 정치에서의 압력술책을 전혀 알지 못하는 척해서는 안 된다.

비판   우선, 밑줄쳐진 번역문은 주어진 문맥 속에서는 전혀 의미가 통하지 않는다. 물론, 이것도 문맥을 파악하지 못한 데서 나온 오류다. 그리고 여기서 얘기하는 '그들'이란 도대체 누구를 가리키는지 이해할 수 없다. 둘째로, 전반적으로 번역문에는 '정확성'이 부족하다. 예를 들어, 둘째 문장과 셋째 문장은 현재완료시제로 되어 있는데도 불구하고, 마치 그것이 최초의 민중집회 때의 일인 것처럼 단순과거시제로 옮겨놓았다. 그리고 마지막으로 두 번째 문장의 impulse를 '충격'이라고 옮긴 것은(만일 이것이 오식이 아니라면) 적절하지 않다. 이런 경우에 더 적합한 '충동'이라는 말이 있기 때문이다.

올바른 풀이   그러나 민주주의는 대개 소란스럽고 보기 흉하다. 특히 사람들이 중대한 문제에 대해서 격한 감정을 갖게 될 때에는. 아마도 최초의 민중집회가 소집된 이래로 자기가 좋아하지 않는 대표들에게는 귀를 기울이지 않는 사회자들이 있어 왔을 것이다. 서로 반대하는 파들이 언제나 방청석을 메우고 상대 대표들의 발언을 봉쇄하려고 해왔다. 우리가 이러한 역사적인 사실에 주의를 기울이는 것이 곧 그것을 용서하는 것은 아니다. 우리는 끊임없이 노력해서 부당한 행동을 하려는 인간의 뿌리를 뽑아버릴 수 없는 충동을 억제할 만큼 튼튼한(민주주의 토의) 절차상의 안전책을 마련해야 한다. 그렇지만 이러한 민주주의 방식을 비판하는 사람들은 마치 자기들이 엊그제 태어나서 정치에서의 압력술책을 전혀 모르는 척해서는 안 될 것이다.

In her newspaper column, "At Wit's End,"
Erma Bombeck replied as follows to an invitation from a California group:
"Yesterday, I received your colorful brochure and
special invitation to be a guest at your nudist ranch.
I hope you will understand when I tell you that I must decline,
as I don't have anything not to wear."

| 문맥과 의미 | **상상력의 필요성** |

상상력이라는 것은, 간단히 말해서, "밖으로 드러나 있거나 주어져 있지 않은 것을 생각해내는 능력"이라고 볼 수 있다. 그런데 우리가 글을 읽을 때에 상상력이 필요한 이유는 다음 세 가지라고 할 수 있을 것 같다.

첫째, 앞에서 얘기했듯이 글이란 불완전하므로 필자가 충분히 나타내지 못한 뜻을 우리 스스로가 찾아내야 한다.

둘째로, 어떤 모르는 말이 나왔는데, 그것을 이해하는 데 도움을 줄 참고서적이나 그것을 알고 있는 사람이 주위에 없는 경우에는 자신의 상상력에 의존하는 수밖에 다른 방법이 없을 것이다.

마지막으로, 다른 언어로 쓰여진 책을 읽을 때 자신의 모국어로는 도저히 충분한 설명을 하기 어렵거나 설명할 수 없는 말이 나왔을 경우에 우리는 우리의 사고체계를 떠나서 그 외국어의 사고체계 속으로 들어가서 이해하려고 노력할 수밖에 없을 것이다. (이런 관점에서 볼 때 영영사전은 특히 고급단계에서는 필요불가결하다.)

모르는 단어가 나오기가 무섭게 사전으로 달려가는 사람들이 있다. 그것은 글을 읽는 바람직한 태도가 아닐 뿐만 아니라 우리의 상상력에 해가 된다. 먼저 문맥 속에서 그 단어의 의미를 생각해 보고 나서 사전에서 확인하는 것이 바람직하다. 예를 들어, 다음 문장의 뜻을 생각해 보자.

Azure sweaters **pick up** the blue in her eyes.

Azure는 '하늘 청색의'이라는 뜻을 갖고 있는데, blue의 동의어다. 논리적인 면에서 볼 때 이 문장은 '청색 스웨터'와 '그녀의 눈의 푸른 색깔'과의 관계에 대한 것인데, 볼드체의 어구가 그 관계를 보여주는 것이라고 할 수 있다. '푸른 눈동자'를 갖고 있는 사람이 '청색' 옷을 입는다면 어떻게 되겠느냐?

의미 청색 스웨터는 그녀 눈의 푸른 색깔과 어울린다.

어떤 오해

The ardent honeymooning of her 75-year-old groom was exhausting the young bride. During a momentary lull while he was shaving, she staggered down to the coffee shop.
"What's the matter with you, dearie?" asked the waitress. "Here you are a young bride with an older husband, and you're the one who looks beat."
Said the bride, "That man double-crossed me. He told me he saved up for sixty years, and I thought he was talking about money."

EXERCISE 32

진한 글자 부분이 문맥 속에서 갖는 의미를 구체적으로, 그리고 다른 사람들이 이해할 수 있는 말로 설명하라.

1. Complete freedom is, of course, **out of the question**, but a reduction of pressure might be possible.

2. You once told me you were not **a natural writer**. My God! You have plainly mastered the craft, of course; but you needed far more than craftsmanship for this.

3. The problem is to learn to read these scientific records accurately. There are pitfalls in any such endeavor. The more **independent** approaches that can be brought to bear on a given problem, the greater are the chances that the pitfalls will be overcome and a meaningful solution achieved.

4. Pity is often a perception of our own misfortunes in those of others; it is a shrewd foresight of the **evils** into which we may fall. We help others in order to engage them to help us in similar circumstances; and the services we render them are, to speak properly, a good we do to ourselves by anticipation.

5. All of us should be able to agree that we need air, water, and land of sufficient quantity to sustain life. We must also recognize air and water and land as finite resources. They can be used up. When we consume them, **there is a planetary cost**.

NOTE

1. 문맥 out of the question (=impossible) ≠ possible
3. **pitfall**: an unsuspected error that one may fall into; trap (함정). **endeavor**: an attempt or effort
   approach: a method. **bring~to bear on/upon**: to cause~to have an effect on
   chance: a possibility or probability. **overcome**: to get over; surmount (극복하다)
4. **pity**: sympathy; compassion. **shrewd**: clever. **engage**: to hire; employ. **render**: to do; give
   문맥 help → service = good. render = do to. anticipation = foresight
5. **sustain**: to provide sustenance or nourishment for (~에게 영양을 공급하다). **finite**: limited. **resources**: 자원
   문맥 must recognize = should be able to agree ("also"라는 문맥으로 보아). consume = use up

6. It is true that the work of the peasant who cultivates his own land is varied; he ploughs, he sows, he reaps. But he **is at the mercy of** the elements, and is very conscious of his dependence, whereas the man who works a modern mechanism is conscious of power, and acquires the sense that man is the master, not the slave, of natural forces.

7. A University of North Carolina English instructor introduced to his class what he termed "one of the finest, most elegant lines of poetry in the English language." He had duly recorded it in all of his notebooks as a constant reminder of its beauty. "**Walk with light!**" he quoted, and then repeated softly and blissfully to himself, "Walk with light...now isn't that a wonderful thing to say to someone?" The class agreed, of course, and wished to know the author.

   "I suppose it's anonymous," said the instructor. "It's written on a sign at an intersection of Franklin Street."

8. In Britain at least, this was generally held to establish that light was a passage of electric and magnetic forces through the ether. **The Continent, however, remained comparatively unconvinced.** In 1879 the Berlin Academy offered a prize for a subject which had some bearing on the question "What is light?"

9. Moscow's tough talk was backed up by extensive Warsaw Pact maneuvers in and around Poland. The war games, originally scheduled to end last week, were prolonged indefinitely. Lengthy nightly television reports gave Poles a

---

NOTE

6. **peasant**: a small farmer; farm laborer.   **cultivate**: 경작하다.   **plough**[plow]: 갈다.   **sow**: 씨를 뿌리다   **reap**: to harvest (수확하다)
   is at the mercy of = depends on.   natural forces = the elements

7. **term**: to call.   **duly**: rightfully; properly.   **bliss**: great joy or happiness.   **anonymous**: with no name known (쓴 사람의 이름이 알려져 있지 않은)

8. 이 구절만으로는 첫째 문장에 나오는 "this"의 내용을 알 수 없다.   **establish**: to prove.   **ether**: a hypothetical invisible substance postulated (in older theory) as pervading space and serving as the medium for the transmission of light waves and other forms of radiant energy (가상적인 눈에 안 보이는 물질로 가정에 의하면 — 종전의 이론에서 — 공간에 퍼져서 빛의 파동과 기타 형태의 빛을 내는 에너지의 전도를 위한 매체 구실을 함).   **have bearing on**: to be related to
   hold that = be convinced that ~

9. **tough talk**: 강경한 발언.   **back up**: to support.   **extensive**: 광범위한.   **Warsaw Pact**: 바르샤바 동맹(국)   **prolong**: to extend; protract (연장하다).   **indefinitely**: 무기한으로.   **chilling**: 몸이 오싹하게 만드는, 몸서리치게 만드는.   **mock** = simulated (모의의).   **precede**: 선행하다
   maneuver = war game (기동훈련)

chilling view of amphibious landings, mock tank battles and simulated aerial assaults. Warsaw Pact maneuvers had preceded the 1968 invasion of Czechoslovakia; **the message was not lost on the Pole**s.

10 Mauriac provided his own eulogy in a recording he made 20 years ago to be released after his death. It reflected a lifelong preoccupation with the possibilities of grace that he had explored in his essays, if not in his other work. "I believe," he said, "as I did as a child, that life has meaning, a direction, a value; that **no suffering is lost**, that every tear counts, each drop of blood, that the secret of the world is to be found in St. John's 'God is love.'"

11 Heart attacks, which take about 550,000 lives each year, occur when the coronary arteries that supply blood to the heart muscle become obstructed. Without oxygen and other nutrients carried in the blood, heart tissue dies or is damaged. If too much tissue is affected, the heart is so weakened that it cannot pump. But even mild damage can kill by disrupting the electrical impulses that govern the heart's rhythmic beating. **Stroke claims another 170,000 lives, and is also caused by impeded blood flow, this time to the brain.**

12 **The number of physical phenomena amenable to scientific explanation increases with each passing decade**, whereas our scientific knowledge of human conduct remains relatively insignificant. The teachings of Aristotle concerning astronomy and physics have long since been superseded, but we have yet to replace his doctrines on ethics.

NOTE
10. **eulogy**: 추도찬사. **release**: 발표하다. **count**: to be of importance
11. **heart attack**: 심장마비. **coronary artery**: (심장의) 관상동맥. **nutrient**: 영양물. **disrupt**: to disturb
    stroke: 뇌졸중
    문맥 impede = obstruct
12. **amenable**: responsive; submissive
    문맥 we have yet to replace his doctrines on ethics = his teachings concerning human conduct have not yet been superseded

13 Across the Channel, French President François Mitterrand is following policies diametrically opposed to those of Thatcher. She seeks obsessively to lower Britain's inflation; he would risk increasing France's 14.5% rate in an all-out drive to create new jobs. She has clamped down on government spending; **he has thrown open the national coffers**. She accepts high interest rates as necessary medication; he damns them as a cruel impediment. She refuses to reflate the British economy; he is committed to expanding the French. The two philosophies could not be farther apart or, in many eyes, their chances of success more evenly matched.

14 It has been remarked that life is an almost continuous experience of having to draw conclusions from insufficient evidence. There are varying degrees of plausibility for many **alternatives**.

15 Throughout Western Europe, Begin's reputation fell to an all-time low. Lord Carrington, the British Foreign Secretary, called in the Israeli Ambassador to warn him that pre-emptive strikes, "with their horrible trail of human destruction, cannot conceivably advance the cause of peace." In Paris and Bonn, top officials **were equally scathing in private**.

16 Beyond the fear of a new war and the squeeze of a chaotic economy, social problems old and new are tearing at the fabric of Israeli society. Ethnic differences, exacerbated by social inequalities, strain relations between the Ashkenazi Jews of Northern Europe and the Sephardi Jews of the Mediterranean and the Muslim world. Religious quarrels set observant Orthodox Jews against the secular values of **less pious Israelis**. Lawlessness

---

NOTE

13. **diametrically**: completely; directly.   **obsessively**: persistently.   **all-out**: wholehearted.   **clamp down on**: to restrict (억제하다).   **coffers**: a treasury; funds.   **damn**: to condemn; curse; criticize adversely.   **reflate** = expand. *cf.* reflation: a type of inflation designed to restore a former price structure, accomplished by decreasing the purchasing power of currency by the use of governmental monetary powers.   **commit**: to bind by a promise; pledge; engage.   **in many eyes**: 많은 사람들의 눈에는 [많은 사람들이 보기에].   **evenly matched** = similar

15. **all-time low**: 지금까지 유례없이 낮은 수준.   **pre-emptive strike**: first strike (선제공격).   **cannot conceivably ~** : ~할 수 있으리라 상상할 수 없다. (conceivably는 문장 부사임).   **cause**: any objective or movement that a person or group is interested in and support.   **scathing**: harsh; caustic (신랄한).

16. **squeeze**: a difficult situation.   **chaotic**: in a completely confused or disordered condition.   **tear at**: ~을 찢으려고 격렬하게 잡아당기다.   **fabric**: the framework or basic structure.   **ethnic**: 인종상의.   **exacerbate**: to make more intense or sharp; aggravate.   **observant**: 엄격하게 종교의 율법을 지키는. *cf.* practicing   **secular**: not religious; worldly (세속적인).   **pious**: devout.   **restive**: nervous or impatient; restless   **compulsory**: required; obligatory (의무적인).

in general has risen sharply in a nation unused to it, and a small but flourishing Israeli "Mafia" has become an embarrassing new entry in international organized crime. A restive younger generation has shown growing dissatisfaction with the lack of job opportunities, the disruptive effects of compulsory military service, housing shortages and the political process.

17 Novelist Günter Grass calls it the city closest to the realities of the age. A 186-sq. -mi. Western outpost perched 110 miles inside East Germany, West Berlin, one of West Germany's eleven states, has always seemed **a kind of metaphor of the times**. At the height of the cold war, cheerful, wisecracking West Berliners turned the old German capital into a symbol of courageous resistance against Soviet encroachment. Twenty years ago last week, Moscow and its East German minions suddenly threw up the infamous 28-mile-long Wall across the city to halt a hemorrhage of people from the Communist empire, and West Berlin became a monument to the division of Europe. With detente, the heroic role faded. The outpost turned inward, and today the city is **a harsh reflection of another kind of reality**: the social crosscurrents that are churning through West Germany. It is in West Berlin that political protest is the shrillest, that the drug problem is the worst, the squatter movement the most militant.

18 It was characteristic, too, that when she met me, a young woman living alone in her country, Saura insisted on "adopting" me. It didn't matter to her that I am an American. "What you need," she told me, "is a good set of parents and lots of good brothers and sisters." Family, tradition and hospitality are the most important things in Saura's life; the material benefits and values of the West — or, more precisely, of Soviet society — are real enough, but emphatically secondary in her **scheme of things**.

NOTE

17. **perch**: to place or set. **wisecracking**: joking. **encroach**: to trespass or intrude; make inroads **throw up**: to raise suddenly or rapidly <핵표현: put up. **infamous**: notorious (악명높은). **hemorrhage** = escape. **a monument to**: ~에 대한 기념비 또는 기념비와 같은 존재. **churn** (의성어): to move or stir **shrill**: unrestrained and irritatingly insistent. **squat**: 남의 땅 (특히 공유지나 입주자가 없는 땅)에 무단으로 입주하다 **militant**: vigorous; aggressive (극성스러운)

18. **adopt**: 양녀로 삼다. **matter**: to be of importance or consequence; have significance. **hospitality**: (손님들에 대한) 친절, 환대. **emphatically**: very strikingly; definitely; certainly. **ethnic**: 인종상의

문맥 **real** = important. **scheme of things** = outlook (things = the world).

How Saura Abdullaeva and the 30 million other Muslim Central Asians **look at the world** is a subject that preoccupies the Kremlin these days. The basic reason: The Central Asian Muslim population of the Soviet Union is growing five times as fast as the country's ethnic Russian population. This means that ethnic Russians soon will be a minority and there may be as many Central Asians as Russians entering the labor force and the military.

19 Here are a couple of generalizations about England that would be accepted by almost all observers. One is that the English are not gifted artistically. They are not as musical as the Germans or Italians; painting and sculpture have never flourished in England as they have in France. Another is that, **as Europeans go, the English are not intellectual**. They have a horror of abstract thought; they feel no need for any philosophy or systematic "world-view." Nor is this because they are "practical," as they are so fond of claiming for themselves. One has only to look at their methods of town planning and water supply, their obstinate clinging to everything that is out of date and a nuisance, a spelling system that defies analysis, and a system of weights and measures that is intelligible only to the compilers of arithmetic books, to see how little they care about mere efficiency. But they have a certain power of acting without taking thought. In moments of supreme crisis the whole nation can suddenly draw together and act upon a species of instinct, really a code of conduct which is understood by almost everyone, though never formulated. The phrase that Hitler coined for the Germans, "a sleep-walking people," would have been better applied to the English.

20 Plato's vision of the Republic was that poets must be exiled lest they should lead men astray. But was it not also Plato's wisdom to complement his reasoning with myths, which evidence man's poetic thinking? Surely **Plato was a man who was at odds with himself**.

NOTE

19. a couple of: two; a few; several.　　**generalization**: a general idea or statement (일반적인 얘기).　　**gifted**: talented.　　**flourish**: to prosper; thrive.　　**world-view**: 세계관.　　**have only to∼to...**: ∼을 하기만 하면 …할 수 있다. →You *have only to* do *it to* see how easy it is. = If only you do it, you will see how easy it is.　　**obstinate**: stubborn; dogged (끈질긴).　　**cling to**: ∼에 매달리다.　　**defy**: to resist completely; foil; baffle (좌절시키다).　　**care about**: to feel concern or interest about.　　**draw together**: to pull together; unite.　　**act upon**: ∼에 따라서 행동하다.　　**species**: sort; kind.　　**code of conduct**: 행동규범.　　**formulate**: to express in a systematic way.　　**coin**: to make up; devise; invent.　　**"a sleep-walking people"**: '자면서 걷는 국민' — 이 것은 주어진 문맥에서는 '자다가도 필요하면 일어날 수 있는 국민,' 다시 말해서, '위기에 즉각 대처할 수 있는 국민'이라는 의미로 쓰였음.　　**be applied to**: ∼에 적용되다

20. lead∼astray = mislead.　　**evidence**: to make evident; indicate; show; bear witness to

영어식 사고방식

4 ENGLISH WAY OF THINKING

1 주의해야 할 전치사

2 한국어와 다른 어순

3 경제적인 동사

4 부정의 논리

5 한국와 다른 수식

주의해야 할 전치사 — 전치사와 이동식 사고

영어의 전치사 (또는 전치사에서 목적어가 탈락된 말)에는 우리말에서 찾아볼 수 없는 특성이 있다. 우리말에서는 '~을 그만두다'는 말을 영어에서는 '~에서 벗어나다' 처럼 어떤 대상을 중심으로 '이동하는' 식으로 나타내는 표현방식이 매우 발달되어 있다.

1
 a. She has **grown into** a beautiful woman.
 b. She **argued** him **into** taking the job.
 c. They **sweet-talked** him back to his job.
 d. He **helped** her **to** her feet.

2
 a. The boy **grew out of** his earlier interests.
  = The boy **outgrew** his earlier interests.
  = The boy **grew bigger than** his earlier interests.
 b. She **argued** him **out of** his decision.
 c. He **talked** her **out of** leaving her job.

의미
1. a. 그녀는 자라서 아름다운 여성이 되었다.
   b. 그녀는 그를 설득해서 그 일자리를 받아들이게 만들었다.
   c. 그들은 달콤한 말로 그를 설득해서 다시 자기 일자리로 돌아가게 만들었다.
   d. 그는 그녀를 도와서 일어서게 했다.
      get to one's feet: 일어서다
2. a. 그 소년은 자라서 종전의 관심거리를 그만두었다.
   b. 그녀는 그를 설득해서 그의 결정을 그만두게 했다.
   c. 그는 그녀를 설득해서 직장을 떠나는 것을 그만두게 했다.

A Father's Advice

"Integrity and wisdom — these are the keys to business success," the old man was telling his son.
"By integrity I mean that when you promise the delivery of merchandise on a certain day you must do so even if it bankrupts you."
"Well," asked the son, "What is wisdom?"
"Don't make such promises."

주의해야 할 전치사 — 전치사와 생략

1 a. He **helped** her **into** the car.
  (He **helped** her **to get** into the car.)
  b. He **helped** her **out of** the car.
  (He **helped** her **to get** out of the car.)

2 a. He **helped** me **out of** my financial difficulty.
  (He helped me **to get** out of my financial difficulty.)
  b. Please **help** me **out**.

3 a. I **asked** some friends **over** for drinks.
  (I asked some friends **to come** over **to my home** for drinks.)
  b. I **had** some friends **over** for drinks.

4 I **had** an acquaintance **in** for a cup of tea.
  (I had an acquaintance in **my home** for a cup of tea.)

5 The next day we were all **snowed in**.
  (The next day we were all snowed in **our home**.)

  cf. 1) She **locked** her husband **out of** her room.
    2) They were **locked out of** the house.
    3) He was **locked** in his room all day long.

의미

1. a. 그는 그녀가 차에 들어가는 것을 도와주었다.
   b. 그는 그녀가 차에서 나오는 것을 도와주었다.
2. a. 그는 나를 도와서 내가 재정적인 어려움에서 벗어나게 해주었다.
   b. 나 좀 도와줘.
   > 순해 여기서는 'me'가 처해 있는 '어려움'을 상대방이 알고 있으므로 그것을 생략했다.
3. a. 나는 친구 몇 사람을 한잔 하러 우리집에 초대했다.
   b. 친구 몇 사람이 한잔 하러 우리집에 와 있었다.
4. 내가 아는 사람 한 분이 차 한잔 하러 우리집에 와 있었다.
5. 그 다음날 우리는 모두 눈이 와서 집 안에 갇혀 있었다.
   cf. 1) 그녀는 자기 방을 잠그고 남편이 들어오지 못하게 했다.
     2) 그들은 안에서 잠겨 있어서 집에 들어가지 못했다.
     3) 그는 밖에서 문이 잠겨 있어서 하루종일 자기 방에 갇혀 있었다.

EXERCISE 33

진한 글자 부분을 주목하면서 전체의 뜻을 파악하라.

1 He means to **cheat** me **out of** my inheritance.

2 I attempted to **reason** him **out of** his absurdities.

3 The crux of Thatcher's argument is that British goods have **priced** themselves **out of** international markets.

4 There are grounds, though, for taking a hopeful view. By far one of the most important of these is the fairly steady, though irregular, drop in the inflation rate from its frightening peaks of 1979-80. During the 1970's, surges of inflation eventually undermined every economic upswing and led to new slumps, which brought about only temporary slowdowns in price rises. But many economists believe that the length and depth of the present recession have **wrung** inflation **out of** the economy more thoroughly than the preceding busts.

5 Gently, he **pushed** me **to** my feet.

6 The book **bored** me **to** distraction.

7 She **argued** her husband **into** doing what she wanted.

8 His impudence **provoked** her **into** slapping him on the face.

NOTE 4. **by far**: considerably; to a great degree; very much; far and away.   **surge**: any sudden, strong increase
문맥 price rises = inflation.   bust = recession = slump

9 The Nixon Administration, of course, is not the first to give undue priority to detente at the expense of Atlantic alliance. At least three administrations in succession, mesmerized by the threat of a mushroom cloud, have concluded that relations with the Soviet Union must take priority over those with Europe. But the best way to avoid **blundering into a nuclear war with Russia** is to maintain a healthy balance of power. And the indispensable ingredient in such a balance is a strong and united Europe. Thus Europe, not Russia, must take priority in our policy-making.

10 He never passes a mirror without stopping to **pat** his hair **into** place.

11 To visitors, the only time the Kennedy children ever seemed to rest was when they were sleeping. And they never seemed to do that. Whenever they gathered together, they were ready to play.

   The Kennedys have always liked touch football. Even in later life, those who **married into** the family had to be good players. Friends remember the time that Bobby Kennedy, in the middle of a game, ran into a fence. His face was covered with blood, but he did not stop playing. Many years later, Jack Kennedy would say to a friend about Bobby's new wife, Ethel: "She's really good. You ought to see her run and throw."

12 At 7:30 on a Sunday night, David Stockman sits alone at a conference table in the cavernous, ornate sanctum of the director of the Office of Management and Budget, poring with total concentration over computer printouts and tables of figures. When a visitor arrives to keep a dinner date, Stockman appears disappointed. "Is it that time already? I need five more minutes." Before the words are out, his gaze has returned to the papers.

   Finally, the OMB director **struggles into** his jacket and overcoat and starts down the corridor. "We've got just two more weeks," he says over his shoulder. The deadline he is referring to is Feb. 18, when Ronald Reagan plans to announce the details of his fiscal program, including radical surgery on the federal budget.

NOTE

9. **give priority to**: ~에 우선권을 부여하다.   **mesmerize**: to surprise very much, especially so as to make speechless and unable to move.   **mushroom cloud** = a nuclear war

12. **cavernous**: very large and deep.   **ornate**: heavily ornamented or adorned, often to excess   **sanctum**: a study or private room where one is not to be disturbed.   **pore over**: to read or study carefully.   **table**: 도표.   **figure**: 숫자.   **radical**: extreme; thorough (철저한).   **federal budget**: 연방정부의 예산

13
a. The acid has **eaten through** the metal.
b. Our holiday has **eaten into** the money we saved.
c. What both Taiwan and South Korea have encountered is a rude lesson in the limits of growth. Even in the boom years, planners in both countries acknowledged that they would one day have to rationalize and modernize their economies if they were ever to make the great leap into the ranks of the rich. But the day of reckoning came sooner than was expected. Protectionism, inspired by the global recession and the 1979 oil crisis, **bit into** foreign sales at just the time that other, less developed countries like China and the Philippines began producing and exporting products of their own at even lower labor costs. Explains Young Yoo, a South Korean economist, "We find ourselves sandwiched between the powerful developed countries and the Third World."

14 Women can move proudly into the security of their new bodies — they can **jog into shape**, lift weights for body tone, wear themselves out in the disco bliss of Jazzercise. But what about men? "Jazzercise is a blowout," one Atlanta woman says. "Remember the first dances you went to, where all the girls ended up dancing with other girls because the boys couldn't dance? So this gives me a chance to dance, which my husband hasn't done since our wedding. But my husband still won't dance. Come to think of it, I'm back to dancing with the girls. Haven't made much progress in the past 25 years, have I?" Wendy May, 34, who teaches aerobics in Atlanta, might argue that progress comes first, then the education of the recalcitrant male: "The discovery is not that it's sexy to be healthy but that it feels good. I think most men are frightened by muscles, maybe even by fitness. Now, though, I don't think they have a choice. They may as well decide it's sexy, because it's here."

NOTE
13. **encounter**: to meet with; face. **rude**: rough, violent, or harsh. **leap**: 도약. **the ranks of the rich**: 부국들의 대열. **the day of reckoning**: the time when one must suffer for a mistake. **protectionism**: 자기 나라의 무역을 보호하는 정책. **inspire**: to cause. **recession**: 일시적인 경기후퇴. **the Third World** = underdeveloped countries

14. **lift weights**: 역기를 들다. **wear oneself out**: (본래 이것은 '자신을 지치게 만들다'는 뜻이지만, 여기서는 다음 의미로 쓰였음) 자신의 살을 빼다. **bliss**: great joy or happiness; any cause of bliss. **Jazzercise** = Jazz+exercise. *cf.* workaholic (일 중독자). **blowout** [slang]: a party, banquet, or celebration. **end up -ing**: 끝에 가서 ~하게 되다. **come to think of it**: 거기에 대해서 생각해 보니. **recalcitrant**: hard to handle or deal with; unruly. **fit**: in good physical condition; healthy. **may as well**: to be very likely to

15. **subject to**: dependent on; contingent or conditional upon. **take effect**: 효력을 발휘하다
   예문 The bill was **voted into** law last month.
   문맥 are voted in = got congressional approval

15 Nearly all of the proposals would be subject to Congressional approval. And even if they are **voted in**, most would not take effect until 1984.

16 About twice a week my wife gets stinking drunk. Her outrageous behavior terrifies me and our teenage son. She becomes abusive and uses obscene language. The only way we can protect ourselves is by **locking her out of our rooms**.

After several hours of yelling she passes out on the floor. I let her sleep there because she is too heavy to move. It is not a pleasant sight for a child to find his drunken mother sprawled out in the corridor when he leaves for school in the morning.

17 a. Your article was **crowded out of** the magazine.

b. In an epoch when colorful volumes **crowd** each other **out** in bookshops, the black-and-white book is more than refreshing; it is a revelation.

18 DEAR ABBY: I am going crazy with this problem. I have two kids, 7 and $1\frac{1}{2}$. Both of them were breast-fed and given lots of love, but we ended up with a couple of thumb-suckers. Where have we failed? Is it hereditary, or what? The older one has outgrown the habit, but I still find her with her thumb in her mouth when she sleeps. It's the younger one I'm worried about.

He keeps his thumb in his mouth all the time, except when he eats or cries. It is really maddening to see him with his thumb constantly in his mouth. I tried applying bitter-tasting medicine on his thumb, but he got accustomed to it and sucks his thumb anyway. I even made a pair of gloves, but his hands are so small and flexible, it's only a matter of time before he frees his thumb and sucks it.

If I scold him, he goes and hides so he can suck his thumb. I am sick and tired of this tug of war with him. My pediatrician is no help. He says to leave

---

NOTE

16. stinking [slang]: to an excessive or offensive degree; very.　**outrageous**: very offensive or shocking; unrestrained (무절제한).　**abusive**: coarse and insulting in language (거칠고 모욕적인 말을 쓰는).　**pass out**: to become unconscious; faint.　**sprawl out**: 네 활개를 쭉 뻗다

18. hereditary: 유전적인.　**apply**: 바르다.　**it is only a matter of time before~**: 시간이 불과 얼마 지나지 않아서　**tug of war**: 줄다리기.　**pediatrician**: 소아과의사.　**foolproof**: very simple to use.　**tamperproof**: 손을 대서 손상할 수 없는　cf. **tamper with**: to interfere with or meddle with, especially so as to damage (손을 대다, 특히 손상하기 위해서).　**device**: a thing devised; plan; a mechanical invention or contrivance

him alone. I have no one to turn to but you, Abby. If you can't find a solution, ask your readers if they know of a foolproof, tamperproof device to keep a child's thumb out of his mouth.

19 *"My policies often change, sometimes radically. But so do circumstances. I like to think of myself as one of those people who adapt themselves to changing circumstances, who react to the changes, and who sometimes help to create them."*
— Moshe Dayan

For millions of people around the world, he was, quite simply, the living symbol of Israel. With his distinctive black eye patch and round boyish face, he was instantly recognizable in any country, in any kind of uniform, even in disguise, which he donned from time to time in the service of his nation's diplomacy. Soldier, statesman and swashbuckling hero of Israel's wars with its Arab neighbors, Moshe Dayan occupied center stage in Israel for more than 30 years. By the time he died last week of a heart attack at 66, Dayan had largely **outgrown his image as a warrior** and become an impassioned advocate of peace.

20 But if Reagan has **grown bigger than** supply-side economics, if he has grasped the meaning of presidential leadership and felt the exhilaration of achieving rather than preaching, he is more likely to succeed in the challenges ahead.

There is another hope held tenderly by some of Reagan's supporters and even a few of his adversaries. It is that he has also escaped his obsession with being consistent. Reagan believes inconsistency discredited Jimmy Carter. That bit of history has some truth, but, as always, one bit is an imperfect guide for other times. Carter was perceived to change positions not for the nation's good but for his personal political fortunes. If Ronald Reagan understood what he said last week about acting for all Americans, it could be the most important declaration of his presidency. That is true consistency.

NOTE

19. **radical**: fundamental; extreme; thorough.   **adapt**: to adjust (적응시키다).   **eye patch**: 안대.   **disguise**: 위장하기 위한 복장.   **don**: to put on (입다).   **swashbuckling**: loudly boasting or bullying.   **heart attack**: 심장마비.   **warrior**: a soldier.   **impassioned**: passionate; ardent.   **advocate**: a person who speaks for or supports something; supporter

20. **supply-side economics**: 공급면에 중점을 두는 경제 철학 또는 정책.   **exhilaration**: excitement.   **preach**: 설교하다.   **tender**: sympathetic; compassionate.   **adversary**: an opponent (반대하는 사람).   **obsession**: great preoccupation (집착).   **consistent**: 일관성 있는.   **discredit**: to damage the credit or reputation of; disgrace

21 DEAR ABBY: I'm glad you advised that 15-year-old girl against dating boys of a different religion if she had no intention of **marrying out of her faith**.

I was raised in a strict Baptist home, but dated boys I knew I could not marry. I fell deeply in love with a Jewish boy, but I married someone else. That was over 30 years ago, and I still dream of my first love. Now I wish I had either married him or not set myself up to fall in love with a man I could not marry.

22 a. How can we **get around** the new taxes and keep some more money for ourselves?

b. Not since 1966, when Gemini 9 was delayed by an electrical malfunction, had a launch been scrubbed with the astronauts already in the cockpit. But it flew off triumphantly two days later — and so did *Columbia*. Working through the night, computer experts in Houston eliminated the hitch by **working around** it. Saturday, the experts switched the computers on early, many hours before the second launch attempt. This time the machines worked in full harmony, and controllers knew they had those electronic gremlins licked. And so, an hour after dawn on Sunday, the go signal was given, the engines thundered and, as the grassy meadows and sandy beaches of Florida's coast trembled, Columbia was finally on its way.

c. His lawyers **found a way around** a California law that prohibits graves on private land.

NOTE
21. **advise~against...**: ~에게 …하지 말라고 충고하다.　**have no intention of -ing**: ~할 의도가 없다.　**faith** = religion.　**raise**: to bring up or rear (기르다, 양육하다).

22-b. **launch**: 발사.　**scrub**: to cancel or call off.　**cockpit**: 조종실.　**astronaut**: cosmonaut (우주비행사). **hitch** (의성어) = malfunction; hindrance; obstacle; entanglement.　**switch~ on**: 스위치를 넣어서 ~을 작동하게 만들다.　**gremlin** = hitch; (본래의 의미) an imaginary small creature humorously blamed for the faulty operation of airplanes or the disruption of any procedure.　**lick**: to overcome; vanquish; control

주의해야 할 수동표현
한국어와 다른 어순

우리말에서는 보통 'A는 B를 능가하다' 라고 나타내는 말을 영어에서는 'A는 B에 의해서 능가되다' 로 나타내는 경우가 흔하다.

1 Dinner **was followed by** dancing.
→ After dinner there was dancing.

2 The deceased **is survived by** his wife alone.

cf. He **survived** his wife by ten years.
 = He **outlived** his wife by ten years.
 = He **lived longer than** his wife by ten years.

3 a. We were **outnumbered by** the enemy.
b. The incumbent **was outvoted by** his opponent.

4 a. The ship **was undermanned**.
b. When discount houses tried to undersell department stores, the latter reduced prices, too, and adopted the slogan "We will not **be undersold**."

▶ We will not be undersold.
 = We will not let others undersell us.

의미
1. 저녁식사 뒤에 춤이 있었다.
2. 고인의 유족으로는 아내뿐이다.
3. a. 아군의 수효는 적군보다 적었다.
b. 재임자는 그의 상대후보보다 표를 적게 얻었다.
4. a. 그 배에는 선원이 부족했다.
b. 할인상점들이 백화점보다 더 싸게 물건을 팔려 하자, 백화점도 값을 내리면서 "우리보다 더 싸게 팔게 내버려두지 않을 것이다"라는 표어를 채택했다.

EXERCISE 34

진한 글자 부분을 주목하면서 전체의 뜻을 파악하라.

1. As a performer of Chopin, Arthur Rubinstein **was rivaled** in the second half of the century only **by** Vladimir Horowitz. He was noted also for his performance of Brahms, Schumann, Schubert, Beethoven, Liszt, Ravel and Debussy, Falla and Albeniz and his Polish compatriot Szymanowski.

2. In times of trouble, it has been Harlow's observation, there are no absolutely correct answers to problems, only approximate ones. As he sees it, a President in command must hold his course, tell the dissenters to go to hell — if possible, making them like it — and inject a bit of fear into his adversaries. "World peace and economic health are the two issues before Reagan now," says Harlow. "The rest **are dwarfed by** them. The President is the whale and he cannot let himself be eaten by the guppies."

3. To be sure, Argentina has certain economic advantages that both Britain and Israel lack. The country is a major grain and beef exporter and, like the U.K., is self-sufficient in oil. Even so, poor economic management over the years has regularly squandered these advantages, unleashing devastating bouts of inflation as weak governments have sought to bolster their popularity by providing easy credit and generous wages for workers. The defeat in the Falklands could mean more of the same. Sums up a Western diplomat in Buenos Aires: "The new government will be forced into a 25% to 30% wage increase (in the public sector), **followed by** hyperinflation, **followed by** more economic problems, **followed by** bank failures and business collapses, **followed by** foreign debt payment problems, **followed by** a fall in government again. Then they'll start all over."

NOTE
1. **noted**: famous; well-known; renowned.   **compatriot**: a fellow countryman
2. **approximate**: more or less correct.   **dissent**: to differ in belief or opinion; disagree.   **inject**: 붙어 넣다
   adversary: an opponent.   **dwarf**: to make small or insignificant.   **guppy**: a tiny freshwater fish
   As he sees it = In his opinion
3. **grain**: 곡물.   **squander**: to spend or use wastefully or extravagantly.   **unleash**: release (풀어놓다)
   devastating: completely destructive; ravaging; ruining.   **bout**: a period; spell (기간).   **bolster**: to prop up; support; strengthen; reinforce.   **hyper-**: over, above, or more than the normal; excessive
   collapse: failure or breakdown

4   Fortunately, things have improved somewhat since Hillary made that assessment. While the Khumbu Valley is something less than Shangri-la today, it remains one of those rare places where reality cannot be contained in postcards, where nature can still overwhelm, where refugees from more earth-bound regions can begin to understand Messner's own reason for climbing. "In the high mountains," he wrote, "the desperate business of living can **be transcended by** the sheer joy of being alive."

5   Thus Peking's oft-repeated condemnation of the Soviet Union as "the superpower that possesses the greatest threat to world peace" has **been superseded by** criticism of both superpowers. Chinese spokesmen lately blame international upheavals from the Middle East to the Falkland Islands on "superpower contention." Moreover, such old anti-American slogans as "running dogs of U.S. imperialism" and "the U.S. is a paper tiger" that were buried when Richard Nixon visited China a decade ago have crept into the political vocabulary again.

6   El Salvador is clearly not another Viet Nam. **The superficial parallels are outweighed by some very real differences.** Among them: El Salvador is not a sprawling jungle 8,000 miles from American shores, the junta is conscientiously trying to carry out an agrarian reform program, and the 4,000 leftist guerrillas are not backed by a force the size of the North Vietnamese army. Nonetheless, President Ronald Reagan and Secretary of State Alexander Haig have invested high stakes in a guerrilla war in a republic the size of Massachusetts. By waging a campaign against "indirect armed aggression" of foreign Communists who are smuggling arms to El Salvador's leftist guerrillas, the Reagan Administration is signaling to the

---

NOTE

4. **somewhat**: to some extent or degree; a little; rather.   **assess**: to evaluate; appraise.   **While** = Though   **Shangri-la**: any imaginary, idyllic utopia or hidden paradise.   **transcend**: to exceed; surpass; excel   **sheer**: pure

5. **oft**: (주로 시에서 사용됨) often.   **condemn**: to pass an adverse judgment on; disapprove of strongly; censure.   **supersede**: to replace.   **both superpowers** = the Soviet Union and the U.S.   **spokesman**: 대변인.   **lately**: recently.   **upheaval**: a sudden, violent change or disturbance in affairs.   **blame~on...**: ~의 탓을 …에게 돌리다.   **contention**: struggle; strife; dispute.   **creep**: 기다

6. **parallel**: a similarity; likeness; resemblance.   **outweigh**: to be more important than.   **sprawling**: 마구 뻗어있는.   **agrarian**: 농토의, 농토의 소유권 또는 분배와 관련된.   **back**: to support.   **stakes**: money.   **wage**: to engage in or carry on.   **armed aggression**: 무력침략.   **smuggle**: 밀수하다.   **draw a line against**: to set a limit to; restrain (억제하다).   **press conference**: 기자회견.   **possibly**: perhaps.   **destabilize**: to upset the stability of (~의 안정을 무너뜨리다, 불안정하게 만들다)

world that a line is being drawn against Soviet expansionism. "The terrorists aren't just aiming at El Salvador," explained Reagan in a White House press conference last week. "They are aiming at the whole of Central and possibly later South America and, I'm sure, eventually North America. What we're doing is trying to stop this destabilizing force of guerrilla warfare and revolution from being exported in here."

7.
a. I can **top** your story with an even funnier one.

b. He lost his job and **on top of that** his wife left him.

c. His house burnt down and his car was stolen and **to crown it all** he lost his job.

d. **Alexander the Drunk?**
Was Alexander the Great also Alexander the Drunk? The short, turbulent life of the man who conquered a world has long baffled scholars. Even as Alexander pushed Greek civilization all the way to the frontiers of India, he seemed to sink into a spiral of blackouts, binges, raging paranoia and morning-after remorse. Prof. John Maxwell O'Brien of Queens College in New York has a theory that is outraging the hero's legion of supporters. Alexander lived his last years, O'Brien contends, with "the classic symptoms of acute alcoholism."

Revel: O'Brien, whose study has just been published in the *Annals of Scholarship*, sees the influence of alcohol at many of the crucial junctures in the last seven years of Alexander's life. In 330 B.C., after a wine-soaked victory revel, he pointlessly torched Persia's ancient capital, Persepolis. Two years later, in a drunken rage, he killed his old friend Cleitus, and then, overcome with grief, tried to kill himself. But it was the death of his apparent lover and most trusted commander, Hephaestion, that sent Alexander over the edge. The 32-year-old conqueror slipped into a grim final year of massacres, purges and end-to-end binges, **capped by** what O'Brien identifies as a fatal alcoholic withdrawal aggravated by malaria.

Such claims predictably do not go down well in Athens — or with some other scholars who have studied Alexander's life. "Within only ten years, Alexander achieved more in conquest and the spreading of civilization than any other man," said Nikos Yalouris, supervisor of antiquities in the Greek Culture Ministry. "The minor evidence as to whether he was an alcoholic is, by comparison, petty." Biographer Mary Renault, who has written several books about Alexander, weighed in with a stout letter defending the hero's image that was printed in *The Times* of London — and prominently featured in Athen's mass-circulation press. None of O'Brien's detractors deny that Alexander, like all Macedonians of his time, drank heavily. But few are willing to slur the great conqueror by association with modern stereotypes of a hapless, debilitated drunkard. Says French scholar Maurice Druon: "An alcoholic? No. A good drinker, yes. But for heaven's sake, after so many victories the man deserved a drink."

Patient to doctor:
"After one checkup you made me quit smoking because I smoked too much. Next you made me quit drinking because I drank too much. Now I'm just back from my honeymoon, so this checkup really scared the hell out of me!"

NOTE   7. **turbulent**: violent; stormy; disorderly; tumultuous.   **baffle**: to make understanding impossible by confusing; puzzle; confound.   **spiral**: 소용돌이.   **blackout**: a temporary loss of consciousness.   **binge**: a drunken celebration or spree (폭음, 폭주).   **raging**: violent.   **paranoia**: 정신이상.   **morning-after remorse**: (일을 저지르고 난) 다음날 아침의 후회.   **outrage**: to cause great anger in.   **legion**: a large number; multitude.   **contend**: to assert; argue; maintain.   **symptom**: a sign (증세).   **acute**: severe (심한).   **crucial**: of supreme importance; decisive; critical (결정적인).   **juncture**: a point of time; moment.   **wine-soaked**: 술에 쏙 빠져 있는.   **revel**: boisterous festivity; merrymaking; celebration.   **torch**: to set fire to (~에 불을 지르다)   **overcome**: to make helpless, overpower or overwhelm (압도하다).   **grief**: deep sadness; acute sorrow   **send ~ over the edge**: ~을 비정상적으로 만들다.   **grim**: fierce; cruel; savage; ghastly.   **massacre**: 대량학살   **purge**: 숙청.   **identify**: ~의 정체를 밝히다.   **a fatal alcoholic withdrawal aggravated by malaria**: 술중독자가 술을 입에 대지 않았을 때에 겪는 치명적인 무기력증에다 말라리아가 겹친 상태.   **go down**: 전해져 내려가다.   **weigh in**: (싸움에) 들어오다.   **stout**: powerful.   **detract**: (명예 따위를) 깎아내리다.   **slur**: to disparage or discredit   **hapless**: unfortunate; unlucky.   **debilitate**: to weaken; enfeeble, enervate

경제적인 동사: '비교' 타동사

영어에는 한 단어 안에 '비교'의 의미가 들어 있는 동사들이 있는데, 이들 가운데 가장 많이 사용되는 것이 'out-동사'다.

1 a. He **outeats** people twice his size. (= eats more than)
　　b. He long **outlived** doctors' predictions.
　　　= He lived far longer than doctors predicted.
　　c. Soccer games **outdraw** presidential speeches.
　　d. The prisoner **outwitted** his guards and escaped.

2 a. A house guest should be careful not to **outstay** his welcome.
　　b. The idea was good once, but it has **outlived** its usefulness.

3 The gains **overbalanced** the losses. (= outweighed)

4 His accomplishment **surpassed** expectations. (= excelled)

5 John **excelled** his class in English. (= was better than)

의미
1. a. 그는 자기보다 두 배 더 큰 사람들보다 더 많이 먹는다.
　b. 그는 의사들이 예언한 것보다 훨씬 더 오래 살았다.
　c. 축구시합은 대통령의 연설보다 더 많은 사람들을 끈다.
　d. 그 죄수는 꾀를 써서 간수들을 물리치고 도망쳤다.
2. a. 남의 집에 손님으로 가는 사람은 주의를 해서 환영받지 않을 정도로 오래 머무르지 말아야 한다.
　b. 그 아이디어는 한때는 훌륭했으나, 지금은 너무 오래 돼서 효용가치를 잃어버렸다.
3. 이득은 손실보다 더 많았다.
4. 그의 업적은 사람들의 예상보다 더 훌륭했다.
5. 잔은 자기반 학생들보다 영어실력이 더 좋았다.

Don't try to awaken a sleepwalker. Better to lead him gently back to bed. The most hopeful note about sleepwalking is that most children outgrow it as they outgrow bedwetting and nightmares.

EXERCISE 35

진한 글자 부분을 주목하면서 전체의 뜻을 파악하라.

1 The advantages of living in a city **outweigh** the disadvantages.

2 People never **outgrow** their need for love.

3 The child has **outgrown** his earlier interests.

4 Since I couldn't **outrun** him, I had to **outfox** him.

5 The football games **outdrew** all the other college sports combined.

6 They still cling to some mummified customs that have long **outlasted** their usefulness.

7 Their marriage **outlasted** their differences.

8 The Bolsheviks brought out a paper called *Pravda* (Truth) in April, and its circulation **outdistanced** the Menshevik paper.

9 He **outvied** them all by the reach and freshness of his imagination and the variety and inventiveness of his resource.

10 Unfortunately, he was **outmatched** in the competition.

11 He was no small man, but **outtowered** by his companion.

12 Though his clothes were a little **outgrown**, there was something attractive about the boy.

13 Hart would try to change military thinking by rewarding and advancing officers who are expert in tactics and innovation, not program managers. "We've got to **outsmart** the enemy," says the Senator, who was shocked to discover that the academies have virtually squeezed out the required study of military history and tactics in favor of the social and political sciences.

14 This was demagogy **outsmarting itself**.

15 Singapore's precocious development is unparalleled in so young a nation. In 1960, when U.S. Economic Historian Walt W. Rostow published *The Stages of Economic Growth,* his classic yardstick of national economies, Singapore was still a British Crown Colony, with a freshly minted home-rule government under Lee Kuan Yew, then just into his second year as Prime Minister. Since then the country has marched swiftly through Rostow's "take-off" period, on through a concerted "drive to maturity," and today stands at the door of the "age of high mass consumption." Rostow, who is now teaching at the University of Texas at Austin, says that Singapore is "right on the edge of what you would call a First World economy." At present growth rates, he predicts, it should surely move up to that rank within the next few years.

Singapore in any case is quickly becoming an industrial market economy. Final figures for 1981 may well show that its per capita gross national product passed $5,000, putting Singapore ahead of most of Latin America, Asia, Africa and Eastern Europe, on a par with Ireland and poised to **outstrip** Spain. That is not enough for Lee, however. By 1990 he wants his country to have reached the level of Japan today, to become a nation of high-technology manufacturing and computerized services in industries such as banking and communications. Lee himself says he will step down as

---

NOTE

13. **advance**: to raise in rank; promote (승진시키다).　**outsmart**: to overcome by cleverness; outwit　**academy**: (군의) 사관학교.　**virtually**: in effect; practically; almost.　**squeeze out**: 짜내다, 없애다
14. **outsmart oneself**: to have one's efforts at cunning or cleverness result in one's own disadvantage; lose by acting too cleverly (자기 꾀에 자신이 불리하게 되다)
15. **precocious**: 조숙한.　**unparalleled**: unequaled; unmatched; unrivaled (비길 데 없는).　**classic**: excellent; standard; authoritative; established.　**yardstick**: any standard of measurement or comparison (척도)　**crown colony**: 직할식민지.　**mint**: to create.　**home-rule**: 국내문제에 대해서는 자치하는.　**concerted**: combined (단합된).　**on a par with**: on an equal footing with (~와 같은 수준인).　**poised**: ready.　**step down**: (관직에서) 물러나다.　**end**: an aim or purpose.　**groom**: to train for a particular purpose.　**turn over the helm**: 통치권 또는 지도자 자리를 넘겨주다

Prime Minister before he turns 65 in 1988. To that end he is not only trying to groom successors, but is pushing his nation to achieve as many of his goals as possible before turning over the helm.

16 Much has been said about the need for love. Yet love means different things to different people at different times in each of their lives. With proper care and guidance, a person grows in his ability to love in much the same way he grows in size and weight. To a helpless baby, love means prompt attention to his needs. Love is shown in the way he is held and cared for. Even a small baby knows when he is wanted. Through love, he develops his sense of trust. Kind attention tells him that he is worthwhile. It helps prepare him for social growth and learning. Without love, he cannot form the framework into which the pieces of his personality must fit. The young child needs love, too. So do teenagers. And how about your parents? **Do people outgrow their need for love?**

AT A CHURCH-COUNCIL DINNER,
my mother and father were seated at the same table as the pastor. Near the end of the meeting, the latter stood to offer some closing remarks, which became quite long-winded. As he rambled on, he lost his place in his notes for the third time.
"Now where was I?" he asked, scratching his head.
To the delight of audience and speaker alike, my mother spoke up and said,
"In conclusion!"

NOTE **16. helpless**: unable to look after oneself or to act without help (자신을 돌보거나 도움을 받지 않고 행동할 능력이 없는)
care for = to take care of; look after.   **framework**: the basic structure (기틀, 기반)

부정의 논리 — **간접부정(완곡부정)**

1 He was **the last** person I had expected to see in such an odd place.
  = Never did I expect to see him in such an odd place.

2 a. He is **above** deceit.
    = He is the last person to deceive.
  b. She is **above** doing such a mean thing.

3 a. The dying man was **beyond** help.
  b. The meaning of the sentence was **beyond** him.
    =He couldn't grasp the meaning of the sentence.

4 These goals are **far from** being realized yet.

5 He is **anything but** a scholar.
  = He is not a scholar at all.

6 **But for** his help, I would have been drowned.
  = If it had not been for his help, I would have been drowned.

7 He was **at a loss** for words.
  = He didn't know what to say.

의미
1. 나는 결코 그런 이상한 곳에서 그를 만나리라 기대하지 않았다.
2. a. 그는 결코 속일 사람이 아니다.
   b. 그녀는 결코 그런 비열한 짓을 할 사람이 아니다.
3. a. 그 죽어가는 사람은 어쩔(치료할) 수가 없었다.
   b. 그는 그 문장의 의미를 이해할 수가 없었다.
4. 이들 목표는 아직도 실현되기에는 요원하다.
5. 그는 결코 학자가 아니다.
6. 그의 도움이 없었더라면, 나는 익사했을 것이다.
7. 그는 무슨 말을 해야 할지 몰랐다.

| 부정의 논리 | **부정 + 부정** |

1 a. There is **no** rule **but** has exceptions.
   = There is no rule that does not have exceptions.
   = There is **no** rule **without** exceptions.
   = **Every** rule has exceptions.

   b. **Who** is there **but** commits errors?
   = There is **no** one **but** commits errors.
   = There is no one that does not commits errors.
   = **Every**one commits errors.

   c. **Scarcely** a week passes **but** a prophet of doom raises his voice in that country.
   = **Scarcely** a week passes **without** a prophet of doom raising his voice in that country.
   = **Almost every** week a prophet of doom raises his voice in that country.

2 They **never** meet **but** they quarrel.
   = They **never** meet **without** quarreling.
   = **Every time** they meet, they quarrel.

3 You **cannot** read this book **but** you will be the better for it.
   = You **cannot** read this book **without** being the better for it.
   = If you read this book, you will surely be the better for it.

의미 1. a. 예외없는 규칙은 없다.
   b. 잘못을 저지르지 않는 사람이 누가 있느냐?
   c. 거의 매주 그 나라에서는 예언자가 나타나서 파멸이 온다고 외친다.
      (거의 매주 그 나라에서는 파멸의 예언자가 나타나서 떠들어댄다.)

2. 그들은 만나기만 하면 말다툼을 한다.

3. 이 책을 읽으면 틀림없이 이득을 얻을 것이다.

| 부정의 논리 | **한국어와 다른 부정의 논리** |

1 a. He was **not, like** his father, optimistic about his future.
   (He was not optimistic about his future + His father was optimistic about his future)
   = His father was optimistic about his future, but he was not.
   b. Boredom saps one's energy **like nothing** else.
   (Boredom saps one's energy + Nothing else does so)
   = Nothing saps one's energy so much as does boredom.

2 A whale is **no more** a fish **than** a horse is.
   = A whale is not a fish, just as a horse is not.

3 He was **not so** stupid **but** he could see the seriousness of the matter.
   = He was **not so** stupid **that** he could **not** see the seriousness of the matter.
   cf. He was so stupid that he could **not** see the seriousness of the matter.
   = He was too stupid to see the seriousness of the matter.

의미 1. a. 그는, 자기 아버지와는 달리, 자신의 장래에 대해서 낙관하지 않았다.
    (※그는, 자기 아버지와 같이, 자신의 장래에 대해서 낙관하지 않았다.)
    주의 괄호 안에 있는 것처럼 옮기면, '그의 아버지도 그의 장래에 대해서 낙관하지 않았다'는 뜻이 되므로 주의하기 바란다.
    b. 권태처럼 사람의 정력을 소모시키는 것은 없다.
 2. 고래가 물고기가 아닌 것은 말이 물고기가 아닌 것이나 마찬가지다.(고래는 말이나 마찬가지로 물고기가 아니다.)
 3. 그는 그 문제가 심각하다는 것을 알 수 없을 만큼 어리석지는 않았다.
    cf. 그는 너무도 어리석어서 그 문제가 심각하다는 것을 알 수 없었다.
    주의 이 구문은 that 이하부터 먼저 옮기는 것이 좋다.

주의 부정적인 뜻과 긍정적인 뜻이 결합되어 있을 때에는 우리말로 옮길 때에 특별히 주의해야 한다.

EXERCISE 36

빈칸에 알맞은 단어를 써넣어라.

1 If you want to learn, you must not be _____ asking questions.

2 Your pronunciation is far from perfect.
   = Your pronunciation leaves _____ to be desired.

3 It's quite a surprise to see you here.
   = You're the _____ man I expected to see here.

4 There can be no man _____ has some faults.

5 I cannot look at this photograph _____ being reminded of my childhood.

6 Everything becomes easy by practice.
   = Nothing is _____ hard _____ becomes easy by practice.

7 He is never too busy to answer letters.
   = No business can _____ him from answering letters.

8 I've got to go at all costs.
   = _____ can stop me _____ going.

9 He is strong in subjects other _____ mathematics.

10 I cannot make myself understood well even in English, much _____ in French.

11 The clearer a business letter is made, the better it is.
   = A business letter can never be made _____ clear.

진한 글자 부분을 주목하면서 전체의 뜻을 파악하라.

1. In their dusty work clothes they looked **anything but** affluent.

2. He is out on an errand but he will be back **in no time**.

3. a. You **cannot** be **too** careful of your health.
   b. Accuracy can **never** be **overdone**.
   c. The danger of vitamin deficiency **cannot** be **overemphasized**.
   d. It's **impossible** to treat a child **too** well. Children are spoiled by being ignored too much or by harshness, not by kindness. Rich kids are often spoiled not by their toys and automobiles, but by parents who are too busy to pay much attention to them.

4. a. We can **no more** explain a passion to a person who has never experienced it **than** we can explain light to the blind.
   b. Up until some four decades ago fashionable ladies would **no more** have thought of exposing themselves to sunshine **than** they would today to rain. For to be pale was then the sign of social distinction.

5. a. There is **nothing** on the earth **but** is affected by the sun.
   b. I could **not** spend an hour in anyone's company **without** getting the material to write at least a readable story about him.
   c. **No** one is so occupied with the business of his calling **but** he finds time to read the newspaper.
   d. There is **none so** wise **but** he is foolish at some time.

6. a. It is **not** true, **as** sometimes claimed, that "health is wealth."
   b. He was **not** guilty of the murder, **as** many people thought him to be.
   c. In the United States institutions of higher learning supported by public funds are **not** absolutely free, **as** are the elementary and secondary schools.

d. Reverie is the groundwork of creative imagination; it is the privilege of the artist that with him it is **not, as** with other men, an escape from reality, but the means by which he accedes to it.

e. The writers of the Bible were **not** learned men, **as** we use that term today. But their great works have lived and been read as have **no** others.

f. Though his book covers little new ground, he tells the Hitler story **as no** non-German could: dispassionately, but from the inside. When he blames the German people for Hitler, as he does, the charge rings true.

7 a. You can't expect to have seen **the last** of him; he'll turn up again like a bad penny.

b. A cut in exports is about **the last thing** that the Korean economy, already groaning under a heavy load of foreign debt, can afford.

8 Yasser Arafat is **nothing if not** a practical man; he is unlikely now to do anything that will undermine growing sympathy in the West for the Palestinians.

9 There **never** was a child **so** lovely **but** his mother was glad to get him asleep.

10 Oil is a buyer's market these days — with prices dropping despite a slump in production. Oil contracts dipped below $30 per barrel on the Rotterdam spot market last week, $2 less than the standard OPEC price. In turn, the availability of large quantities of crude at such steep discounts is putting stiff pressure on the world's large oil companies to roll back some prices at the pump. Already, independent refiners and marketers have aggressively begun to reduce gasoline prices in Britain and some European countries — and more cuts are likely soon.

　　Oil production is dropping too. Worldwide crude output fell during the first six months of 1980, after five years of steady increases. OPEC output was off most steeply — by more than 5 percent — while North Sea producers bucked the trend and posted a 13 percent gain.

　　Slack consumer demand in the United States is a major reason behind the supply glut. For the week ending Aug. 15 U.S. oil imports average 4.2 million barrels per day, down nearly 40 percent from the 1979 figure. Few experts, however, think the present buyer's market for oil will last long. Oil companies seem eager to spend record sums on exploration, and despite falling crude prices, drilling rigs are in strong demand as offshore development picks up. Last week a Norwegian firm chartered one seven-year-old unit for a record $84,000 per day — hardly an indication that the price of oil, in the long run, is going **anywhere but** up.

Success Story

I was interviewing applicants for the position of junior sales manager and had narrowed the list to four people. As a final test I gave the applicants a barometer and told them to determine the height of a particular building using their barometers. The person who used the most initiative would get the job. A couple hours later they returned and each told me how he did it.

The fourth applicant said, "I knew that you were looking for someone who knew how to handle people, not a mathematician. So I introduced myself to the building manager and said that if he told me how tall his building was, I'd give him a barometer."

He got the job.

NOTE

10. dip: to drop slightly, usually temporarily.   **spot market**: 현물시장.   **crude** = crude oil (원유).   **steep**: unreasonably high or great; exorbitant; excessive.   **stiff**: powerful; high or excessive.   **roll back**: to reduce (prices) to a previous or standard level.   **at the pump**: 석유 생산지에서.   **buck**: to resist stubbornly.   **post**: to register (기록하다).   **glut**: oversupply (초과공급).   **record** (adj.): 기록적인.   **drilling rig**: 석유채굴장비.   **pick up**: to improve.   **in the long run**: in the end; ultimately. *cf.* **in the short run**: for the moment; in the immediate present

| 한국어와 다른 수식 | **영어는 형용사를 좋아한다** |

1 **Slow tears** rose to her eyes. 〔영어식 표현〕
= Tears **slowly** rose to her eyes. 〔한국어식 표현〕

2 He doesn't speak **much English**.
= He doesn't speak English **much**.

3 The Smiths spend **an occasional night** in a cheap hotel.
= The Smiths **occasionally** spend a night in a cheap hotel.

4 Bill was **a casual visitor** to the museum while in college.
= Bill **casually** visited the museum while (he was) in college.

5 Often, while Pierre worked at some chemical experiment, she prepared **hasty meals** which they ate as they continued their task.
(=meals in haste)

6 As *Columbia* landed safely on the hard-packed dirt of the dried lake bed at California's Edwards Air Force Base, the watching world, even the cool hands at Mission Control Center in Houston, **breathed a collective sigh of relief**. (= all breathed a sigh of relief)

의미
1. 눈물이 서서히 그녀의 눈에 솟아올랐다.
2. 그는 영어로 얘기를 많이 하지 못한다.
3. 스미스 씨 부부는 가끔 하룻밤을 값싼 호텔에서 보낸다.
4. 빌은 대학에 다닐 때 띄엄띄엄 그 박물관을 찾아갔다.
5. 흔히, 삐에르가 어떤 화학 실험을 하고 있는 동안, 그녀가 서둘러 식사준비를 해서 작업을 계속하며 식사를 했다.
6. 컬럼비아 우주왕복선이 캘리포니아의 에드워즈 공군기지에 있는 마른 호수 바닥의 단단히 굳어진 땅에 안전하게 착륙하자, 지켜보던 세상 사람들은, 심지어 휴스턴에 있는 비행통제본부의 냉철한 전문가들까지도, 모두 안도의 한숨을 쉬었다.

| 한국어와 다른 수식 | **수식어와 피수식어 사이의 관계** |

필자는 언젠가 영어를 잘 아는 분이 educated guesses가 말이 되느냐고 얘기하는 것을 듣고 속으로 무척 놀란 적이 있었다. 필자가 알기로는 영어에 이런 표현이 많이 있기 때문이었다. 물론, '과학적으로' 따져보면, educated guesses는 말이 되지 않는 것 같아 보인다. 왜냐 하면, '짐작'이란 말이 '교육을 받은'이란 말의 '주체'가 될 수 없기 때문이다. 그러나 이런 경우에 educated라는 말은 based on knowledge or experience(지식이나 경험에 밑바탕을 둔)라는 뜻을 갖는다. 다음 예문을 보면서 조금 더 생각해 보기로 하자.

There was a satisfied look on his face.

앞에서처럼 따진다면, a satisfied look도 말이 되지 않는다. 왜냐하면 '표정'이 '만족을 받은' 동작의 '주체'가 될 수 없기 때문이다. 그러나 그렇게 보는 것은 피상적인 관찰이다. 왜냐하면, 주어진 문장은 다음 문장의 변형으로 볼 수 있기 때문이다.

He looked satisfied.

이렇게 바꾸어놓고 보면, 첫째 예문에서 satisfied라는 형용사의 수식을 받는 말은 He라는 것을 알 수 있다.

1. She shook **an astonished head**.
   = She shook her head in astonishment.

2. It took mankind **untold** ages to get out of its barbarous state.

3. I am on **speaking terms** with her.

4. The actual **speaking vocabulary** of most people is small.

5. He has **a reading knowledge** of English.
   = He knows enough English to read it.

6. He shook his head and raised **an emphatic finger** indicating that he would not pay more than a pound.

7 They killed **an estimated 60 villagers.**
= It is estimated that they killed 60 villagers.

8 His beat had been **a frenetic 140** when he finished the operation.

의미
1. 그녀는 놀라서, 머리를 흔들었다.
2. 인류가 야만상태에서 벗어나는 데에는 엄청나게 많은 세월이 필요했다.
3. 나는 그녀와 얘기를 주고받는 사이다.
4. 대부분의 사람들이 실제로 말할 때 사용하는 어휘수는 적다.
5. 그는 영어를 읽을 수 있을 정도로 알고 있다.
6. 그는 머리를 흔들고 힘차게 손가락을 치켜들고 1파운드 이상은 지불하지 않겠다는 뜻을 표시했다.
7. 추산에 의하면 그들은 60명의 마을사람들을 살해했다고 한다.
8. 그가 그 수술을 끝냈을 때 그의 맥박은 광적으로 높은 140이었다.

> While my car was being fixed I took the bus to the supermarket. Halfway through my shopping I realized that in my condition — $8\frac{1}{2}$ months pregnant — I wouldn't be able to carry the groceries home. When I asked the young store manager if he delivered, he looked me over and said,
> "Only groceries, madam."

EXERCISE 37

진한 글자 부분을 주목하면서 전체의 뜻을 파악하라.

1. She took a draw on her cigarette and blew **a healthy beam of smoke** toward my face.

2. He does not smoke, **drinks an occasional Scotch**, worries about his waistline and his men, to whom he is a father figure.

3. Nearby islands were reflected in the water, and on them we could see **an occasional human figure** moving about.

4. A recent opinion poll found that **a startling 69%** of the French population worry that "things were getting worse."

5. Although most workers returned to their jobs after the Gdansk accords promised free unions and other political concessions, strikes broke out **in scattered areas** last week.

6. Perhaps stymied by her spirited defense, the court went into **an unexplained recess**, leaving the debate phase to be finished later, possibly next week.

7. Americans do not use silverware for eating bread. They hold it in their fingers, usually breaking it first. A person is considered peculiar if he anchors a slice of bread firmly on his plate with his fork, butters the whole thing with his knife, and then cuts it up and eats it with his knife and fork, thus **avoiding greasy fingers**.

NOTE
5. **accord**: an agreement (합의, 협정). **concession**: 양보
6. **stymie**: to hinder or obstruct; block; impede. **go into recess**: 휴정하다. **debate phase**: 심의과정
7. **silverware** = forks and knives. **peculiar**: out of the ordinary; strange; odd; queer. **anchor**: to keep fixed

8   Despite its **studied frivolity**, the novel is concerned with a very interesting subject. It is true that one may read half the book, with much pleasure and some impatience, before this becomes clear, but on page 158 precisely, the author drops her enigmatic allusions for long enough to tell us, plainly, that she is writing about money.

9   Serious dissension within the troika, in turn, could be paralyzing to the Reagan Administration. Below the top group, talent is disquietingly thin, even though the staff is **deceptively large**. There are about 350 people on the White House staff; about 40 report to Deaver and 25 to Meese. That most of the others are in Baker's jurisdiction is no accurate guide to his influence.

10 The president's initiation of a crusade recently brought to light the plight of **uncounted** numbers of citizens who, at a time of unprecedented prosperity, are unable to keep their heads above the financial disaster level. This spring the nation is in for another shock, when the subject of military pay increases comes before Congress. The American people will then **get a good hard look at** a situation that must fill all but the thickest-skinned citizen with a sense of shame: the financial plight of the men who protect our country.

11 Congress has been a major stumbling block in the year-long fight for **higher judicial pay**. The lawmakers refuse to let judges get a pay raise unless they also give themselves one. Congress has been miserly with the judicial branch. It repeatedly has blocked presidential recommendations for increases under a law designed to make federal pay scales comparable to those in private industry.

NOTE

8. **studied**: deliberate.   **frivolous**: not properly serious.   **enigmatic**: perplexing; baffling.   **allusion**: an indirect reference; casual mention.   **plainly**: clearly; frankly

9. **dissension**: a difference of opinion; discord; disagreement or, especially, violent quarreling or wrangling   **troika**: 레이건 대통령의 세 수석보좌관인 Edwin Meese, Michael Deaver, James Baker를 가리킴.   **disquiet**: to make uneasy; disturb.   **deceptively**: misleadingly.   **jurisdiction**: the range or sphere of authority (관할 영역)

10. **initiation**: start (시작).   **crusade**: vigorous, concerted action for some cause or idea, or against some abuse.   **bring to light**: to make known to the public; reveal; disclose; unveil.   **plight**: a sad situation   **unprecedented**: unexampled; unheard-of.   **in for**: certain to have or get (usually an unpleasant experience)

11. **stumbling block**: an obstacle (장애물).   **judicial**: of judges (판사들의).   **miserly**: stingy (인색한)   **designed to (do)**: ~하는 것을 목적으로 하는

12 a. It is **a rare writer** who is his own best critic.

b. We spend our lives in motor cars, yet most of us do not know enough about a car to look in the gas tank when the motor fails. Our lives today would not move smoothly without electricity, but it is **a rare man or woman** who, when the power goes off, knows how to look for a burned-out fuse and replace it.

13 Before leaving Warsaw, the Pope **paid unannounced visits to** monuments commemorating his homeland's tragic ordeal in World War II.

Anyway

People are unreasonable, illogical and self-centered.
    Love them anyway.
If you do good, people will accuse you of selfish ulterior motives.
    Do good anyway.
If you are successful, you will win false friends and true enemies.
    Succeed anyway.
Honesty and frankness make you vulnerable.
    Be honest and frank anyway.
The good you do today will be forgotten tomorrow.
    Do good anyway.
The biggest people with the biggest ideas can be shot down by the smallest people with the smallest minds.
    Think big anyway.
People favor underdogs but follow only top dogs.
    Fight for some underdogs anyway.
What you spent years building may be destroyed overnight.
    Build anyway.
Give the world the best you have and you'll get kicked in the teeth.
    Give the world the best you've got anyway.

하이픈 – 형용사

> 한국어와 다른 수식

하이픈은 두 단어 이상을 결합해서 명사로 만들거나 명사를 연결해 주는 구실도 하지만, 하이픈의 보다 더 중요한 기능은 명사를 형용사로 만들거나 두 단어 이상을 합쳐서 형용사로 만드는 것이다.

1 명사 만들기 : give-and-take

2 명사의 연결

The modern **citizen-worker-consumer-voter** demands two things: steady employment and reasonably stable prices.

3 명사를 형용사로 전환

a. middle class [명사]
b. middle-class [형용사]

4 형용사 만들기

1) 형용사＋과거분사

    a **deep-rooted** evil 뿌리깊은 악
    a **far-sighted** politician 장기적인 안목을 가진 정치가
    an **open-minded** man 개방적인 의식을 가진 사람
    a **solar-heated** house 태양열로 난방되는 집

2) 형용사 또는 부사＋현재분사

    a **good-looking** girl 미모의 여성
    a **strange-looking** animal 이상하게 생긴 동물
    a **hard-working** student 열심히 공부하는 학생

3) 명사＋과거분사

    a **man-made** satellite 인공위성
    a **money-oriented** society 금전지향적인 사회
    a **Seoul-born** pianist 서울에서 태어난 피아니스트
    a **bone-tired** official 뼛속까지 지쳐있는 관리

4) 명사+현재분사

    a **self-effacing** man 자신을 내세우지 않는 사람
    smoke-producing fuel 연기를 내는 연료
    mouth-watering smell 군침이 나게 만드는 냄새
    bone-chilling cold 뼈를 시리게 하는 추위

5) 명사+형용사

    a **color-blind** man 색맹인 사람
    a **world-famous** artist 세계적으로 유명한 화가
    duty-free goods 관세가 면제되는 상품
    a **tone-deaf** man 음정을 구분 못하는 사람, 음치

6) 구 또는 문장 형용사

    a **live-in** housekeeper 입주 가정관리인
    a **keep-out-of-war** position 전쟁에 들어가지 않겠다는 입장
    a **forget-me-not** look 나를 잊지 말아 달라는 표정
    She wore her usual **don't-worry-everything-will-be-fine** look.
    그녀는 보통 자기가 짓는 '걱정 말아-모든 일이 잘 될 거야' 하는 표정을 띠고 있었다.

Lines of Resistance

One Sunday morning after services, my husband told our priest that he felt there was a lack of friendliness among members of the congregation and that people were reluctant to greet one another in church. Agreeing, our priest said that he had devised a plan to change things.

    During services the next Sunday, the priest described the situation to the congregation and said that the following Sunday we would have a brief pause to allow parishioners to turn to those seated behind them and greet them with a friendly hello. After the service, my husband turned around to the woman behind us and said, "Good morning." She looked at him in shocked indignation. "That doesn't start until next Sunday!" she snapped.

EXERCISE 38

진한 글자 부분을 주목하면서 전체의 뜻을 파악하라.

1. They're **short-handed** at the gate. (= short of hands)

2. She looked at herself in the tall mirror, **wonder-struck**. (= struck with wonder)

3. He is a **philosopher-turned** poet.

4. A lot of **achievement-oriented** people worry about being left behind.

5. The **Korean-born** American novelist won his recognition as a writer in his early thirties.

6. Korean hospitality is **world-famous**. (= famous the world over)

7. Some blacks, however, are taking a **wait-and-see** attitude toward the New Administration.

8. It was a **once-in-a-lifetime** chance for a student of politics like Jack Kennedy.

9. One fellow says he's going to observe Thanksgiving with a **broad-breasted** turkey and **narrow-minded** relatives.

10. Supporters see the Carter Administration's efforts to create a Rapid Deployment Force as a **better-late-than-never** remedy for the perceived decline of American military might.

NOTE   10. Rapid Deployment Force: 신속배치군.   might: power; strength

11 Ever since the early 1920's, federal budget directors have been complaining about the **"use it or lose it"** syndrome: a curious disease that causes government agencies — worried about the implications of a surplus at year-end — to go to enormous and creative lengths to make sure that every nickel of the taxpayers' money is spent.

12 She studied welding at a vocational school, but when she applied for a job with an aluminum company, she was greeted with the predictable "**Are you serious?**" look. She talked her way into a job, for which she had to commute 110 miles a day. That forced her to quit after a year, but she remembers with pride, "When I left, the company vice president said I was probably the best aluminum welder he had ever employed."

13 The **fail-safe, error-checking** computer even did its own trouble-shooting. When something went wrong, it would examine itself and flash a message that would tell the operator what was amiss and how to fix it.

*Most people live too far
within self-imposed limits.*

NOTE

11. **federal budget director**: 연방정부의 관리예산청장 (director of the Office of Management and Budget).
    go to enormous and creative lengths: 무척 그리고 창의적으로 (새로운 방법을 고안해서) 애를 쓰다. **every nickel of the taxpayers' money**: 자기들 부서에 할당받은 예산 전부
    문맥 syndrome = diesase
12. **welding**: 용접. **commute**: 통근하다. **vice president**: 부사장
13. **fail-safe**: 고장을 막는 장치를 갖추고 있는. **error-checking**: 잘못을 점검하는. **trouble-shoot**: (기계가) 고장난 곳을 찾아내어 수리하다. **fix**: to repair (수리하다)
    문맥 amiss = wrong

표현의 미학
5 EXPRESSION

1. 표현의 범위
2. 핵표현의 발견: 표현의 색채화
3. 말의 유희: Pun

표현의 범위 — 의미의 발전

말은 구체적인 것을 가리키는 데(1차단계)서부터 추상적인 것(2차단계)과 표현의 효과를 높이기 위한 수사적인 것(3차단계)으로 발전한다고 볼 수 있다. 다음 예문을 통해서 이러한 발전과정을 이해하고, 기본표현을 이용해서 2차 및 3차적인 표현을 만드는 요령을 터득하도록 노력하라.

1
 a. She's grown **out of her shoes**.
 b. She's grown **out of her silly love**.

2
 a. Her debts **amount to** over $50,000.
 b. Her words **amount to** a refusal.

3
 a. These shoes **wear out** quickly.
 b. All this talking **wears** me **out**.

4
 a. He **cut** useless branches **off** the tree. 〔1차 물리적인 단계〕
 b. He **fasted** his illness **off**. 〔2차 추상적인 단계〕
 c. She **screamed** her head **off**. 〔3차 수사적인 단계〕

의미
1. a. 그녀는 자라서 자신의 신발을 신지 못하게 되었다. 〔신체적 성장〕
   b. 그녀는 자라서(철이 들어서) 어리석은 자신의 사랑에서 벗어나게 되었다. 〔정신적 성장〕
2. a. 그녀의 빚은 합쳐서 5만 달러 이상이 된다.
   b. 그녀의 말은 거절하는 것이나 마찬가지다.
3. a. 이 신발은 빨리 닳아서 신을 수 없게 된다.
   b. 이 모든 얘기는 나를 녹초가 되게 만든다.
4. a. 그는 쓸모없는 가지들을 그 나무에서 잘라 버렸다.
   b. 그는 단식을 해서 자신의 병을 떨쳐 버렸다.
   c. 그녀는 머리가 떨어져 나가라 비명을 질렀다.

MIGRATORY BIRDS in the United States were tagged by the Department of the Interior with metal strips reading "Wash. Biol. Surv." — for Washington Biological Survey. The code was changed, so the story goes, after a farmer from Arkansas wrote to the department:
"Dear Sirs, I shot one of your crows. My wife followed the cooking instructions attached — she washed it, boiled it and served it. It was the worst thing we ever ate."

EXERCISE 39

진한 글자 부분을 주목하면서 전체의 뜻을 파악하라.

1. She **dieted off** 20 pounds.

2. He usually **sleeps off** his fatigue.

3. He'd annoy me, and I went down the stairs to my mailbox, simply to **walk off** my annoyance. I wasn't eager to see the mail.

4. The ability to **laugh** things **off** will save you many an awkward situation in social life.

5. At 38, after two decades of heavy drinking, O'Neil **swore off** liquor. Except for isolated lapses, he abstained for his remaining 29 years.

6. She was in her limousine, **talking her silly head off** with two women.

7. When boys get to the age of fifteen or sixteen, they **eat their heads off**.

8. Our guide was so anxious for us to see everything of interest that he **walked us off our feet**.

9. It would be foolish to **stand upon one's dignity** in a place where there is hardly room to **stand upon one's feet**.

NOTE   **5. lapse**: a small mistake; a failure in correct behavior, belief, duty, etc.

10 During semester break our neighbor's daughter invited her boyfriend to a home-cooked meal, an invitation he eagerly accepted. At dinner he was soon into his third large helping, while everyone watched in amazement.

After the fourth plateful he complimented the hostess on her cooking. Then, noticing the dessert fork next to his plate, he asked, "What's this fork for?"

Without hesitation his girlfriend answered, "That's in case the first one **wears out.**"

A woman wearily laid her purse on the counter in the jewelry department
where I was working. I asked if I could help her.
"No, dear," she said.
"I only want to look around to get my mind off the exasperating hour
I just spent with my psychiatrist. He is so stubborn
that I suppose I'll never get him around to my way of thinking!"

NOTE 10. break: a pause for rest. compliment: to praise. in case: for fear that
         plateful = large helping

표현의 색채화

어떤 하나의 표현에서 가장 기본이 되는 단위를 필자는 '핵표현'(Nuclear Expression)이라고 부른다. 모든 표현은 그것의 핵표현에서 파생된 것이라 볼 수 있으므로, 핵표현에 대한 이해는 영어의 기본구조의 파악과 직결된다.

1 **get to one's feet** = **stand up** 일어서다 [핵표현]

    a. **leap** to one's feet 펄쩍 뛰어 일어서다
    b. **spring** to one's feet 용수철이 튀기듯이 빨딱 일어서다
    c. **run** to one's feet 달리듯이 벌떡 일어서다
    d. **shoot** to one's feet 총알같이 일어서다
    e. **stagger** to one's feet 비틀거리며 일어서다
    f. **stumble** to one's feet 넘어질 듯하며 일어서다
    g. **struggle** to one's feet 애를 써서 일어서다

2 **put～to death** : ～을 죽이다

    a. **beat**～to death 때려서 죽이다
    b. **burn**～to death 태워서 죽이다
    c. **club**～to death 곤봉으로 치거나 때려서 죽이다
    d. **freeze**～to death 얼려서 죽이다
    e. **starve**～to death 굶겨서 죽이다
    f. **stone**～to death 돌로 쳐서 죽이다
    g. **shoot**～to death 총으로 쏴서 죽이다

3 **make one's way～** : **go～** 가다

    a. He **felt his way toward** the door in the dark.
    b. She **pushed her way through** the crowd.
    c. He **elbowed his way through** the crowd.
    d. They **shot their way through** the crowd.
    e. The Han River **winds its way into** the Yellow Sea.
    f. They **wormed their way up** the rock.
    g. He **worked his way through** college.

> h. He **earned part of his way through** college by selling books.
> i. He could **eat his way to** better health.
> j. He tried to **explain his way out of** the difficult situation.
> k. Americans admire the self-made man — the man who, with neither money nor family influence, **fights his way to** the top.

의미 3. a. 그는 어둠 속에서 더듬으며 문 쪽으로 갔다.
  b. 그녀는 밀면서 군중 속을 뚫고 갔다.
  c. 그는 팔꿈치로 밀며 군중 속을 뚫고 갔다.
  d. 그들은 총을 쏘며 군중 속을 뚫고 갔다.
  e. 한강은 구불구불 흘러서 황해로 들어간다.
  f. 그들은 벌레처럼 기어서 그 바위 위로 올라갔다.
  g. 그는 일을 해서 학비를 벌어 대학을 나왔다.
  h. 그는 책을 팔아서 학비의 일부를 벌어 대학을 나왔다.
  i. 그는 식사로 건강이 더 좋아질 수 있었다.
  j. 그는 해명을 해서 그 어려운 입장에서 빠져 나오려고 했다.
  k. 미국인들은 자수성가한 사람을 찬양한다 — 다시 말해서, 돈도 가족의 영향력도 없이 노력해서 정상에 오르는 사람을 말이다.

The husband confided to his wife.
"My boss suddenly lost his temper today and told me to go to hell."
"Then what did you do?" asked the wife.
"I came home immediately," the husband meekly replied.

EXERCISE 40

주어진 문장과 의미가 같도록 빈칸에 적당한 단어를 써넣어라.

1. a. She expressed her thanks with a smile.
      = She _____ her thanks.

   b. He approved with a nod.
      = He _____ his approval.

진한 글자 부분을 주목하면서 전체의 뜻을 파악하라.

2. a. I **played away** a month on account of illness.

   b. They used to **sing away** their weariness at the day's end.

   c. He once **drank and talked away** an entire night with Ernest Hemingway.

   d. There is no pleasanter way of **idling away** an hour or two than by reading an interesting story.

   e. For the third time in four months my husband has **gambled away** his entire two weeks' paycheck. I don't want to leave him. We have three swell kids. Tell me what to do before I go crazy.

3. a. No one **expects an early end to** the controversy.

   b. Most economists **see no quick end to** the inflationary pressures.

   c. The exasperated chairman **gaveled** the meeting **to a temporary close**.

   d. Khomeini has avoided comments on the hostage issue since February, when he turned the matter over to Parliament. He may have decided to intervene again in an effort to eliminate a divisive and paralyzing issue between Iran's secular moderates, who **favor a quick end to** the crisis, and the religious hard-liners.

NOTE

2b. weariness: fatigue (피로)
2e. swell [slang]: first-rate; excellent
3c. exasperate: to annoy very much; make angry; vex.   **bring~to a close**: ~을 정지시키다
3d. hostage: 인질.   **turn~over**: ~을 넘겨주다.   **secular moderate**: 비교도(회교신도가 아닌) 온건파 사람.   **religious hard-liner**: 종교를 믿는 (회교도) 강경파 사람

e. At precisely 11 a.m. one day last week, air raid sirens across Israel sounded a single, high-pitched "all clear" blast for two minutes, and the country came to a standstill. On Jaffa Road in the heart of Jerusalem, pedestrians froze in their tracks. Lounging border troops **sprang to attention**. Vehicles braked to a halt in the middle of intersections. Bus passengers **rose to their feet** — as did people all across the nation. In stores, restaurants and offices, conversations stopped, forks were put down, typewriters and business machines hushed. It was Israel's Memorial Day. In the silent vigil, Israelis remembered the dead of the five wars they have fought since the creation of the state in 1948.

Then, at sunset, the next day's observance began, this one in joy rather than sorrow. The day of mourning was followed by the festive Independence Day, this year marking the 33rd year of Israel's existence as a state. Jerusalem's King George Street was closed to traffic as young people linked arms to dance the hora and began the celebration. Some of the merriment lasted through the night with springtime abandon.

4
a. I wish they'd invent a washing machine that always **turned out** an even number of socks.

b. India has one of the largest film industries in the world. Its producers **crank out** more than 400 feature films each year. Demand is so insatiable that the industry is run on a shift basis and there is never a day when it is completely shut down. Movie theaters open as early as 9 a.m.

c. The rush to use the chips has propelled the nation's automakers into headlong competition to come up with new applications. When Toyota last year introduced the world's first chip-operated voice synthesizer to warn drivers of low fuel and fluid levels in their cars, Nissan Motor **hustled out** its competing versions within weeks.

> **NOTE**
>
> **3e. come to a standstill**: 정지하다.　**pedestrian**: walker (보행인).　**spring to attention**: 재깍 차렷자세를 취하다 < come to attention: 차렷자세를 취하다.　**brake to a halt**: 브레이크를 잡아서 정지하다 < come to a halt: 정지하다　**rise to one's feet**: to rise; stand up < get to one's feet.　**the five wars**: the 1948-49 war following independence, the 1956 Suez War, the Six-Day War of 1967, the 1969-70 War of Attrition, and the 1973 October War.　**abandon**: unrestrained freedom of actions or emotions; freedom from control
>
> **4a. turn out**: 내놓다.　**even number**: 짝수. *cf.* odd number (홀수)
>
> **4b. crank out** < turn out: to produce.　**insatiable**: that cannot be satisfied (충족시킬 수 없는) < satiate: to satisfy to the full.　**shift**: 교대 근무반 또는 교대근무시간 → I work on the night shift at the factory.　**shut down**: to cease operating (가동을 중지하다).
>
> **4c. headlong**: uncontrollable (걷잡을 수 없는).　**come up with**: to produce.　**hustle out** = to turn out hurriedly (서둘러서 만들어내다).　**versions** = cars

d. Young Cheever maintained family traditions by attending Thayer Academy, but then managed at age 17 to get himself kicked out for smoking and laziness. Within a year, his short story *Expelled* appeared in *The New Republic.* He spent some time in Boston with his older brother Fred, then took a cheap room in Manhattan and **pounded out** short stories to pay the rent. At 22, he sold a piece to *The New Yorker*, and he and the magazine grew up together.

e. *A comedian on Warsaw radio told the story of a teacher trying to explain that glass is made from sand. The children burst into laughter at the very thought — glass from sand! Asked why he was giggling, one boy replied: "Oh, we know they make you tell us those things."*

Polish authorities have made teachers tell students many things — and now Poles want to set matters straight. After months of negotiations, the independent teachers' union persuaded officials to make major changes in history texts — including material dealing with the Soviets. From now on, teachers say, "the subject matter must be based on truth."

Work has already begun. Some textbooks are being revised under the guidance of a "didactic committee," headed by Marian Marek Drozdowski, one of the country's most respected historians. Authors are also **cranking out** new works, and publishers plan to market a bigger, more modern set of schoolbooks. In particular, the changes will do away with some of the interpretive excesses of the existing curriculum. Instead, children will be given the facts — and encouraged to arrive at their own conclusions. "The truth is difficult for everybody," says one expert. "But it is the only way of educating our children."

5 The venerable Oxford English Dictionary certifies 414,825 words of the Queen's English. The 13-volume work trickled out between 1884 and 1928, and in 1957 Robert Burchfield was offered the chance to edit the first updated supplement. So far, his labor has yielded only two volumes; the third is in the works and he hopes the fourth and final will be on sale by

---

NOTE

4d. kick out = to expel. **pound out** = to turn out by pounding on a typewriter (타자기를 쳐서 만들어내다)

4e. giggle: 낄낄 웃다. **set straight**: to put right; correct (바로잡다). **subject matter**: the thing or things considered in a book, course of instruction, discussion, etc. (교과내용). **do away with**: to get rid of; eliminate; remove (제거하다)

5. venerable: worthy of respect; impressive. **trickle out**: 찔끔찔끔 또는 드문드문 나오다. < come out. **so far**: thus far; till now. **yield**: to produce. **in the works**: in the process of being planned or done. **bloody** [British slang]: cursed; damned

1985. He is already looking forward to completing his "bloody war with words" and to his retirement.

What is Burchfield's favorite of the 414,825 words? "*Finished*," he declares with a smile. "As in 'I've *finished* the dictionary.'"

6 Right now there are almost 2 million personal and home computers in the U.S., and manufacturers will ship nearly 2 million more this year. One company alone, Timex, is **turning out** copies of its $99.95 computer at the rate of one machine every ten seconds. As a rule of thumb, Columnist Art Buchwald has suggested, "For every home computer sold in America, there is a computer widow somewhere."

"Sports widow, computer widow, you name it, that's me," says Actress Elaine Grant, 25. Three months ago, her husband brought home a $250 Commodore VIC 20. "I have to laugh sometimes," she says. "When friends come, Jerry immediately drags them over to show them the computer. Some may actually understand what's going on, but most just stand there and smile and can't wait to get away." Jerry, 42, a violinist with the Boston Symphony Orchestra, and his son David, 9, now while away the hours playing games, composing music and deciphering complex programs. "Jerry has begged me to show some interest," Elaine confesses, "but I can't. It's ugly. It makes obnoxious noises. It has about 80 zillion things stuck to the back of the TV. Hair dryers self-destruct in my hands, so why should I touch the computer?"

Many women, rather than join the computer revolution, have **hammered out** peace pacts with their mates. In Palo Alto, Calif., a woman who spent five years with an Atari programmer finally imposed a 15-minute limit on uninterrupted talk about his work. In Atlanta the wife of a former camera bug who switched to home computers uses travel to protect their relationship. Says she: "I insist that we go to our place at the lake every weekend to get him away from the computer."

NOTE 6. **ship**: to send out. **as a rule of thumb**: 주먹구구로. **you name it**: 이름을 대어보라. **can't wait to get away** = are impatient to get away (어서 그 자리를 떠나고 싶어한다). **while away**: to spend (time) in a pleasant or idle way. **decipher**: to make out the meaning of (해독하다). **obnoxious**: very unpleasant; offensive. **zillion**: a very large, indefinite number (엄청난 숫자). **self-destruct**: to be automatically destroyed. **hammer out**: to work out by careful thought or repeated effort (해머로 치듯이 주의하거나 반복적인 노력에 의해 만들어내다). **peace pact**: 평화협정. **mate**: spouse (배우자). **imposed a 15-minute limit on uninterrupted talk about his work**: 그가 (집에서) 자신의 업무에 관해서 마음대로 (방해받지 않고) 얘기할 수 있는 시간을 15분으로 제한했다. **bug** [slang]: an enthusiast or devotee. → He's a shutterbug. (그는 사진광이다.)

7

a. Correspondent Barry Kalb happened to be reading about terrorism in Italy when word reached him at the TIME Rome bureau that Pope John Paul II had been shot in St. Peter's Square. He **pieced together** the grim sequence of events and then rushed to Gemelli Hospital to pursue reports on the Pope'condition.

b. The new Prime Minister decided early on to retain many of his predecessor's domestic programs, such as literacy lessons and unemployment relief, and, as a consequence, found himself committed to programs that will cost at least $2.5 billion over the next three years. To foot the bill and to **whittle down** Jamaica's balance of payments deficit ($700 million last year), the Prime Minister, a Harvard-educated sociologist before he turned to politics, **put together** a complicated financial package.

c. And the people's affection for Washington shows in more indirect circumstances still — in those quiet, unguarded moments when visitors and residents as well set aside words like access and power and amble among the monuments as subconscious patriots. Children are more demonstrative. They shout up at Lincoln's capacious ears, or take the Capitol three steps at a clip, acting as if they owned the place.

   They cannot take the Capitol these days. Piles of wood lie on the steps, where workmen are **hammering together** the viewing stands for the Inauguration.

d. The man who **pulled together** the agreement on the P.L.O.'s evacuation of Lebanon, a triumph of delicate diplomacy, worked so secretly and with such an abhorrence of publicity that many of his top colleagues in the Middle East literally did not know how he was faring.

NOTE

7a. piece together: 조각을 붙여서 조립하다 < put together: 조립하다.   **grim**: frightful; ghastly; horrible (무서운)

7b. early on: 초기에. *cf.* later on (나중에).   **literacy lessons**: 문맹자를 위한 읽기와 쓰기 교육.   **commit**: to bind as by a promise (약속 따위로 묶다).   **foot**: to pay.   **whittle down**: to cut down gradually, as if by whittling away with a knife (마치 칼로 깎아버리듯이 점차 깎아내리다, 줄이다).   **balance of payments deficit**: 수지적자

7c. unguarded: 자신에 대해서 경계하지 않는, 허심탄회한.   **A and B as well** = both A and B.   **set aside**: 옆으로 제쳐놓다.   **access**: 문자 그대로는 '접근'을 의미하는데, 여기서는 '그가 빽이 든든한 사람이다'에서 '빽'과 같은 뜻을 갖고 있다.   **amble**: to walk in a leisurely manner.   **capacious**: spacious (넓직한).   **clip**: a rapid pace (빠른 걸음)   **hammer together**: 해머로 쳐서 조립하다.   **the Inauguration**: 대통령 취임식

7d. pull together: to put together by pulling.   **agreement**: 협정.   **evacuation**: withdrawal (철수)   **abhorrence**: loathing; detestation; aversion (싫어함).   **publicity**: 대중에게 알려지는 것.   **fare**: to get on (잘척 해 나가다).   **shuttle back and forth**: 왕래하다.   **itinerary**: 여행일정.   **arduous**: laborious; onerous; strenuous (힘드는).   **let alone**: not to mention (~는 더 말할 나위도 없고).   **bypass surgery**: a surgical operation to provide passage for a fluid, as blood, around a diseased or blocked part or organ   **medication**: a medicine

For more than eleven weeks, Philip Charles Habib shuttled back and forth across the Middle East, following an itinerary that would have been arduous for a young man, let alone a 62-year-old official who has suffered four heart attacks and undergone bypass surgery. Habib carried all his medical records with him, as well as his medications. He likes to rest for a while in the afternoon, but there was little time for that during the talks.

8
a. The principal industrial economies see little prospect of **exporting their way out of** the current downturn as long as the United States is also in trouble.

b. No longer can the poor count on **working their way steadily toward** a better life. And no longer do Americans share the great expectations of generations past. For the first time, public-opinion polls show that the average U.S. citizen is not at all sure that his children's lot will be better than — or even as good as — his own.

c. Ever notice how the nose has **poked its way into** our language? If you're angry, your nose is out of joint; if you're inquisitive, you're nosy; if you nose out an opponent, you're a winner; if you keep your nose to the grindstone, you're a hard worker; if you can be led by the nose, you're submissive; if your nose is in the air, you're snobbish.

d. One of Kennedy's first acts in the White House was to order 200 books on the presidency put on his shelves for easy access. "Roosevelt got most of his ideas from talking to people," Kennedy told Historian James MacGregor Burns. "I get most of mine from reading."

Of Kennedy's ten favorite books, eight was history and biography. He devoured the 407-page *Sir Robert Walpole: The Making of a Statesman* in one evening. Eyeing China, J.F.K. called for two of Mao's books. Seeking

---

NOTE

8a. **industrial economy**: 산업경제국가.   **downturn**: 경기하향추세
　　　문맥 trouble = downturn

8b. **the poor** = poor people.   **public-opinion poll**: 여론조사
　　　문맥 count on = expect.   lot = life

8c. **poke**: to push or jab.   **inquisitive**: curious; prying.   **snobbish**: 거만한

8d. **access**: approach; a way or means of approaching, getting, using, etc.   **devour**: to consume; take in greedily.   **eye**: to watch carefully.   **call for**: to demand.   **account**: an explanation; description   **point**: an impressive or telling argument; a helpful hint or suggestion.   **accord**: an agreement (협정)   **rest on**: to be based on.   **convulsive**: violently disturbing (세상을 뒤흔드는).   **will do well to (do)**: ~하는 것이 좋을 것이다.   **fraught**: filled, charged, or loaded (with)

insights into world trouble spots, he dug into Che Guevara's accounts of guerrilla war.

All of this makes a forceful point in these days because both Jimmy Carter and Ronald Reagan seemed to view the world as having been created at the same time they were born. Carter's repeated failures to understand the Soviets and be prepared for their actions can be blamed at least in part on his ignorance of the history of U.S.-Soviet relations. His big success, the Camp David accords, surely rested on his determined study of the history of the Middle East conflict. Reagan's convulsive acts both domestically and internationally come too often from nothing more than prejudice inspired by ideology. Reagan and his advisers would do well to consider how the young Kennedy **read and thought his way safely through** a time fraught with peril.

e. When forester Robert Perschel walks through the Connecticut woods these days, the leaves look as if marksmen had used them for target practice. And as woodpeckers **tap out** their staccato counterpoint, Perschel hears the ominous sound of less benign critters. "It's eerie to actually hear insects devouring the forest," he says.

The gypsy moth has returned to the Northeast. For the second year in a row, billions of caterpillars are draping oaks in fuzzy brown tinsel and turning the spring finery of birch and hawthorn into winterscapes of bare branches. In 1980 the insects **munched their devastating way through** 5.1 million acres in a dozen states from Maine to Maryland. Many states had record damage — the 2.5 million acres defoliated in New York was five times the previous high — and this year seems to be even worse. Entomologists in Massachusetts have counted enough egg masses (caterpillars-in-waiting) to defoliate some areas ten times over. Weakened by last year's plague and by the continuing drought, many

---

NOTE 8e. **woodpecker**: 딱따구리. **tap out**: '딱딱' 두들겨(찍어) 내다. **counterpoint**: 대위법식 멜로디. **benign**: favorable; beneficial. **critter (dialect)**: creature. **less benign critters**: 딱다구리보다 덜 이로운 동물들(즉, 산림에 해를 끼치는 동물들). **eerie**: uneasy; frightening. **for the second year in a row** = for two consecutive years (2년 동안 계속해서). **caterpillar**: 애벌레. **drape**: to cover. **fuzzy**: 솜털 같은. **tinsel**: thin sheets **turn the spring finery of birch and hawthorn into winterscapes of bare branches**: 장식해 놓은 것처럼 아름다운 자작나무와 산사나무의 파아란 모습을 앙상한 가지만 남아있는 겨울철의 모습으로 바꾸어 놓다. **munch**: to chew steadily, often with a crunching sound (이것은 씹을 때 나는 소리를 흉내낸 의성어임). **record**: 기록인 **entomologist**: 곤충학자. **defoliate**: to strip (trees, etc.) of leaves. **crossbreed**: 이종교배시키다, 잡종을 만들다. **hitchhike on**: to get a ride on; ride on. **bust**: a financial collapse; economic crash (경기몰락) **stem**: to stop or check. **predator**: 다른 동물을 잡아먹는 동물 ≠ **prey** (다른 동물에게 잡아먹히는 동물). **bounce back from**: to recover from. **infestation** = plague; trouble. **reduce their maples' greenery to paupers' rags**: 자기들의 푸른 단풍나무 잎을 가난뱅이의 누더기옷처럼 만들어 놓다.

trees will die because they aren't strong enough to replace leaves eaten by the caterpillars. "All of New England will have serious problems," warns Charles Schwalbe of the Department of Agriculture's gypsy-moth laboratory on Cape Cod. "In some states, the damage will be unprecedented."

Man does not get much help from nature in fighting the gypsy moth because the insect, a European immigrant, has few effective natural enemies in the United States. The plague was born when a French naturalist in Massachusetts tried to crossbreed silkworms and gypsy moths and lost about a dozen of the creatures to a gust of wind in 1869. The moth hitchhiked on breezes and people to reach Connecticut in 1905, New York in 1922, Pennsylvania in 1934 and Michigan in 1954. Researchers have tried controlling it with imported parasites like wasps and flies — so far without notable success — but they habitually return to pesticides.

The gypsy moth rides a boom-and-bust cycle as unsettled as the stock market. "If we leave it alone the population will crash," says Charles Hood, chief of the bureau of insect-pest control in Massachusetts. "It has always happened before." When it will happen is another question, but ultimately nature always stems her own plagues by balancing predators and prey. Scientists feel certain that most forests can bounce back from even the worst infestations. That, of course, is little comfort to gardeners watching the insects reduce their maples' greenery to paupers' rags.

9

After the war MacArthur returned to West Point as one of its most innovative superintendents. At the age of 42 he married; seven years later he was divorced. He did a tour of duty in the Philippines, and then, in 1930 he became Army Chief of Staff in Washington. It was a post his father had sought but never received. Two years later, MacArthur ordered the forcible eviction of hungry veterans, the "bonus marchers," from their Washington encampment, a totally unnecessary action that only left anger and bitterness. He also began to speak of himself with such third-person grandiloquence as, "MacArthur has decided to go into

---

NOTE

9. **innovative**: 혁신적인. **superintendent** = principal (교장). **do a tour of duty in**: ~에 가서 복무하다
forcible: done or effected by force (강제적인). **eviction**: ejection (추방). **encampment**: a camp
bitterness: strong feelings of hatred, resentment, cynicism, etc. **third-person** (형용사): 3인칭의
grandiloquence: 거창하게 말하는 것. **incipient**: just beginning to exist; inchoate (초기 단계의). **in the air**: current or prevalent (진행되거나 널리 퍼져있는). **brain-truster**: 행정고문 노릇을 하는 전문가. **take on**: to accept; undertake. **whip into shape**: to put into the proper or desired condition by vigorous action (채찍질을 하듯이 힘찬 노력으로 형성하거나 바람직한 상태로 가져오다). **dead end**: 막다른 골목

active command in the field. There is incipient revolution in the air."

In fact, the only revolution turned out to be the New Deal, and Roosevelt's brain-trusters regarded MacArthur with as much suspicion as he did them. After leaving the office of Chief of Staff in 1935, he retired from the U.S. Army and took on the job of **whipping into shape** the largely nonexistent army in the Philippines, which were being prepared for independence from the U.S. So far as anyone, including himself, could see, the job was a dead end.

10 Another approach will be to scrap certain government regulations. Today, for example, firms that produce new drugs or pesticides often must **struggle** for as long as 13 years **through** a regulatory labyrinth before getting a product on the market.

11 It's a Swiss joke that the nation's warplanes need good brakes — because a Mach 2 jetfighter can **scorch across** Switzerland in 4.73 minutes flat. One of our planet's tiniest countries, it is smaller than West Virginia; but Europe's oldest republic wields power and influence far beyond its size. Strictly a have-naught nation in natural resources — no oil, no coal, no gold, no uranium — Switzerland nevertheless became the richest nation on earth in 1978: its per-capita income **streaked to** a matchless $13,853 a year, **elbowing** oil-gorged Kuwait **to** second place ($13,000) and the United States **to** a humble eighth ($9,646)

12 While recuperating from surgery, my neighbor became cantankerous and refused to follow the doctor's orders to take a ten-minute walk three times a day. His wife coaxed and cajoled, then nagged. Nothing moved him.

In desperation, she **lit upon** a solution. Three times a day she turned on every light in the house. Her husband cringed at the waste, and it took him ten minutes three times a day to walk around and turn the lights off.

NOTE

10. **scrap**: to get rid of or abandon as useless; discard. **regulation**: 규제. **firm**: a business company (기업체) **pesticide**: any chemical used for killing insects, weeds, etc. (살충제, 제초제). **a regulatory labyrinth**: 미로처럼 복잡한 여러 가지 규제(= a labyrinth of regulations). **get a product on the market**: 생산품을 시장에 내놓다

11. **scorch across**: 쏜살같이 지나가다. **wield**: to exercise (행사하다). **naught**: nothing. **streak**: to move at high speed; go fast. **matchless**: peerless (맞먹을 상대가 없는)

12. **recuperate**: to recover (회복하다); get well again. **cantankerous**: bad-tempered (성질이 나쁜); quarrelsome; perverse (완고하게 말을 잘 안 듣는). **coax**: 달래다, 감언으로 꾀다. **cajole**: to coax with flattery and insincere talk (아첨과 허무맹랑한 말로 꾀다). **nag**: 잔소리하다, 바가지를 긁어 괴롭히다. **light upon a solution**: 번쩍 해결책이 떠오르다 < come upon, hit upon (~가 떠오르다). **cringe**: to cower (벌벌 떨다). **waste**: 낭비

말의 유희 — Pun

일반적으로 영-미인들은 우리나라 사람들보다 말에 대한 관심이 더 많다. 그래서 영어에는 pun이 매우 발달되어 있는데, 이것은 같은 단어나 또는 발음이 같거나 비슷한 단어가 두 가지 이상의 의미를 갖도록 해학적으로 사용하는 것을 말한다.

1 For years, I was proud when my boss called me his **right-hand man.** Then it occurred to me — he's left-handed.

2 Did you hear about the snake charmer who married the undertaker? They have towels marked "**Hiss**" and "**Hearse**."

3 Said the Northern girl: "Men are all **alike**."
Agreed the Southern girl: "Men are all **Ah like**, too."

4 One day, after my kindergarten class sang "The Old Gray **Mare**," I asked, "What is an old gray mare?" One little boy piped up, "He's the guy that runs the city."

유희
1. 일반적으로 one's right-hand man이라고 하면 자신의 오른팔처럼 '자기에게 매우 도움이 되거나 믿을 만한 사람'(one's most helpful or reliable man)을 의미하는데, 여기서는 듣는 이의 그런 기대를 무너뜨림으로써 해학이 발생한다.
2. Hiss는 뱀이 내는 소리를 흉내낸 말로(the snake charmer와 관련되며) His를 생각나게 하고, Hearse는 영구차를 의미하는데 (이것은 the undertaker와 연결되며), Hers를 생각나게 함으로써 주어진 말이 웃음을 자아내게 해준다.
3. **Ah** like = **I** like
4. the guy that runs the city = **mayor**

Puns are Fun!

Wilton Lackaye was on the program for a speech at a gathering in Chicago.
It was late in the evening, and everyone had been bored by the other speakers.
When the toastmaster announced,
"Wilton Lackaye, the famous actor, will now give you his address,"
Lackaye arose and said,
"Toastmaster and gentlemen, my address is the Lambs Club, New York."
He sat down to tremendous applause.

EXERCISE 41

진한 글자 부분을 주목하면서 전체의 뜻을 파악하라.

1. "I understand the bank is **looking for** a cashier."
   "I thought they hired one a month ago."
   "He's the one they're **looking for**."

2. A husband and wife sat in front of their fireplace. She asked, "Can you see **figures** in the fire?"
   "Yes, dear," replied her spouse.
   "What kinds of **figures**?" the wife persisted.
   "Forty dollars a cord for the wood," he sighed.

3. The congressman's wife shook him vigorously in the middle of the night. "Wake up, Adam!" she whispered frantically. "There's a thief in **the house**!"
   "No way," came the sleepy reply. "In the Senate, maybe. In **the House** — never."

4. Three men were driving to London in a noisy old car, and hearing was difficult. As they neared the city one asked, "Is this **Wembley**?"
   "No. It's **Thursday**."
   "Me, too. Let's stop and have a drink."

5. If my husband has to leave his music shop unattended during business hours, he puts a note on the door. I visited the shop one day to find two waiting customers chuckling about the message: "**Bach** in five **minutes**."

NOTE

2. **cord**: 목재를 재는 단위로 128입방피트(길이 8 feet×높이 4 feet×넓이 4 feet).
3. **vigorously**: forcefully (힘차게); energetically.　**whisper frantically**: 미친 듯이 속삭이다 (이것은 '소리없는 아우성'과 같은 역설적인 표현인데, 현대인의 미적 감각은 이런 것에 아름다움을 느낄 수 있도록 훈련이 되어 있습니다).　**no way** [slang]: no.
   House (the House of Representatives): 하원
4. **near**: to come or draw near to; approach

6   It was a typical family evening — Father sat in his favorite chair reading the paper; the baby sat at his feet playing with a toy; Mother sat in her favorite chair knitting. Father happened to glance down at the baby. "Baby's **nose is running**." he said.

   Mother dropped the knitting on her lap in disgust. "Don't you ever think of anything but horse racing?"

7   A friend who had worn glasses since she was a child decided to buy a pair of contact lenses. She hoped they would put an end to her "wallflower" days.

   The next week, we went to a local dance, where her new appearance made her much in demand. On the way home, she said excitedly, "Now I know why they call them **contact lenses**."

8   Little Johnny's father found him holding his pet rabbit demanding, "Five plus five, how much is that?"

   "What are you doing?" Johnny's perplexed father asked.

   "My teacher says that rabbits **multiply** quickly," Johnny replied indignantly, "but this dumb bunny can't even add."

9   A mayoral candidate, standing in front of a San Diego office building at eight o'clock one morning during the last election, stuck out his hand as a pretty girl dashed toward the entrance. "Hi," he said. "I'm Lee Hubbard. I'm **running for** mayor."

   She smiled but didn't slow down. "Hi," she said. "I'm Tania Smith and I'm **running for** work."

10 The hospital emergency room where I worked received word that a child named Billy Cash was en route with his mother. A new orderly was asked to watch for their arrival.

   The orderly stood his post at the entrance like a soldier. When the door

---

NOTE

6. **one's nose is running**: ~의 콧물이 흘러나오고 있다.   **in disgust**: 넌더리가 나서
7. **wallflower** [colloq.]: a person, especially a girl, who merely looks on at a dance, etc. as from shyness or from lack of a partner (수줍음 때문이나 파트너가 없기 때문에 무도회 따위에서 구경만 하는 사람, 특히 여자)
9. **stick out**: ~을 내밀다.   **run for mayor**: 시장이 되기 위해 출마하다
10. **emergency room**: 응급실.   **word** = a message.   **en route** = on the way (to the hospital)
   orderly: a male hospital attendant, usually without special professional training.   **lurch forward**: 쏜살같이 앞으로 나가다.   **somewhat**: a little; rather (다소)   **taken aback**: startled and confused (놀라고 어리둥절한); surprised.   **do**: to be enough (되다, 충분하다)

finally swung open, revealing a small boy and a woman, the orderly lurched forward, shouting, "Is this **Cash**?"

Although somewhat taken aback, the woman managed to answer calmly, "Well, I have insurance. Will that do?"

11 Following a lot of dull, long-winded speakers at a sports dinner, a well-known athlete, noticing some guests who had dozed off, started his speech: "Friends and **nodding** acquaintances."

12 Last year, as a young cellist, I was working hard at the Bowdoin College Summer Music Festival. In her letters, my mother occasionally included clippings on subjects that interested me. One such enclosure was an inspiring article on Yo Yo Ma, a 23-year-old Indonesian-American cellist. In the top margin my mother had written: "Enjoy this article on Yo Yo Ma...Love from **Yo Ma Ma**!"

13 The Military Affiliate Radio System is commonly called MARS by the civilian and military radio operators who belong to it. Part of their job is to make telephone "patches" via radio to enable overseas servicemen to talk with their families and friends at home. Recently, one of the members called a woman and identified himself by saying. "Hello, this is the **MARS** radio station calling." There was a moment of silence; then her excited voice came back: "Hello, Mars. Hello, Mars. This is Earth."

14 A horse breeder showed us one of his prize mares and then pointed to her filly. "This little beauty was born on the first day of the fourth month," he said. "We named her **April Foal**."

15 Overheard next to the very-tightly-fitting-designer-blue-jeans counter of a department store: "Is it all right if I try this one on for **thighs**?"

NOTE

11. **long-winded**: speaking or writing at great, often tiresome length (장황하게 얘기하는). **doze off** (= drop off, nod off): to fall asleep unintentionally (졸다). **nodding acquaintance** (본래의 의미): 만나면 목례로 인사할 정도로 아는 사람
13. "**patches**": '통신' cf. dispatch: a message. **identify oneself**: 자신의 신분(신원)을 밝히다. **Mars**: 화성
14. **breeder**: 사육가. **prize**: worthy of a prize; first-rate. **mare**: a fully mature female horse, specifically, a female horse that has reached the age of five. **filly**: a young female horse, specifically one under five years of age. **foal**: a young horse
15. **try~on for size**: ~을 크기가 맞는지 입어보다

16 A man was talking to his neighbor. "Guess what! I got a nice new Cadillac for my wife."

The other man patted his friend on the shoulder. "Say," he said, "sounds like you made a pretty good trade."

17 For many years I was a university theater director. My wife was once asked by one of her clients about her plans for the upcoming weekend. "I think I'm going to watch my **husband's play**," she replied. "Oh," the client said. "How many do you have?"

18 A sailor had been shipwrecked on a small island for several months with a crew of 12 men and one woman. When he was finally rescued and returned home, an elderly aunt was very interested in the situation of so many men and one woman alone on a deserted island. "About this woman," said the aunt, "was she **chaste**?"

Replied the sailor, "Oh, yes, Auntie — all over the island!"

Father: Do you know what happens to liars when they die?
Son: They lie still.

NOTE
16. **say**: 놀라움, 감탄 따위를 나타내는 감탄사
18. **chaste**: 정숙한. *cf.* chased

APPENDIX 1

모범 시험 문제

1. 주제의 파악
2. 논리적인 관계의 파악

01　주제의 파악

주제 파악과 관련된 문제에는 주제(the main idea)를 묻는 것, 제목(the title)을 고르는 것, 글의 목적(purpose)을 묻는 것, 글의 논조(tone)를 묻는 것 등이 있다. 다음 문제들은 모두 **TOEFL** 기출 문제들이다.

지문을 읽은 다음 문제에 알맞은 답을 고르시오(해답은 p.260에 있음).

문제 1

Because a large proportion of the land in Hawaii is rugged and mountainous, the state has little space in which to grow crops. Some areas are also covered with hard, black lava on which nothing can grow. Even so, Hawaii produces large quantities of farm products. The volcanic soil in the valleys and lowlands is very fertile, and the warm climate makes it possible to grow crops all year long. Rainfall is plentiful on the northern and eastern sides of each island. Much of the land of the southern and western sides of each island receives too little rainfall for most crops to grow well, but in many of the places where rainfall is light, wells and mountain streams supply water for irrigation.

The main purpose of the passage is to describe the Hawaiian _____.

(A) geography　　　　　　　(B) market system
(C) farming conditions　　　(D) settlement patterns

요령　반복되어 나오는 key words에 밑줄을 치면서 빠른 속도로 읽어나가라.

설명　이 구절에서 밑줄쳐진 말들이 바로 key words다. 이것으로 보아 A, B, D는 정답이 될 수 없다는 것을 금방 알 수 있다.

해석　하와이에 있는 땅의 대부분은 울퉁불퉁하고 산이 많기 때문에, 농작물을 재배할 수 있는 공간이 거의 없다. 어떤 지역은 또한 단단하고 검은 용암으로 덮여 있어서 아무것도 자랄 수가 없다. 그럼에도 불구하고, 하와이는 많은 양의 농산품을 생산한다. 계곡과 저지대의 화산 토양은 매우 비옥하고, 그리고 기후가 따뜻해서 일년 내내 농작물을 재배할 수 있다. 각 섬의 북쪽과 동쪽 지역에는 강우량이 풍부하다. 각 섬의 남쪽과 서쪽 가운데 많은 지역에는 강우량이 너무 적어서 대부분의 농작물이 자랄 수 없지만, 강우량이 적은 지방 중 여러 곳에는 우물과 산개울이 관개용 물을 공급해 준다.

표현　**rugged**: rough (험한); uneven (울퉁불퉁한).　　**lava**: 용암.　　**fertile**: producing abundantly (비옥한).　　**irrigation**: 관개

문제 2

Soon after the Louisiana Purchase was made in 1803, Meriwether Lewis and William Clark were chosen by President Thomas Jefferson to head an expedition. They were to explore the newly acquired, but unknown, territory. The journal of their extraordinary trip of eight thousand miles, which lasted twenty-eight months, is enthralling reading today. They used their eyes and ears along the way — recording land formations, rivers, possible future routes, plant and animal life, and the habits and attitudes of the Indians.

What is the main topic of the passage?

(A) The lives of two expedition leaders
(B) The Louisiana Purchase
(C) The Lewis and Clark exploration
(D) The mapping of a new territory

요령 먼저 논제(topic)를 파악하라.

설명 1. 첫째 문장에 제시되어 있는 논제로 보아 B와 D는 정답이 될 수 없다는 것을 알 수 있고,
2. 이 구절의 줄거리는 탐험대 지도자들의 '생활'이 아니라 '탐험'이므로 A도 정답이 될 수 없다.

해석 1803년에 루이지애나 매입이 이루어진 직후, 메리웨더 루이스와 윌리엄 클라크는 한 탐험대를 지휘하도록 토마스 제퍼슨 대통령에 의해 선발되었다. 이들이 탐험하기로 되어 있는 곳은 새로 구입했으나 사람들에게 알려져 있지 않은 이 영토(루이지애나)였다. 8,000 마일에 걸친 이들의 놀라운 여행에 대한 일지는 — 이 여행은 28개월간 계속되었다 — 오늘날에도 매혹적인 읽을거리가 되고 있다. 이들은 답사길에 눈과 귀를 이용해서 지형, 강, 장래에 건설할 가능성이 있는 길, 식물과 동물의 생태, 그리고 인디언들의 습관과 태도를 기록했다.

표현 **purchase**: buying. **head**: to be in charge of; lead. **expedition**: 탐험대. **last**: 지속하다, 계속되다
enthrall: to captivate; fascinate (매혹시키다). **reading**: any material printed or written to be read (읽을거리 — 이 단어는 의미와는 달리 이런 뜻으로 사용될 때에는 불가산 명사로 취급된다는 점에 주의하라). **land formation**: 지형

| 문제 3 |

Muscles produce heat when the body is in motion, but when the body is at rest, very little heat is generated except by the metabolic activity of the internal organs. In fact, the internal organs are the source of most body heat. The temperature of an organ such as the liver, for example, is much higher than the overall body temperature. The blood carries heat away from the internal organs to the lungs and skin and heat is then released by the lungs through respiration and by the skin through contact with the air.

What is the main topic of the passage?

(A) Ways of relaxing the body   (B) Instability of internal organs
(C) Sources of body heat   (D) Paths of the circulatory system

요령   A, B, D는 논제인 "body heat"와 관계가 없으므로 정답이 될 수 없다

해석   근육은 신체가 움직일 때 열을 발생시키나, 신체가 쉬고 있을 때에는 내부 기관의 신진대사 활동에 의해서를 제외하고 열이 거의 발생되지 않는다. 사실, 내부 기관이 대부분의 신체 열을 발생시키는 곳이다. 예를 들어, 간장과 같은 기관의 온도는 전반적인 체온보다 훨씬 더 높다. 혈액이 열을 내부 기관으로부터 폐와 피부로 옮겨주면, 열은 다시 폐에 의한 호흡을 통하여, 그리고 피부에 의한 공기와의 접촉을 통하여 방출된다.

표현   **muscle**: 근육. **at rest**(= not in motion) ≠ in motion. **generate** = produce. **metabolism**: 신진대사 **liver**: 간, 간장. **release**: to send out. **respiration**: breathing (호흡)

> 문제 4

As the American colonies in the seventeenth century prospered and trade increased among them, an efficient way of hauling goods overland was needed. The answer was the Conestoga wagon. It had a boat-shaped body and was suited for mountain trails. No matter how the wagon was tilted, the cargo stayed in place. For feeding the horses, there was a trough attached to the rear end. A Conestoga had six or seven overhead bows, or arches, with the ones in the center being a little lower than the ones on the end. These bows supported a covering of white canvas that protected the goods from the weather. The wagon was capable of carrying up to eight tons, though for each ton a horse had to be added to the team.

The best title for this passage would be _____.

(A) A Seventeenth-Century Transport Vehicle
(B) Shipbuilding in the Seventeenth Century
(C) The Increase in Trade in the American Colonies
(D) Early Roads in Colonial America

요령 Topic Sentence에 주의하라.

설명 첫째 문장에 논제가 제시되어 있다.

해석 17세기에 미국에 있는 (영국의) 식민지들이 번성하고 이들 사이에 교역이 증가하자, 육로로 상품을 수송하는 효율적인 방법이 필요하게 되었다. 이에 대한 해결책이 대형 포장마차였다. 이 마차는 보트 모양의 차체가 있었고 산길에 적합했다. 이 마차는 아무리 기울어져도, 짐은 제자리에 머물러 있었다. 말에게 먹이를 주기 위해, 이 마차의 뒤쪽 끝에는 여물통이 하나 부착되어 있었다. 대형 포장마차에는 6개 또는 7개의 활모양의 받침대(또는 아치라고도 했음)가 있었는데, 중앙에 있는 받침대들이 끝에 있는 것들보다 약간 더 낮았다. 이 받침대들은 흰 천으로 된 덮개를 지탱해 주었고, 이 덮개는 짐을 눈과 비와 바람으로부터 보호해 주었다. 이 마차는 최고 8톤까지 짐을 실어나를 수 있었다. 1톤마다 말 한 필씩을 붙여야 했지만.

표현 **haul**: to transport (운반하다, 수송하다). **overland**: by land (육로로). **tilted**: 기울어진. **in place**: 제자리에, 정해진 곳에. **trough**: 구유, 여물통. **be capable of**: ~할 능력이 있다. **up to**: as many as; a maximum of (최고 ~까지)

| 문제 5 |

Human environmental interference has halted the approach of a new ice age and will mean a warmer global climate, a local researcher has said. Among the possible consequences, Professor David G. Bridges believes, will be a shrinking of the Great Lakes and inland waters, a northward shift of the agricultural belt into Canada, and a melting of glacial ice that could raise ocean levels. A future increase of atmospheric carbon dioxide, caused by the burning of coal, oil, and gas, will be an overwhelming weather influence. The effect of this use of fossil fuels will be a drier Midwest climate with drastic effects on agriculture, commerce, and recreation. "After overpopulation and the shortage of food, this is probably the most serious problem mankind faces," Professor Bridges said.

The main topic of the passage is the _____.

(A) world's changing climate
(B) approaching ice age
(C) shrinking of the Great Lakes
(D) shifting of the Canadian agricultural belt

요령   Topic Sentence를 찾아라.

설명   1. 첫째 문장의 내용으로 보아 B는 정답이 아님을 알 수 있고.
2. C와 D는 열거된 여러개 가운데 하나이므로 줄기가 아니라 가지에 불과하다는 것을 알 수 있다.

해석   인간이 자연 환경에 손을 댐으로써 새로운 빙하시대의 접근이 정지되었고, 지구의 기후가 더 따뜻해질 것이라고, 이곳의 연구가가 말했다. 이 결과로, 데이비드 G. 브리지스 교수에 의하면, (미국의) 오대호와 내륙 수역이 줄어들고, 농업지대가 북쪽으로 이동해서 캐나다로 들어가고, 빙하의 얼음이 녹아서 바다의 수위가 높아질 수 있는 일 따위가 발생할 수 있으리라고 한다. 석탄, 석유, 가스의 연소로 말미암은 장래 대기 중의 이산화탄소 증가는 기후에 엄청나게 큰 영향을 끼칠 것이다. 이러한 화석 연료의 사용으로 중서부의 기후가 더욱 건조해져서, 농업, 상업, 레크리에이션이 크게 영향을 받게 될 것이다. "과잉 인구와 식량 부족 다음으로, 이것이 아마 인류가 직면한 가장 심각한 문제일 것이다"라고 브리지스 교수가 말했다.

표현   **halt**: to stop.   **shrink**: 줄어들다.   **waters**: 수역(강·호수·바다 따위),   **shift**: movement (이동).   **glacial**: 빙하의   **carbon dioxide**: 이산화탄소.   **overwhelming**: 압도적인, 압도적으로 큰.   **fossil fuel**: 화석 연료.   **drastic**: severe; harsh; extreme (심한)

| 문제 6 |

Like all insects, it wears its skeleton on the outside — a marvelous chemical compound called chitin which sheathes the whole of its body. This flexible armor is tremendously tough, light and shatterproof, and resistant to alkali and acid compounds which eat the clothing, flesh and bones of man. To it are attached muscles so arranged around catapult-like hind legs as to enable the hopper to hop, if so diminutive a term can describe so prodigious a leap as ten or twelve feet — about 150 times the length of the one-inch or so long insect. The equivalent feat for a man would be a casual jump, from a standing position, over the Washington Monument.

The title below that best expresses the ideas of this passage is:

(A) The Grasshopper vs. Alkali and Acid.
(B) The Champion Jumper.
(C) A Marvelous Insect.
(D) Man Meets His Conqueror.

요령 실마리(clue)를 찾아라.

설명 "Like all insects"라는 말로 보아서 이 구절의 논제는 '어떤 곤충'이라는 것을 알 수 있다. 따라서 B와 D는 정답이 될 수 없다. 그리고 이 구절은 이 곤충의 여러 가지 놀라운 점들에 관한 얘기이므로 A도 정답이 될 수 없다.

해석 모든 곤충들과 마찬가지로 이것은 몸의 외부가 껍질로 덮여 있는데, 이 껍질은 놀라운 화합물로 키틴질이라고 불리며, 이 곤충의 몸 전체를 싸고 있다. 이 신축성 있는 갑옷은 무척 단단하고 가볍고 깨어지지 않으며, 사람의 옷과 살과 뼈를 부식하는 알칼리와 산성 혼합물에 대한 저항력을 갖고 있다. 이 갑옷에는 근육이 달라붙어 있는데, 이 근육들은 석궁(石弓)처럼 생긴 뒷다리 주위에 배열되어 있어서 잘 뛰는 이 곤충으로 하여금 깡충 뛸 수 있게 해준다. 만약 깡충 뛴다는 빈약한 말이 10 또는 12피트나 되는 엄청난 도약을 묘사해 줄 수 있다면 하는 말인데, 이 곤충은 1인치 정도의 자기 몸 길이의 약 150배를 깡충 뛸 수 있다. 이에 비길 만한 묘기를 사람이 한다면 아무런 준비 없이 선 자리로부터 워싱턴 기념비(높이가 555피트임)를 뛰어넘는 일이 될 것이다.

표현 **skeleton**: 골격, 뼈대, 껍질. **compound**: 화합물, 혼합물. **sheathe**: to enclose or cover (싸거나 덮다). **flexible**: 신축성 있는. **shatterproof**: 깨어지거나 부서지지 않는. **eat**: 부식하다. **catapult-like**: 석궁처럼 생긴. **hind leg**: 뒷다리. **diminutive**: very small; tiny. **prodigious**: amazing; of great size; enormous; huge. **feat**: a remarkable deed; exploit. **casual**: not planned

| 문제 7 |

While observing rats in the laboratory, a scientist in a North American university developed the idea that rats might perform better on tests involving complex behavior if they lived in a rich environment rather than a small barren cage. The scientist therefore took several young rats home where they became family pets and were exposed to a variety of conditioning and experiences. Such rats performed better in a maze than the rats that had been raised in laboratory cages. Later, additional rats were raised in large cages furnished with a variety of objects which the rats could climb, manipulate, and explore. Scientists were able to show that there was a critical period, shortly after weaning, in which exposure to an enriched environment produced a maximum effect on behavior.

Which of the following would be the best title for the passage?

(A) Barren Cages in a University Laboratory
(B) How to Raise Rats at Home
(C) The Critical Period in the Development of Young Rats
(D) The Effect of an Enriched Environment on Rats

요령 줄기와 가지를 엄격하게 구분하라.

설명
1. 첫째 문장만 보아도 A와 B는 정답이 될 수 없다는 것을 알 수 있다.
2. 이 구절의 '줄기' (주제)는 '쥐와 생활환경과의 관계'이므로 C는 정답이 될 수 없다. 중요한 점이기는 하지만, C는 하나의 가지에 불과하기 때문이다.

표현 **develop**: 개발해내다.　**perform/do well on a test**: 시험에서 잘 해내다.　**involving**: requiring (요구하는)　**barren**: dull (무미건조한); boring (따분하게 만드는).　**pet**: 애완동물.　**be exposed to**: ~에 노출되어 있다　**condition**: to influence; to develop a conditioned reflex or behavior pattern.　**maze**: 미로 → amaze (정신이 혼미할 정도로 놀라게 만들다).　**raise**: to bring up (기르다); rear.　**furnished with**: ~로 갖추어져 있는.　**object**: 물체.　**manipulate**: to handle or use.　**critical**: decisive (결정적인); crucial.　**shortly**: in a short time; soon　**wean**: 젖을 떼다

| 문제 8 |

In its typical feeding position, a sea otter swims along on its back as it uses a rock to crack the shellfish on which it feeds. Then, tucking the rock into a pocketlike fold of skin under its arm (in which it also often keeps a supply of extra food), it will turn and dive to the bottom for more shellfish. Otters have been seen playing with rocks and shells, throwing them from one paw to another for hours at a time.

Mother otters usually shelter their young on their chests. If they have to leave the pups for any length of time, mother otters may wrap them in the strand of a kelp plant to keep them from drifting away. Although an otter is large at birth — five to six pounds — it receives maternal care until it is three or four years old, by which time, like its parents, it can dive to depths of 100 feet or more.

What is the main topic of the passage?

(A) Why the sea otter lives in the water
(B) How the sea otter cares for its young
(C) Habits of the sea otter
(D) Feeding behavior of the sea otter

설명 주어진 구절에는 sea otter의 feeding, playing, caring for its young에 관한 얘기가 나오므로 B와 D는 정답이 될 수 없고, A에 대한 언급은 전혀 찾아볼 수 없다.

해석 전형적으로 먹이를 잡아먹을 때에, 해달은 등을 물에 대고 헤엄쳐 가면서 돌을 사용해서 자기 먹이가 되는 조개를 깨뜨려 먹는다. 그리고 나서, 그 돌을 팔 밑에 있는 호주머니처럼 생긴 주머니에 넣고 (여기에는 또한 흔히 여분의 먹이를 보관한다), 몸을 뒤집어 조개를 더 잡기 위해 밑바닥으로 잠수한다. 해달이 돌과 조개를 갖고, 그것을 한쪽 발로부터 다른 쪽 발로 던지면서 한 번에 수 시간 동안 노는 것을 사람들은 보아 왔다.

어미 해달은 대개 새끼를 가슴에 안고 보호한다. 만일 어미가 새끼를 잠시라도 떠나야 하는 경우에는, 어미는 새끼를 해초 가닥 속에 싸서 떠내려가지 않게 하기도 한다. 비록 해달은 출생시에 크지만 — 몸무게가 5 또는 6 파운드 — 3 또는 4세가 될 때까지 어미의 보호를 받는데, 이 때에 이르면, 어버이와 마찬가지로, 100 피트 이상의 깊은 곳까지 잠수할 수 있다.

표현 **on its back**: 등을 (물에) 대고. **feed on**: ~을 잡아먹고 살다. **pup**: young (새끼). **maternal**: 어미의, 어머니의. *cf.* paternal

| 문제 9 |

For nearly a century before there was such a thing as a space program, a view of space was possible. People could see detailed views of the Moon, explore Mars, and study the geometric beauty of Saturn's rings. All of this was made possible by a small group of artist-astronomers who made a career of illustrating how other worlds in space might look.

Lucien Rudaux, a French artist, was the first to combine his artistic talents with his knowledge of astronomy. His paintings show a mixture of skilled observations, brilliant imagination, and painstaking attention to detail. As a result, many of his works have come surprisingly close to actual conditions on distant planets. His painting of Mars included moonlike craters that were first photographed by the Mariner 4 probe in 1965. His 1930 painting of a dust storm looks remarkably like a photograph of a storm taken by Orbiter 2 in 1976.

The artist-astronomers, including Rudaux, stimulated interest in outer space by painting what eventually turned out to be precise portraits of the planets.

What is the main idea of the passage?

(A) The amazing accuracy of space artists

(B) The popular success of Lucien Rudaux

(C) The imaginations of great artists

(D) The similarities of the Moon to Mars

요령 논제를 찾아라.

설명 이 구절의 논제는 "artist-astronomers"이므로 B, C, D는 정답이 될 수 없다

표현 **space program**: 우주탐험계획. **Mars**: 화성. **geometric**: 기하학적인. **Saturn**: 토성. **artist-astronomer**: 화가 겸 천문학자. **make a career of**: ~을 생업으로 삼다. **brilliant**: distinguished; excellent (뛰어난). **illustrate**: 그림을 그려서 보여주다. **painstaking**: very careful (매우 주의깊은, 세심한). **come close to**: ~에 근접하다(가깝다). **crater**: 분화구. **probe**: 우주탐사를 위한 도구를 갖춘 우주선. **dust storm**: 먼지 폭풍. **stimulate**: 자극하다. **outer space**: 지구 밖의 세계(외계). **turn out**: to prove (판명되다). **eventually**: finally; ultimately; in the end

| 문제 10 |

When traveling through space or a uniform medium, light moves along straight lines. The paths are called light rays. The direction of light rays can be changed by using lenses, mirrors, and prisms. Optics is the study of how light rays are affected by bouncing off or passing through materials. When light crosses the boundary from one transparent material to another (from air to glass, for example), its direction generally changes. This bending of light rays is termed refraction. The amount of refraction is different for each of the various wavelengths of light, with blue light bent more than red. The shorter the wavelength, the greater the angle of refraction. Through refraction, white light can even be broken up into light of differing wavelengths, so that its component colors are visible. Smooth surfaces return light by bouncing back the rays. This process is called reflection. A light ray bounces off a polished surface the same way a ball bounces off a smooth wall: the ball rebounds at an angle equal to the angle at which it hits. Thus, reflection does not depend on the wavelength of the light.

What is the main topic of the passage?

(A) The behavior of light rays

(B) The development of optics

(C) The meaning of refraction

(D) Different sources of light rays

설명
1. 광학에 대한 정의는 본문에 나와 있으나, '광학의 발전'에 대한 언급은 없다.
2. '굴절'은 이 구절의 가지 하나에 불과하다.
3. '광선의 원천'에 대한 언급은 없다.

표현 **uniform**: 단일 형태의, 형태가 같은, 균일한.   **optics**: 광학.   **affect**: to have an effect on; influence (~에 영향을 끼치다).   **boundary**: 경계.   **transparent**: 투명한.   **term**: to call by a term; name (~라고 부르다).   **refraction**: 굴절.   **component**: 구성하는, 이루는.   **bounce back**: 튀어서 되돌아가게 하다.   **bounce off**: 튀어서 ~로부터 떠나다   **reflection**: 반사.   **(in) the same way** = as (접속사)

| 문제 11 |

The conventions of national accounting allocate to services all output that does not come from the four goods-producing sectors: agriculture, mining, manufacturing, and construction. The service sector thus embraces distributive services such as wholesale and retail trade, communications, transportation, and public utilities; producer services such as accounting, legal counsel, marketing, banking, architecture, engineering, and management consulting; consumer services such as restaurants, hotels and resorts, laundry and dry-cleaning establishments; and nonprofit and government services such as education, health, the administration of justice, and national defense.

The United States economy in 1929 employed 45 percent of the working population in the production of goods; by 1977 that sector employed only 32 percent. Employment in the service sector therefore increased from 55 to 68 percent of the working population. Most of the shift came in the three decades after the end of the Second World War. Between 1948 and 1977 employment in goods production declined by 12 percentage points; the decline in manufacturing employment accounted for two-thirds of that decline.

What is the primary topic of the passage?

(A) The service sector of the United States economy
(B) The problem of unemployment
(C) The United States economy after the Second World War
(D) The growth of government services

표현 convention: 관례, 관습. accounting: 회계. allocate: to allot (할당하다). mining: 광업. embrace: to include (포함하다). wholesale: 도매. retail trade: 소매업. utility: the service of electricity, gas, water, telephone, etc. legal counsel: 법률상의 상담. establishment: 업소, 업체. the administration of justice: 사법 행정. shift: change (변화). account for: to be the cause or source of

| 문제 12 |

Rhythm in literature is a more or less regular occurrence of certain elements of writing: a word, a phrase, an idea, a pause, a sound, or a grammatical construction. We are also accustomed to this recurrence in the alternate heavy and light beats in music. Our love for rhythm seems to be innate: witness the responses of a small child to lively music. Children love to beat on toy drums or empty boxes. They stamp their feet and chant nursery rhymes or nonsense syllables, not unlike primitive dancers. As children grow older, they are taught to restrain their responses to rhythm, but our love of rhythm remains. We live in rhythms; in fact we are governed by rhythms.

Physiologically, we are rhythmical. We must eat, sleep, breathe, and play regularly to maintain good health. Emotionally we are rhythmical, too, for psychologists say that all of us feel alternate periods of relative depression and exhilaration. Intellectually we are also rhythmical, for we must have periods of relaxation following periods of concentration. It naturally follows then that rhythm, a fundamental aspect of our lives, must be a part of any good literary work — whether poetry or prose.

What is the main idea of the passage?

(A) Rhythmic patterns in literature are helpful to physicians and psychologists.
(B) Rhythmic patterns in literature are among the natural manifestations of rhythm in all facets of life.
(C) Rhythm tends to be more accentuated in music than in poetry.
(D) Rhythm tends to be more regular in literature than in other facets of life.

표현   **depression** ≠ exhilaration.   **relaxation** ≠ concentration

ANSWER KEY

1. C 2. C 3. C 4. A 5. A 6. C 7. D 8. C 9. A 10. A
11. A 12. B

02 논리적인 관계의 파악

(A) 다음 빈칸에 알맞은 말을 고르시오(해답은 p.287에 있음).

1 It is exhilarating to be alive in a time of awakening consciousness, but it can also be painful, confusing, and _____. 〈고려대 대학원〉

   (A) exciting   (B) harmful
   (C) indifferent   (D) disorienting

> **요령** 빈칸에 들어갈 말은 우선, exhilarating과 대조적이어야 하고; 둘째로, painful과 confusing과 조화를 이룰 수 있어야 한다. 그리고 it이 가리키는 것은 to be alive in a time of awakening consciousness라는 점을 생각하고 '사람들의 의식이 깨어나면 어떤 일이 벌어질지'를 생각해 보라.

2 That which determines us, from given premises, to draw one inference rather than another, is some habit of mind, whether it be constitutional or _____. 〈고려대 대학원〉

   (A) unlawful   (B) acquired
   (C) conditional   (D) rational

> **요령** 'whether X or Y'에서 Y는 X와 대조적인 것이어야 한다.
>
> **표현** **constitutional**: inherent; innate; inborn (선천적인)

3 I am in favor of sports as recreation, but it is my belief that no sport should be permitted to become an end in itself. Amusements cannot be cultivated at the expense of the serious business of life. Man must _____. 〈고려대 대학원〉

   (A) keep physically fit   (B) help his team to win
   (C) put work before play   (D) learn how to lose

> **표현** **put X before Y**: X를 Y보다 더 중시하다

4 You cannot judge by appearances. Because of their clumsy appearance and slow, ponderous movements, bears have earned a reputation of stupidity. Among zoo keepers, however, it is agreed that, of all the animals they handle, bears are among the most _____. 〈고려대 대학원〉

   (A) dangerous   (B) stupid
   (C) intelligent   (D) peaceful

5 Education is not simply a process of filing and storing facts and ideas in their appropriate cranial niches. Even more basic is the eradication of false ideas and unsound ways of thinking. Elimination is often more important than _____. (고려대 대학원)

   (A) education (B) understanding
   (C) exclusion (D) acquisition

   요령 the eradication of false ideas and unsound ways of thinking = Elimination
         a process of filing and storing facts and ideas in their...niches = ?

6 You do not educate a person's palate by telling him that what he has been in the habit of eating is disgusting, but persuading him to try _____. (고려대 대학원)

   (A) a dish of properly cooked food
   (B) a dish of overboiled cabbages
   (C) an invariable diet of high protein
   (D) a dish of poorly prepared food

7 Man, unlike other forms of life, is not a captive of his past — of his heredity and habits. — but is possessed of a high degree of _____. (고려대 대학원)

   (A) friability   (B) mutability
   (C) plasticity   (D) liability

   요령 엄격하게 사고하라 : X에 사로잡혀 있지 않다면 X와 다를 수 있는 능력이 있을 것이다.

8 Fears of massive unemployment have greeted technological changes ever since the Industrial Revolution. Far from destroying jobs, however, rapid technological advance has generally been accompanied by high rates of job _____. (서울대 대학원)

   (A) deprivation (B) creation
   (C) derision   (D) loss

9 They might occasionally suffer from partial abuse of delegated authority; but the _____ principle of government was wise, simple, and beneficent. (서울대 대학원)

   (A) general   (B) particular
   (C) specific (D) special

10 For John Stuart Mill, liberty is both a means and an end, a condition of the general welfare and _____ component of personal happiness. (서울대 대학원)

   (A) extrinsic (B) intrinsic
   (C) insignificant (D) infinite

   요령 a condition 이하와 앞의 진술(statement)과의 관계를 생각해 보라.

11 Human cognitive systems, when seriously investigated, prove to be no less marvelous and _____ than the physical structures that develop in the life of the organism. (서울대 대학원)

   (A) simple (B) intricate
   (C) broad (D) responsible

   논리 두 가지 이상의 정보(information)의 조각을 한 자리에 묶어서 제시할 때에는, 그 두 정보의 조각 사이에는 반드시 어떤 합당한 관련이 있어야 한다. 다음 두 진술이 논리적으로 성립되는지 따져보라.
   (a) 그 지역에는 돌과 물이 많다.
   (b) 그 지역에는 범죄와 행복이 많다.
   '돌' 과 '물' 은 자연의 일부라는 점에서 관련이 있으나, '범죄' 가 많은 곳에 '행복' 이 많을 리가 없을 것이다. 그러므로, 빈칸에는 marvelous와 조화를 이룰 수 있는 말이 필요하다.

12 No man should be praised for his goodness if he lacks the strength to be bad; in such cases goodness is usually only the effect of indolence or _____. (고려대 대학원)

   (A) desire for praises (B) saucy impudence
   (C) impotence of will (D) a sense of public disgrace

   요령 'X or Y' 에서 Y는 X와 대조적이거나 유사한 것이어야 하는데, 여기서는 어떤 경우인지 생각해 보라.
   표현 effect = result

13 Since music is perceived subjectively, so the argument runs, does this not reduce criticism to mere personal opinion? And if this is so, what makes one critic's opinions any truer than another's? This objection can be disposed of on the broadest philosophical level. Since all things perceivable are perceived subjectively, the charge of subjectivity must either be levelled against every other human endeavour, or _____. (서울대 대학원)

   (A) it must be withdrawn from criticism
   (B) it must be observed objectively
   (C) it should be limited to music
   (D) it can be applicable to every other branch of art

14. The social structure is built on the right and need of society to control, indeed, coerce, certain behavior from the individual. Religion, morality, ethics, style and fashion, public education, civil law, constitutional law, criminal procedures all help set up _____.

    (A) avenues of persuasion   (B) methods of integration
    (C) mechanisms of conformism   (D) means of repression

    요령 개인이 사회의 규범에 따라서 행동하는 것이 integration인지 또는 conformism인지 생각해 보라.

15. Because plastics do not have traditional associations in the art world, they present a fresh, _____ medium with which the sculptor can experiment.

    (서울대 대학원)

    (A) stereotyped   (B) mass
    (C) innovative   (D) reactionary

    요령 빈칸에는 fresh와 어울릴 수 있는 말이 필요하다.

16. The economic world is extremely complicated. As we noted, it is usually not _____ to make economic observations under the controlled experimental conditions characteristic of scientific laboratories.

    (서울대 대학원)

    (A) possible   (B) serious
    (C) comfortable   (D) beneficent

17. Any officious fool who enlightens us about our fault is persecuted with hatred, not because his accusation is false, but because he assumes that superiority which we are not willing to grant him, and because he has dared _____.

    (고려대 대학원)

    (A) to detect what we desired to conceal
    (B) to tell us what he has known all along
    (C) to publicize what we desired to hide
    (D) to conceal whatever defects he has himself

    요령 enlightens와 accusation이 detect에 가까운지 publicize에 가까운지 따져보라.

18 Those who are regarded as inferior elements of society may play an important role in the shaping of history. Their importance lies in the readiness with which they are collectively swayed in any direction. They can be easily persuaded to take risks and _____.　(고려대 대학원)

(A) to plunge into some united action
(B) to consider the consequences of their action
(C) to work for a noble political cause
(D) to reap rewards from the risks taken

> 요령　collectively swayed in any direction이라는 말에 해답의 실마리가 들어 있다.

19 Over the years different concepts in home management have been studied and considerable knowledge of each has developed, but, until recently, little has been done to _____ the concepts together.　(서울대 대학원)

(A) pore　　　　　　　(B) concern
(C) tie　　　　　　　　(D) clarify

> 요령　문제해결로 이끌어주는 '실마리' (clue)를 찾아라. 여기 실마리는 together라는 단어다.

20 We have the technology and knowledge to change the earth, and we have learned to manipulate nature to our advantage, but until recently we had failed to see that our manipulations could destroy both nature and us. Inherent in the harmonious operation of our whole environment must be an awareness of the _____ of all life.　(서울대 대학원)

(A) independence　　　(B) dependence
(C) interdependence　　(D) dependent

21 The more developed countries have the most exact and adequate _____ data available, whereas the less developed and younger nations, and unfortunately many of those with the most outstanding health problems, tend to have the least satisfactory information about their people.　(서울대 대학원)

(A) vital　　　　　　　(B) popular
(C) populous　　　　　(D) financial

> 요령　우선, 대조적인 내용을 보여주는 whereas에 주의하라.

22. There appears to exist an inverse relationship between the birth rate and the degree of development of a nation. Thus, the greater the degree of industrial and scientific progress, and elevation of the standard of living, the more the birth rate tends to be _____. (서울대 대학원)

(A) sustained   (B) higher
(C) depressed   (D) stabilized

> 문맥 depressed(= lower) ≠ higher

23. We do not hate those who injure us if they do not at the same time wound our self-love. We can forgive anyone sooner than those who lower us in our opinion. We as often dislike others for their virtues as for their vices. The reason is that _____. (고려대 대학원)

(A) we naturally hate whatever makes us despise ourselves
(B) we envy anyone who possesses more virtues than vices
(C) we know that we are not as virtuous as we would like to think
(D) we naturally hate those who have false pretensions

> 요령 문맥을 잡아라 ― 여기서는 wound our self-love → lower us in our opinion → ?

24. I thought that I ought to reject as downright false all opinions which I could imagine to be in the least degree open to doubt — my purpose being to discover whether, after so doing, there might not remain, as still calling for belief, something entirely _____.

(A) doubtful   (B) indubitable
(C) credible   (D) cogent

> 요령 Key words를 잡아라 ― 여기서는 open to doubt.

25. His father, a self-made man and by the time of Paul Cezanne's birth a successful banker, had a domineering personality that succeeded in terrifying his son into severe neurosis by the time he was grown up and in making him _____. (서울대 대학원)

(A) happy with his father all the more
(B) subservient to his father all his life
(C) confident with his father in everything
(D) superior to his father in any respect

> 문맥 subservient ≠ domineering

26 The popular story that Beethoven, when asked for the meaning of the opening theme of his Fifth, replied, "Thus Fate knocks at the door," is probably not _____. Such literalness seems unlikely in one who was so completely the tone poet. (서울대 대학원)

(A) credulous (B) authentic
(C) false (D) incredible

27 The problem of philosophy in the seventeenth and eighteenth centuries were related to the advances of science then. Much work in philosophy was an attempt to find foundations for the new science, and many philosophers were scientists. Kant was among these, and his philosophy was such an attempt _____ the foundations of science which had been opened unexpectedly in his boyhood. (서울대 대학원)

(A) to dispute (B) to close a gap in
(C) to exclude (D) to justify exclusively

주의 빈칸에는 뒤에 나오는 opened와 연결될 수 있는 말이 필요하다!

28 Cezanne effectively ended his long friendship with Emile Zola, as much because of neurotic distrust and jealousy as from disappointment at Zola's "popular" writing, which his antisocial and single-minded genius found _____. (서울대 대학원)

(A) tolerable (B) informative
(C) incomprehensible (D) justifiable

문맥 antisocial and single-minded ≠ "popular"

29 Even in a totalitarian state, it is indispensable that there should exist the freedom of opinion which causes opposing opinions to be debated, if only as a way of ascertaining the condition of things. As time goes on, that is [becomes] less and less easy; critical discussion disappears as the internal opposition is liquidated. That is why the early successes of despots have usually been followed by _____. (고려대 대학원)

(A) an irreparable mistake
(B) the silencing of opposition
(C) the sullen disobedience of the ruled
(D) the growing discontent of the populace

> 참고 is 다음에 나오는 [becomes]는 편집자인 본인(김영로)이 생각하기에는 그 자리에는 후자가 더 적절하다는 것을 나타낸다. 이 괄호 [ ]는 교정하거나 정보를 보충하기 위해 편집자가 사용하는 부호이다.

30 In the Pacific Islands, hurricanes come at intervals of a few years; even earthquakes are quite in the cards; and then, however strongly your house may have been built, it is bound to come down. The _____ is that people, building in those localities, do not attempt to put up massive buildings.

(서울대 대학원)

(A) singular face   (B) profound truth
(C) natural result   (D) suggestive point

> 요령 '인과관계' (causality)를 생각하라.
> 문맥 put up = build

31 Scientific studies of the sex cell development in mice, cattle and man have provided parts of the story from which the process (as a whole) can be deduced. Until recent years the results were often thought to be _____ and hence the origin of germ cells has been the subject of unceasing debate for some 50 years or more.

(서울대 대학원)

(A) inconclusive   (B) incredible
(C) indigenous   (D) indisputable

> 요령 논리적인 관계를 보여주는 장치인 "hence"라는 말에 주의하라.

32 More than 2,000 different substances are used as food additives. Yet most food specialists hold the belief that long continued and widespread dietary intake of a substance with no harmful effects coming to light does not constitute adequate proof of its _____ for lifetime consumption.

(서울대 대학원)

(A) efficacy   (B) safety
(C) usefulness   (D) virtue

> 표현 hold the belief that~ = believe that~

33 Health in ourselves and in our animals is often taken for granted until something goes wrong. So interest is initially aroused rather by disease than health. This bias in the wrong direction is liable to persist and often colors a farmer's thinking about his stock _____.　　　　　　　(서울대 대학원)

(A) to his advantage　　　　　(B) in a harmless way

(C) to his own great disadvantage　(D) and make it more colorful

34 The accumulation of capital requires abstention from immediate consumption. A worker who has to grow all his own food can barely take time out to improve his tools. But if he can save or borrow enough to feed himself and keep warm while he is working on his tools, he can ultimately produce a better crop, more than is needed to keep him alive. _____.
　　　　　　　　　　　　　　　　　　　　　(고려대 대학원)

(A) The resulting surplus goes into the formation of his capital

(B) The resulting surplus becomes available for his consumption

(C) The crop then can be used as animal feed

(D) The crop can be retained for possible emergency

> **요령**　주제를 붙잡아라!

35 Formerly philosophers thought of mind as having to do exclusively with conscious thought. But of late it has been shown that we are unaware of a great part of what we perceive, remember, will and infer; and that a great part of the thinking of which we are aware is determined by that of which we are not conscious. It has indeed been demonstrated that our unconscious psychic life _____.　　　　　　　(서울대 대학원)

(A) is sorely determined by our conscious thought

(B) far outruns our conscious

(C) did not influence our conscious thinking at all

(D) is largely determined by other factors than our conscious mind

> **요령**　복잡한 것은 단순하게 만들어서 생각하라. 이 문제를 푸는 데 실마리가 되는 내용을 요약하면 다음과 같다:
> 과거 : mind = conscious thought
> 최근 : unconscious mind > conscious mind
>
> **문맥**　aware (= conscious) ≠ unaware

36 Despite all the inventive marvels of the present day, Edison declares that "We are only beginning to get the benefits of machinery. In some directions we have progressed a fair amount. In other directions we have scarcely done anything. But the most that we have done in any line is _____ as compared with what can be done." (서울대 대학원)

(A) brilliant (B) enormous
(C) insignificant (D) remarkable

37 There has been some speculation about the effects that a four-day workweek would have upon industry. Some industries would certainly benefit — those associated with _____. (고려대 대학원)

(A) steel (B) food
(C) clothing (D) leisure

38 By the 1920s, endocrinologists had discovered what they took to be a real difference between the two sexes: separate male and female hormones. Later, it was discovered that men had significant amounts of estrogen, the female hormone. That discovery showed how _____ sex differences really were. (서울대 대학원)

(A) precarious (B) significant
(C) big (D) biological

39 Hegel's position in the history of philosophy is undoubted. But one can _____ the dangers of Hegel's thought without denying his greatness: distinction and danger are twins. (서울대 대학원)

(A) follow (B) concede
(C) agree to (D) be influenced by

40 If all the scientific papers, and reports written about saccharin were laid end to end, they would reach from Madison Avenue to the Mayo Clinic. Few medical issues have been subjected to so much _____. (서울대 대학원)

(A) pressure (B) scrutiny
(C) criticism (D) praise

요령 엄격하게 생각하라 : 모든 과학논문의 목적이 "criticism"이라고 볼 수 있는가?

41 A man will be proportionately more powerful, that is, he will come closer to being a real human being — in direct ratio to his mastery of his language. A man who has a language consequently possesses the world expressed and implied by that language. For _____, as observed.　　　　　　(고려대 대학원)

(A) mastery of language affords remarkable power
(B) language is a tool for efficient communication
(C) reality cannot be totally contained in language
(D) foreign language are hard to master

42 In their evolution of defenses against predators many burrowing and nest-building animals have developed special techniques; examples are dumb nests, multiple burrows, false entrances and emergency exits. Marsh wrens may build as many as a dozen fake nests to _____ the chances that a fox or racoon will discover the real one which is carefully concealed.　(서울대 대학원)

(A) improve　　　　　　(B) miss
(C) reduce　　　　　　 (D) stand

> 요령　문맥으로 보아 'dumb = fake ≠ real' 이라는 관계를 파악할 수 있다.

43 U.S. interest in Asia, which goes back to the day of the American Revolution, has always been alive not for colonial gain, but essentially to keep any other single power from dominating the affairs of the vast region of the world, and _____.　　　　　　(서울대 대학원)

(A) inviting the United States in
(B) shutting the United States out
(C) invading the United States
(D) subjugating the United States

> 문맥　the vast region of the world = Asia

44 An instrument is efficient to the extent to which the using of it enables the purpose, for which the instrument is designed, _____. An inefficient instrument is bad; an efficient instrument is good. An instrument is for use.　　　　　　(서울대 대학원)

(A) to be efficient　　　　(B) to be inefficient
(C) to be achieved　　　　(D) to be used

> 요령　상식적으로 생각해 보라.

45 This ubiquitous importance of water makes it a hub around which the wheel of biological research must be built. It makes water a dominant factor in the food industry so much so that a knowledge of the behavior of water and its interactions with proteins will lead to steady _____ in the preservations of food. (서울대 대학원)

(A) degeneration (B) dispute
(C) importance   (D) improvement

46 No weakness of the human mind has more frequently incurred animadversion, than the negligence with which men overlook their own faults, however flagrant. It seems generally believed that the mind has no faculties by which it can contemplate its own state, as _____. (고려대 대학원)

(A) the eye cannot see itself
(B) one hand clapping makes no sound
(C) the rolling stone gathers no moss
(D) confession does not make a legal case

> **주의** 모르는 단어가 나오더라도 당황하지 말라 : 주어진 문제를 푸는 데에는 "animadversion"이라는 단어의 뜻을 모르더라도 지장은 없다. 중요한 것은 주제 또는 논리적인 관계를 파악하는 일이다.

47 A discussion of the nature of any intellectual effort is more difficult than the mere _____ of that particular intellectual effort. It is hard to understand the mechanism of an airplane, and the theories of the forces which lift and which propel it, than merely to ride in it, to be transported by it or even to steer it. (서울대 대학원)

(A) continuance   (B) exercise
(C) exertion   (D) understanding

48 The domestic torment Jane Carlyle endured in her long marriage to Thomas Carlyle is of a particular opacity due to the naturalness of so much of it, to its origin in the mere strains of living. The conflicts were _____. (고려대 대학원)

(A) of an exceptional kind, unlike any found in the households of the time
(B) of a pathological nature due to Carlyle's nervous disorders
(C) not of a remarkable kind or different from those suffered in any household of the time

(D) were worthy of study for the light they throw on the working of the mind of a literary genius

요령 실마리를 찾아라!

49 Gout is the aristocrat of diseases. Ancient philosophers and physicians attributed it to high living, and it has often afflicted men of exceptional talent. Michelangelo suffered from it, as did Galileo and Martin Luther. Gout was called the physician's shame because _____ could be done to treat it. (서울대 대학원)

(A) so little (B) so much
(C) something (D) everything

50 Copernicus did not believe that God would have created so clumsy a system. He decided to complete changes observed in the positions of the sun and planets in complete mathematical detail. He hoped to prove to astronomers and calendar makers that the sun-centered theory worked at least as well as its antique rival in reducing the complex and irregular planetary motions _____, while providing new evidence for an understanding of the structure of the universe. (서울대 대학원)

(A) to provable theories (B) to unprovable theories
(C) to predictable order (D) to unpredictable disorder

(B) 주어진 passage를 완성하기에 알맞은 것을 고르시오(해답은 p.287에 있음).

51 From a purely selfish point of view, it is not advisable to let people know that you think they are stupid. You might be wrong, in which case they will quite justifiably _____.

(A) form the same opinion of you
(B) concur with your opinion
(C) continually ask you for advice
(D) defer to your ability to judge others

주의 **in which case** = and in that case. **concur**: to agree. **defer to**: to give in to; yield to

52 During the Great Depression, one state of the United States passed a law forbidding anyone to bring poor or needy people into the state. The United States Supreme Court declared the law unconstitutional, saying that any American has the privilege of moving from place to place regardless of _____.

(A) religion (B) education
(C) citizenship (D) income

주의 needy: not having enough to live on; very poor. cf. A friend in need is a friend indeed.

53 We think of the earth underneath us as being solid, but volcanoes and earthquakes are evidences of violent internal stirrings. Slower and more gentle movements are going on constantly in all earth's inner and outer areas, causing changes that may take thousands of years to become evident. No mountain or plain is _____.

(A) natural (B) moving
(C) volcanic (D) permanent

문맥 stirrings = movements

54 During the seventeenth century, Thomas Dekker wrote that his age thought better of a gilded fool than of a threadbare saint. His point was that a person's true worth cannot be judged by _____.

(A) anyone (B) intelligence
(C) personality (D) appearances

55 In the past raincoats were made of water-repellent materials whose solid composition allowed no ventilation. For this reason, raincoats were uncomfortable in hot weather. A porous material now has been invented in which the openings are too small to let water molecules through but large enough to allow ventilation for the wearer. Raincoats of this material provide both protection and _____.

(A) comfort (B) warmth
(C) dryness (D) lightness

56 Forest fires can completely destroy a large area of timber. If the fire is severe enough, it can burn away all vegetation that holds the soil in place and can leave the area ripe for erosion. For this reason, land that has been ravaged by fire should be _____.

(A) patrolled by rangers   (B) completely abandoned
(C) protected from fire   (D) replanted immediately

57 The human body is designed, both structurally and functionally, for a considerable amount of physical activity. Exercise may produce detrimental as well as beneficial effects, however, depending on an individual's own physical health. Exercise is not a panacea or a one-ingredient prescription for good health. It should be _____.

(A) chosen carefully   (B) left alone
(C) done strenuously   (D) required of all students

58 In many respects, the literature of the Romantic period is a direct reaction to the literature of the Augustan period that preceded it. Whereas the Augustans were rational, the Romantics were highly emotional. Whereas the poetry of the Augustans were classical and regular, Romantic poets often wrote experimental and erratic verse. While the Augustans eschewed excess in any form, the Romantics revelled in extremes. Augustan respect for polished and refined skill was replaced by Romantic emphasis on individual creative impulse and inspiration. Indeed, the relationship between the Augustans and Romantics might be meaningfully described as one of _____.

(A) influence   (B) purpose
(C) contrast   (D) similarity

59 One of the most important pieces of equipment in a school library is the unabridged dictionary. It is a rare day when at least one of the staff or a faculty member does not make use of this authoritative book. Not even the most eminent scholars have _____.

(A) the services of a trained assistant
(B) an unabridged dictionary at home
(C) complete knowledge of their language
(D) a vocabulary of above-average size

60 The progress of a nation is dependent on its members to maintain an equal emphasis on thinking and on doing. Unfortunately, the spirit of some countries is like a pendulum swinging between the two extremes of quick activity and sober reflection rather than, as it should be, _____.

(A) influenced by persons of reason

(B) evenly balanced between them

(C) indifferent to social reforms

(D) alert to the need for doing

문맥   activity = doing.   reflection = thinking.   sober ≠ qucik

61 We cannot give our children the assurance that there will be no more devastating war, no depressions to be weathered, no great social upheaval to be survived. But we can make every effort to see that our children live in security and as happily as possible so that they will be prepared to meet _____.

(A) the uncertainties of the future   (B) either poverty or war

(C) the common enemy   (D) any natural disasters

주의   **weather**: to pass through safely.   **meet**: to deal with

62 John Locke, a philosopher of the eighteenth century, believed that the association of ideas is one of the chief mental processes. If two experiences have occurred together in the past, an occurrence of one of them in the future will frequently cause a person to _____.

(A) form a new idea   (B) recall the other

(C) forget the past   (D) dissociate the two

63 With the advent of mechanization, the workers who had previously performed the tasks by hand complained that the machines were taking their jobs away from them. Of course, this particular complaint was true, but if the overall employment picture is considered, it is clear that machines do not take jobs away without providing other jobs, for machines _____.

(A) restrict the purchasing power of the operators

(B) do away with only the highest-paid jobs

(C) have to be built and repaired by workers

(D) can produce goods more cheaply than can handworkers

> 주의　**picture**: a situation; condition; state of affairs

64. Moulds can be very annoying when they develop on our food or on our clothes. One useful thing they accomplish, though, is to cause dead plants and animals to decay. You might say that moulds are _____.

(A) killers of plants and animals　(B) nature's garbage disposers
(C) annoying in all ways　(D) useful in every way

> 주의　**though**: however (그러나)

65. Sir Walter Raleigh, once popular with Queen Elizabeth, was less popular in his later years. After the succession of James I, Raleigh was tried on a charge of having conspired against the king's life. He was sentenced to die, but on the scaffold his sentence was commuted to life imprisonment. His bearing during the trial had been so admirable that public opinion had _____.

(A) turned to support him　(B) caused his execution
(C) no influence in court　(D) brought a not-guilty verdict

> 주의　**bearing**: manner (태도).　**execution**: putting to death (사형집행, 처형)

66. Some reformers have urged that our language be purified by discarding all words of foreign origin for which there are equivalent words in our native tongue. These reformers are doomed to failure, for many such words are used so frequently that they seem _____.

(A) fantastic and affected
(B) completely alien to us
(C) an intrinsic part of our language
(D) replaceable by native equivalents

> 주의　**affected**: not natural; artificial; pretentious (가식적인). **intrinsic**: belonging to a thing; essential; inherent (고유의, 본질적인, 필요불가결한)

67 Sigmund Freud, the founder of psychoanalysis, repeatedly emphasized the pervasive importance of the acts and gestures that individuals unrealizingly perform. To understand the underlying truth of people's intentions and attitudes, place little credence in what they proclaim openly; seek, rather, real meanings _____ .

(A) by probing their earliest childhood memories
(B) in the unconscious gestures and words that escape them
(C) in the dreams that they remember
(D) by insisting that they say what they mean

> 주의 **place credence in**: to give credence to; trust in; believe

68 The value of a scientific hypothesis will be proportionate to the care and completeness with which its basis has been tested and verified. That is to say, the guess of the fool will be worthless, while the tentative theory of the scholar will _____ .

(A) be obscure   (B) be inspired
(C) have validity   (D) be random

> 문맥 be worthless(=have no value) ≠ have validity(=have value)

69 The problem of whether or not we possess free will is entangled with that of moral responsibility. It is difficult to comprehend how we can be held responsible for actions that we could have determined no other way. The existence of several genuine alternatives from which we may choose appears to be a necessary prerequisite of _____ .

(A) action   (B) forming good habits
(C) moral responsibility   (D) determinism

70 A great educator once said that the mark of an educated person is the ability to make a reasoned guess on the basis of insufficient information. The educator's point was that whenever we face decisions, we show intelligence if we act in the best possible way in spite of _____ .

(A) promises   (B) uncertainties
(C) self-confidence   (D) convictions

71. The noblest deeds require nothing but simple language; they are spoiled by emphasis. It is insignificant matters that stand in need of high-flown words, because it is the expression, the tone, and the manner that alone give them effect. But noble deeds _____.

(A) precede exhortations
(B) are usually exaggerated
(C) are seldom expressed
(D) speak for themselves

문맥 stand in need of = require

72. A fox served soup in a flat bowl to a bird that could not eat it with its long beak. Then the bird invited the fox for dinner and served the soup in a long-necked pitcher into which the fox could not get its mouth. The fox complained, but the bird said, "You deserve this for the way you treated me." The story has a moral: _____.

(A) it is not good to hold a grudge
(C) return good for evil
(B) one good turn deserves another
(D) the offender is often repaid in kind

73. Historians are always careful to check the reliability of sources of information. Some documents are forged; authors may be so prejudiced that they cannot make fair judgements; and even honest people can be mistaken. Historians must avoid such _____.

(A) pitfalls
(B) precautions
(C) accuracy
(D) facts

74. We should consider carefully the source of our information. We should seek out both sides of a question and form the habit of having suspended judgement and an open mind receptive to _____.

(A) no influence
(B) radio reports
(C) tradition
(D) new evidence

주의 suspended judgment: 판단보류. receptive to: ~을 받아들이는

75 Repetitions in discussion are often a great waste of time, but sometimes the frequent restatement of the problem at hand saves time, for it _____.

(A) precludes lengthy discussions
(B) results in frivolous side remarks
(C) maintains an atmosphere of compromise
(D) keeps many irrelevant matters from being discussed

76 The surface waters of the Arctic Ocean hold the smallest amount of dissolved salts because melting ice causes dilution; conversely, in the tropics, where great evaporation occurs, the salinity of the ocean's surface water is _____.

(A) greatest   (B) average
(C) evaporated   (D) diluted

77 Architecture is sometimes called "the mother of the arts." In the sense that a mother gives birth to children, this is a misnomer. Rather, perhaps, "the nurse of the arts" might be more appropriate, for architecture originally _____.

(A) directly preceded painting
(B) depended on painting and sculpture
(C) competed with painting and sculpture
(D) supported and encouraged painting and sculpture

78 Newton's third law of motion states that for every action there is an equal and opposite reaction. When a gun is fired, the force that pushes the bullet forward is equal to the force with which the gun recoils. Space vehicles, having left the earth's atmosphere, can maneuver by firing small rockets in the direction _____.

(A) of the earth
(B) in which they wish to go
(C) at right angles to their destination
(D) opposite to their destination

79 The taxes are indeed very heavy, and if those laid by the government were the only ones, we might easily discharge them. We are taxed twice as much by our idleness, three times as much by our pride, and four times as much by our folly; and from these taxes the commissioners cannot free or _____.

(A) tax us
(B) punish us
(C) deliver us
(D) collect from us

80 Passive acceptance of the teacher's wisdom is easy to most children. It involves no effort of independent thought, and it pleases the teacher. Yet, the habit of passive acceptance is a disastrous one in later life. It causes people to seek a leader and to accept as leader _____.

(A) a person who is unworthy
(B) a person from their own ranks
(C) one whom they do not know personally
(D) whoever is established as such

81 In dealing with the problems of his time, Socrates used a method of proper definition. He divided and subdivided in order to distinguish between the widely differing and often contradictory meanings that hide behind a word. In brief, his method was a protest against the _____.

(A) aristocratic idea of education
(B) careless use of general terms
(C) complex nature of the Greek language
(D) insistence on precise, meticulous definition

82 Temperature denotes the intensity of heat in a substance. A milliliter of water and a liter of water may have the same temperature, but the heat in the liter of water will be a thousand times as great as the heat in the milliliter of water, because there is a thousand times as much water in the liter. The amount of heat in a substance is in direct ratio to the volume or amount of the substance. Temperature and heat are _____.

(A) increased with volume
(B) the same
(C) not the same
(D) of equal intensity

83. People are always talking about originality; but what do they mean? As soon as we are born, the world begins to work upon us, and this goes on to the end. And after all, what can we call our own except energy, strength, and will? If I could give an account of all that I owe to great predecessors and contemporaries, there would be but _____.

(A) little time required
(B) few faults to explain
(C) a few to whom I am indebted
(D) a small balance to my credit

84. Historically, a person convicted of a felony was required to forfeit all property, real or personal; but a person convicted of a misdemeanor did not have to give up any property. Initially, then, one could tell the class of crime of which a person had been convicted by the _____.

(A) type of trial
(B) penalty imposed
(C) nature of the crime
(D) guilt of the accused

> 문맥   did not have to give up = was not required to forfeit (forfeit = give up)

85. Of all the existing barriers to the transmission of ideas and knowledge, perhaps the most subtle is our unwillingness to listen to what is being communicated and our unwitting distortion of what we do hear. The ideological aspects of our culture give each of us a frame of reference into which we fit ideas and knowledge. In general, those communications that do not fit neatly into our preexisting frame of reference are _____.

(A) accepted by the majority
(B) given further study
(C) accepted without equivocation
(D) disregarded or unconsciously altered

> 주의   frame of reference: the standards by which a person compares something to form an attitude or make a judgment or analysis (태도를 정하거나 판단 또는 분석을 하기 위해 어떤 사람이 사용하는 표준)

86. Although the sequence of night and day may appear invariable in our experience, it does not follow that under all conditions this succession would remain unchanged. For the succession of night and day is a derivative sequence caused by the sun and is, therefore, _____.

(A) hypothetical
(B) sequential
(C) conditional
(D) experiential

> 문맥   unchanged = invariable

87 Euphemism is a way of speaking in which an inoffensive term is substituted for a harsh or offensive term. A euphemist would say that a liar is a person who exaggerates. Such a person would also speak of a frugal individual rather than of _____.

(A) a spendthrift
(B) a miser
(C) a euphemist
(D) a philanthropist

> 문맥   speak of a frugal individual rather than of a miser = say that a miser is a person who is frugal

88 According to this author, that which one reads fertilizes a seed of thought and is not the seed itself. One should utilize reading to _____.

(A) enhance one's knowledge of current views
(B) aid the growth of already existent thoughts
(C) provide the raw material from which thoughts are created
(D) develop the ability to express thoughts clearly

89 To know truth and to recognize error — these are the fundamental goals of science, related but not identical. When we believe something that is indeed true, we as a consequence may avoid accepting a false assertion. We often can recognize the falsity of several interpretations of a phenomenon, however, without _____.

(A) rejecting its true interpretation
(B) making any mistakes
(C) believing another false interpretation
(D) knowing its true interpretation

90 Traditionally, it has been supposed that natural structures exemplify perfect regularity in both their construction and their functioning. Thus, the atom has been pointed out as the acme of orderly consistency. Recent findings, however, have indicated the complete untenability of these assumptions about natural phenomena. Indeed, we are now forced to concede that nature is _____.

(A) fully predictable
(B) the exemplar of perfection
(C) disdainful of accuracy and precision
(D) governed by unalterable laws

91 The separation of thought and action in education is regrettable. When students are encouraged to absorb facts rather than to learn to apply skills, education becomes _____.

(A) an invaluable part of worthwhile living

(B) the passive reception of information

(C) the translation of thoughts into actions

(D) an esoteric function performed by only a few

> 문맥   facts = information

92 In some scientific journals, sentences bulge with unnecessary words and phrases that weaken the article's emphasis and even hide the ideas that the writer is trying to express. One would never guess from a look at these writings that science _____ .

(A) encourages research

(C) requires no knowledge of language

(B) takes prides in natural resources

(D) is renowned for its efficiency

93 Changes in developing science are not to be compared to the tearing down of old buildings to make way for new ones, but rather to the gradual evolution of a zoological type. We must not believe that discarded theories have been _____.

(A) either sterile or in vain   (B) seriously considered

(C) used in shaping new ideas   (D) of any purpose in present research

94 If the majority of hard, green apples you have tasted in your life have been sour, then you are apt to derive a tentative law that all hard, green apples are sour. You may occasionally, however, find a hard, green apple that is sweet. To the extent that there are exceptions to your law, your confidence in the law is decreased. We accept the law of gravity because of the lack of exceptional cases. Confidence in any natural law is inversely proportional to the _____.

(A) number of observations on which it is based

(B) amount of variation in results

(C) number of things that it can explain

(D) carelessness of the experimenter

> 주의   be inversely proportional to: ~에 반비례하다.   variation = exception

95 Milton's life is probably the best known in English literature, and his forceful personality is so clearly and indelibly impressed on all his works that we are acquainted with him almost more intimately than we are with many of our contemporaries, or even ourselves. He is, thus, in this respect, very different from Shakespeare, _____.

(A) whose life is revealed in his plays

(B) whose biography is also complete

(C) who is the great enigma of our literature

(D) who has a more forceful personality

96 *The Guinnes Book of World Records* cites the shortest correspondence on record as one between author Victor Hugo and his publishers, Hurst and Blackett. Hugo, on holiday and anxious to know how his latest novel, *Les Miserables*, was selling, wrote to his publishers the simple inquiry, "?" Not to be outdone for brevity, they indicated the novel's immediate popularity to Hugo with their reply of "_____".

(A) ?   (B) Bravo!

(C) !   (D) Miserable success

> 주의 Not to be outdone for brevity: 간결함에서 뒤지지 않기 위해

97 For a concrete illustration of the prevalent avoidance of independent thought, listen to the conversation of a group of people who have just attended a movie together. During the film one or two individuals have experienced decided sensations and emotions, which they now describe vigorously. The rest of the crowd jolts out of passive indifference to nod in habitual assent, thus _____.

(A) dividing the party into fractions

(B) expressing their originality

(C) uniting in enthusiasm about the film

(D) creating a semblance of unanimity

98. Occasionally, a clear-sighted individual frees some area of investigation from the unprofitable tradition by which it has been fettered. All too often, however, this evidence used to overthrow tradition becomes formalized into a new revered tradition that in time becomes an impediment to progress. The rigid conventions that now restrict our range of activity were probably initiated by _____.

(A) independent thinkers
(B) irrational rebels
(C) cringing traditionalists
(D) pure chance

문맥 fetter = impede = restrict.   conventions = traditions

99. There is no place for dogma in science. The scientist is free to ask any question, to doubt any assertion, to seek for any evidence, to correct any error. Where science has been used in the past to erect a new dogmatism, that dogmatism has found itself incompatible with the progress of science; in the end, the dogma has yielded, or science has _____.

(A) grown
(B) advanced
(C) assented
(D) suffered

100. In his farewell address George Washington urged: "Promote as an object of primary importance institutions for the general diffusion of knowledge." Jefferson said in 1820: "I know of no safe depository of the ultimate powers of the society but the people themselves; and if we think them not enlightened enough to exercise their control with a wholesome discretion, the remedy is not to take it from them, but to inform their discretion by _____."

(A) freedom
(B) education
(C) democracy
(D) legislation

ANSWER KEY(A)

1. D	2. B	3. C	4. C	5. D	6. A	7. C	8. B	9. A	10. B
11. B	12. C	13. A	14. C	15. C	16. A	17. C	18. A	19. C	20. C
21. B	22. C	23. A	24. B	25. B	26. B	27. B	28. C	29. A	30. C
31. A	32. B	33. C	34. A	35. B	36. C	37. D	38. A	39. B	40. B
41. A	42. C	43. B	44. C	45. D	46. A	47. C	48. C	49. A	50. C

ANSWER KEY(B)

51. A	52. D	53. D	54. D	55. A	56. D	57. A	58. C	59. C	60. B
61. A	62. B	63. C	64. B	65. A	66. C	67. B	68. C	69. C	70. B
71. D	72. D	73. A	74. D	75. D	76. A	77. D	78. D	79. C	80. D
81. B	82. C	83. D	84. B	85. D	86. C	87. B	88. C	89. D	90. C
91. B	92. D	93. A	94. B	95. C	96. C	97. D	98. A	99. D	100. B

APPENDIX 2
READING SELECTIONS

다음에 나오는 10편의 글은 줄이지 않고 원문을 그대로 실은 것입니다. 이제 혼자 힘으로 읽어보십시오. 당신의 학문이나 인생에 많은 도움이 될 것입니다. 여기에 실린 글에 필자의 손을 대지 않은 이유가 있습니다. 너무도 잘 쓰여진 글들이라 다칠세라 손을 대기가 두렵기 때문입니다.

우리도 노력만 하면 영어로 글을 쓸 수 있다는 것을 보여드리기 위해 필자가 쓴 글도 한 편 실어놓았습니다.

"나"를 찾겠다! — 도대체 "나"라는 존재는 누구인가? 서구의 젊은이들 중에는 자기를 찾아나서는 사람들이 상당수 있는 것 같습니다. 이 넓은 세상에서 자신이 설 자리를 안다는 것이 얼마나 중요한 일입니까? 다음 글은 한 유명한 해학가의 눈에 비친 젊은이들의 이러한 모험의 단면입니다.

* 이 글은 <Reader's Digest>에서 뽑았습니다.

Lost and Found

BY ART BUCHWALD

One of the reasons why colleges are suffering from underenrollment is that many high-school students are taking a year off to "find themselves."

I was at the Thatchers' home the other night when their son, Rolf, announced that he had decided he would not go to any of the universities that had accepted him. He wanted to spend time bumming around the country.

"Why?" Thatcher asked.

"Because I have to find myself," Rolf said.

"How can you find yourself any better bumming around the country than going to college?" his father asked him.

"Because it's not happening at school. It's happening out there."

"What's happening out there?" Mrs. Thatcher asked.

"I don't know. That's what I have to find out."

Thatcher said, "Willy Grugschmid has been on the road for three years now trying to find himself. The only time he knows where he is is when he has to call collect and ask his parents for money."

"It takes some people longer to find themselves than other people," Rolf said defensively.

"Where will you go?" Mrs. Thatcher asked.

"I thought I'd hitchhike to Nevada. Blair Simmons is living on unemployment insurance in Reno. He's with several kids who are trying to find themselves. Then I'll go to Arizona. I know some guys there who are working for the Indians making Navajo blankets."

"How do you find yourself making Navajo blankets for the Indians?" Thatcher wanted to know.

"You work with your hands," Rolf said, "and that gives you time to think."

"Rolf," Thatcher said, "no one admires your adventurous spirit more than I do. But I have just so much money set aside for your college education, and costs are rising every day. By the time you find yourself, I may not be able to send you to college. Couldn't you go to college first, then find yourself later?"

"No," Rolf said. "If I go to school in the fall, I won't be able to concentrate because I'll know I'm missing something out there."

"What?" Thatcher demanded.

"If I knew, I wouldn't miss it. You see, I have to establish my own identity. If I can't do it in this country, then I plan to go to South America with Edna."

"Edna?" Mrs. Thatcher gasped. "Is Edna trying to find herself, too?"

"Yes. She has a Volkswagen, and she's invited me to go with her."

"How do her parents feel about it?" Thatcher asked.

"They're pretty mad, but Edna says if she doesn't go she'll wind up going to school, then getting married, and finally she'll become a mother. She sees no future in that."

"Suppose she becomes a mother in South America?" Mrs. Thatcher asked.

"It's not going to be that kind of trip," Rolf said angrily. "We each have our own sleeping bag."

"It gets cold in the Andes," Thatcher warned.

"Well, anyway," Rolf said, "I just thought you should know I'm not going to college until I find myself."

"I guess there isn't much we can do then, is there?" Thatcher asked. "Will you do us one favor, though? As soon as you find yourself, will you let us know?"

"How will I do that?" Rolf asked.

"Put an ad in the Lost and Found column."

세상을 살아가는 방법에는 여러 가지가 있겠지만, 평범하게 사는 것과 비범하게 사는 것 두 가지로 요약할 수 있습니다. 그러나 아무도 어느 것이 더 낫다고 단정할 수는 없습니다. 왜냐하면 이것은 개인의 인생관에 관한 문제이니까요. 만일 당신이 비범하게 사는 길을 원한다면, 이 글을 읽으십시오. 이 글은 재벌들이 보통 사람들과 다른 점을 잘 보여줍니다.

* 이 글은 <Reader's Digest>에서 뽑았습니다.

What Makes Tycoons Tick?

BY ARTHUR M. LOUIS

What is special about tycoons? What distinguishes the men who run the major companies from those who never reach the top?

Tycoons differ from one another in so many ways that they occupy the entire spectrum from extroverts to recluses, from free-spenders to tightwads, from charmers to bores. But they do have many things in common, qualities that appear to be standard equipment for anyone who aspires to be the boss.

It is well known that long hours of hard work are required to reach the top in business. Probably most people assume that this hard work is the means to an end, to success. But the work can be an end in itself. Tycoons, by and large, are driven by a passion for work that is quite as powerful as any other human drive. Their work takes precedence over wives, children, vacations and hobbies. Businessmen who lack this overpowering commitment will almost certainly be eclipsed by those who do have it.

Tycoons cheerfully admit that they are workaholics. Robert Edward (Ted) Turner III, the flamboyant young Atlanta entrepreneur and sailing champion, told an interviewer, "I've provided for my family, but I'm still running. Why? It's fun. I couldn't quit." Harry Gray, chairman of United Technologies, once had office files and a secretary moved into his hospital room after a serious accident, and continued working for months while flat on his back.

Tycoons are often so intent on work that they look upon vacations as a nuisance. William A. Marquard, chairman of American Standard, Inc., takes long weekends instead of vacations. "After the fourth day I start to get itchy," he says. John Brooks Fuqua, founder of the Fuqua Industries conglomerate in Atlanta, once scheduled a two-week vacation in Switzerland. But he was back in his office early, explaining, "When you've seen one castle, you've seen them all."

The tycoon needs an extraordinary amount of energy to satisfy this passion for work. Many a talented young businessman has failed to get ahead simply because he wasn't built to take the grind. "It becomes clear pretty soon if you can't do the job," remarks C. Peter McColough of Xerox. Tex Thornton of Litton Industries makes the same point: "Thoroughbreds are bred to race. It's the same with people. It's something that's inborn."

To confess fatigue is often regarded by tycoons as an admission of weakness or a lack of dedication. "This can be a problem for subordinates," one tycoon admits. "You think everyone's on the same wavelength you are, and you find that you're wearing out your staff."

What else motivates successful businessmen to work so hard? Money may draw people to business in the first place, but it is not what motivates them to reach the very top. Power is.

Some top businessmen are quite frank about their addiction to power, a raw word that does not sit very well with the inhabitants of a democracy. John Weller Hanley, chief executive of the Monsanto Company, recalled that even as a teenager he felt the urge to persuade people to do what he wanted them to do. Working at a soda fountain, he would pressure his customers into taking an egg in their malted-milk shakes. Donald Nelson Frey worked his way up to group vice president at Ford by age 44 — but that wasn't enough. "I just had to run a whole business," he explains. He left and eventually became chief executive of Bell and Howell, a mere fraction of Ford's size — but the fraction was all his.

The whole system of executive perquisites — tangible evidence that the tycoon is someone special — is tailored to the tycoon's need for power. There are company jets to take him to the far corners of his empire and helicopters to fetch him from his summer home. If he needs a new suit or a haircut, the tailor or the barber will come to him.

Tycoons are extremely competitive and take intense pleasure in winning. People who disdain or fear competition never get very far, because business really boils down to an endless series of hard-fought contests.

It is surely no coincidence that a disproportionately large number of tycoons competed in sports. Donald Kendall of Pepsico and Robert Anderson of Rockwell International both attended college on football scholarships, and David Mahoney of Norton Simon won a basketball scholarship. Mahoney recalls that "the coaches I had in school were among the most important people in my life. Their whole idea was that you have to reach out, that you can, you should, put out your best — and if you put out your best you should win." Mahoney says he bitterly hates to lose. "Show me a good loser, I'll show you a loser," is a favorite apothegm.

Most tycoons possess intelligence well beyond the ordinary. Nevertheless, persistence is more important than intelligence for the man who hopes to reach the top in business. "Men of very high intellectual caliber are often strikingly ineffectual," writes Peter F. Drucker, the renowned management consultant. "They often fail to realize that a single insight is not in itself achievement and performance." His sentiment is echoed by Henry Singleton, the founder of Teledyne. "Many people who don't have extraordinary intelligence do extraordinary things," Singleton says. "They just keep plugging away."

Tycoons are compulsively curious. This trait manifests itself quite early in their careers — the budding tycoon refuses to stay put in his office and wanders into other departments, asking questions, offering suggestions, generally making a nuisance of himself. Even after he has moved up, the tycoon remains obsessed with details. John DeButts, former chief executive of AT&T, occasionally tagged along with maintenance men and helped them install telephones or repair cables. In a Fortune profile of DeButts, one of his vice presidents recalls "accompanying the boss past a room in which 70 or 80 people were working at desks. 'John,' I said, 'I wonder what all those people are doing.' DeButts, with a slight edge to his voice, replied, 'Donald, I know what they're doing.'"

Tycoons also possess certain other traits that make them different. They are masterful opportunists, keenly alert to any chance for personal advancement. They are tougher and more aggressive than other people. They also know how to get along, how to ingratiate themselves with their superiors on the way up.

Above all they are True Believers. They believe in their jobs; they believe in their products; they believe in their companies; and they believe in the free-enterprise system. And why shouldn't they? It has worked for them.

3

전쟁! 그것은 결코 단순히 인명을 앗아가는 비극에 그치는 것이 아닙니다. 그것은 멀쩡한 사람들을 순식간에 미치광이로 만드는 가장 무서운 비극입니다. 제2차 세계대전 때의 독일인들을 생각해 보십시오. 그러기에 그것은 우리 모두가 해결해야 할 최대의 과제입니다. 여기 그 광란과 죄없는 피압박민족이 당하는 고통을 보십시오. 비록 짧지만, 이것은 많은 감동을 주는 글입니다. 필자는 이런 것이 명문이라고 생각합니다.

* 이 글은 <TIME>에서 뽑았습니다.

"They Hassle People at Whim"

Nafez Nazzal is a Palestinian who became a U.S. citizen and earned a Ph. D. in history from Georgetown University in Washington, D.C. A part-time reporter for TIME since 1977, he lives in the town of El-Bireh with his wife and two sons. His account of what life was like for one Palestinian on the West Bank last week:

An army truck screeches to a stop in front of our neighbor's house. Twelve soldiers jump out shouting. Clutching their clubs and guns, they barge onto the porch. They think that some boys who threw stones are hiding there. Our neighbor insists that there is no one except her in the house. To no avail. They demand that she give them the key to the upstairs flat. She says the owner is on a trip to the U.S., but they are not convinced. Three of them go back to their truck, get axes and saws and knock the steel door off its hinges. There is no one inside. My four-year-old son is terrified. Over and over again he says, "Bad soldiers...bad soldiers."

Shortly afterward we hear shots. The radio announces that a 17-year-old boy was killed when bullets were fired in the air to disperse protesting youths. He must have been flying in the air, I think to myself.

Stillness falls on our small town. The dead boy is taken to his home. Slowly and stoically, men, women and children come to pay their respects. In pain and anger the family carry their son to his resting place. The funeral cortege is broken up by soldiers who fire in the air and lob tear-gas canisters into the crowd. On the way home from the funeral, I see an 80-year-old man being dragged by soldiers from his front porch and forced at gunpoint to clear the streets of debris.

We awaken the next day to find all the streets leading to the center of town closed off with barbed wire, the type often used to fence confiscated land in preparation for the establishment of a settlement. An army jeep with a loudspeaker announces a curfew; no one is to step outside his home for 48 hours. A whole town seems to be placed in solitary confinement.

My son develops a severe case of bronchitis on the following day. Violating the curfew, I bundle him up and sneak through back alleys to the doctor's house. My anxiety grows, and then I feel anger and frustration as I try to pacify my son's whining demands for candy when we pass the closed stores. Just how does one explain these things to a child?

Anyone who lives on the West Bank cannot escape some sort of contact with the Israeli soldiers. For many of us, this is often brutal and dehumanizing. They hassle people at whim. They stop and search cars, sometimes even knocking off the hubcaps. They demand to see identity cards, and woe to that person who has forgotten to carry his with him. After being harassed once, I make certain I have my ID at hand before I even get dressed in the morning.

Occasionally, long and miserable nights are spent outside by people who have been roused from their sleep by soldiers and ordered to line up in the street until the following morning because someone in the neighborhood had thrown a stone at a passing Israeli vehicle. The authorities say that residents are collectively responsible for anything that happens in their neighborhood.

There is an Arab proverb to the effect that hearing about a situation is nothing compared to witnessing it with one's own eyes, not to mention living in it. It has been a frightening week in the West Bank. The feeling today is that peace has never been so far out of reach.

엄청난 악이 만들어 놓은 처참한 지옥 속에서도 식을 줄 모르는 한 '연약한' 여인의 뜨거운 인간애를 보십시오. 죄없는 사람들에게 고통을 가하는 악마들이여, 이 아름다운 인간 앞에서 무릎을 꿇고 회개하라. 그리고 자기 자신밖에 모르는 그릇된 지성인들이여, 이 여인에게서 동료 인간들에 대한 한없는 사랑을 배우라!

* 이 글은 <TIME>서평란에서 뽑았습니다.

"The Pole of Cold and Cruelty"

BY PATRICIA BLAKE

"Poetry is power," observed Osip Mandelstam, Russia's great 20th century poet who died some time in the late '30s in a Soviet concentration camp. "Poetry is respected only in this country — people are killed for it. There's no place where more people are killed for it."

In Stalin's time, certainly, poetry had the power to arouse the wrath of a dictator bent on destroying his country's intellectual and spiritual resources. At the same time, poetry had the power to console Stalin's victims, as has been amply documented in the writings of survivors of Stalin's gigantic Gulag of prisons, camps and places of exile. A compelling example is Eugenia Ginzburg's description of solitary confinement in a maximum-security prison in Yaroslavl. A former schoolteacher and an ardent Communist, Ginzburg was arrested in 1937, like millions of other innocent citizens caught up in Stalin's Great Terror. Lying in a glacial underground punishment cell, where rats scuttled past her face, she asked herself: "What was I to do? Of course — there was always, poetry! I recited Pushkin, Bolk, Nekrasov and Tyutchev." She then composed a poem of her own:

> *A flagstone is my only cushion,*
> *But Pushkin, sitting in one corner,*
> *Sings me a song...*

> *And, unseen by any guard,*
> *Another priceless friend*
> *Comes into my cell —*
> *His name is Alexander Blok.*

"Poetry, at least, they could not take away from me!" she thought. "They had taken my dress, my shoes and stockings, and my comb, they had left me half naked and freezing, but this it was not in their power to take away, it was and remained mine. And I should survive even this dungeon."

That haunting passage is from *Journey into the Whirlwind*, the first volume of Ginzburg's memoirs, published in the U.S. in 1967. There, she began recounting the 18 years she spent in the Gulag, mostly in the Arctic death camps of Kolyma. In this, the second volume (*Within the Whirlwind*), Ginzburg, who died in 1977, picked up her story about "the gradual transformation of a naive young Communist idealist into someone who had tasted unforgettably the fruits of the tree of the knowledge of good and evil."

Evil abounds in the world evoked by Ginzburg. The Kolyma region where she was ultimately imprisoned was the largest and most terrible of the Stalin-era concentration-camp complexes, stretching a thousand miles from the Arctic Ocean to the Sea of Okhotsk. Alexander Solzhenitsyn has called Kolyma "the pole of cold and cruelty." It was a place of massacre, where 3 million died, the men digging for gold under the permafrost, the women felling trees at temperatures of -56° F. Young men dispatched to the mines quickly succumbed to tuberculosis. Ginzburg, who acted for a time as a medical assistant, reckoned that "something like a thousand" died in her arms. Among her own ordeals was a 46-mile forced march across the frozen taiga, while seven husky, well-fed guards escorted her in relays.

Excerpt

"There, inside the barbed wire, I came across this gift for sharing the happiness of others. I had always noticed that people's faces light up when they are watching some little wild animal that has strayed into a built-up area. How their faces are transformed!

> The same transformation occurred in the faces of prisoners when one of their number was being released. It was an expression of selfless joy. To see a squirrel or a hedgehog that by some miracle has strayed into a town garden is to make contact with nature. To see someone emerging on the far side of the barbed wire was to make contact with freedom."

How did she survive to bear witness to these unspeakable happenings? In his moving introduction to her book, the German Nobel-prizewinning novelist Heinrich Böll notes that though many shared Ginzburg's experience, "very few can narrate it, even fewer can write about it, and it is these few who transform personal experience into testimony." Ginzburg tells us that her book was the "main object" of her life in captivity. Like Solzhenitsyn, she committed names, facts and events to memory by incorporating them into long rhymed poems that she could more easily memorize.

Once again, poetry, her own and that of others, was the thread that tied her to humanity. Poetry served her also when she was reunited with her younger son Vasya. (Her elder had died of hunger after her arrest.)

By then the 16-year-old Vasya was a stranger. He had been four when his mother was taken away, and he was dispatched to one of the orphanages for the children of the enemies of the people. In Kolyma, mother and son found a means of communicating with each other by reciting poetry during their first night together. Those lines, she recalls, were "a bulwark against the inhumanity of the real world…a form of resistance." Vasya (who grew up to be the brilliant Russian novelist Vasili Aksyonov) told her: "Now I understand what a mother is…you can recite your favorite verses to her, and if you stop she will go on from the line where you left off."

The most remarkable feature of Ginzburg's narrative is the decency and kindness she encountered in the Arctic inferno. She describes the kinship that developed among political prisoners as "the strongest of all human relationships," citing innumerable examples of their virtually suicidal generosity to one another. Alongside her portraits of cruel or monstrously indifferent guards and camp administrators are some of men and women capable of acts of compassion. One camp commander, whom she describes as a "peculiar specimen," intervened again and again to save her and her camp lover, later her husband, the prisoner-physician Anton Walter.

Ginzburg experienced not only friendship and love in Kolyma but also snatches of happiness. The post-Stalin years found her desirous, not of bloody vengeance, like many ex-prisoners, but of telling her story of good and evil to Russia and the world. As her husband observed, "You just aren't very good at hating."

How striking is the difference between Ginzburg's account of the camps and that of Solzhenitsyn, whose governing passion in the writing of *The Gulag Archipelago* was an unconquerable rage. No outsider in the West can hazard a judgment as to why the experience of the Gulag should have softened the heart of one prisoner while it hardened the purpose of another. Unquestionably, both pieces of testimony contain their own profound truth.

5

여기 또 한 사람이 있습니다. 이름도 없는 한 사나이가 차디찬 한 겨울의 강물 속에 있습니다. 동료 인간들을 구하기 위해 자신을 바친 하느님의 친동생같은 사나이가 있습니다. 하느님보다 먼저 섬기고 싶은 한 인간이 있습니다. 영원히 섬기고 싶은 한 인간이 있습니다.

* 이 글은 <TIME> Essay란에 실렸던 것입니다.

The Man in the Water

BY ROGER ROSENBLATT

As disasters go, this one was terrible, but not unique, certainly not among the worst on the roster of U.S. air crashes. There was the unusual element of the bridge, of course, and the fact that the plane clipped it at a moment of high traffic, one routine thus intersecting another and disrupting both. Then, too, there was the location of the event. Washington, the city of form and regulations, turned chaotic, deregulated, by a blast of real winter and a single slap of metal on metal. The jets from Washington National Airport that normally swoop around the presidential monuments like famished gulls are, for the moment, emblemized by the one that fell; so there is that detail. And there was the aesthetic clash as well — blue-and-green Air Florida, the name a flying garden, sunk down among gray chunks in a black river. All that was worth noticing, to be sure. Still, there was nothing very special in any of it, except death, which, while always special, does not necessarily bring millions to tears or to attention. Why, then, the shock here?

Perhaps because the nation saw in this disaster something more than a mechanical failure. Perhaps because people saw in it no failure at all, but rather something successful about their makeup. Here, after all, were two forms of nature in collision: the elements and human character. Last Wednesday, the elements, indifferent as ever, brought down Flight 90. And on that same afternoon, human nature — groping and flailing in mysteries of its own — rose to the occasion.

Of the four acknowledged heroes of the event, three are able to account for their behavior. Donald Usher and Eugene Windsor, a park police helicopter team, risked their lives every time they dipped the skids into the water to pick up survivors. On television, side by side in bright blue jumpsuits, they described their courage as all in the line of duty. Lenny Skutnik, a 28-year-old employee of the Congressional Budget Office, said: "It's something I never thought I would do" — referring to his jumping into the water to drag an injured woman to shore. Skutnik added that "somebody had to go in the water," delivering every hero's line that is no less admirable for its repetitions. In fact, nobody had to go into the water. That somebody actually did so is part of the reason this particular tragedy sticks in the mind.

But the person most responsible for the emotional impact of the disaster is the one known at first simply as "the man in the water." (Balding, probably in his 50s, an extravagant mustache.) He was seen clinging with five other survivors to the tail section of the airplane. This man was described by Usher and Windsor as appearing alert and in control. Every time they lowered a lifeline and flotation ring to him, he passed it on to another of the passengers. "In a mass casualty, you'll find people like him," said Windsor. "But I've never seen one with that commitment." When the helicopter came back for him, the man had gone under. His selflessness was one reason the story held national attention; his anonymity another. The fact that he went unidentified invested him with a universal character. For a while he was Everyman, and thus proof (as if one needed it) that no man is ordinary.

Still, he could never have imagined such a capacity in himself. Only minutes before his character was tested, he was sitting in the ordinary plane among the ordinary passengers, dutifully listening to the stewardess telling him to fasten his seat belt and saying something about the "no smoking sign." So our man relaxed with the others, some of whom would owe their lives to him. Perhaps he started to read, or to doze, or to regret some harsh remark made in the office that morning. Then suddenly he knew that the trip would not be ordinary. Like every other person on that flight, he was desperate to live, which makes his final act so stunning.

For at some moment in the water he must have realized that he would not live if he continued to hand over the rope and ring to others. He *had* to know it, no matter how gradual the effect of the cold. In his judgment he had no choice. When the helicopter took off with what was to be the last survivor, he watched everything in the world move away from him, and he deliberately let it happen.

Yet there was something else about the man that kept our thoughts on him, and which keeps our thoughts on him still. He was *there*, in the essential, classic circumstance. Man in nature. The man in the water. For its part, nature cared nothing about the five passengers. Our man, on the other hand, cared totally. So the timeless battle commenced in the Potomac. For as long as that man could last, they went at each other, nature and man; the one making no distinctions of good and evil, acting on no principles, offering no lifelines; the other acting wholly on distinctions, principles and, one supposes, on faith.

Since it was he who lost the fight, we ought to come again to the conclusion that people are powerless in the world. In reality, we believe the reverse, and it takes the act of the man in the water to remind us of our true feelings in this matter. It is not to say that everyone would have acted as he did, or as Usher, Windsor and Skutnik. Yet whatever moved these men to challenge death on behalf of their fellows is not peculiar to them. Everyone feels the possibility in himself. That is the abiding wonder of the story. That is why we would not let go of it. If the man in the water gave a lifeline to the people gasping for survival, he was likewise giving a lifeline to those who observed him.

The odd thing is that we do not even really believe that the man in the water lost his fight. "Everything in Nature contains all the powers of Nature," said Emerson. Exactly. So the man in the water had his own natural powers. He could not make ice storms, or freeze the water until it froze the blood. But he could hand life over to a stranger, and that is a power of nature too. The man in the water pitted himself against an implacable, impersonal enemy; he fought it with charity; and he held it to a standoff. He was the best we can do.

번잡한 도시에서 정신없이 끌려가다 보면 때로는 주저앉고 싶은 생각이 듭니다. 그동안 까맣게 잊고 살아온 아늑한 자연의 품 안으로 돌아가고 싶은 때가 있습니다. 너무 빨리 달리는 차를 멈추고 내려서 잠시 쉬고픈 때가 있습니다. 좀 느긋하게 살고픈 마음이 있습니다. 가끔은 뒤도 돌아보면서.

* 이 글은 필자가 대학 3학년 가을에 쓴 것으로 <THE KOREA TIMES> (November 24, 1968)에 실린 것을 손을 대지 않고 그대로 실었습니다.

Fall Leads Man 'Inward'

BY KIM YOUNG-NO

O you poor creature! Where are you going with such a machine-like pace, downcast eyes red and bleary with dust? Where is your soul? You are so absent-minded, so shackled by and so tied to your routine which runs on as monotonous a track as that of the train, preoccupied all your waking hours with nothing but trifles and squabbles, killing your priceless, irrecoverable time with no pangs in your mind.

Poor slave! You are so badly shorn all of you and yours that there is no leisure left in your mind even to stop your mechanical walk to raise your head to see this speckless autumn sky over your head. Blind, though you have eyes; deaf, though you have ears; you cannot smell, though you have your nose; you cannot sing the delights of nature, though you have your mouth. O miserable creature, for what are you living?

Thus speaks a Zarathustra in a deep corner of my innermost self. It is a voice, faint and distant, which comes through the tide of the season of "return to nature," knocking on the door of my mind every now and again when I happen to cock my head, exhausted to the core of every cell with hours of brains-racking work at school, to those lovely gingko trees and dazzling maples, gorgeously clad in their autumnal garments, in the brilliant foliage of which shafts of the setting sun are basking in a gentle breeze, exchanging caresses in eager affection and reluctant adieus.

Theirs, however, is not a world of hustle and bustle, but of placidity and serenity. They never try to tempt you; they are merely there, enjoying themselves in a manner, calm and serene, like an old woman, well settled in her senior years, living contentedly in the reminiscences of green days of spring and of naked joys under the baking suns of summer.

But that is enough to captivate the sensitive eyes and ears of mind. My mind, long dormant and secluded in its narrow domain all through the sweating and stormy days of summer, is wide awake by now and drifts in the crisp breeze to a deep mountain valley, my usual spiritual resort while I am in dire distress, where under the splendid canopy of sprawling trees a grandiose autumnal feast is taking place amid a grand symphony of the pleasant murmurings of little streams, of the merry tunes of small birds, and of the whisperings of the cool breeze.

Have you ever heard a finer orchestra? The Beethoven's Sixth? No, it is not equal to that natural song of most melodious harmony. In what a lovely manner they are performing what is composed by no other beings but by their own hearts and minds, so exquisite and so delicate. What is more, their tune sometimes outruns a storm in vigor. It flows and flows, allowing no other voice to interfere in it.

There you have lost your word! How small and meager a man is in the great immensity of the universe! He is merely a grain of sand in the vast Sahara. And perhaps much, much, much less than that, I wonder.

You want a shout of your own there in the valley? Good, then move just a little and keep some distance from the scene and shout as much as you please. You will get whole-hearted rejoinders from the Echo. She is so friendly to everyone if only one is first kind enough to her. She is really a true friend of the lonely heart, who knows no perfidious things. But remember it is all from your own MIND!

Poor creature, you are still much of a snob. Take off, at least, your coat. The breeze is so sorry. She cannot caress your breast.

Good! You are now with Nature — in her tender arms and breast, surrounded by her pretty, brisk angels. How wonderful!

How about taking a walk through this leaf-carpeted lane flanked by flaming maples and pine trees? Forget all and just enjoy some strolling around, the sun is still way up in the sky. If lucky, you'll soon find yourself at an elegant temple, however weathered and shaky it may be, which stands surrounded by a fine grove of pine trees, commanding a wonderful view, at a sunny and cozy nook in the valley.

Remember, however, you should keep your head lifted high all the time lest this rare journey in a wonderland should be spoiled by unexpected "earthly" things.

Well, have you taken 108 turns round the tower, delicately cut in stone, in the garden? According to the Buddhistic legend here, it will relieve you of all those "108 agonies of life."

Now turn your head to the priests there and watch how they go about their work. What a simple life they are leading! The simple food they eat, the simple robes they wear, the simple, unsophisticated look on their unfurrowed faces — their life is simplicity itself, a true embodiment of simple life. Even time, the "Merciless Destroyer," has not left its scratches on their shiny foreheads, as serene as the statue of Buddha.

You have now spent a lot of time here, the sun is now on the western mountain top, tinging the whole world in auras of burning red and yellow. A lovely picture! You could not forget those tantalizing looks of the setting sun. What does he miss so much, shooting so ardent backward glances over his shoulders?

But the appearance often deceives. Please don't be mistaken about this falling season. Autumn's looks should not be allowed to be compared to those of a fretful old woman who watches the fleeting of steady-paced time with an uneasy, tearful eye, looking, on the other hand, back through the roughly-drawn lines on her face into her good old days with a sort of miserable nostalgia.

The word "fall" is quite appropriate to depict the most essential characteristic of the season. The falling leaves show us to where we all eventually return. Well may you recall here a line from T.S. Eliot: "All pilgrimages lead home," home where we all start from. Thus leaves are on their way back home, the bosom of the earth which mothered and brought them up all through the drowsy days of spring and the scorching droughts and the nuzzling floods of capricious summer days, like a dedicated mother tends her dear children with an ever warm heart and mind.

Autumn thus enables us to see not merely the surface of Nature, but beneath it, far, far down into the deep, consequently, the innermost self of our beings. It leads us into a long journey inward, as Dag Hammarskjold put it.

Autumn is also a season of ascent, for the ever-highering firmament yonder. Thus God shows us here the most wonderful harmony between Earth and Heaven — in other words, the most spectacular example of the resolution of what William Butler Yeats called "antinomies" of life. If you turn to history, you will find many star-like examples who pursued all their lives this ultimate goal of life, most outstanding among them are Heraclitus, Virgil, Christ, Buddha, Confucius, and many others.

O you steady Nature, you always travel far ahead of this poor creature, leaving behind only your shadows, elusive like the rainbow in the empty air, a mirage in the desert. This morning, not this morning alone but every morning, I got up to find you already way up in the eastern sky. Tonight again, as usual, I must stop here to sleep, to get some rest for this exhausted soul.

But you never pause even a second — your wheels are on the constant, eternal turning around. How could I, so much so slow-paced like this, keep pace with you? Please let me know the way! The argument that man is at once a transtemporal and transspatial being seems ridiculous, at least at this moment. O thou steady-paced Nature!

살아 있는 모든 사람들이 가끔은 생각해 보아야 할 한 가지 엄숙한 사실이 있습니다. 그것은 우리에게 주어진 시간이 제한되어 있다는 것입니다. 그러기에 사람은 누구나 보람있게 살기를 갈망합니다. 여기 사랑하는 딸을 바깥 세상으로 내보내는 대학 졸업식에서 한 아버지가 들려주는 얘기를 들어 보십시오. 아마 당신이 인생을 보람있게 살아가는 데 도움을 얻을 수 있을 것입니다.

* 이 글은 <Reader's Digest>에서 뽑았습니다.

"Dig Into the World"

BY ALAN ALDA

The best things said come last. People will talk for hours saying nothing much and then linger at the door with words that come with a rush from the heart.

We are gathered at a doorway today. We linger there with our hand on the knob chattering away like Polonius to Laertes. Now remember, *Neither a borrower nor a lender be...* and don't forget, *This above all: To thine own self be true...*

But the very best things said often slip out completely unheralded, preceded by, "Oh, by the way." In real life, when Polonius had finished giving all that fatherly advice to his son — who probably wasn't paying much attention anyway — he must have said, "Oh, by the way, if you get into any trouble, don't forget you can always call me at the office."

As we stand in the doorway today, these are my parting words to my daughter. There are so many things I want to tell you, Eve.

The first thing is: don't be scared. You're being flung into a world that's running about as smoothly as a car with square wheels. It's okay to be uncertain. You're an adult in a time when the leaders of the world are behaving like children. Where the central image of the day is a terrorist one: humane concerns inhumanely expressed. And the only response to this is impotent fury. If you weren't a little uncertain. I'd be nervous for you.

Adulthood has come upon you and you're not all that sure you're ready for it. I think that sometimes I'm not ready for adulthood either — yours or mine.

The day before yesterday you were a baby. I was afraid to hold you because you seemed so fragile. Yesterday, all I could feel was helplessness when you broke your nine-year-old arm. Only this morning you were a teenager. As I get older, the only thing that speeds up is time. But if time is a thief, time also leaves something in exchange: experience. And with experience, at least in your own work you will be sure.

Love your work. If you always put your heart into everything you do, you really can't lose. Whether you wind up making a lot of money or not, you will have had a wonderful time, and no one will ever be able to take that away from you.

I want to squeeze things great and small into this lingering good-by. I want to tell you to keep laughing. You gurgle when you laugh. Be sure to gurgle three times a day for your own well-being. And if you can get other people to join you in your laughter, you may help keep this shaky boat afloat. When people are laughing, they're generally not killing one another.

I have this helpless urge to pass on maxims to you, things that will see you through. But even the Golden Rule doesn't seem adequate to pass on to a daughter. There should be something added to it. Here's my Golden Rule for a tarnished age: Be fair with others, but then keep after them until they're fair with you.

It's a complex world. I hope you'll learn to make distinctions. A peach is not its fuzz, a toad is not its warts, a person is not his or her crankiness. If we can make distinctions, we can be tolerant, and we can get to the heart of our problems instead of wrestling endlessly with their gross exteriors.

Once you make a habit of making distinctions, you'll begin challenging your own assumptions. Your assumptions are your windows on the world. Scrub them off every once in a while, or the light won't come in. If you challenge your own, you won't be so quick to accept the unchallenged assumptions of others. You'll be a lot less likely to be caught up in bias or prejudice or be influenced by people who ask you to hand over your brains, your soul or money because they have everything all figured out for you.

Be as smart as you can, but remember that it's always better to be wise than to be smart. And don't be upset that it takes a long, long time to find wisdom. Like a rare virus, wisdom tends to break out at unexpected times, and it's mostly people with compassion and understanding who are susceptible to it.

The door is inching a little closer toward the latch and I still haven't said it. Let me dig a little deeper. Life is absurd and meaningless — unless you bring meaning to it, unless you make something of it. It is up to us to create our own existence.

No matter how loving or loved we are, it eventually occurs to most of us that deep down inside, we're all alone. When the moment comes for you to wrestle with that cold loneliness, which is every person's private monster, I want you to face the damn thing. I want you to see it for what it is and win.

When I was in college, 25 years ago, the philosophy of existentialism was very popular. We all talked about nothingness; but we moved into a world of effort and endeavor. Now no one much talks about nothingness; but the world itself is filled with it.

Whenever that sense of absurdity hits you, I want you to be ready. It will have a hard time getting hold of you if you're already in motion. You can use the skills of your profession and other skills you have learned here, dig into the world and push it into better shape.

For one thing, you can try to clean the air and water. Or you can try to make the justice system work, too. You can bring the day a little closer when the rich and privileged have to live by the same standards as the poor and the outcast.

You can try to put an end to organized crime — that happy family whose main objective is to convince us they don't exist while they destroy a generation with drugs and suck the life from our economy.

You can try to find out why people of every country and religion have at one time or another found it so easy to make other people suffer. (If you really want to grapple with absurdity, try understanding how people can be capable of both nurture and torture; can worry and fret over a little girl caught in a mine shaft, yet destroy a village and everyone in it with hardly the blink of an eye). You can try to stop the next war now, before it starts, to keep old men from sending children away to die.

And while you're doing all of that, remember that every right you have as a woman was won for you by women fighting hard. There are little girls being born right now who won't even have the same rights you do unless you act to maintain and extend that range of equality. The nourishing stew of civilized life doesn't keep bubbling on its own. Put something back in the pot for the people in line behind you.

There's plenty to keep you busy for the rest of your life. I can't promise this will ever completely reduce that sense of absurdity, but it may get it down to a manageable level. It will allow you once in a while to bask in the feeling that, all in all, things do seem to be moving forward.

I can see your brow knitting in that way that I love. That crinkle between your eyebrows that signals your doubt and your skepticism. Why — on a day of such excitement and hope — should I be talking of absurdity and nothingness? Because I want you to focus that hope and level that excitement into coherent rays that will strike like a laser at the targets of our discontent.

I want you to be potent; to do good when you can, and to hold your wit and your intelligence like a shield against other people's wantonness. And above all, to laugh and enjoy yourself in a life of your own choosing and in a world of your own making. I want you to be strong and aggressive and tough and resilient and full of feeling. I want you to be everything that's you, deep at the center of your being.

I want you to have chutzpah. Nothing important was ever accomplished without chutzpah. Columbus had chutzpah. The signers of the Declaration of Independence had chutzpah. Laugh at yourself, but don't ever aim your doubt at yourself. Be bold. When you embark for strange places, don't leave any of yourself safely on shore. Have the nerve to go into unexplored territory.

Be brave enough to live life creatively. The creative is the place where no one else has ever been. You have to leave the city of your comfort and go into the wilderness of your intuition. You can't get there by bus, only by hard work and risk and by not quite knowing what you're doing. What you'll discover will be wonderful. What you'll discover will be yourself.

Well, those are my parting words as today's door closes softly between us. So long, be happy…

Oh, by the way, I love you.

8

세상에 이처럼 훌륭한 인간이 언제 또 나올 수 있을까요? 주여, 비록 제가 공식적으로 등록된 당신의 아들은 아닐지라도, 이럴 때에는 당신의 이름을 부르고픈 심정을 이해해 주소서. 광활한 대우주의 작은 한 점 지구에 태어난 '하나의 돌' — 정말 당신은 위대한 인간이었습니다. 제가 당신을 위대한 사람으로 섬기고 있는 것은 물리학자로서 당신의 위대한 공헌보다는 동료 인간에 대한 당신의 잔잔한 사랑 때문입니다. 주여, 이런 분들을 저희에게 더 많이 보내주소서.

* 이 글은 역시 <Reader's Digest>에서 뽑았습니다.

Unforgettable Albert Einstein

BY BANESH HOFFMANN

He was one of the greatest scientists the world has ever known. Yet if I had to convey the essence of Albert Einstein in a single word, I would choose simplicity. Perhaps an anecdote will help. Once, caught in a downpour, he took off his hat and held it under his coat. Asked why, he explained, with admirable logic, that the rain would damage the hat, but his hair would be none the worse for its wetting. This knack for going instinctively to the heart of a matter was the secret of his major scientific discoveries — this and his extraordinary feeling for beauty.

I first met Albert Einstein in 1935, at the famous Institute for Advanced Study in Princeton, N.J. Einstein had been among the first to be invited to the Institute, and was offered carte blanche as to salary. To the director's dismay, Einstein asked for an impossible sum: it was far too small. The director had to plead with him to accept a larger salary.

I was in awe of Einstein, and hesitated before approaching him about some ideas I had been working on. My hesitation proved unwarranted. When I finally knocked on his door, a gentle voice said, "Come" — with a rising inflection that made the single word both a welcome and a question. I entered his office and found him seated at a table, calculating and smoking his pipe. Dressed in ill-fitting clothes, his hair characteristically awry, he smiled a warm welcome. His utter naturalness at once set me at ease.

As I began to explain my ideas, he asked me to write the equations on the blackboard so that he could see how they developed. Then came the staggering — and altogether endearing — request: "Please go slowly. I do not understand things quickly." This from Einstein! He said it gently, and I laughed. From then on, all vestiges of fear were gone.

Burst of Genius. Einstein was born in 1879 in the German city of Ulm. He had been no infant prodigy; indeed, he was so late in learning to speak that his parents feared he was a dullard. In school, though his teachers saw no special talent in him, the signs were already there. He taught himself calculus, for example, and he told me that his teachers seemed a little afraid of him because he asked questions they could not answer. At the age of 16, he asked himself whether a light wave would seem stationary if one ran abreast of it. It seems an innocent question, but this shows Einstein going to the heart of a problem. From it there would arise, ten years later, his theory of relativity.

Einstein failed his entrance examinations at the Swiss Federal Polytechnic School, in Zurich but was admitted a year later. There he went beyond his regular work to study the masterworks of physics on his own. Rejected when he applied for academic positions, he ultimately found work, in 1902, as a patent examiner in Berne, and there, in 1905, his genius burst into fabulous flower.

Among the extraordinary things he produced in that memorable year were his theory of relativity, with its famous offshoot, $E = mc^2$ (energy equals mass times the speed of light squared), and his quantum theory of light. These two theories were not only revolutionary, but seemingly self-contradictory as well: the former was intimately linked to the theory that light consists of waves; while the latter said that it consists somehow of particles. Yet this unknown young man boldly proposed both at once — and he was right in both cases, though how he could possibly have been is far too complex a story to tell here.

Mental Magic. Collaborating with Einstein was an unforgettable experience. In 1937, the Polish physicist Leopold Infeld and I asked if we could work with him. He was pleased with the proposal, since he had an idea about gravitation waiting to be worked out in detail. Thus we got to know not merely the man and the friend, but also the professional.

The intensity and depth of his concentration were fantastic. When battling a recalcitrant problem, he worried it as an animal worries its prey. Often, when we found ourselves up against a seemingly insuperable difficulty, he would stand up, put his pipe on the table, and say in his quaint English, "I will a little tink," (he could not pronounce "th") then he would pace up and down, twirling a lock of his long, graying hair around his forefinger.

A dreamy, faraway and yet inward look would come over his face. There was no appearance of concentration, no furrowing of the brow — only a placid inner communion. The minutes would pass, and then suddenly Einstein would stop pacing as his face relaxed into a gentle smile. He had found the solution to the problem. Sometimes it was so simple that Infeld and I could have kicked ourselves for not having thought of it. But the magic had been performed invisibly in the depths of Einstein's mind, by a process we could not fathom.

When his wife died he was deeply shaken, but insisted that now more than ever was the time to be working hard. I vividly remember going to his house to work with him during that sad time. His face was haggard and grief-lined, but he put forth a great effort to concentrate. Seeking to help him, I steered the discussion away from routine matters into more difficult theoretical problems, and Einstein gradually became absorbed in the discussion. We kept at it for some two hours, and at the end his eyes were no longer sad. As I left, he thanked me with moving sincerity, but the words he found sounded almost incongruous. "It was a fun," he said. He had had a moment of surcease from grief, and these groping words expressed a deep emotion.

Ideas From God. Although Einstein felt no need for religious ritual and belonged to no formal religious group, he was the most deeply religious man I have known. He once said to me, "Ideas come from God," and one could hear the capital "G" in the reverence with which he pronounced the word. On the marble fireplace in the mathematics building at Princeton University is carved, in the original German, what one might call his scientific credo: "God is subtle, but he is not malicious." By this Einstein meant that scientists could expect to find their task difficult, but not hopeless: the Universe was a Universe of law, and God was not confusing us with deliberate paradoxes and contradictions.

Einstein was an accomplished amateur musician. We used to play duets, he on the violin, I at the piano. One day he surprised me by saying that Mozart was the greatest composer of all. Beethoven, he said, "created" his music, but the music of Mozart was of such purity and beauty that one felt he had merely "found" it — that it had always existed as part of the inner beauty of the Universe, waiting to be revealed.

It was this very Mozartean simplicity that most characterized Einstein's methods. His 1905 theory of relativity, for example, was built on just two simple assumptions. One is the so-called principle of relativity, which means, roughly speaking, that we cannot tell whether we are at rest or moving smoothly. The other assumption is that the speed of light is the same no matter what the speed of the object that produces it. You can see how reasonable this is if you think of agitating a stick in a lake to create waves. Whether you wiggle the stick from a stationary pier, or from a rushing speedboat, the waves, once generated, are on their own, and their speed has nothing to do with that of the stick.

Each of these assumptions, by itself, was so plausible as to seem primitively obvious. But together they were in such violent conflict that a lesser man would have dropped one or the other and fled in panic. Einstein daringly kept both — and by so doing he revolutionized physics. For he demonstrated that they could, after all, exist peacefully side by side, provided we gave up cherished beliefs about the nature of time.

Science is like a house of cards, with concepts like time and space at the lowest level. Tampering with time brought most of the house tumbling down, and it was this that made Einstein's work so important — and so controversial. At a conference in Princeton in honor of his 70th birthday, one of the speakers, a Nobel Prize winner, tried to convey the magical quality of Einstein's achievement. Words failed him, and with a shrug of helplessness he pointed to his wristwatch, and said in tones of awed amazement, "It all came from this." His very ineloquence made this the most eloquent tribute I have heard to Einstein's genius.

Sand Sense. Although fame had little effect on Einstein as a person, he could not escape it; he was, of course, instantly recognizable. One autumn Saturday, I was walking with him in Princeton discussing some technical matters. Parents and alumni were streaming excitedly toward the stadium, their minds on the coming football game. As they approached us, they paused in sudden recognition, and a momentary air of solemnity came over them as if they had been reminded of a world far removed from the thrills of football. Yet Einstein seemed totally unaware of the effect he was having on them, and went on with the discussion as though they were not there.

We think of Einstein as one concerned only with the deepest aspects of science. But he saw scientific principles in everyday things to which most of us would give barely a second thought. He once asked me if I had ever wondered why a man's feet will sink into either dry or completely submerged sand, while sand that is merely damp provides a firm surface. When I could not answer, he offered a simple explanation.

It depends, he pointed out, on surface tension, the elastic-skin effect of a liquid surface. This is what holds a drop together, or causes two small raindrops on a windowpane to pull into one big drop the moment their surfaces touch.

When sand is damp, Einstein explained, there are tiny amounts of water between grains. The surface tensions of these tiny amounts of water pull all the grains together, and friction then makes them hard to budge. When the sand is dry, there is obviously no water between grains. If the sand is fully immersed, there is water between grains but there is no water surface between them to pull them together. This is not as important as relativity; yet, as his youthful question about running abreast of a light wave showed, there is no telling what seeming trifle will lead an Einstein to a major discovery. And the puzzle of the sand does give us an inkling of the power and elegance of Einstein's mind.

Cosmic Simplicity. Einstein's work, performed quietly with pencil and paper, seemed remote from the turmoil of everyday life. But his ideas were so revolutionary that they caused violent controversy and irrational anger. Indeed, in order to be able to award him a belated Nobel Prize, the selection committee had to avoid mentioning relativity, and pretend that the prize was awarded primarily for the work on the quantum theory. Political events upset the serenity of his life even more. When the Nazis came to power in Germany, his theories were officially declared false because they had been formulated by a Jew. His property was confiscated, and it is said that a price was put on his head.

When scientists in the United States, fearful that the Nazis might develop an atomic bomb, sought to alert American authorities to the danger, they were scarcely heeded. In desperation, they drafted a letter which Einstein signed and sent directly to President Roosevelt. It was this act that led to the fateful decision to go all out on the production of an atomic bomb — an endeavor in which Einstein took no active part. When he heard of the agony and destruction that his $E = mc^2$ had wrought, he was dismayed beyond measure, and from then on there was a look of ineffable sadness in his eyes.

There was something elusively whimsical about Einstein. It is illustrated by my favorite anecdote about him. In his first year in Princeton, on Christmas Eve, so the story goes, some children sang carols outside his house. Having finished, they knocked on his door and explained that they were collecting money to buy Christmas presents. Einstein listened, then said, "Wait a moment." He put on his scarf and overcoat, and took his violin from its case. Then, joining the children, he accompanied their singing of "Silent Night" on his violin.

How shall I sum up what it meant to have known Einstein and his works? Like the Nobel Prize winner who pointed helplessly at his watch, I can find no adequate words. It was akin to the revelation of great art that lets one see what was formerly hidden. And when, for example, I walk on the sand of a lonely beach, I am reminded of his ceaseless search for cosmic simplicity — and the scene takes on a deeper, sadder beauty.

9

젊은 시절의 Sartre — 분명히 그는 익지 않은 떫은 과일이었습니다. 만일 그가 젊은 시절부터 인간에 대한 진정한 애정을 갖고 가슴 속에서 우러나온 철학을 했더라면 얼마나 더 많은 공헌을 했을까? 필자는 가끔 이런 시건방진 생각을 해봅니다. 그러나 사회정의 실현을 위한 그의 '행동하는 지성'을, 만년에 젊은 시절의 과오를 인정하고 다시 인간을 포용한 그의 솔직한 태도를, 그리고 늙기를 거부하는 그의 정열을 필자는 존경합니다.

* 이 글은 Sartre가 1980년 사망했을 때 <Newsweek>에 실렸던 것입니다.

Jean-Paul Sartre (1905-1980)

Jean-Paul Sartre objected in principle to obituaries: he believed that one person cannot confer meaning on another without, Medusalike, freezing him into stone. Everyone, he argued, is free to "make himself" and this "project" in self-creation can be terminated in only two ways: by surrendering individual freedom or by death. Sartre's own Promethean project came to a close last week when the ailing philosopher — perhaps the best-known intellectual of his generation — died of heart failure in a Paris hospital at the age of 74.

In the course of his prodigious career, Sartre produced some four dozen volumes of philosophy, psychology, fiction, biography, plays and literary criticism as well as sundry political tracts, film scenarios and articles. From an early preoccupation with absurdity and nothingness, he moved in middle age to questions of social justice and commitment. Although he never joined the French Communist Party, Sartre was always a man of the left longing for a truly popular revolution in France. With the abortive student revolt of May 1968, he entered a Maoist phase, deriding culture as bourgeois and trying, against his own elitist inclinations, to subordinate the aims of the intellect to the communitarian goals of youthful radicals. And then, in an altogether unexpected turn of mind, Sartre revealed during the last weeks of his life that he had embraced such mellow — almost bourgeois — values as hope, fraternity, the family and democracy.

'Bad Faith': Despite the diversity of his enthusiasms, Sartre was known chiefly as an existentialist, the popular but imprecise label for a mood as well as a movement among modern European thinkers in the period shaped by two world wars. Existentialists stressed the anxious individual's search for meaning and personal integrity in a world that provided no coherent explanation of what things are in themselves or why anything — including man — should exist.

Sartre built his existentialist philosophy on the notion that "existence precedes essence," that man has no nature which defines who he is or what he must do. On the contrary, each person must define himself for himself, from moment to moment, by making choices and living with the results. He regarded life as a never-ending process of self-creation in which the present cancels out the past and the future erases the present. To allow others — a spouse, an enemy or society — to define us is to become guilty of "bad faith" toward one's self. Thus, as he suggested in his famous play "No Exit," "Hell is other people."

By writing a beguiling autobiography of his early years, Sartre in effect dictated the terms in which he himself was to be understood. Sartre felt fortunate that his father died shortly after Jean-Paul was born because without a father, he wrote, "I have no superego." In his psychological explorations, Sartre drew a sharp Cartesian distinction between the massive, unknowable world of external things and the fluid, everchanging inner world of human consciousness. In his major philosophical work, "Being and Nothingness" he enlarged these psychological insights into a full-blown ontology of human existence.

Anxiety: But it was through his more accessible literary works, such as his novel "Nausea" and plays like "No Exit" that Sartre gained a wide popular audience for his view of the human condition as angst-ridden and despairing. Yet Sartre himself stood apart from the world he depicted. He dramatized anxiety, he said late in life, because "It was the fashion." What's more, he added, "I was never in despair, nor did I imagine despair in any way at all as something that could belong to me." Indeed, much of Sartre's literary work seems in retrospect to have been aimed at jarring the complacency of the bourgeoisie.

In the postwar years, when existentialism became an international vogue, Sartre continued to produce books from his small apartment in Montparnasse and to share his life with his companion of 50 years, writer Simone de Beauvoir.

Increasingly, Sartre's thought turned in the direction of political action. To him, there could be no separation between the intellectual and the active life; indeed, there was a moral obligation to weld them together. He was often a fellow traveler with the Communists, but broke away after the Soviet invasion of Hungary in 1956. He publicly opposed de Gaulle during the Algerian war but failed in his repeated efforts to be thrown into jail. "Sartre," de Gaulle explained, "is also France."

Revolt: In 1964, he refused the Nobel Prize in Literature, explaining that "A writer must refuse to allow himself to be transformed into an institution." Then came the students' revolt of 1968, and Sartre — almost alone among the Parisian intellectuals — continued to support the radicals despite their failure to incite a revolution among the workers.

By 1974, Sartre had lost practically all use of his left eye — the right had been blind since childhood — and high blood pressure had reduced his daily walk to less than half a mile. In losing the ability to write, he said, "I have lost my reason for being."

In his final months, he revealed an unsuspected calmness in his life and revisionism in his thinking. Surprisingly, he joined a number of conservatives in condemning the Soviet invasion of Afghanistan as well as supporting the U.S. boycott of the Moscow Olympics. In a series of interviews in the weekly *Le Nouvel Observateur*, the philosopher of lonely commitment said he had been wrong to think that "Hell is other people." "I left each individual too independent in my theory of others," he concluded. "Today, I consider that everything which occurs in one consciousness in a given moment is necessarily tied to, often engendered by...the existence of others... What is real is the relationship between thee and me." At the end of his life, Sartre proclaimed that "The left no longer exists" — he saw conservative politicians in control throughout the West — and that democracy "ought to be the way for men to live." But he continued to object to one intrusive tendency of other people — their treatment of him as an old man. "An old man never feels like an old man," the aged existentialist insisted. "It's the others who are my old age."

10

학문에서 가장 중요한 것은 방법이라고 볼 수 있습니다. 이런 점에서 Bacon은 정말 거인이었다고 할 수 있습니다. 왜냐하면 그는 현대과학의 방법론과 과학적인 추리방법을 최초로 체계화했기 때문입니다. 너무도 잘 알려져 있는 그의 '네 가지 우상'을 생각해 보십시오. 우리 인간이 빠지기 쉬운 편견을 얼마나 체계적으로 보여주고 있습니까? 이 글은 과학적인 방법론에 관심이 있는 분들은 한번쯤 읽어볼 만한 글이라 생각됩니다.

* 이 글은 <THE HISTORY OF SCIENCE>라는 책에서 뽑았습니다.

Bacon and the Experimental Method

BY C.D. BROAD, LITT. D., F.B.A.
Knightbridge Professor of Moral Philosophy in
the University of Cambridge

I will begin by giving you a very brief sketch of Bacon's life, so that you may have some idea of the kind of man that he was and the society in which he moved. He was born at York House, Strand, London, in January 1561, i.e. about two years after Queen Elizabeth came to the throne. His father was Nicholas Bacon, who held the office of Lord Keeper; and his mother was Anne Cook, whose father had been tutor to Edward VI. So we may say that Bacon's family belonged to the higher ranks of the civil service. Bacon was a very bright precocious boy, and Queen Elizabeth used to enjoy talking to him. He was sent to Cambridge as an undergraduate of Trinity College at the extremely early age of thirteen, and he left two years later. He then took up the study and practice of law, which became his profession. The Queen employed him much in legal and political business, but she seems not to have really liked him or trusted him, and he held no important office under her reign. After the accession of James I in 1603 Bacon's advancement was rapid, for the King greatly admired him. He became Lord Keeper, Lord Chancellor, and in 1620 Viscount St. Albans. He was now a very wealthy man, but a tragedy was approaching. He had always been careless with money and extravagant in his mode of life, and he had followed the common practice of his day in taking presents from suitors, though he always asserted that he had not allowed this to influence his legal judgments. However that may be, he was tried on a charge of corruption, pleaded guilty, was condemned, and had to pay a fine of £40,000 (an immense sum in those days), lost his office, and was banished from the court. This happened in 1621. Bacon lived on for another five years, a broken man. He died in April 1626. His last illness is said to have been caused by his getting out of his carriage in freezingly cold weather in order to try the experiment of stuffing the carcase of a fowl with snow to test the preservative effects of a low temperature.

Though Bacon was an able, and up to a point successful, lawyer and politician, his heart was not in that work. His one fundamental interest was to discover and propagate a general method by which men might gain scientific knowledge of the ultimate laws and structure of matter, and might thus acquire ever-increasing practical control over nature. He saw that, in order to collect the data from which the laws of nature were to be extracted by his methods, a huge organisation of research would be needed. Vast numbers of men and women, at various levels, would have to be employed, and expensive buildings and apparatus would be required. All this would be very costly. The only hope of getting adequate supplies of money and sufficient authority and prestige to start and continue such a scheme was for Bacon himself to become a rich and prominent man and for him to persuade the King and powerful noblemen and churchmen to back it. In order to do this he must be ready to turn a blind eye to their vices and follies, to humour their whims, and to play upon their weaknesses by flattery. Bacon was nothing if not thorough, and he analysed and practised with his usual acuteness and assiduity the arts of worldly success. I believe that, like many other clever idealistic men, he started by seeking wealth and power wholly, or at any rate mainly, as a means to a high impersonal end, but gradually slipped into pursuing them for their own sake. I suspect also that, as often happens with such men, he was not quite so clever, and those whom he used and despised were not quite so stupid as he imagined, and that he was seen through and distrusted much more than he realised.

If we are to appreciate Bacon's originality, farsightedness and breadth of vision and be fair to his limitations and mistakes, we must see him against the background of the science of his own day and not against that of ours. The fundamental science of dynamics, for instance, did not exist. It was founded during Bacon's lifetime by Galileo(1564-1642), who also invented the telescope and noted with it the spots on the sun and the irregularities on the moon's surface. In astronomy it was still generally held that the earth was the fixed centre of the universe, and that the sun and the planets revolved about it, the latter in complicated epicyclic orbits. The discovery of the three fundamental laws of planetary motion was made in Bacon's lifetime by Kepler(1571-1630). It was not until long after Bacon's death that Newton provided the first example of a scientific theory on the grand scale and in the modern sense, by explaining those laws and correlating them with the phenomena of falling bodies through his hypothesis of universal gravitation. Bacon's older contemporary Gilbert(1540-1603) had discovered some elementary facts about natural magnets, but the existence of electricity was unknown and its connexion with magnetism was unsuspected. Chemistry, as a science and not a mere set of recipes, did not come into existence for another hundred and fifty years. Learned men commonly accepted without question the Aristotelian theory that earthly bodies are composed of the four elements, earth, air, fire and water, and that heavenly bodies are fundamentally different, being composed of a superior fifth element, called the quintessence.

Corresponding to this lack of scientific knowledge was a lack of power over nature. The only available devices for obtaining mechanical energy were clockwork, waterwheels, and windmills. All land transport was on foot or by horse, and all water transport by rowing or sailing. Men were constantly at the mercy of local and seasonal food shortages and gluts, and were periodically decimated by epidemics, whose causes they did not understand and which they had no rational means of combating. Bacon was impressed by this impotence and its evil consequences, and he could not be expected to foresee, what we have learned since, that men can bring even greater evils upon themselves by abusing the power which science gives them than they suffered when they were powerless in the face of natural forces.

Now Bacon was completely convinced that the ignorance of nature and the consequent lack of power over nature, which had prevailed from the earliest times up to his day, were by no means inevitable. They sprang, not from any fundamental imperfection in the human mind, nor from lawlessness or inextricable complexity in nature, but simply and solely from the use of a wrong method. He felt sure that he knew the right method, and that, if only this could be substituted and applied on a large enough scale, there was no limit to the possible growth of human knowledge and human power over nature. Looking back after the event, we can see that he was right, and we may be tempted to think that it was obvious. But it was not in the least obvious at the time; it was, on the contrary, a most remarkable feat of insight and an act of rational faith in the face of present appearances and past experience.

What was wrong with the methods in use up to Bacon's time? The fundamental defects, as Bacon clearly saw, were the following. In the first place there was an almost complete divorce between theory, observation and experiment, and practical application. Plenty of experiments of a kind had been done, and a certain number of disconnected empirical rules or recipes had been discovered. But the experiments were made in the main by men like alchemists and quacksalvers. These were often, though by no means always, charlatans or half-crazy enthusiasts. But, even when they were honest and sensible men, they did their experiments with some immediate practical end in view, such as turning lead into gold or discovering a universal medicine for all diseases. They were not guided by any general theory; they did not seek to discover the all-pervading laws and the minute structure of matter; and they worked in isolation from each other, keeping their results secret rather than pooling them. Bacon valued science both as an end in itself and for the immense power over nature which he believed that it could give. He thought that the failure of contemporary physics to have any useful practical applications was a sign that it was on the wrong track. But he was firmly convinced that it is fatal for scientists to work shortsightedly at the solution of this or that particular problem. Let them concentrate, he thought, on discovering by suitably designed experiments and appropriate reasoning the fundamental laws and structure of nature. Then, and only then, could they make innumerable practical applications with complete certainty of success. Anyone who reflects on how our modern applications of electromagnetism, of chemistry, and of medicine depend respectively on the theoretical work of Faraday and Maxwell, of Dalton and Avogadro, and of Pasteur, will see how right Bacon was in this.

The second defect which Bacon found in the science of his time was on the theoretical side. During the twelfth century, when Europe had reawakened from barbarism and men had again begun to take a scientific interest in external nature, it happened that the works on physics of the Greek philosopher Aristotle were rediscovered. It happened also that the greatest and most influential thinker of the Middle Ages, St. Thomas Aquinas (1226-1274), became an enthusiastic disciple and advocate of Aristotle. Now St. Thomas was a daring innovator who had to face strong opposition. But Aristotle's physics and logic were so much better than anything else available at the time, and St. Thomas was so much abler than his opponents, that the Aristotelian methods and concepts scored a complete triumph. Thenceforth they were accepted uncritically and handed down from one generation to another. Scientists decided all questions, not by investigating the observable facts, but by appealing to the infallible authority of Aristotle, just as present-day Communists appeal to that of Marx, and Engels and Lenin. Now this would have been disastrous, even if Aristotle's physics had been sound. But although he was a very great man, his strength lay in natural history and in certain branches of deductive logic. He was no mathematician, and his theories of physics and astronomy were much inferior to those of certain other Greek philosophers.

Bacon rightly accused the learned men of his time of accepting on authority sweeping general principles, which Aristotle himself had reached by hasty and uncritical generalisation from a few rather superficial observations. Using these as premises, they proceeded to deduce conclusions about nature and to hold elaborate wrangles with each other by means of Aristotle's favourite form of reasoning, which is called the 'syllogism'. The following argument is an example of a valid syllogism: All metals are good conductors of heat, and all good conductors of electricity are metals; therefore all good conductors of electricity are good conductors of heat. Some arguments in syllogistic form are valid and others are not. Aristotle formulated the rules for distinguishing between valid and invalid syllogistic arguments. That was a very considerable achievement, but, to put it familiarly, it rather 'went to his head', and made him overestimate the importance of the syllogism. What he failed to do was to suggest any method for establishing generalisations, like 'All metals are good conductors of heat', which are needed as premises before any syllogistic argument can get started.

Bacon saw that syllogistic reasoning, however well it may be adapted for tripping up an opponent in the law courts or in Parliament, is utterly useless for discovering the laws of nature and for applying them to the solution of practical problems. What was wanted was a method by which we could slowly and cautiously rise from observed facts to wider and deeper generalisations, testing every such generalisation at each stage by deliberately looking out for possible exceptions to it, and rejecting or modifying it if we actually found such exceptions.

That process is called 'induction'. Of course, as Bacon quite well knew men have always been practising it to a certain extent in an unconscious and unsystematic way. What Bacon did was to abstract and exhibit the general principles of such reasoning, so that in future men might perform it consciously with a full knowledge of what they were doing. Perhaps his greatest service here was to show the importance of testing every generalisation by devising and performing experiments which would refute it if the result turned out in a certain way, and would confirm it if the result turned out in a certain other way.

Bacon realised that every man inherits or acquires certain mental kinks, of which he is generally quite unaware. These tend to lead us astray in our thinking, and we need to be put on our guard against them. Bacon calls these kinks by the quaint name of 'Idols'. Besides the tendency to accept on authority the dogmas of some prominent person or sect, which Bacon calls 'Idols of the Theatre', he enumerates three others, 'Idols of the Tribe' are certain unfortunate mental tendencies common to the whole human race: for instance, the tendency to notice facts which support one's beliefs and fall in with one's wishes, and to ignore or pervert those which do not. Then there are 'Idols of the Market Place'. These arise from the fact that many words and phrases embody the false beliefs and inaccurate observations of our remote ancestors, and are thus, so to speak, crystallised errors which we swallow unconsciously. Lastly, there are 'Idols of the Cave'. These are sources of error or bias which are peculiar to each individual, depending on his particular temperament and the special circumstances of his upbringing.

It is time for me to bring this chapter about Bacon to an end, though there is much more that I would like to tell you about him and his work. In conclusion I would say that he was not a practising scientist, and it would be quite unfair to judge him from that point of view. His service to science was to criticise the existing bad methods, to try to formulate the methods which should be substituted for them, and to paint a glowing picture of the power which men might acquire by such means over nature. Perhaps his main defect here was his failure to see the enormously important part which mathematics was to play in the development of science. But in other respects he showed great insight and most remarkable foresight, and he clothed his thoughts in a garment of wit and wisdom which makes his writings one of the glories of English literature.

영문독해 능력 향상의 핵심은 바로 직독직해

4th Edition

영어 순해

김영로 지음

Exercise 뜻풀이 | 여담 뜻풀이

넥서스

EXERCISE 1

1 a. 민주주의는 이론적으로는 좋으나 실천하는 것은 잘 안 된다.(민주주의의 이론과 실천과의 관계)

b. 이것은 이론적으로는 좋아 보이나 실천은 잘 안 될지 모른다.

2 a. 그는 학교에서 (공부를) 잘 하고 있다. (그와 학교 공부와의 관계)

b. 나는 확신한다, 내가 그 시험을 잘 봤다고. (나와 그 시험과의 관계)

c. 대부분의 아이들은 아주 잘 자란다, 아주 안 좋은 음식을 먹어도. (아이들의 영양 섭취와 성장과의 관계)

d. 몇 종의 물망초는 서늘하고 습한 곳에서 가장 잘 자라나, 다른 종들은 건조한 토양에서 잘 자란다. (물망초의 성장과 토양과의 관계)

e. 인도에서 열한 살 소녀가 아들을 낳았는데, 보도에 의하면 둘 다 건강하게 집에서 잘 지내고 있다고 했다. (산모와 아기의 건강 관계)

f. 헬렌은 자라는 동안에는 아무 탈이 없었다. 그러나 대학 4학년 때에는 집으로 보내는 편지가 불규칙적이기 시작했다. 전화로 얘기할 때에는 딴 일에 정신이 빠져있는 것 같았다. (헬렌과 정신 건강과의 관계)

g. "네가 술을 끊은 것은 단순히 그녀가 하라고 해서란 말이니?"
"그래."
"그리고 네가 담배를 끊은 게 같은 이유니?"
"맞아."
"그리고 네가 도박을 그만둔 것도 그녀를 위해서야?"
"그랬지."
"그럼, 그러고도, 왜 그녀와 결혼하지 않았지?"
"음, 내 생각에 내가 이렇게 단정하고, 바람직한 사람이 되었으니까, 결혼을 더 잘 할 수 있을 거라고 생각했지." (나의 향상과 결혼과의 관계)

> 요점 모든 진술은 어떤 것에 관한 얘기다. 따라서 그것이 무엇에 관한 얘기인지를 알면 그것의 의미를 파악하는 것이 쉬워진다.

3 a. 내가 생각하기에 나는 그 시험을 잘 본 것 같다.

b. 노조들은 정부의 그 계획이 법률로 제정되면 어려움을 겪게 될 것이다.

c. 1983년에, 텔레비전 광고가 9% (물가 상승율을 제하고) 성장하리라고, 업계의 관측통들이 말한다.

워터슨의 예측에 의하면 신문의 항목별 광고가 지난 한 해 동안에는 실적이 그렇게 좋지 않았으나 곧 나아지고, 이렇게 되면 전 업계가 정말로 두드러지게 성장하리라고 한다.

4 a. 이 약은 잘 듣는다, 호흡에 문제가 있을 때에.

b. 어떤 여자가 자신의 손목시계가 가지 않자 제조회사에 편지를 썼다. 회답이 없자, 그녀는 그 회사에 전보를 쳤는데, 내용은 이러했다. "저에게 귀사의 손목시계 하나가 있습니다. 몇시죠?" 이것이 효과가 있었다. 그들은 그녀에게 새 손목시계 하나를 보내주었다.

5 a. 인간사가 때로는 너무도 꼬인다. 그렇지만 사정은 언제나 결국은 풀린다.

b. "걱정하지 마라, 탐. 내가 일을 해결하려고 노력하고 있다."

c. "쟌은 아직 어느 대학원으로부터도 입학 허가를 받지 못했다."
"틀림없이 그는 일이 잘 풀릴거야."

> 주의 복수형 acceptances로 보아 그가 지원한 학교가 복수임을 알 수 있다.

EXERCISE 2

1 a. 그는 나를 걷게 해서 녹초가 되게 만들었다.

b. 그는 걸어서 녹초가 되었다.

2 a. 그는 굶어 죽었다.

b. 그는 스스로 굶어서 죽었다.

3 a. 어제판 뉴욕 타임스에 비극적이면서 희극적인 기사 한 편이 있었는데, 그 내용은 아주 뚱뚱한 어떤 여자가, 그녀의 유일한 소망이 몸무게가 주는 것이었는데, 다이어트를 하다가 죽었다는 것이었다.
   b. 단지 재채기 소리만 내도 수많은 사람들이 "감기에 걸리지 않기를"이라고 인사를 하지만 정작 감기에 걸려서 죽어라 기침을 하면 역겹다는 듯이 바라볼 뿐이다.
   c. "Nathaniel이 저에게 말했어요, 그가 죽도록 제가 바라야 한다고요. 그래서 그렇게 했어요. 그랬더니 그가 죽었어요."
      "그러나 그건 가능하지 않아. 누가 죽기를 바란다고 그가 죽는 건 아니야."

4 a. 그는 허겁지겁 음식을 먹기 시작했다. 며칠 동안 음식을 못 본 것처럼.
   b. 날마다 나는 걸어서 행복을 얻고 걸어서 모든 질병에서 벗어난다. 나는 걸어서 가장 좋은 생각을 하게 되었다.

5 a. 넌 자라서 네 형의 옷을 입을 수 있을 거야, 멀지 않아서.
   b. 그녀는 곧 경험을 쌓아서 그 일을 하게 되었다, 처음에는 그 일을 할 자격이 없었지만. (그녀와 그 일과의 관계)

   > a에서의 성장(growing)이 신체적인 것이라면, b에서의 성장은 정신적인 것이다.

6 a. 기억해라, 우리가 너를 웃음거리로 만들어서 정계에서 쫓아낼 수 있다는 것을.
   b. 그는 심각하게 자살을 생각했으나, 그것이 부당하다고 생각해서 자살을 그만두었다.
   c. 설득을 통해 어떤 사람을 편견에서 벗어나게 하려고 하지 마라. 그것은 설득을 통해서 갖게 된 것이 아니었으므로 설득을 통해서 없앨 수는 없다.
   d. 그녀는 그 위험한 공연을 못하게 그를 설득할 수 없자, 헬렌에게 말려 달라고 부탁했다.
   e. 추측컨대 그가 얘기하려고 했던 것은 다만 그가 생각하기에 쿠바와 협상해서 앙골라에서 물러가게 하는 것이 백인 소수민족과 협상해서 남아프리카 공화국의 권좌에서 물러가게 하는 것보다 더 쉬울 거라는 뜻이었던 것 같다. 그러나 그게 그가 (실제로) 한 말은 아니었다.

7 a. 그 영리한 젊은이는 말로 무슨 일에서든지 빠져나올 수 있다고 생각했다. 아주 어려운 중간고사 시험에 어쩔 줄 몰라 그는 이런 변명을 시험지 표지에 썼다. "하느님만 해답들을 아십니다. 즐거운 성탄을 보내십시오!"
      그가 답안지를 되돌려 받았을 때 거기에는 이렇게 적혀 있었다. "하느님은 A를 받으시는데, 자넨 F를 받네. 즐거운 새해를 맞이하길!"
   b. 결코 내가 이해하지 못할 것은 어른이 된 자식들이 부모에게 의지해서 살아가는 것이다. 마찬가지로 이해할 수 없는 것은 부모들이 이런 사태가 벌어지도록 기꺼이 내버려 둔다는 것이다. 내가 결혼에 실패했을 때 나는 집으로 엄마에게 달려가지 않고, 나 자신의 생활을 개선하고, 두 가지 직업을 갖고 일을 해서 빚에서 벗어나려고 했다. 내가 부모에게 부탁한 것은 사랑과 심적인 지원뿐이었는데, 이것이 어른이 된 자식이 부모에게 부탁해야 하는 것 전부여야 한다.

EXERCISE 3

1 알랑 들롱은 말하길 자기가 젊음을 유지하는 방법은 "사랑을 많이 하고 물을 많이 마시는 것"이라고.

2 정직한 정치가란 매수되면 매수된 상태로 남는 사람이다.

3 성인으로서 우리들 중의 일부는 믿었다, 분노는 매력이 없고, 받아들일 수 없는 감정이라고. 우리는 계속해서 믿었다, 만일 우리가 분노를 표출하면 사람들은 우리를 벌하기 위해 비난할 거라고.

4   우리는 유머감각이 있어야 이 미친 세상에서 미치지 않을 수 있다.

5   스프링스틴의 명곡들에 담겨 있는 현실적인 메세지는 이런 것들이다. 즉 실업자들의 아픔, 부모들의 삶에 대한 이해를 통해서 사이가 멀어진 부모들과의 화해, 비록 현실이 미국의 꿈(이상)에 미치지 못하더라도 계속해서 희망을 갖는 것이다.

6   나는 나의 신체적인 단점들 때문에 비참했다. 나는 너무 말랐다. 내 머리는 빗질한 상태로 있질 않았다. 나는 춤을 추지 못했다. 만일 어떤 여자 아이가 내게 미소를 지으면 나는 얼굴이 붉어져서 고개를 다른 곳으로 돌리고, 그 아이를 못 본 척했고, 답례로 미소를 짓지 못했으며, 단 한 마디도 할 수 없었다.

7   a. 그는 코카인을 끊었다고 말한다.
    b. 중독 분야의 많은 전문가들의 말에 의하면 담배를 끊는 것이, 정말 중독되어있는 경우에는, 코카인을 끊는 것보다 더 어렵다고 한다.
    c. 만일 코카인을 일년만 하지 않으면, 아마 코카인을 다시 하지 않을 것이다.

8   a. 많은 새 업체들이 첫 해에 이윤을 내는 것은 어렵다. 수지를 맞추고 영업을 계속하는 것만 해도 잘 하는 것이다.
    b. 가장 훌륭한 그런 컨설턴트들은 1년에 10만 달러 보다 상당히 더 많이 벌 수 있다. 그러나 그가 아는 대부분의 컨설턴트들은 고전하고 있다 — 그래서 가족들의 생활을 망치며 겨우 근근이 생활하고 있다.
    c. 내가 태어난 것은 1921년 10월 22일 오전 4시였다, 인디애너 주, 하트포드 시에서. 나의 아버지가 의사 선생님에게 물으셨다. "얼마를 드려야 합니까?" 의사 선생님이 대답하셨다, "제가 여기로 올 때 타이어 공기가 빠져 있었습니다. 제 타이어를 갈아주신다면 그것으로 서로 갚을 게 없는 것으로 하죠."

9   a. 에이즈 바이러스에 노출이 되어 양성 반응이 나타났지만 건강하게 느끼는 사람은 어떻게 하면 건강을 유지할 수 있을까? 확실한 대답은 할 수 없지만 건강을 유지하기 위해 노력하는 것은 합당한 일이다.
    b. 그 물은 깨끗했다.
       → 그 물은 테스트해 보니 깨끗했다.
    c. 그는 테스트 결과 이해력이 높았다.
    d. 그 차는 테스트해 보니 시내 운전보다 고속도로 운전에 더 좋았다.
    e. 현재 추산에 의하면 테스트 결과 에이즈 바이러스 감염 양성 반응으로 판명되는 세 사람 중에서 한 사람만 에이즈에 걸릴 거라고 한다.
    f. 한 연구에 의하면 취학 전 아이들에게 부모가 적극적으로 참여하여 책을 읽어 준 아이들은 테스트 결과 다른 아이들보다 6~8개월 앞선 것으로 드러났다.

10 a. 그 일식 날은 흐렸다.
    b. 그 일식 날은 동이 틀 때 흐렸으나, 서서히 개이기 시작해서 천문학자들은 희망을 갖게 되었다.

11 a. 그의 생애는 근면이 보상을 받는다는 것을 광고해 주는 것 같았다.
    b. 내 인생이 당신이 나와 당장 자리를 바꾸고 싶어할 정도로 언제나 좋은 삶이었던 것은 아니다.

EXERCISE 4

1   a. 교회에 대한 사랑이 그 가족에는 강하다.
    b. 남성 우월주의가 아직도 많은 독일의 기업체에 널리 퍼져 있다.
    c. 우리들은 예정된 시간에 늦어서 성질들이 예민해져 있었다.

2   a. 우리는 커피와 설탕이 얼마 남아 있지 않다.

b. 오늘날 세계는 마음의 평화는 적고 긴장과 압박은 많다.

3 a. 너는 보통이다.
   b. 너는 대략 보통이다.
   c. 처음에 성공하지 못하더라도 보통은 하는 것이다.

4 a. 그의 말이 내게는 거짓으로 들린다.
   b. 이 주장은 전에 많이 들어봤던 것 같다.
   c. 그 가정은 허구처럼 들리지만 실현될 수 있다.

5 a. 그들은 자기들의 요구사항에 대해 확고했다.
   b. 그녀는 확고히 믿고 있다, 이것은 국가적인 비극이라고.

6 a. 내 등골이 오싹해졌다, 그 무서운 광경을 보자.
   b. 그 생각은 바닷물이 마를지도 모른다고 걱정하는 것이나 마찬가지로 터무니없는 것 같다.
   c. 제기랄! 이 TV는 뭐가 문제야? 내가 특별히 보고 싶어하는 것이 있을 때마다 화면이 흐려지니 말야.

7 a. 어렸을 적에 그는 흔히 굶으면서 지냈다.
   b. 그들은 흔히 수개월 동안 고기 없이 지냈다.
   c. 파업은 언제나 일어날 가능성이 있다, 근로자들이 수개월 동안 임금을 받지 않고 지낼 가능성이 있으니까.
   d. 그는 자기가 구할 수 있는 것이면 무슨 육체 노동 일이라도 맡아 했다, 흔히 오랜 기간 동안 일이 없이 지내면서.

8 a. 한국인들은 실내에서는 신발을 신지 않는다.
   b. 자연이 옷을 입는 방식은 인간의 방식과는 정반대다. 여름에 자연은 가장 무거운 옷을 입지만 겨울에는 옷을 벗고 지낸다.
   c. 그는 나에게 말했다, 네가 20년 동안 브래지어를 착용하지 않았다고. 그의 말에 의하면 클랜튼 여자들 대부분은 브래지어를 착용하지 않는다고 한다.

EXERCISE 5

1 a. 지금은 경제적으로 어려운 시기인지라, 우리는 겨우 가족들이 입는 것과 먹는 것을 해결할 수 있을 뿐이다.
   b. 우리는 가족들이 먹는 것과 입는 것을 겨우 해결할 수 있을 뿐, 휴가 가는 것은 할 수 없다.

2 a. 스티브에게 샌드위치를 만들어 주다가 오늘 밤은 볼일 다 보겠는 걸!
   b. "자네 올해 담배 농사로 돈 좀 벌었나?" "그래, 자식이 1년 더 담배를 피우게 할 수 있을 만큼만 벌었다네."

3 a. 식사에 들어가기 전에, 그들은 머리 숙여 기도했다.
   b. 음식이 도착해서 내가 먹기 시작할 때 보니까 나나는 먹지 않고 있었다.

4 수영하려면 옷을 모두 벗어야 한다. 진리에 도달하려면 훨씬 더 내적인 의미에서 옷을 벗어야 한다. 모든 내면의 옷, 생각, 관념, 이기심 등을 벗어 버리고 충분히 아무것도 우리 마음에 걸친 것이 없어야 한다.　　　—쇠렌 키에르케고르

5 어떤 사람들은 살아가는 수단으로 죽음에 대한 두려움에 의존하고, 어떤 사람들은 살아가는 수단으로 삶의 기쁨에 의존한다. 전자의 사람들은 죽으면서 살고, 후자는 살면서 죽는다. 언제 내가 죽든, 나는 살면서 죽을 작정이다.
　　　　　　　　　　— 호리스 캘른

6 내가 만일 한 사람의 상심을 막는다면,
　내 삶은 헛되지 않으리.
　내가 만일 한 생명의 고통을 덜어 주거나,
　한 통증을 진정시키거나,
　한 마리 기절하는 개똥지빠귀를
　제집에 다시 올려 놓을 수 있다면,
　내 삶은 헛되지 않으리.
　　　　　　　　　　— 에밀리 디킨슨

EXERCISE 6

1. a. 나는 다음주에 학기말 리포트 한 편을 제출해야 한다.
   b. 친구 몇이 오늘 저녁에 우리 집에 한잔 하러 온다.

2. a. 토요일 밤의 치통으로 월요일 오전 일찍 나는 치과에 가 있었다.
   b. 비록 33개 주와 컬럼비아 특별구가 시트 벨트법을 시행하고 있지만, 많은 사람들은 아직도 시트 벨트를 착용하는 수고를 하지 않는다.
   c. 교역 수지가 흑자이고 인플레이션이 잡혀 있으므로, 우리는 지금 우리의 통화의 지속적인 안정을 위한 조건들이 갖추어져 있다.

3. a. 그는 그 계약을 서류로 작성하자고 주장했다.
   b. 일단 목표를 정하면, 그것을 써 놓아라. 성취도가 높은 사람들은 자기들의 성취는 자기들이 목표를 적은 그 순간에 시작되었다고 말한다.

4. a. 유모차가 뒤집혔다.
   b. 너 저 유모차 뒤집겠다, 더 조심하지 않으면.

5. a. 그 공은 유리창을 깨뜨리고 지나갔다.
   b. 너 저 공 어디로 차는지 주의해라. 그렇지 않으면 유리창을 깨뜨리고 지나갈 테니까.

6. a. 그는 곧 돌아올 거야.
   b. 언제 그가 돌아오리라 예상하니?

7. a. 너는 우리 팀에 소속되어 있다.
   b. 나는 네가 우리 팀에 소속되길 원한다.

8. a. 그는 이 집에 있다.
   b. 나는 그가 이 집에 있는 것을 원하지 않는다.

9. a. 내 생각에 그가 나를 통제하려고 하는 것 같아서, 나는 그의 통제에서 벗어나고 싶었다.
   b. 만일 제시카가 곤경에 빠지게 되더라도, 그녀는 언제나 이리저리 노력해서 무사히 빠져나갈 것이다.

10. a. 그 말은 매여 있지 않다.
    b. 그 동물들은 매어 놓은 것을 풀고 달아나 버렸다.
    c. 이 기둥은 (고정된 상태에서) 느슨해지고 있는데 곧 쓰러질 것이다.
    d. 그 쇠사슬은 그의 손에서 풀렸다.
    e. 내 머리카락은 (빗어 놓은 상태서) 풀린다, 내가 달릴 때.

11. a. 나는 전혀 그 유혹을 떨쳐버릴 수가 없었다.
    b. 밤새도록 유전 채굴 장비 위에서 사람들이 채굴 파이프를 더 깊이 페이너 호수 밑 땅속으로 밀어 넣고 있었다. 약 1,240 피트에서 그 파이프는, 39톤 무게의 강철 막대인데, 땅에 박혀버렸고, 그들은 그것을 빼낼 수 없었다.
    c. 산화는, 물론, 생명 자체에 필수 불가결하다. 왜냐하면 우리의 신체는 산소를 음식물에 가해서, 말하자면, 불꽃 없이 연소시켜서 필요한 에너지를 얻기 때문이다. 그러나 산화가 언제나 이롭지는 않다고 최근의 과학 이론은 주장한다. 산소가 원자와 결합할 때 그것이 때로는 전자를 뒤흔들어서 빠져 나오게 한다. 전자가 부족한 원자는, "프리 래디컬"이라고 알려져 있는데, 자동적으로 다른 전자를 구하게 되어 연쇄반응을 일으키는데, 이것이 세포에 손상을 끼칠 수 있다.

12. a. 그들은 그가 범죄를 저지르는 것을 현장에서 잡았다.
    b. 그녀는 백화점에서 물건을 훔치다가 잡혔다.
    c. 나는 탐이 총을 하나 슬쩍하는 것을 보았다.
    d. 공교롭게도, 내가 찾아갔을 때 조던은 연습 중이었다.
    e. 나는 그녀가 여러번 거짓말하는 것을 보아서 그녀에 대한 존경심을 잃었다.

f. 아이들은 예측할 수 없다. 우리가 다음에 무슨 모순되는 것을 하다가 그들에게 걸릴지 알 수 없다.

g. "이봐, 나 발가 벗었어, 마시!"
"그게 무슨 뜻이니?"
"나 샤워중이었단 말이야!"
"다시 전화할까?"

h. 나의 남편은, 40대인데, 새 취미가 생겼다. 그는 음란한 전화를 한다. 그는 번호를 닥치는 대로 돌려서, 전화로 그녀와 "정사"를 한다. 나는 그가 그것을 여러번 하는 것을 보았다. 그는 실제로 아무 잘못된 짓을 하는 게 아니고, 그것은 다만 아무에게도 해를 끼치지 않는 오락이라고 말한다. 그러고는 나에게 용서해 달라고 빈다.

13 a. 우리의 수요는 일년에 약 12% 성장하고 공급은 일년에 약 2% 성장하여, 10%의 물가 상승을 낳는다.

b. 심장병은 국민들의 가장 큰 건강 문제인데, 1967년 이래로 20% 줄었다. 미국 심장학회에 의하면, 뇌졸중은 3분의1이 줄었다고 한다. 평균 수명은 증가해서 기록적인 73세가 되었다. 콜레스테롤 논란 때문에 미국인들의 소고기 소비량은 10년 전보다 6파운드 줄었다. 또한 미국인의 술 소비량은 4% 줄었다. 비록 젊은층, 특히 여성들 사이에서 흡연율이 다소 증가하고 있지만, 180만 명의 연장자층의 흡연가들이 담배를 끊었다. 아주 최근까지도 쾌락과 자기 표현에 열중하고 있다고 생각되던 이 나라에서 이것은 적지 않은 성과일 것이다.

EXERCISE 7

1 a. 앨리스는 건강하다. 그녀는 건강을 유지하기 위해 노력한다.

b. 나는 건강하지 않다. 나는 건강해지기 위해 노력해야 한다.

2 a. 어리석게 행동하지 마라. 정신 차려라 (=현명하게 행동해라).

b. 너 제 정신이 아닌가 보다, 그런 여자와 결혼할 생각을 하는 걸 보니. 난 최선을 다해 네가 제 정신을 되찾게 해야겠다.

3 a. 과거와 똑같은 일이 일어나지는 않는다.

b. 나는 기적이 일어나리라 기대했다, 그때 거기서, 그런데 기적이 정말 일어났다. 그러나 중요한 변화가 흔히 그러하듯이, 그것은 상당한 기간에 걸쳐 일어났다.

4 a. 우리가 깊은 믿음과 감정을 갖고, 일어나리라고 기대하는 것은, 틀림없이 일어난다.

b. 사람들이 걱정하는 일 대부분은 결코 일어나지 않는다. 프랑스의 수필가 몽떼이뉴는 이 점을 웅변적으로 잘 얘기했다. "나의 인생은 재난의 연속이었는데 — 그 재난 대부분은 결코 일어나지 않았다."

5 a. 더 작은 일들이 일어남에 따라, 우리는 더 큰 일들이 일어나게 만들 수 있다.

b. 모든 사람은 타고난 창조 능력을 갖고 있다, 비록 창조 능력의 수준과 창조하는 것의 유용성 정도에 있어서는 차이가 있지만.

6 a. 일단 하나의 새로운 관념을 생각해내면, 그것을 없앨 수는 없다.

b. 물리학자들은 지금 '스스로 창조하는 우주'에 대한 얘기를 하고 있는데, 우주는 저절로 생긴다는 것이다, 마치 핵보다 작은 입자가 때로는 어떤 높은 에너지 과정에서 저절로 생기듯이.

7 a. 아이들을 돌보아라, 내가 점심을 준비하는 동안.

b. 얼른 샌드위치 두어 개 만들어 줄게.

c. 그들은 모두 식당으로 물러갔는데, 거기에는 놀라운 진수성찬이 마치 누가 요술이라도 부린 것처럼 차려져 있었다.

d. 만일 그녀가 반 시간을 소비해서 식사를 준

비하면, 그녀는 그것이 진수성찬이라고 생각한다. 너 못봤니, 그녀가 얼마나 빨리 식사를 준비하는지?

8 a. 이 책을 쓰면서 나는 많은 것을 배웠다.
    b. "아무리 애를 써도, 나는 이것을 제대로 조립하지 못 하겠다."
      "설명서 읽어봤니?"

9 a. 그들은 당장 구조대를 만들기 시작했다.
    b. 전담반을 만들어서 이것을 진행시켜라.

10 a. 그는 영화 제작을 위한 자금 조달을 위해 노력하고 있었다.
     b. 영화 제작자들이 흔히 자금을 조달하는 방법은 상영권을 미리 비디오테이프 배본업자들, 케이블 TV 방송국과 외국 영화 상영업자들에게 판매하는 것이다.

11 a. 날마다 열심히 일하여 간신히 생계를 마련하는 사람은 골치아픈 철학적인 물음에 대해 곰곰이 생각할 시간이 없다.
     b. Jobs와 Wozniak이 밴 한 대와 계산기 두 개를 팔아 간신히 1,300 달러를 긁어 모아 Apple Computer사를 Jobs의 차고에 열었을 때, 그들이 놀라운 성공을 거둘 가능성은 너무도 멀어 보였다.

12 a. 우리는 우리의 행동을 한 곳에 모아야 한다. — (다시 말해) 우리는 조직적으로 행동해야 한다.
     b. '부활' (다시 온전한 사람이 되는 것)은 여러 가지로 불린다. '다시 태어난,' '치유,' 혹은 단순히 '우리의 행동을 조직하는 것'으로. 무엇이라 부르든지, 그 행동이 아무리 크든 작든, 우리들의 삶의 깨어진 조각들을 다시 모아 온전하게 만들려는 충동은 다 같다.

13 a. 건강한 사람들은 두뇌가 정리되어 있다.

     b. 친구들 말에 의하면, 그녀는 전보다 더 행복하고, 더 안정되어있다고 했다.
     c. 그녀는 자기들이 이것에서 무사히 빠져나가게 될 것이라고 그 남자를 안심시켰다.
     d. "처음에는 나는 혼란에 빠져있었다."라고 그녀가 말했다. "나 자신을 주체할 수 없었다. 몇 분이 지나서야 나는 나 자신을 진정시킬 수 있었다."
     e. 울음을 그치고 진정해라, 그가 돌아오기 전에.

14 a. 나는 무너져선 안 돼. 날 온전하게 장악해야 해.
     b. 온전함과 건강이라는 말은 같은 고대 영어 "hal" ('건전한', '완전한'을 뜻함)에서 나왔다. 우리는 직관적으로 안다. 우리가 말하는 것만 보면, 우리는 '갈라진'이란 느낌을 좋아하지 않는다는 것을. 상심했거나, 실망했거나, 상처를 받았을 때, 우리는 말한다. '난 나 자신을 끌어당겨 모아야 해.' '나는 봉합해 놓은 곳이 갈라지고 있어.' 혹은 나의 인간 관계가 '갈라지고 있다'고. 우리는 '무너짐'과 '깨어짐'이란 말을 한다. 우리들 자신에 대해 기분이 좋고 우리들의 삶이 순조로울 때, 우리들은 말한다. "나는 완전하다는 느낌이 든다." "나의 삶이 통합되고 있다." 혹은 "마침내, 나는 그 문제에 대해 한 마음이다"라고.

EXERCISE 8

1 a. 그녀는 그 문제를 이해하는 것을 완전히 실패했다 (= 그녀는 그 문제를 전혀 이해하지 못했다).
    b. 그녀는 그 문제를 완전히 이해하지는 못했다.

2 a. 그는 면도로 자기 턱수염을 깍아버렸다.
    b. 그는 면도로 이틀 자란 자기 턱수염을 깍아버렸다.

3 a. 나는 너와 함께 있고 싶지 않다.
   b. 나는 일 분도 더 너와 함께 있고 싶지 않다.

4 a. 나는 옷도 없다.
   b. 나는 한 번 갈아입을 옷도 없다.

5 a. 온전한 정신은 매우 드물다. 거의 모든 남자와 모든 여자는 약간의 정신 이상을 갖고 있다.
   b. 비록 겉으로는 탄력성이 없어 보이지만, 뼈는 상당한 탄력성을 갖고 있어 골절이 상당한 충격을 버틸 수 있게 해 준다.

6 a. 그는 명상에 대해 상당한 전문가가 되었다.
   b. 모든 사람에게 모든 것이 되려고 하면 대개 아무에게도 별것 아닌 존재가 된다.

7 a. 그는 자기 중심적이지만, 조금도 가식은 없다. 이렇게 전혀 가식 없는 점이 그를 견딜 만한 사람으로 만든다.
   b. 네가 그 시합에 이길 가능성은 조금도 없다.

8 a. 나는 혼이 났다, 눈이 오는데 집에 오느라고.
   b. "나는 미적분 때문에 혼이 나고 있다. 이 과목을 포기할까 생각한다."
   "계속 해봐. 포기하지 말고."

9 a. 집으로 다시 돌아와서, 나는 어떤 종류의 일과와 정상적인 생활 비슷한 것을 다시 시작하려고 했다.
   b. 그러나 수도에서 새 정부는 질서 비슷한 것조차 유지하는 데에도 어려움을 겪고 있다.
   c. 그 식당은 프랑스 음식에 아주 가까운 음식을 내놓는다.

10 a. 범죄 집단들이 거리를 돌아다니면서 강도질과 공격을 해도 거의 처벌을 받지 않았다.
   b. 그들은 서로 바라보았다, 애정에 아주 가까운 감정으로.
   c. 새 차는 지난 번 우리 차가 갖고 있던 동력에 전혀 못 미치는 동력을 갖고 있다.

   d. 그는 사설 탐정 같아 보이지 않았다.
      → 그는 전혀 사설 탐정 같아 보이지 않았다.
      → 그는 전혀 그녀가 생각하는 사설 탐정 같아 보이지 않았다.

11 a. <u>종잡을 수 없이 많은 미신들</u>과 호전적인 부족신에 대한 편협한 관념들로부터 일신론적인 신앙이 발생했는데, 이것은 이원론과 부합하지 않았다.
   b. <u>어떤 지역의 물</u>의 생사를 좌우하는 것은 주로 일정한 양의 물에 용해되어 있는 산소를 그 물이 유지하는 능력이다. 이 용해된 산소를 물고기들이 호흡한다. 그것이 없으면 그들은 질식해서 죽는다.

   > 주의 a chaos of superstitions와 any body of water에서 핵심은 superstitions와 water이고 a chaos of와 any body of는 수식어구다.

12 a. 내가 지금까지 들어본 성공한 사람들은 자기가 처한 여건에서 최선을 다했지, 여건이 더 좋아질 때까지 기다리지 않았다.
   b. 시인들은 사람들과 삶에 관심을 갖고 있으며, 시라는 매체를 이용하여 인생에 대해서 자신들이 이해한 것과 인생에 대해서 자신들이 보는 대로의 진실을 전달한다. 그들은 "개념의 느낌"과 그 "개념 밑에 놓여 있는 경험"을 우리에게 전달하려고 한다. 그들은 한 민족과 한 국가, 한 문명의 가장 깊은 내면에 놓여 있는 정신을 풀이한다. 왜냐하면 시는 인생을 몇 가지 면에서 드러내거나 풀이하는 것이기 때문이다. 시의 소재는 감정에게 알려져 있는 대로의 인생인데, 감정은 보편적이며 지속적이다. 더구나, 시인은 인생 전체에 흐르는 영원한 리듬을 감지한다.

13 a. 돈으로 우리는 무엇이든지 우리가 생각하기에 더 큰 행복으로 데려다 줄 것을 살 수 있다.
   b. 비록 의료업이 대부분의 어린이 질병을 정복했다고 하지만, 어린이들은, 여전히 많이, 잠자리에 들어야 할 시간에 잠이 오지 않게 하는 질병(이것이 무엇이든지 간에)에 걸려 있는 것 같다.

14 a. 그는 그녀에게 미소를 짓고 있었는데, 그녀는 알았다, 그것이 가짜 미소라는 것을.

b. 많은 정부들은 외환 시장에 개입해서 환율이 자기들이 생각하기에 그릇된 방향으로 지나치게 멀리 가는 것을 막으려고 한다.

15 a. 그 파티는 계속되었는데 그것이 얼마나 오랫동안이었는지 나는 모른다.

b. 그녀는 태어났다, 주님만이 아시는 해에 말이다.

c. 많은 사람들이 바라는 여성 이미지에 맞추기 위한 노력으로, 나는 나 자신을 굶겼고 하늘만이 아는 화학물질로 만든 약을 복용했다.

EXERCISE 9

1 우리는 웃음으로써 많은 걱정들을 제거할 수 있다, 달리 제거할 수 없는 걱정들을.

> 주의 앞의 문장에서는 to death가 무엇과 관련되는지 알기 어렵다. 따라서 이런 어순은 피해야 한다.

2 좋은 시는 산문으로 옮길 수가 없다.

3 대화의 진정한 기술은 적절한 말을 적절한 곳에서 하는 것뿐만 아니라, 적절하지 않은 말을 아무리 하고 싶어도 안 하는 것이다.

4 토테미즘을 실천하는 (다시 말해 식물이나 동물 또는 대상을 신으로 숭배하는) 사람들은 대개 선택해서 숭배한다, 그 지역에 중요한 대상들을 말이다.

5 보는 것은 우리들의 눈뿐만 아니라 두뇌의 활동인데, 두뇌는 일종의 선택하는 기계로서 작용한다. 두뇌에 제시된 모든 영상들 중에서, 두뇌가 선택해서 인식하는 것은 과거의 경험에 의해 배운 세계와 가장 잘 맞는 것들이다.

6 엑스레이는 대상을 통과할 수 있다. 그래서 작은 부분들을 볼 수 있게 만든다, 달리 볼 수 없는 것들을 말이다.

7 나는 생각했다, 마땅히 완전히 그릇된 것으로 내가 배척해야 한다고, 내가 생각하기에 조금이라도 의심할 여지가 있는 모든 견해들을. 왜냐하면 나의 목적은, 그렇게 한 뒤에, 여전히 믿기를 요구하는, 전적으로 의심할 여지가 없는 어떤 것(견해)이 남아 있을지를 알아내는 것이었기 때문이다.

8 많은 재능이 세상에서 상실된다, 약간의 용기가 부족하기 때문이다. 날마다 이름없는(= 성공하지 못한) 사람들이 사라진다, 용기가 부족해서 시작하지 못했고, 만일 우리가 시작하게 만들 수 있었더라면 십중팔구 크게 성공했을 사람들이 말이다.

EXERCISE 10

1 a. 1650년 이후 3세기 동안에, 세계의 인구는 다섯 배 증가해서 1950년에는 합계 약 25억이 되었다.

b. 그는 주식을 1995년부터 1996년까지 보유하여, 자본 수익을 약 3.7% 얻고, 거기다가 3.6%의 배당 수익을 얻어, 합계 수익 7.3%를 얻었다.

c. 미국인들은 3월에 지갑을 닫아 소매가 1% 떨어지게 만들었는데, 이것은 2년 이상 동안에 일어난 가장 급격한 하락이다.

2 a. 수소 원자 두 개가 산소 원자 한 개와 결합하여 물을 만든다.

b. 탄소와 수소가 산소와 결합하여 빛과 열을 생산한다.

c. 돈을 벌면 온 세상 사람들이 공모하여 당신을 신사라 부른다.

d. 고요한 마음과 젊은 심장, 뛰는 피, 이것들이 합쳐 기적을 낳는다.

e. 두 개의 힘이 협력하면, 그들은 합쳐서 하나의 더 큰 힘이 된다. 그러나 두 개의 힘이 직접 서로 반대하면, 그들의 힘은 감소된다.
  f. 칼슘은, 인체 내에서 가장 풍부한 무기물인데, 인과 함께 작용하여 뼈와 치아를 유지한다.
  g. 인터페론이 면역세포와 협력하여 암을 포함하는 여러가지 질병과 싸운다는 증거가 있다.
  h. 이 지역 경찰이 FBI와 협력하여 그 범인들을 찾고 있다.

3 a. 이 책에는 완전히 새로운 관점이 들어있는데, 그것은 과거의 지혜와 과학 지식을 결합해서 현재의 문제들을 해결하려는 것이다.
   b. 심리언어학은 심리학과 언어학 양쪽의 이론과 경험적 자료를 이용하여 언어 사용의 기초를 형성하는 심리적 과정들을 연구한다.
   c. 행동의학은 심리학과 의학의 지식을 결합하여 질병을 평가하고 진단하는 방법, 치료 방법, 특히 예방 방법을. 재활은 물론, 연구한다.

   참조 어떤 것을 할 때 두 가지를 이용하는 경우에는 use는 물론, combine과 bring together도 이용할 수 있고, 둘째 동작은 'to+동사원형'이나 'in+동명사'로 연결한다.

   주의 우리들 자신을 치유하는 데에 작용하는 같은 원칙들이 다른 사람들을 치유하는 데에도 작용한다.

4 a. 경험론자들은 관찰과 실험을 이용하여 무엇이 옳은지를 결정한다.
   b. 철학자들은 보통 논증에 의해 자신들의 이론이 옳다는 것을 증명하고 다른 사람들의 이론이 그르다는 것을 증명한다.

5 a. 녹색 식물은 햇빛을 이용하여 이산화탄소와 물을 당분과 산소로 바꾼다.
   b. 근육은 마그네슘을 이용하여 탄수화물을 이용 가능한 에너지로 바꾼다.
   c. 그는 공산주의 철학을 이용하여 생명의 기원에 관한 자신의 견해들이 옳다는 것을 증명한다.

   참조 use = rely on = draw on

6 a. 박쥐는 청각을 이용하여 밤에 날아다니면서 먹이를 찾는다.
   b. 그 화가는 어린시절의 기억들을 이용하여 그의 그림들을 그렸다.
   c. 우리는 건조한 날씨를 이용하여 집에 페인트 칠을 했다.
   d. 우리는 중력을 이용하여 성군과 은하계의 구조를 설명한다, 팽창하는 우주의 전반적인 움직임은 물론이고.

   참조 rely on(= depend on) = draw on = take advantage(= use) = look to. 이런 관찰은 영어를 이해하기 위해서 뿐만 아니라 영어를 구사하기 위해서도 필요하다.

7 a. 미세한 식물들(식물성 플랭크톤)이 바다의 생태계의 기반을 이루는데, 빛을 동력원으로 이용하여 전분을 합성한다.
   b. 그들은 부모에게 의존하여 금전적인 도움을 받는다.
   c. 두뇌는 혈액에 의존하여 계속해서 산소와 포도당을 공급받는다.
   d. 동물은 다른 생물, 궁극적으로 식물에 의존해야 먹이를 공급받을 수 있다. 그것은 또 식물의 활동에 의존해야 계속해서 산소를 공급받아 호흡할 수 있다.

8 a. 질문이 복잡할 때에는 처음 머릿속에 떠오르는 답을 제시하지 마라. 시간을 내서 곰곰이 생각해 보라.
   b. 암컷 두꺼비는 수컷의 구애의 소리를 들을 때 테너는 경멸하고 베이스를 선호한다.
   c. 당시 원시주의자 히피들은 언제나 현대 문명을 비판하고, 행동과 말을 반대하며 단지 존재하는 것을 선호했다.

9 a "난 오늘 어머니 생각을 많이 해왔다."
     "가서 뵙지 그래."
   b. 잠시 쉬며 물 한 모금 마신 뒤에, 연사는 계속해서 야생 사자들의 습성에 관해 얘기했다.

10 a. 그 결과, 제1차 세계 대전 후로 점점 더 많은 관객들이 극장을 버리고 영화관으로 갔다.

b. 마지막 순간에 Bob은 근소한 차이로 Henry를 밀어내고 일등을 차지했다.

11. a. 놀라운 비율로, 서유럽 고등 학생들은 독일어를 포기하고 영어를 선택해 오고 있다, 주로 자기들이 생각하기에 영어가 더 쉽게 배울 수 있다는 이유 때문이다.
    b. 런던 남부 Wandsworth 학교들은 긴 여름방학(본래 의도는 학생들로 하여금 수확을 돕게 하려는 것이었는데)을 버리고 8주 5학기제를 채택해 왔다.
    c. 성숙은 인내다. 그것은 기꺼이 당장의 쾌락을 포기하고 장기적인 이득을 위하는 것이다.
    d. 민주당원들은 레이건의 3년에 걸친 일률적인 소득세의 대폭적인 삭감안을 거부하고 훨씬 폭이 좁은 1년에 걸친 감축안을 지지한다.

12. a. 전화 교환원이 잠자기 끼어들어 말했다. "75센트를 더 내야 통화를 계속하실 수 있습니다"라고.
    b. 지금과 같은 전자 시대의 삶은 아이들에게는 무척 힘들다. 두 6학년 학생들이 어느날 오후에 낚시질을 하고 싶어 무전기를 갖고 갔다. 이 말이 선생님에게 들어가자, 그는 무전기를 다른 학생한테 빌렸다. 선생님이 무전기를 켜자, 아니나 다를까, 그 무단 조퇴한 아이들의 소리가 들렸다. 그러자 그는 재빨리 끼어들어 명령했다. 가능한 빨리 교실에 나타나라고, 그들은 그렇게 했다.

    참고 a에서는 두 번째 동작을 분사로, b에서는 to부정사로 연결했다.

13. a. 지식을 얻으면 순진함을 잃는다.
    b. 사람들을 대개 유명해지면, 사생활을 잃는다.

14. a. 문명은 오늘날 목재에 의존하여, 세계의 자연 자원에 커다란 손실을 끼친다.
    b. 보호무역정책은 단기적인 혜택을 특별한 이익 집단들에게 제공할지 모르나 많은 더 큰 손해를 나머지 사람들에게는 가져온다.

15. a. 우리들은 새 친구들을 사귀고 옛 친구들을 잃을 수는 없다.
    b. 일반적으로, "속독"은 많이 읽는 것을 중시하고 이해는 소홀히 한다.
    c. 오락을 개발하고 일을 희생할 수는 없다. 사람은 마땅히 일을 노는 것보다 중시해야 한다.
    d. 수없이 여러가지 방법으로 인간은 자연 환경을 이용하여 당장은 이득을 얻지만 결국은 손해를 입는다.

16. a. 질서가 한 곳에 발생하면 그 대가로 무질서가 다른 곳에 발생된다.
    b. 우주의 한 지역에 질서가 증가하면 언제나 그 대가로 무질서가 다른 지역에 증가한다.
    c. 엔트로피 법칙에 의하면, 질서가 지구나 우주의 어떤 곳에 만들어지면 그 대가로 더 큰 무질서가 주위 환경에 일어나게 된다.

17. a. 누구든지 법을 위반하면 그 대가로 벌을 받는다.
    b. 그는 사람이다, 만일 그에게 거절하면 해를 입힐 그런 사람 말이다.

18. a. 우리는 그 집을 팔아 손해를 보았다.
    b. 그 제철소는 지금 가동하여 많은 수익을 낸다.

19. a. 1902년에, 그 책은 출판되어 평론가들의 칭찬을 받았다.
    b. 일과 놀이는 둘 다 우리들의 행복을 위해 필요하다. 우리는 어느 하나를 중시하고 다른 하나를 제외해선 안 된다.
    c. 나는 깊은 잠에서 깨어나서 차츰 깨달았다. 내가 집에 있지 기숙사에 있지 않다는 것을 말이다.
    d. 얼마나 여러번 우리는 어떤 재미있는 책 여러 페이지를 꿈꾸며 지나가다가 깨어나서 깨달았더냐, 우리가 전혀 모르고 있다는 것을, 무엇을 읽었는지.

20. a. 그는 담배를 많이 피워 자신의 건강에 해를

끼쳤다.
  b. 그에게 해가 되겠지만, 얘기해야겠다. 그가 죄수들이 고문당하도록 내버려 두었다는 것을.

21 a. 지식과 지식에 대한 탐구는 여러 세기에 걸쳐 계속되어 오면서 엄청난 혜택을 사람들에게 가져다 주었다.
  b. 우리들 서구인들은 과학상의 발견과 그것의 응용을 200년 동안 집중적으로 고무해온 결과 우리들은 방대한 물질적인 혜택을 얻었다.

22 a. 일상 생활에서 우리는 대단히 많은 말을 사용하지만 논리적인 정확성은 전혀 무시한다.
  b. 누구든지 다른 사람들을 도와주면서 자신의 이득을 생각하지 않는다면 그는 근본적으로 이타주의자다.

23 나는 그 문제 대해서 한 시간 이상 동안 곰곰이 생각해 보았으나 아무 결과도 얻지 못했는데, 그때 갑자기 해답이 번쩍 내 머릿속에 떠올랐다.

24 일류 지성인의 징표는, F. Scott Fitzgerald가 말했듯이, 두 개의 모순되는 주장을 머릿속에 동시에 갖고 있으면서도 미치지 않을 수 있는 능력이다.

25 돌이켜 보면, 우리는 진실로 알 수 있다, 개인의 권리라는 개념이 확장되어 나가서 점점 더 많은 사람들이 그 권리를 갖게 되었고, 마침내 모든 사람들이 그 권리를 갖게 되었다는 것을 말이다.

26 해마다 많은 책들이 발행되지만, 이들 중의 다수는 일시적인 관심만 끌다가 사라져갈 뿐이다, 차츰 서가와 독자들의 마음으로부터. 그리고 소수만 남아 돌아다닌다, 책이 읽히는 동안에는.

27 모든 자신의 변화 과정에서, 물은 결코 상실되지 않고, 사라졌다가는 다만 다시 다른 형태로 나타나서 끊임없이 자연과 문명에 봉사한다.
  주의 제1 동작(정동사), 제2 동작(분사), 제3 동작(부정사), 제4 동작(전치사구)

참고 지금까지 공부해온 예문들을 잘 살펴보면 동작과 동작을 연결해 주는 장치로서 부정사와 분사, 그리고 전치사와 접속사가 얼마나 중요한 역할을 하는지 알 수 있을 것이다.

28 헤겔에 의하면, 하나의 이론이 나오면 그것에 반대해서 반론이 나와 종합론을 만들어 내는데, 이것이 그러면 새 이론이 된다고 한다.

29 헤로인을 거래한 사람은 5만 달러의 벌금과 최고 30년 교도소 복역형을 선고 받을 수 있는데, 적어도 6년을 복역해야 가석방 자격을 얻을 수 있다. 메타콸론을 거래하는 사람은 최고 10년의 교도소 복역에다가 3만 달러의 벌금형을 선고 받을 수 있는데, 4년을 복역해야 가석방될 수 있다.

EXERCISE 11

1 정치 및 경제적 보수주의자로, 그는 강한 사회적인 양심을 보여주었는데, 이러한 양심은 말보다는 행동에서 나타났다.

2 중학생을 위한 지질학 책의 저자인 골든 씨는 현재 중학생을 위한 천문학 책을 쓰고 있다.

3 소련은 동독에 대한 외교적인 승인 문제를 회피했다.

4 그녀는 약 3년 전에 한국전(6·25 사변) 고아들을 돌보려는 특정한 목적으로 한국에 도착했다.

5 지극히 중요한 과정인 광합성은 지구 위에 있는 거의 모든 생물들의 궁극적인 영양 공급의 원천이다.

6 과거의 투쟁, 미래의 열망과 현재의 긴장이 한데 얽혀, 그녀는 결코 진정한 안식을 누리지 못하고 있다.

7 이 새로운 교육제도가 강조하는 것은 스스로 지식을 얻는 것이 가장 좋다는 사실이다. 다시 말해서, 실제 경험을 통해 얻어지는 지식이 가장 잘 이해되고 가장 오래 기억된다는 것이다.

　　요령 의미는 문맥 속에서 결정되므로 반드시 거기서 찾아야 한다.

8 사로이언은 관습을 따르지 않는 작가로 자신의 자유분방한 '민중 얘기' (소설)에 걷잡을 수 없는 활력과 밝은 낙관론을 부여했고, 예술과 상업적인 관습에 열렬히 저항했다. 아르메니아 이주민의 아들로 태어나서, 그는 학교를 그만두고 15세에 글을 썼으며, 26세에 이르러서는 자기 자신을 천재라 선언했다.

9 아가사 크리스티(유명한 추리소설가)가 고고학자와 결혼해서 사는 것을 어떻게 생각하느냐는 질문을 받았다.
　　"고고학자는 여성이 가질 수 있는 가장 훌륭한 남편입니다"라고 그녀는 대답했다. "나이가 많아지면 많아질수록, 그는 아내에게 그만큼 더 많은 관심을 갖게 되니까요."

　　어렵 여러분 이런 재치있는 얘기를 들으면 웃을 줄 알아야 됩니다.

EXERCISE 12

1 거의 모든 사회에는 거의 모든 시대에 유한 계층이 있었는데. 이 계층의 사람들은 힘든 노동으로부터 면제받았다.

2 그는 전형적인 미국 사업가의 전형적인 본보기인데, 이런 사람은 기꺼이 큰 위험을 무릅쓰고 큰 보상을 받으려고 한다.

3 알프스의 식물들이 더 높은 곳으로 이동하고 있다, 지구의 온난화 때문에. 이러한 이동으로 말미암아 결국은 수십 종이 사라질 가능성이 있다.

4 이렇게 세상을 선과 악의 투쟁으로 보는 견해(세계관)는 Greenberg의 핵심적이고 한결같은 주제 중의 하나인데, 이 견해는 어린시절을 텍사스 주 휴스턴의 어느 빈민가에서 보냄으로써 길러진 것이다.

5 Mary는 SAD 즉 계절적 정서증을 앓고 있는데, 이 질환의 특징은 심한 계절적 감정의 동요다.

6 일본 교육자들은 '학교 거부증'의 증가에 놀라고 있는데, 이것은 아이들의 심리적인 질환인데, 이런 아이들은 너무 스트레스를 받아 의욕을 잃어서 학교에 가질 못한다.

7 지방질과 단백질과 달리, 탄수화물은 근육과 간에 포도당으로 저장되는데, 이것은 쉽게 이용할 수 있는 동력원이서 우리의 신체는 필요한 대로 이용할 수 있다.

8 예술가는 공통 분모를 (다시 말해 우리들에게서 유사한 것을) 찾아서 그것을 이용하여 작품을 만들어 내야 한다, 우리들을 통합해 줄 뿐만 아니라 분리해 주는 작품을 말이다.

9 누구나 직관을 갖고 있다. 그러나 직관의 작은 목소리는 대부분의 사람들에게는 들리지 않는다. 왜냐하면, 이들의 사고는 중심에서 벗어나 있기 때문이다. 그들의 사고가 중심에 모아질 때, 직관의 목소리는 더 똑똑히 '들린다.'

10 a. 영국의 회사들은 기록적인 금액을 작년에 광고에 썼는데, 이것은 영국의 경제 부활이 임박했다는 것을 보여준다.
　b. 작은 일들에 대한 그의 기억은 지워져버렸는데, 이것이 그가 늙어가고 있다는 징조다.
　c. 그 과학자들은 자기들의 연구가 유용하기를 바랐는데, 이것이 그들이 인류의 혜택을 위해 일하고 싶어했다는 것을 보여준다.
　d. 어쩌면 남플로리다가 직면한 가장 슬픈 난관은 아이티 난민들의 참상일 것이다. 사법 관리들이 한 달에 약 500명의 아이티인들을 플로리다의 해안에서 체포하는데, 아마 그 수에 상당하는 아이티인들이 잡히지 않고 잠입할 것이다. 아이티로부터 600

마일의 여행은 흔히 무척 힘드는데, 이것은 얼마나 필사적으로 아이티인들이 자기 나라를 떠나고 싶어하는지를 보여준다.

11 생명공학자들이 사용하는 가장 잘 알려져 있고 가장 많은 논란을 불러 일으킨 기술이 유전자 결합인데, 이것은 다른 생물의 유전자를 식물이나 동물 혹은 미생물에 삽입하는 것이다. 과학자들은, 예를 들어, 쥐의 성장 호르몬을 새앙쥐의 DNA에 도입하여 더 큰 새앙쥐를 만들어냈고, 개똥벌레 유전자를 담배에 도입하여 어두운 곳에서 빛을 내는 담배를 만들어냈다. 유전 공학은, 그러나, 암소와 개구리를 '교배시켜서' (즉 이들 둘의 유전자를 결합해서) 새로운 종을 만들어내지는 못한다.

12 오래전부터 월 스트리트에서 전해 내려오는 얘기에 의하면, 30세까지 첫 백만 달러를 벌지 못하는 사람은 결코 그런 돈을 벌 수 없다고 한다. 1776년에 아담 스미스는 젊은이들이야말로 위험을 겁내지 않고 자신만만하게 성공을 희망한다고 기술했는데, 바로 이런 자질들이 새로운 기업체를 창설하는 데에 필요하다. 정말이지, 많은 기업인들이 아주 젊은 나이에 성공을 이루었다. 많은 예 가운데 하나로, 빌 게이츠(26세)는 1975년 2학년 때에 하버드 대학을 중퇴하고 마이크로소프트라는 회사를 창설했는데, 개인용 컴퓨터를 위한 소프트웨어를 만드는 이 회사의 1981년 매상은 1,500만 달러였다.

13 해마다, 수천 명의[또는 수많은] 미국인들이 화재로 사망한다. 많은 경우에, 사망 원인은 너무 많은 피부가 타버려서 필요불가결한 신체 기능들이 붕괴되기 때문이다. 필수적인 체액이 흘러나오고, 신체의 타고난 방어력이 너무 약해져서 박테리아에 의한 감염을 싸워서 물리칠 수 없게 된다. 이러한 화상으로 말미암은 신체 기능의 악화를 막기 위해, 의사들은 피부가 타버린 곳에 환자의 신체 중에서 손상을 입지 않은 부분으로부터 피부를 이식하려고 하지만, 흔히 남아 있는 피부가 너무 적어서 할 수 없이 돼지나 시신의 피부를 이용하게 된다. 이질적인 조직이기 때문에, 이렇게 이식된 피부는 대개 3일 내지 25일이 지나면 거부반응을 보이게 된다. 이상적인 해결책은 인조 피부가 되겠지만, 과학자들은 지금까지 이러한 목표를 달성하지 못했다. 그러나 지난 주에 보스턴의 한 연구 팀의 발표에 의하면, 놀랍게도 소가죽, 상어 연골과 플라스틱 등의 재료를 배합해서 인조 피부를 만들어내는 데 성공했다고 한다.

주의 thousands of : 1. several thousand (수천의, 수만의)
2. a large number of (다수의, 수많은)

14 2,500만 명으로 추산되는 미국인들이 읽기장애를 갖고 있는데, 이 증세는 수년 동안 여러 가지 시험에 의해 알아낼 수 있었다. 읽기장애자들은 흔히 왼손잡이나 양손잡이들인데, 글자를 뒤집어서 읽거나(d를 b로), 단어를 거꾸로 읽거나(saw를 was로), 어순을 혼동하거나 (please hurry up을 please up hurry로), (내리) 뺄셈을 왼쪽에서 오른쪽으로 해나가거나, 차례차례 따져나가는 사고에 어려움을 겪는 경향이 있다. 이러한 문제점에도 불구하고, 이들은 지적으로 뛰어나며 재주가 좋아서 (속이면서) 저학년생활을 헤쳐 나아간다. 읽기장애자들은 에디슨, 아인슈타인, 패튼 장군, 넬슨 록펠러, 그리고 브루스 제너처럼 위대한 업적을 이룰 수가 있다. 그러나 이들은 흔히 정신지체아나 정서적으로 불안한 아이로 잘못 진단[판정]을 받는다.

주의 여러분, 제가 마지막 번역문에서 '아이' 라고 옮긴 이유를 아세요? 여기서 얘기하는 they는 '어른' 이 아니기 때문입니다. 이런 '작은' 면에도 세심한 주의를 기울이세요. 그래야만 여러분의 영어가 정확해지고, 여러분의 사고가 '엄격성' (rigor)을 갖게 됩니다.

EXERCISE 13

1 a 나는 그를 화나게 만들 말을 아무것도 하지 않았다.
b 나는 아무 말도 하지 않았는데, 그것이 그를 화나게 만들었다.

2 아무 것에도 매달릴 수 없는 사람은 실패하기 마련이다, 무슨 일을 떠맡든지 간에.

3 나를 이루는 것은 과거의 나와 현재의 나, 그리고 미래의 나다.

4 효과적인 지식은 자신의 지식의 한계에 대한 지식이 포함되어 있는 지식이다(다시 말해서, 효과적인 지식은 자신의 지식의 한계를 알고 있는 지식이다).

5 진정으로 매력 있는 여성은 젊은이를 성숙한 사람으로, 노인을 젊게 해주고, 중년의 남자에게 자신감을 줄 수 있는 여성이다.

6 로봇은 산업이 물려받은 모든 질병에 대한 만병통치약이 아니다.

7 면전에서 칭찬해주는 사람을 믿지 말아라.

8 칸트는 나에게 강력하고 지워버릴 수 없는 인상을 주었는데, 나는 그 후에 내가 읽은 어떤 철학자에게서도 그와 같은 인상을 경험하지 못했다.

9 강사들을 가장 당황하게 만드는 것들 가운데 하나는 청중이 시계를 보는 것이다. 나는 언젠가 존 어스킨에게 그런 괴로운 체험이 화나는 일이라고 생각하지 않느냐고 물어보았다.
 "아니에요, 사람들이 시계를 흔들기 시작하기 전까지는 아니죠!"라고 그가 대답했다.
 여러분, 이런 마음의 여유가 부럽지 않습니까? 유머의 의의가 바로 여기에 있겠죠.

10 사랑은 창의적인 것으로, 받는 사람과 주는 사람의 삶을 모두 크게 윤택하게 해준다. 그것은 세상에서 아무리 많이 주어도 지나치다고 할 수 없는 유일한 것이다. 진정한 사랑에는 아무것도 대신해줄 수 없는 힘과 자제력이 있으므로, 그것은 결코 해를 끼치거나 억제하거나 망치지 않으며, 혜택을 줄 수 있을 뿐이다.

11 아마도 과학은 원칙적으로 인간의 구조와 행동을 물리적인 자연의 일부로 설명할 수 있을지 모른다. 그러나 분명히 인간은 그렇게 해서는 완전히 설명되지 않는다. 관념과 이상주의, 이해[이성]와 감정처럼 인생에 인간적인 의미를 부여하는 영역이 완전히 설명에서 제외되기 때문이다.

12 우리 일요학교 교사들은 교대로 강의를 했다. 대개 이들은 다음과 같은 말로 강의를 끝냈다. "자, 어린이 여러분, 이 얘기의 도덕[교훈]은 … 입니다."
 어느 날, 자기 차례가 된 브라운 양이 얘기를 특별히 신나게 만들어 주어서, 어린이들은 기뻤다. 그러자 한 남자아이가 브라운 선생님이 더 자주 가르쳐줄 수 없느냐고 물었다. "우리는 그 선생님을 무척 좋아해요", 그가 설명했다. "왜냐하면 그 선생님에게는 아무 도덕이 없으니까요."
 여러분, 이거 농담입니다. 좀 지나치기는 하지만요.

13 딘 러스크는, 전 국무장관으로 지금은 아테네에 있는 조지아 대학교에서 국제법 교수로 있는데, 끊임없이 인터뷰에 응해달라는 부탁을 받으므로 자연히 준비가 잘 되어 있다. 지난 봄 어느 날, 이 대학교의 스튜디오(여기서 텔레비전 대담 프로를 녹화하기로 되어 있었다)에 일찍 도착한 그는 방송 담당자들이 준비를 끝마치는 동안 무대 위 자기 자리에 앉아 노트해 온 것을 훑어보고 있었다. 무대감독이 5분 후에 시작한다고 발표하자, 러스크는 호주머니에서 콤팩트를 꺼내서 분첩을 꺼낸 뒤에 자신의 대머리에 발랐다. 그렇게 하지 않으면 거기에 텔레비전 조명이 반사될 것이기 때문이었다. 그러고 나서 그는 콤팩트를 치우고 시작할 준비가 되었다고 말했다.

14 미국의 여러 지역에서는 1870년 이래로 기록상 최악이 될지도 모를 겨울을 경험하고 있다.

15 나는 그를 무척 좋아했으나, 어떤 면으로 보아도 세상 사람들이 얘기하는 식으로 그와 "사랑에 빠져" 있지는 않았다.

16 새로 나온 한 백과사전은 인간의 지식이 증가함에 따라서 축소되도록 계획되어 있다.
 대부분의 백과사전들은 새로운 발견이 이루어짐에 따라서 내용을 추가할 필요가 있다. 그러나 〈무지의 백과사전〉(이것은 과학분야에서 인간이 모르는 것을 요약한 사전이다)에서는 새로운 사실이 발견됨에 따라서 내용이 삭제되어야 한다. 예를 들어, 어떻게 중력이 작용하는

지, 어떻게 해서 식물이 꽃을 피우는지, 또는 왜 사람들은 약물과 알코올에 중독되는지 등에 관해서 말이다.

이 책은 최근 뉴욕의 퍼거먼 출판사에 의해 발행되었는데, 여기에는 60명의 저명한 과학자들이 자기 전공 분야에서 이해하지 못하는 것에 대해서 기고한 글들이 들어 있다.

17 어쩌면 역사상 처음으로 축구시합이 웃음 때문에 지연된 적이 있었다. 5천 명의 아테네 축구 팬들이, 작년 그리스 팀과 중국 팀 사이에 시범경기가 시작되기를 기다리다가, 중국 국가가 확성기로부터 울려나오는 줄 알고 일어서서 엄숙하게 조용히 서 있었다. 경기장에 나와 있던 중국 팀은, 그리스인들이 모두 일어서 있는 것을 보고 그리스 국가가 연주되고 있는 줄 알고서 또한 차렷자세를 취했다.

그 때 낭랑한 여성의 목소리가 낯선 음악 위에 솟아나와서, 그 지방에서 생산되는 치약의 좋은 점들을 칭찬했다.

18 다리에 부상을 입었지만, 클라크(6세)는 꺼려하지 않고 학교에 다녔다. 취학전학교 후반에 다니는 동안에 그는 기꺼이 점점 더 많은 시간을 어머니와 떨어져서 보내려고 해 왔다. 부모님이 열렬히 학교에 관한 얘기를 하시면, 클라크는 그들의 말씀대로 학교를 받아들였다. 선생님이 그에게는 부모님의 연장으로, 그들과 마찬가지로 인정을 통해서는 즐거움을, 비판을 통해서는 고통을 줄 수 있는 힘을 갖고 있는 것으로 생각되었는데, 클라크에게는 그런 즐거움이나 고통이 중요했다. 클라크는 선생님이 제의하는 방법이 무엇이든지 그 방법대로 (학교활동에) 참여했다. 만일 자기 조가 커다란 소방서 그림을 그리게 되면, 클라크는 자기에게 맡겨진 부분을 열심히 그렸다. 그리고 자기 조에서 소방서 방문에 관한 얘기를 하게 되면, 클라크는 거기에 맞게 귀를 기울였다. 선생님이 생각하기에 클라크는 좋은 공부하는 버릇을 갖고 있었다. 혼자 내버려두게 되면, 그는 다른 아이들보다 훨씬 더 오랫동안 자기 공부에 열중했는데, 다른 아이들은 그런 경우에 너무도 쉽게 공부를 잊어버리고 놀거나 (친구와) 얘기하려 들었다.

19 우리 가운데 누구든지 종교 분야에서 선입관으로부터 어느 정도까지 자유로울 수 있느냐는 의문의 여지가 있다(즉, 우리가 종교 분야에서 어느 정도까지 선입관으로부터 해방될 수 있는지는 의심스러운 문제다).

20 폴란드의 군사적 움직임 뒤에는 소련의 그림자가 위협적인 모습으로 나타났다. 정말이지, 만일 야루젤스키 장군 정부가 그런 단속조치를 취하지 않았더라면, 소련이 틀림없이 그렇게 했을 것이다. 바르샤바에 소련의 고위 관리들(빅토르 쿨리코프 장군을 포함해서)이 자리잡고 있었다는 사실은 대리침략이나 다름없는 이 조치를 계획하는 데에 소련이 직접 관여했으리라는 것을 암시해 주기까지 했다. 일 년 이상 동안, 소련은 폴란드 자유노조가 해 온 것처럼 직접적으로 공산주의 정부에 도전할 수 있는 노조운동을 무한정으로 용납하지 않겠다는 것을 분명히 밝혀왔다. 왜냐하면 이 운동은 사실상 피지배자의 동의에 의한 정치(즉, 민주정치)를 요구하는 거나 다름이 없기 때문이다.

EXERCISE 14

1 보석 가게에서 반지 하나를 훔치다가 들킨 사람이 애원했다. "제발 경찰을 부르지 말아주세요. 제가 기꺼이 그 반지 값을 지불하겠습니다."

계산원이 그에게 청구서를 제시하자, 그는 이렇게 말했다. "이건 제가 쓰려고 계획했던 것보다 액수가 좀 많군요. 더 싼 걸 보여주실 수 있습니까?"

> 예답 이 양반 정말 두껍군요. 하기야, 사정상 어쩔 수 없기도 하겠지만.

2 알루미늄이 그토록 여러 가지 용도에 사용될 수 있는 것은 알루미늄의 속성 때문인데, 이러한 속성은 너무도 다양해서 마치 몇 개의 다른 광물의 속성 같아 보일 정도다.

3 어느 여름, 매사추세츠 주 낸터컷 섬에 있는 거의 모든 가게와 식당 창문에 커다란 표지가 붙어있었는데, 거기에는 맨발로 다니는 사람들이

들어오는 것을 금지한다는 내용이 적혀 있었다. 그러나 눈에 띄는 예외가 하나 있었다. 중심가에서 떨어져 있는 한 작은 가게에서는 대담하게 "맨발 환영"이라는 표지를 붙여놓았다. 그 가게는 그 지방의 샌들 만드는 가게였다.

참고 Massachusetts 주가 속해 있는 미국의 New England 지방은, 그 이름이 암시하듯이, 보수적인 곳이다.

4 독서는 경험의 보충에 불과한 것이 아니다. 좋은 독서는 경험 그 자체다. 힘과 통찰력과 진실을 갖고 쓸 수 있는 저자는 자신이 인식한 것을 통해 독자가 주위 세계를 이해할 수 있도록 도와줄 수 있다. 그러므로 위대한 저술가들의 지혜와 이해를 멀리하는 사람은 다른 방법으로 얻을 수 없는 매우 값진 경험을 멀리하는 셈이다.

책을 통해서, 우리는 우리 자신의 시대와 모든 시대의 가장 훌륭한 지성인들이 누구나 흥미를 갖는 소재에 대해서 얘기하는 것을 들을 수가 있다.

5 다윈은, 세계를 한 바퀴 돈 뒤에, 여생 전부를 자기 집에서 보냈다. 마르크스는, 몇몇 혁명을 불러일으킨 뒤에, 여생을 대영박물관에서 보내기로 작정했다. 대체로 조용하게 살아가는 것이 위대한 사람들의 특징이며, 이들의 즐거움은 겉눈으로 보기에 신나는 그런 종류의 것이 아니었음을 알 수 있을 것이다. 위대한 업적은 끈질긴 노력 없이는 불가능하다 — 그러한 노력은 당사자의 관심을 모두 빼앗아갈 뿐 아니라 너무도 어렵기 때문에 더 많은 힘을 요하는 여흥에 쓸 수 있는 정력이 거의 남지 않는 법이다.

6 이탈리아인들은 점점 더 약해지고 효율성이 떨어지는 정부와의 엄청난 간격에도 불구하고 생존하고 있다. 그들은 통제 불능의 복지제도, 무질서한 학교와 사회 서비스 (공공시설) 체계, 그리고, 아마 무엇보다도 가장 나쁜, 너무도 팽창되어 있고 비능률적이어서 족쇄와 올가미라고 조롱받는 관료제도에도 불구하고 살아남아 있다. 지난 11월 일련의 강력한 지진이 남부 이탈리아에 발생해서, 마을들을 송두리째 무너뜨려 고립시켰고, 3,000명의 사망자를 내고, 30만 명이 집을 잃게 만들었다. 구호의 손길이 재빨리 쏟아져 들어왔는데, 여기에는 미국의 원조 5천만 달러도 포함되어 있었다. 지금까지 관료조직의 비능률 때문에, 미국의 원조자금 가운데에서 불과 420만 달러만이 이재민을 돕기 위해 사용되었을 뿐이다. 그것은 분명히 놀랄 만한 일이 아니다. 13년 전에 시칠리아 섬의 벨리체 지역을 뒤흔들어 놓았던 지진의 생존자들이 아직도 임시 주택에서 살고 있다는 점을 고려해볼 때 말이다.

EXERCISE 15

1 우리는 금전지향적인 사회에 살고 있으므로, 우리가 돈을 지나치게 값지게 여기는 것은 당연하다.

2 a. 기회가 주어진다면, 그들은 자기들의 삶을 더 낫게 만들 수 있을지 모른다.
b. 경험이 없다는 점을 고려해 볼 때에, 그들은 일을 잘 했다.

3 a. 너 도대체 자신을 누구라고 생각하기에, 나에게 이래라 저래라 하고 명령을 하느냐?
b. 너 도대체 자신이 무엇을 하고 있다고 생각하느냐? 나에게 입을 닥치라고 하니 말이다.

4 그는 누워서 눈을 뜨고, 커튼 틈새로 시냇물처럼 흘러들어오는 아침 햇살을 바라보고 있었다.

5 자신을 과대평가하는 것으로 유명한 동료직원이 꼼꼼하게 보관하고 있는 여러 서류철에서 서류 하나를 찾으려던 중에, 나는 우연히 커다란 서류철 하나를 발견했는데, 거기에는 두꺼운 서체로 "실수들"이라는 제목이 붙어 있었다. 호기심에 압도되어, 나는 그것을 펴 보았다. 그 서류철 안에는 아무것도 없었다.

어구 여러분, 웃으세요. 이거 해학입니다.

6 우리 아파트에 어린 소년이 새 광고판을 하나 세웠는데, 거기에는 50센트로 세차를 해주겠다는 내용이 적혀 있었다. 나는 재빨리 그의 제의를 이용했는데, 내가 그의 첫고객이라는 것을

알고 그에게 일을 잘 했다고 25센트를 더 주었다. 약 10분 뒤에 그의 광고판 곁을 지나가다 보니 재미있게도 이제 거기에는 이렇게 적혀 있었다. "세차. 75센트 — 경험 있음."

예답 어린이는 어른의 거울! — 이 유머에는 어른 세계의 한 면이 너무도 생생하게 그려져 있군요.

7 우리 마을에서는 날마다 오후 6시에 소방서 사이렌이 울린다. 어느 날 저녁 그것이 저녁 7시 15분에 울렸다. 걱정이 된 마을 사람들이 소방 트럭들이 어디로 가는지 보려고 모였다.

트럭들이 소방서를 떠나지 않자, 우리는 무슨 영문이냐고 물어보았다. "화재가 일어난 게 아닙니다"라는 대답을 우리는 들었다. "소방대원들이 회의를 하고 있는데, 충분한 인원이 나타나지 않았습니다."

8 어느 날 저녁, 우리 시누이댁에서는 미국기를 특별한 날에만 달 게 아니라 날마다 달기로 결정했다. 그 다음날 아침에 그들은 그 결정을 실천에 옮겼다. 현관에 있는 받침대에 기를 꽂은 뒤에 곧 현관 문에 노크 소리가 났다. 우리 시누이가 문가에 나가보니, 우체부가 서 있었다. 기를 가리키면서, 그가 물었다. "어째서 오늘 기가 날리고 있죠?"

설명을 들은 뒤에, 집배원은 발걸음을 옮기면서 말했다. "감사합니다. 휴일에 제가 근무하고 있는 게 아닌지 확인해 보고 싶었을 뿐입니다."

9 미국의 가장 유명한 소설가 가운데 한 사람으로서 더스 패서스는 긴 생애를 통해서 작가란 역사를 만드는 사람이라는 자신의 믿음에 충실해 왔다. 내일의 문제는 과거에 대한 연구로 가장 잘 해결될 수 있다고 믿고, 그는 미래의 세대들이 보고 이해할 수 있도록 주변 세계의 모습과 소리를 정확하게 묘사하는 데에 자신의 생애를 바쳐왔다. 20세기의 미국을 묘사한 작품으로, 더스 패서스의 소설을 능가하는 것은 없다.

10 휴버트 험프리 부통령이 얼마 전에 워싱턴에서 교육자들에게 연설을 하고 있었는데, 자신의 교직 경험에 대해서 다소 자세히 얘기했다. 그의 교직 경험에는 짧은 기간 동안 한 미네소타 대학에서 정치학 부교수로 근무한 기간이 포함되어 있다. 험프리는 이렇게 말했다. "제가 저의 교직배경에 관해서 말씀드리는 것은 공직의 불안정한 장래로 보아 여러분이 혹시 저를 검토해 보고 싶어하실지도 모르기 때문입니다."

11 다른 모든 일과 마찬가지로, 독서 역시 지나칠 수가 있다. 지나치게 탐닉한다면, 독서는 악이 된다 — 그런데 이 악은 일반적으로 악이라고 인정하지 않기 때문에 그만큼 더 위험하다. 그러나 지나친 독서는 자기 탐닉 가운데 유일하게 마땅히 받아야 할 비난을 받지 않는 형태다. 이 사실은 놀라운 일이다. 왜냐하면 솔직하게 자신과 다른 사람들을 관찰해 보면 누구나 지나친 독서는 자신의 시간을 집어삼키고, 정력을 낭비하며, 사고력을 타락시키고, 현실로부터 관심을 다른 곳으로 돌리게[외면하게] 만든다는 것을 분명히 알 수 있기 때문이다.

EXERCISE 16

1 그는 그 질문에 다소 놀라는 것 같아 보였다. 왜냐하면 그것은 논의되고 있는 문제와 아무 관련이 없는 것 같아 보였기 때문이었다.

2 처음에는 내 능력에 자신이 없었으나, 나는 마침내 자신을 갖는 법을 알게 되었다.

3 증세가 나타날 때까지 기다려서는 안 된다. 왜냐하면 찾아내서 치료를 받지 않으면, 고혈압은 환자를 사망하게 만들기 때문이다. 그것은 살금살금 소리없이 사람을 죽이는 병이다.

주의 이 글은 전형적인 구어체 영어로 쓰여져 있음에 주의하라.

4 그는 확고한 개인주의적 사고방식을 갖고 있었지만, 협력할 줄 아는 사람이었다.

5 옛날의 런던 시에서는 화재가 드물지 않았는데, 그것은 좁은 거리들이 미로처럼 복잡하게 얽혀

있었고, 나무로 만든 집들이 빽빽하게 몰려 있었기 때문이었다.

6 이상하게도 그리스인들(옛날의 그리스인들을 가리킴)은, 발달하고 예리한 두뇌를 갖고 있었지만, 현미경이나 망원경을 만들 수 있다는 사실을 한번도 깨닫지 못했다.

7 지난 30년 동안에 언어교수 방법론에 상당한 발전이 있어왔지만, 우리는 어렵지 않게 "문장은 논리적으로 연결되어야 한다"는 원칙에 어긋나는 교과내용을 찾아볼 수 있다. 현재 나와 있는 청각 어학 교재들은 구조를 강조하느라, 흔히 어휘와 의미에 충분한 주의를 기울이지 않은 결과 많은 문형연습문제에는, 설령 논리적으로 연결되어 있다고 하더라도, 다만 희박하게 연결되어 있는 문장들이 들어 있다.

8 정치 분야에서 또한 여성들은 중요한 역할을 담당한다. 국회에 선출된 여성들이 많지 않았고, 비록 2개 주에 여자 지사가 있었지만, 여자 대통령은 한 명도 없었다. 그렇지만 여성은 유권자로서 너무도 중요하므로 공직 후보자라면 누구나 여성들의 태도를 의식하지 않을 수가 없다. 여성들은 1920년에야 투표권을 갖게 되었는데, 여성 투표권(의 실시)은, 많은 사람들이 예측한 것처럼 여성들이 남편과 같은 쪽에 투표함으로써 주어진 문제의 찬반에 던져질 투표의 총수를 단순히 두 배로 증가시키지는 않았다. 그 대신 여성들은 문제점과 후보자들에 관한 연구를 통해 스스로 결정을 내리기 시작했다.

> **참고** He was not guilty of the murder, as many people thought him to be.

9 품위있게 차를 조금씩 마시면서, 그는 교육이라는 것은 놀라운 일이라고 말했다.

10 비록 반대로 설교를 하고 있지만, 세상은 돈을 많이 쓰는 사람을 좋아한다.

11 의사가 가지 말라고 충고했는데도 불구하고 그는 미식축구 경기를 보러 갔다.

12 교육에 관한 문제는 흔히 논의된다. 마치 사회제도와 아무런 관련이 없는 것처럼. 그러나 교육은 사회제도 안에서 이루어지며, 그 사회제도를 위해서 이루어진다. 이것이 교육 문제에 대한 해답들이 만족스럽지 않은 가장 흔한 이유들 가운데 하나다.

> **주의** 주어진 영어 문장이 하나로 이루어져 있다고 해서 반드시 그것을 우리말로 옮길 때에 하나로 만들어야 할 이유는 없다. 왜냐하면, 첫째, 영어는 한국어와 구조적으로 다르고, 둘째, 같은 내용을 꼭 한 가지로만 나타낼 수 있는 것이 아니기 때문이다.

13 그리하여 역사가 막 되풀이될지도 모른다는 증거가 쌓이고 있다. 여러 나라의 실업가들이 오늘날 무기를 공산주의자들에게 팔아서 돈을 벌고 있다, 이들의 선배들이 제2차 세계대전이 발발할 때까지 히틀러를 도와서 돈을 벌었듯이. 많은 서구인들은, 마땅히 그렇게 생각하지 말아야 하는 데도 불구하고, 공산진영이 커다란 전쟁을 일으키는 위험을 무릅쓰지 않을 거라고 맹목적으로 생각하고 있다. 이와 같은 종류의 오산[잘못된 생각]이 1930년대 말에 있었다.

14 a. 그는 거기에 혼자 갔다, 내가 그렇게 하지 말라고 충고했는데도 불구하고.

　b. 어떤 여성이 비행기에 올라왔는데, 그녀는 너무 많은 시간을 터미널에 있는 술집에서 보낸 게 분명했다. 스튜어디스는, 그렇게 하지 않는 것이 더 나을 거라고 판단했지만, 마티니 한 잔을 달라는 그녀의 요구를 들어주었으나, 몇 분 뒤에 한 잔 더 채워달라는 요구를 거절했다. 매우 화가 난 그 승객은 다그쳐 물었다. "아가씨, 이름이 뭐죠? 아가씨를 보고하겠어요."
　"제 이름요?" 스튜어디스가 말했다. "분명히, 그건 바로 여기 있죠." 그녀는 자신의 제복에 붙어 있는 명찰을 가리켰다.
　승객은 그 명찰을 뚫어지게 바라보았다. 그녀는 눈을 깜박거린 뒤 다시 들여다보았다. 그런 뒤 그녀는 다시 자기 자리에 푹 주저앉았다. "아가씨가 맞는가 봐요"라고 그녀는 중얼거렸다. "그걸 읽을 수가 없군요."

EXERCISE 17

1 그는 그 문제에 관해서 아무것도 모르는 척했다.

2 "저 과부가 누구냐?"고 그가 물었다, 관심이 없는 척하면서.

3 무엇인가 형용할 수 없는 어떤 것이 그 방에 남자가 살고 있다는 것을 얘기해 주는 것 같았다.

4 그리하여 지구가 우주의 중심이라는 생각은 파괴되었다.

5 항공우주국에서는 그 계획이 80억 달러가 소요될지도 모른다고 생각했다. 그래도 약 30억 달러가 모자라는 비용을 제의받자, 이 기관에서는 낙관하는 척하며, 그 돈을 받아들여서 그 계획을 시작했다.

6 식사 중에 나는 대통령에게 이렇게 말했다. 대부분의 대통령 고문들은 곧 중동에서 전쟁이 다시 일어날 위험성을 '약 60~70% 사이'로 보고 있는 것 같다고.

7 미국의 재벌 카네기는 부자로 죽는 것은 불명예스러운 일이라고 말하고, 백만장자는 다만 가난한 사람들을 위해서 재산을 신탁받은 사람이 되어야 한다고 주장했다.

8 플로리다 주의 한 십대 소녀와 유타 주의 30세 남자가 자살했는데, 이들이 남겨놓은 쪽지에는 레논의 죽음 때문에 슬퍼졌다는 내용이 적혀 있었다.

9 카터는, 레이건이 장래에 미국이 무력을 증강하겠다고 위협함으로써 소련에게 겁을 주어서 기존 무기를 대폭 감축하게 할 수 있다고 생각한다고 해서 그를 어리석을 정도로 단순하다고 말하는데, 카터의 이 얘기는 옳다.

10 그녀의 얼굴에 있는 주름살 하나하나가, 그녀의 부드럽고 졸리는 듯한 목소리의 음조 하나하나가 그녀가 자신의 삶에 전적으로 만족하고 있다는 것을 얘기해 주었다.

11 노동자들은 상관이 올바른 결정을 내릴 것으로 믿는다. 왜냐하면 노동자와 경영자는 함께 일한다는〔동지라는〕생각이 널리 퍼져 있기 때문이다. 일본 기업에서는 일반적으로 경영자가 일반 직원으로부터 승진하는데, 이것이 노동자와 경영자는 동지며 동고동락한다는 생각을 더해 준다.

12 이 견해에 의하면, 대폭적인 지출삭감과 일 년에 걸친 약간의 세금 인하는 가능한 최악의 경제사태, 즉 물가상승에 의한 경기후퇴를 초래할 수 있을 것이다. 그래서 일부 경제고문들은 백악관〔행정부〕측에 자체의 조세 계획을 위해서 끝까지 싸우라고 얘기하고 있는데, 그러나 바로 그 순간에 행정부는 대열을 가다듬고 서 있는〔자신들의 조세계획을 통과시키려고 투쟁하는〕민주당원들을 견제하느라 애를 먹고 있다. 국회에서 장기적인 논쟁이 예상될 뿐만 아니라, 행정부 내에서도 의견이 분열되리라 예상된다.

> 참고 '대폭적인 지출삭감과 1년에 걸친 약간의 세금 인하'는 민주당의 방안이다.

13 확실히, 오늘날 동-서 관계의 상태에서는 소련의 공격을 유발할 만한 것이 아무것도 없다. 그러나 서구의 전략가들은 소련의 정책이 갑자기 바뀔 가능성을 배제할 수 없다. 갑자기 소련이 군사적으로 위협해 온다면, 나토는 그것을 믿을 만하게〔확실하게〕저지할 수 없을 것이다, 현재의 병력수준과 많은 서구 정부들의 현재의 경제적·정치적 약점들을 갖고서는. 수적인 면에서 볼 때에, 오늘날 북대서양 조약기구는 병력 수, 총기, 탱크, 그리고 비행기에서 상대측〔소련측〕보다 뒤떨어진다. 이것은 주로 소련 군대의 대대적인 증강이 가져온 결과다.

14 대부분의 공식 지표에 의하면, 이탈리아의 경제는 심각한 어려움 속에 놓여 있는 것으로 나타난다. 물가상승률은 거의 21%로 치닫고 있으며 산업 생산은 지난 8월 이래로 5.4% 떨어졌

고, 실업자는 150만 명이다. 심한 타격을 입은 이탈리아의 화폐 리라는 계속해서 가치가 떨어지고 있고, 정부의 적자는 연말까지 적어도 312억 달러에 이를 것으로 예상된다. 밀라노의 보르사 발로리는, 이탈리아에서 제일 가는 증권거래소인데, 지난달에 갑자기 3일 동안 문을 닫았는데, 이것은 급격한 주식 매각으로 주가가 한 시간에 20% 떨어진 후에 올 공황을 막기 위해서였다. 이런 일은 1917년 이래로 일어난 적이 없었는데, 그때는 이탈리아가 제1차 세계대전 때에 카포레토에서 굴욕적으로 패배한 직후였다.

15 아마도 TIME지 경제학자 위원회 위원들의 가장 고무적인 예측은 물가상승률이 떨어지리라는 것이다. 이들에 의하면, 그것은 금년에 약 8.6% 연비율로 끝날 것으로 예상되는데, 이에 비해 1980년 4/4분기에는 13.2%였다. 세계 석유시장에서 석유가 약간 남아돌기 때문에 석유 가격이 현재 단단히 묶여 있는데, 이것이 최근의 물가상승의 주요 원인들 가운데 하나를 제거해 줄 것이다. 집값은 소비자 물가지수의 약 4분의 1을 차지하는데, 1년 전보다는 올랐지만 매매가 저조하기 때문에 집값의 인상은 점차 줄어들고 있다. 금년 지금까지의 풍작과 가축의 대량생산으로 앞으로 몇 개월 동안 식량 가격의 증가가 완화될 가능성이 있다. 마지막으로, 미국 달러의 가치 상승으로 수입 상품의 가격이 떨어져 국내 기업들은 제품의 가격을 계속 억제해야 할 것이다. 케네디 대통령의 수석 경제고문이었던 월터 헬러는 미국이 "금년 대부분의 기간 동안 물가상승의 감소를 사실상 보장받은 거나 다름없다"고 결론짓는다.

16 한없이 다양한 법률, 규제, 관습과 전통이 전 세계의 임신중절의 실시에 영향을 미치고 있다, 비록 일반적으로 법률이 관대해지는 경향을 보이고는 있지만.

EXERCISE 18

1 우리는 지난 몇 개월 동안 상당히 곤란을 겪어 왔다, 남편에게 직장이 없어서.
　참고　진한 글자 부분 = because my husband has been out of work

2 스미스 씨 부인은 바빴다, 세 아이와 병약한 남편, 연로한 어머니를 돌봐야 했기 때문에.
　참고　진한 글자 부분 = because she had three children, an invalid husband and an aged mother to look after

3 그 젊은 부부에게는 이미 그들 사이에 태어난 아이가 있는데, 또 한 아이를 임신하고 있다.
　참고　진한 글자 부분 = and another child is on its way

4 나는 연단에 올라갔는데, 그 때 내 마음 속에는 (얘기할) 아무런 준비가 되어 있지 않았다.
　참고　진한 글자 부분 = when I had nothing ready in my mind

5 나는 아이들이 주위에 있을 때에는 아무것도 읽을 수가 없다.
　참고　진한 글자 부분 = when children are around

6 그들은 같은 집에서 거의 1년 반 동안 살았으나, 단 한 마디 말도 그들 사이에 오가지 않았다.
　참고　진한 글자 부분 = but not a single word was spoken between them

7 발판을 잃어버리자, 올리버는 대륙을 따라서 목적없는 방랑을 다시 시작했다.
　참고　진한 글자 부분 = When the earth was cut away from his feet

8 그는, 머리를 숙이고 앉아서, 그 문제에 대해서 생각하고 있었다.

9 나는 서 있었다, 바늘처럼 꼿꼿이, 어깨는 뒤로 젖히고, 머리는 높이 쳐들고, 내 눈은 그녀의 눈을 피하면서.

10 전쟁이 이라크와 그밖의 세계 도처에서 오늘날

끊임없이 계속되고 있으므로, 전쟁 없는 세계라는 그 목표는 여전히 달성하기가 먼 것 같아 보인다.

> 참고 진한 글자 부분 = As fightings in Iraq and elsewhere in the world today are going on incessantly

11 이스라엘이 중동문제 해결에 관해서 아랍국들과 직접회담을 갖겠다고 주장하고 있으므로, 성공적인 평화협정이 체결될 가능성은 요원한 것 같다.

12 북쪽에 있는 공산주의 정권이 아직도 온갖 짓을 다해서 남한을 비방하고 있으므로, 한국의 재통일은 여전히 요원해 보인다.

13 한편, 보도에 의하면 그 회의를 위한 가장 유망한 장소는 서울과 부산인데, 후자가 가능성이 더 높다고 한다.

> 참고 진한 글자 부분 = and that the latter is a stronger possibility

14 버나드 버렌슨은 미술사가였는데, 인생을 사랑했다. 거의 90세였을 때에 그는 이렇게 말했다, "나는 기꺼이 길 모퉁이에 서서, 손에 모자를 들고, 지나가는 사람들에게 자기들이 사용하지 않은 시간을 그 모자 안에 떨어뜨려 달라고 부탁하고 싶다."

15 전체 인구 가운데 거의 60%가 아직도 토지에 생계를 의존하고 있으므로, 그 나라는 무엇보다도 먼저 영농방법의 현대화를 위해 더 많은 노력을 기울여야 한다.

16 스웨덴에서는, 차를 몰고 빨간 신호등이 켜져 있을 때에 어떤 교차로를 지나가게 되면, 사진이 자동으로 찍힌다. 위반한 사람은 우편으로 자기 차가 교통신호를 무시하고 지나가는 것을 보여주는 사진 한 장 — 여기에는 시간과 날짜가 찍혀 있다 — 과 벌금을 내라는 명령서를 받게 된다. 편리하게도, 300크로노의 벌금을 거주 지역의 은행이나 우체국에서 지불할 수 있다.

> 주의 대명사 you의 용법에 주의하라.

17 어린 두 아들을 데리고 온 어떤 어머니가 서둘러 여섯 개들이 맥주통을 사기 위해 슈퍼마켓에서 계산하고 있었다. 잔돈을 정확하게 준비하려고, 이 어머니는 한 아들에게서 3센트를 빌렸다. "그때 일이 벌어졌답니다"라고 그녀가 말한다. "거기에서 임신 8개월 되는 제가 서 있는데, 네 살짜리 아들 녀석이 소리를 질렀습니다. '엄마, 내 동전 갖고 맥주 사지 마!'"

18 몹시 춥고 이슬비가 내리는 어느 아침 6시였는데, 한 무리의 사냥꾼들이 고통스럽게 오리사냥을 위한 매복장소에서 기다리고 있었다. 마침내 한 사냥꾼이 — 그의 손은 (추워서) 시퍼렇고 눈썹에는 얼음이 맺혀 있었는데 — 모든 사람이 속으로 생각하고 있던 것을 큰 소리로 얘기해 주었다.

"여러분," 그는 소리가 나게 이를 떨면서 말했다. "난 이 즐거움을 더 이상 견딜 수 없는 것 같네."

> 예문 이것은 고급 유머입니다. 여기에서는 pleasure라는 말이 상례를 벗어나서, stand라는 말과 '부딪혀 마찰 함으로써 웃음을 자아냅니다. 이런 관점에서 볼 때에, 유머는 '일반적인 것의 파괴' 또는 '파격'이라고 볼 수 있습니다.

19 린든 B. 잔슨 대통령 행정부 시절에 사람들 입에 계속해서 오르내리던 농담 가운데 하나가 대통령의 다이어트였다. 잔슨 대통령 부인은 그가 다이어트를 하도록 최선을 다했는데, 그는 간혹 무슨 수를 써서라도 자기가 좋아하는 높은 칼로리의 음식물을 먹으려 했다.

어느 날, 워싱턴 새너터스 야구 경기에서, 대통령석 부분에 앉아 있던 많은 사람들 중에서 누군가가 핫도그를 주문해서 주위에 돌리기 시작했다. 갑자기 대통령이 허리를 굽히고, 머리를 두 무릎 사이에 넣은 채, 핫도그 하나를 꿀꺽 삼키는 모습이 보였다. 또다시 다이어트를 지키지 않아서, 그는 버드 여사 (자기 부인)가 텔레비전으로 그 경기를 구경하다가 그가 핫도그를 먹는 걸 볼까봐 겁이 났던 것이다.

20 뉴저지 주 애틀랜틱 시티 경찰국에서 풋내기 경찰관으로 있을 때에, 나는 해안 보도의 순찰을 배당받았다. 거의 날마다 나는 거리에서 부모를 잃어버린 아이를 만났다.

어느 날 오후, 나는 어린 남자아이가 혼자 서

있는 걸 보았는데, 그 아이는 분명히 길을 잃은 것 같았다. 나는 우선 그의 신뢰를 얻으려고 노력했다 — 나는 그를 가장 가까운 아이스크림 판매대로 데리고 가서 그에게 콘을 하나 사주었다. 시간은 지나갔으나 그 아이의 부모가 보이지 않아서, 그 다음 단계는 순찰차를 불러서 그를 본부로 데려가는 것이었다. 나는 그 아이에게 내가 전화하러 가는 동안 꼼짝말고 그 자리에 있으라고 얘기했다. 내가 돌아와 보니, 그는 아무 데에도 보이지 않았다.

몇 분 안에 순찰차가 도착했는데, 순찰대원 한 사람이 그 아이가 어디에 있느냐고 내게 물었다. 나는 나 자신이 바보스럽다는 생각이 들었다. 길잃은 아이를 잃어버렸다고 얘기한다는 것은 굴욕적인 일이다. 그러나 나는 그 순찰대원에게 사정을 얘기하고 그 아이의 모습을 설명해 주었다.

"그 아이에게 무엇을 사주었소?"라고 대원 한 명이 물었다.

"아이스크림 콘요. 왜요?"

"왜냐하면" 그 경찰관이 말했다, "그 녀석은 여기서 불과 몇 구간 떨어진 곳에 사는데, 당신은 아마도 그가 먹을 걸 얻어 먹으려고 사기친 다섯 번째 풋내기일 거요!"

21 그 총잡이는 폭력배로 거의 풍자될 정도였는데, 그를 심문한 사람들 중에 하나는 그를 "대폭력배"라고 불렀다. 메흐멧 알리 아으자는 — 23세의 터키의 청부 살인자로 그는 적어도 한 차례 놀라운 살인을 저지른 기록을 갖고 있었는데 — 마음만 먹었다면 팔레스타인인이나 라틴 아메리카인으로 통할 수 있었고 실제로 거의 그렇게 통했다. 그의 이념적인 기반은 엉성했고(확고하지 않았고), 그가 내세우는 주장을 보면 그는 모든 것에 반대하는 사람으로 보였다. 그는 터키의 극우파 출신이었지만, 교황을 살해하기 위한 그의 2년 동안의 원정은 무정부주의적인 좌파의 목적에도 마찬가지로 쉽게 부합할 수 있는 것이었다. 세계에서 가장 많이 수배되고 있는 범인들 가운데 한 사람으로, 그는 서유럽을 떠돌아 다녔으나 붙잡히지 않았고, 이탈리아에 도착했을 때에는 옷을 잘 입고 있었고, 잘 무장되어 있었으며 현금을 많이 갖고 있었다.

주의 이 글은 교황저격사건에 관해서 <Newsweek>에 실린 기사에서 뽑은 것입니다. 상당히 어려우니, 잘 연구해 보시기 바랍니다.

22 윌리엄 가르시아는 성공한 캘리포니아의 마취 전문의사였는데, 그의 생활은 40세에 붕괴하기 시작했다. 그는 심한 자동차 사고를 냈고, 그 다음에 결혼상의 문제점들이 표면으로 나타나서, 아내와 별거 끝에 이혼하게 되었다. 기분이 침울하고 죄의식이 들어서, 그는 마약을 복용하게 되었다. 그는 애리조나에 있는 어느 정신 병원에 들어갔으나, 6주일만에 캘리포니아로 돌아와서 — 다시 마약을 복용했다. 비록 그럭저럭 의사노릇을 계속했으나, 의사로서의 명성이 손상을 입었다. 42세에, 마약 복용 때문에 완전히 쇠진하고 의사로서의 경력마저 무너지자, 가르시아는 어느 모텔에 투숙해서 고의로 헤로인을 과다하게 복용했다.

가르시아의 자살 시도는 실패했다. 그러나 해마다 우리를 불안하게 만들 정도로 많은 의사들이 자살에 성공하고 있는 게 사실이다. 많은 사람들의 자살이 보고되지 않고 넘어가기 때문에 정확한 통계숫자를 얻기가 어렵지만, 각기 다른 전문가들의 추산에 의하면 의사 10만 명 당 36~77명이 해마다 스스로 목숨을 끊는다고 하는데, 이것은 전체 인구의 자살률의 적어도 3배가 된다. 바꾸어 말하면, 130명 이상의 의사들이 해마다 자살을 하는데, 이 숫자는 하버드 의과대학 졸업생 숫자와 거의 맞먹는다. 모든 지적인 전문직업들 중에서, 의사들의 자살률이 가장 높을지도 모른다. 가르시아 씨는, 지금은 로스 앤젤레스의 자살예방센터에서 근무하고 있는데, 이렇게 얘기한다. "의사들의 통계수치로 보아서, 나는 살아남게 된 것이 매우 다행한 일이라고 생각합니다."

비록 하는 일이 '도전적'이고, 사회적인 지위[명성]와 비교적 부유한 생활을 누리지만, 의사들은 긴 근무시간과 싸워야 하고, 단 하나의 실수로 환자를 불구자나 무능력자로 만들거나 죽게도 만들 수 있다는 의식과 싸워야 한다. 이러한 압박감은 이들의 사생활에 영향을 미친다. 로스 앤젤레스의 정신과 의사 로버트 리트먼은 이렇게 말한다. "대체로, 의사들은 좋고 안정된 반려자가 아닙니다. 이들은 돈을 잘 벌지만, 사랑에는 형편없답니다."

참고 서양 사람들이 이상적으로 여기는 직업은, 안이한 것이 아니라, 자신의 능력을 충분히 발휘할 수 있을 만큼 도전적(challenging)이고 동시에 노력하는 만큼의 보상을 주는(rewarding) 것입니다.

EXERCISE 19

1 그런 악랄하게 잔인한 행동이 가해지는 것을 볼 때에 피가 끓어오르지 않는다면 교육을 제대로 못 받은 사람일 것이다.

2 20세기의 급속한 과학기술의 발전은 경악할 만큼 우리의 자연자원을 고갈시킨 대가로 이루어져 왔다.

3 호로비츠는 몇몇 절친한 친구들과 소박한 기쁨을 즐기는데, 이들 친구들은 정기적으로 그를 방문하며, 그는 누가 조금만 격려해 주어도 그들을 위해 피아노를 친다.

4 이 비자는 새로 신청하면 갱신할 수 있다.

5 한 번만 읽어서는 전체의 가치를 얻을 수 없는 책들이 많이 있다.

6 더 자세히 바라보자, 그는 그 어두운 물체가 죽은 나무라는 것을 알았다.

7 훌륭한 작가는 현명하게 주제를 선택하고, 철저하게 자료를 모은다.

8 식자들이 어떤 책에 관해서 뭐라고 얘기하든지 간에, 그리고 아무리 한 목소리로 그것을 칭찬하든지 간에, 그것이 당신에게 흥미를 주지 않는다면 그것은 당신에게 아무 소용이 없다.

9 위대함을 찬양하느라 우리는 위대한 저술에서 흔히 볼 수 있는 오류를 지나쳐버리기 쉽다. 이런 경향 때문에, 나는 오류를 찾아내기 위해 일반적으로 받아들여지고 있는 이론들을 검토하는 것이 필요하다고 믿는다.

10 만일 소비가 현재의 비율로 계속되면, 세계에 매장되어 있는 구리와 납, 주석은 이 세기가 바뀔 때에 이르면 고갈될 것이다. 그리고 현재의 소비 비율이 계속된다면, 세계에 매장되어 있는 철광석은 백 년이 지나지 않아서 고갈될 수 있다.

11 외국인 관찰자를 가장 당황케 하는 특징들 가운데 하나는 미국인이 지니고 있는 강하고도 사라질 줄 모르는 꿈이다. 자세히 조사해 보면, 그 꿈은 미국인의 생활의 현실과 거의 관계가 없다는 것을 알 수 있다. 고향에 대한 꿈과 그리움을 생각해 보라. 이 말만 들어도 거의 모든 우리나라 사람들은 눈물을 흘릴 수 있다.

12 언어는 인간 사회의 필요불가결한 도구다. 그것은 개인들이 서로를 이해하고 함께 하나의 공동체로서 작용할 수 있게 해주는 수단이다. 정말이지 어떤 인간 조직체도 언어가 없다면 형성될 수도 오랫동안 유지될 수도 없을 것이다. 분명히, 언어가 없다면 현대 사회의 복잡한 구조는 전적으로 불가능할 것이다.

13 희극 배우 조이 비숍이 〈투나잇 쇼〉의 사회자로 있을 때 그는 자필서명을 받으려는 사람들에게 시달렸다. 어느 날, 누군가가 거리에서 그를 멈추게 하고 조이 비숍이 아니냐고 묻자, 그는 공손하게 미소를 짓고 대답했다. "아닙니다. 다만 조이 비숍을 닮았을 뿐이에요."

그러고 나서 다시 생각한 끝에, 그는 그 여성에게 조이 비숍의 팬이냐고 물어보았다. 그녀는 공손하게 미소를 짓고 대답했다. "아니에요. 다만 조이 비숍의 팬처럼 보일 뿐이죠" — 그러고서 그녀는 떠나버렸다.

[해설] 이 양반이 다음에는 그런 '무례'를 저지르지 않았겠죠.

14 의사 한 사람이 어느 날 정신병원 목욕탕에서 정신병 환자들이 목욕하는 것을 지켜보고 있었다. 갑자기 그들 중에 한 사람이 소리쳤다. "이제 의사 선생님이 목욕하실 시간이다." 그러자 또 한 사람이 외쳤다. "그를 물에 빠뜨려 죽입시다." 그가 소리치자, 목욕탕 안에 있던 모든 사람들이 의사 주위에 모여서 뚫어지게 그를 바라보았. 그들은 그를 익사시켜야 한다고 주장했다.

자신의 위험을 깨닫자, 의사는 묘안을 하나 생각해냈다. "좋습니다, 여러분." 그가 말했다.

"그러나 지금 의사에게 한바탕 소리쳐서 신나게 해준 뒤에 익사시키도록 하면 어떨까요?"

이 합당한 제의에 당장 동의하자, 요란한 함성이 그 건물에 울려 퍼졌다. 이 심상치 않은 소리가 나자, 말할 필요도 없이, 당장 관리인들이 목욕탕으로 달려왔다.

15 미국의 "마르크스 공포증"은 전 세계에 걸쳐서 민주주의를 증진하려는 미국의 노력에 단 하나의 최대 장애물임이 틀림없다. 미국 정부가 니카라과에 원조를 제공하기를 꺼려함에 따라 아마도 이 나라는 소련의 손에 들어가게 될 것이다. 미국은 사회주의라는 말만 나와도 불안에 떠는 일을 그만두어야 한다. 또한 미국은 아르헨티나와 칠레와 같이 미국이 지지하는 몇몇 정부에 대해서도 경계해야 한다.

독재국가들이 민주주의와 인권을 가장 존중한다고 공언하는 나라의 친구이자 동맹국이 될 수는 없다. 미국은 니카라과에서와 같은 민주주의를 위한 실험에 대해서 이해해 주어야 한다.

16 노르웨이는 서방세계에서 가장 엄격한 음주운전법을 보유하고 있다. 누구든지 차를 몰고 가다가 혈액 내에 0.05% 이상의 알코올이 있는 것이 밝혀지면 적어도 3주일 동안 특별 시설에 갇혀서 지내야 한다. 이곳에서 범법자들은 가구를 만들거나, 스노 타이어에 징을 박거나, 전기 일을 하거나, 자질구레한 가사 일들을 한다. 복역하는 것 외에, 처음 이 법을 위반하면 일년 동안 면허를 정지당하고, 5년 이내에 다시 형 선고를 받으면 영원히 면허를 정지당한다.

거의 아무도, 아무리 그가 영향력이 있더라도, 처벌을 면할 수 없다. 지난 4년 동안에 그런 시설형을 선고받은 약 2만 명의 노르웨이인들 가운데 몇 명은 유명 인사들이었는데, 여기에는 국회의원들도 포함되어 있었다.

17 남편과 내가 처음 만난 것은 우리가 아이다호에서 교사로 있을 때였다. 우리는 뉴멕시코에 있는 나의 고향에서 봄 방학 중에 결혼할 계획이었다. 우리는 그토록 먼 거리를 차를 몰고 가야 하기 때문에, 우리가 근무하는 지역의 학교 감독관에게 편지를 써서 그 여행을 할 수 있도록 이틀간의 개인 휴가를 받을 수 있느냐고 물어보았다. 감독관의 회답에 의하면, 학교 이사회가 개인휴가를 위한 타당한 이유를 결정하는 데에 결혼은 포함시키지 않는다는 것이었다. 그런 규정이 없으므로, 그분의 얘기에 의하면, 그 이틀을 의료휴가로 우리에게 제공하겠다는 것이었다 — 우리 둘이 분명히 상사병을 앓고 있다는 전제로!

어구 법률 집행이 이렇게 웃길 때가 있군요!

EXERCISE 20

1 자신이 설교하는 것을 실천하는 것은, 사람들이 인정하듯이, 그리 간단하지〔쉽지〕 않다.

2 그런 종류의 마찰은 마땅히 자살과 같은 것이라고 말할 수 있다.

3 나는 만일 내가 사람들의 결점만 보고 장점에는 눈이 어둡다면 마땅히 비난을 받을 수 있을 것이라 생각한다.

4 아랍인들은 이스라엘이 휴전 이래로 지금까지 가장 많이 혜택을 입어 왔다고 주장하는데, 그들의 주장은 다소 정당성을 갖고 있다.

5 희생 그 자체에는 아무것도 칭찬받을 만한 것이 없다. 그러므로 사람은 자신을 희생하는 일을 하기 전에, 마땅히 그것이 그만한 가치가 있는지를 자신에게 물어보아야 한다.

6 요컨대, 우리 모두 영양섭취에 관한 그 상원 분과위원회의 충고에 주의를 기울이는 것이 — 그리고 우리의 설탕 소비를 줄이는 것이 — 아마 우리에게 이로울 것이다.

7 앞으로 미국에 불법적으로 들어오는 외국인들의 수효를 억제하기 위해서, 행정부는 알면서도 그런 이주민을 채용하는 고용주들에게 제재조치 — 이것은 많은 벌금형이라 추측된다 — 를 가할 것을 고려하고 있다.

8 화국봉은 모택동의 승인을 얻어 총리가 된 것으로 추측되나, 모주석이 그를 자신의 후계자로 지명했다는 증거는 없다. 그러므로 아마 수주일 — 비록 수개월은 아니라고 하더라도 — 이 지나야 분열되어 있는 중국 지도층이 공산당의 새로운 주석 선출에 대해서 합의할 수 있을 것이다.

9 5년 뒤에, 모든 유럽 공동체 가맹국 수뇌들이 모네에게 명예유럽시민의 칭호를 수여했는데, 그는 지금까지 그런 명예를 받은 유일한 사람이었다. 그런데 그럴 만한 충분한 이유가 있었다. 그의 생각은 숭고한 것으로서 — 그것은 유럽 국가들을 뭉치게 해서 평화와 범세계적인 협력에 이바지하게 하려는 것이었다. 그런데, 놀라울 정도로 그의 꿈은 개가를 올려 왔다.

10 존스 씨는 대부분, 시골에 은퇴해서, 누이동생과 살았는데, 이 동생을 그는 매우 사랑했다. 이 숙녀는 이제 30세를 약간 지났는데, 이것은 마음씨가 나쁜 사람들의 생각으로는 노처녀라고 불러도 마땅한 나이였다. 그녀는 예쁘다기보다는 좋은 품성을 지닌 그런 종류의 여성이었다.

11 디트로이트 시의 즉결 재판소에서 있었던 한 재판에서, 무례한 제의를 했다고 피고를 고소한 어떤 젊은 여성이 자신에게 물었다고 주장하는 질문을 진술하라는 요구를 받았다. 그녀가 그것을 되풀이하는 것은 난처한 일이어서, 그녀는 그것을 종이 쪽지에 써도 좋다는 허락을 받았다. 판사와 검사, 피고측 변호인이 그것을 읽은 뒤에, 그것은 배심원들에게로 넘겨졌다. 각 배심원이 그것을 읽고, 옆에 있는 배심원에게 주었다.

어떤 매력적인 여성 배심원이 그것을 읽은 뒤에, 자기 오른쪽에 있는 남자에게 전하려 했으나 그는 졸고 있었다. 아무 말 없이, 그녀는 팔꿈치로 그를 찌르고 그에게 그 종이 쪽지를 주었다. 잠에서 깬 그 배심원은 그 쪽지를 읽고, 그녀에게 미소를 보낸 다음, 고개를 끄덕이고 그 쪽지를 자기 호주머니에 집어 넣었다! (맙소사!)

12 낯선 사람을 소개받자마자, 그곳에 있는 모든 사람이 대답을 듣고 싶어하는 첫 번째 질문들 가운데 하나는 그가 어떻게 먹고 사느냐는 것이다. 여기에는 그럴 만한 충분한 이유가 있다. 왜냐하면 그 누구도 흠잡을 데 없이 합법적으로 생계를 유지하는 법을 배우기 전까지는 완전한 사람이 아니기 때문이다.

EXERCISE 21

1 그는 너무 뚱뚱해서 자기 발가락에 손이 닿지 않는다.
 (= He is so fat that he cannot touch his toes.)

2 그 홍수로 그 마을의 많은 사람들이 집을 잃었다.

3 노동을 절약해 주는 공학기술의 도입으로 많은 사람들이 일자리를 잃게 되었다.

4 미국이 주도해서 올림픽경기를 거부함으로써 소련은 수백만[수천만 또는 수억] 달러의 재정 손실을 입었다.

5 주말에 시내 중심가[영업지역]에 있는 세 업소를 태워버린 화재는 방화로 추정된다.

6 52세에, 그는 회교혁명의 계속에 대한 주된 희망이었으나, 이 혁명은 공포정치를 해왔기 때문에 이란은 분파로 갈라져서 서로 으르렁거리며 싸우고 있다.
 주의 우리말로 옮기기에 쉽지 않은 예문입니다. 제가 어떻게 처리했는지 잘 살펴보세요.

7 플로리다의 어느 공군기지 게시판에 붙어 있는 공고문 : "다음 사병들은 오늘 오후에 보급실에서 선행 메달을 가져가기 바랍니다. 이 명령에 따르지 않으면 징계처분을 받게 될 것입니다." (이거 너무했군요!)
 여담 여러분, 이런 글을 보시면 웃을 줄 아셔야 합니다. 이것은 익살이니까요!

8 그는 자기 나이를 안 밝히려고 한다. 글로 발표된 추산에 의하면 70대 초반이라고 하지만, 그는 그보다 훨씬 더 젊고 활기가 있어 보이고, 마치 기계로 잰듯이 규칙적으로 일 년에 소설 세 편을 써낸다.

9 정확하게 브레즈네프가 앓고 있는 병이 무엇인지는 철저하게 비밀로 지켜지고 있고, 그것은 소수의 크렘린 내부인사에게만 알려져 있다. 사람들이 추측해온 질병에는 턱암, 기종, 심장병, 통풍, 그리고 백혈병이 포함되어 있다.

10 고등학교에서 체제에 대한 순응을 덜 강조하면 대학생들은 독립적인 사고에 대한 준비가 더 잘 되어 있을 것이다.

11 향후 25년 동안 과학의 발전으로 사망의 원인으로서 전염병이 제거되고, 새로운 동력원이 개발되고, 방사능 폐기물 처리가 해결되며, 문제를 해결할 뿐만 아니라 빚어낼 컴퓨터가 나올 것이다.

12 이집트가 당면한 문제들은 쉬운 해결이 불가능하다. 1인당 국민소득은 일년에 469달러에 불과하고 이 나라의 중산층은 구매가능한 주택이 극도로 부족해서 고통을 받고 있다. 산업은 사실상 침체상태에 놓여있고, 생산적인 외국인의 투자는 빈혈상태에 있다. 이집트는 현재 식량의 반을 수입한다.

13 이집트에서는, 겉은 번드르르하게 부유해 보이지만 경제의 핵심은 허약하다. 새로운 교역정책과 외국인의 투자로부터 나오는 수입은 너무도 뚜렷이 최상의 부유층에게 흘러 들어가고 있다. 그러나 동시에, 대다수 이집트인들은 인구 과잉, 필요불가결한 공공시설의 고장과 생산직 일자리의 부족과 씨름하고 있다.

14 대부분의 사람들은 등화관제 때에 계속해서 전등을 켜기 위해 집이나 아파트의 창문을 두꺼운 검은 종이나 은박지로 덮어 놓았다. 그 이유는 공습에 대한 두려움이라기보다는 스스로 민방위대원 노릇을 하는 젊은이들과 어린이들이 시끄럽게 소리치기 때문이다. 조금이라도 불빛이 창으로 보이면 사방에서 "불을 끄세요"라는 소리가 일제히 터져나온다.

EXERCISE 22

1 그 법안은 어렵게 상원에서 통과되었다.

2 a. 케네디는 새로운 방법으로 일을 처리했다.
 = Kennedy did things in a fresh way.
 b. 사고는 혼란스러운 방법으로 새로운 역사를 만든다.
 = Accidents make new history in a disconcerting way.

3 그는 많은 고대 작가들에 관해서 피상적으로 알고 있었다.

4 그녀의 얼굴은 창백해졌는데, 그녀는 헛되이 미소를 지으려고 했다.

5 (고대) 그리스인들은 형태적으로 철학과 자연과학을 구분하지 않았다.

6 그녀는 늦게 파티에 나타났다.
 = She appeared late at the party.

7 수년 동안 그는 자기 집에서 비정기적으로 변호사 노릇을 했다.
 cf. practice medicine: 의사 노릇을 하다

8 비록 패배했지만, 우리 팀 선수들은 키가 더 크고 더 강한 상대팀 선수들을 상대로 용감하게 방어했다.

9 교육에 관한 문제는 마치 사회제도와 아무런 관련이 없는 것처럼 흔히 논의되지만, 사실, 교육은 일정한 사회제도 안에서 이루어지고 또 그

사회제도를 위해 이루어지는 것이다.

10 노래로 하는 상업광고는 최근에 만들어졌다.

11 이성을 가진 사람이라면 아무도 네가 한 말에 기분이 상하지 않을 것이다.

12 공연예술로서 무용은 미국에서는 비교적 최근에 발생했다.

13 그 자동차는 완전히 파손되었지만, 운전자는 다행히도 살짝 베인 상처와 찰과상을 입고 화를 면했다.

14 칼의 팔이 아픈 것은 최근에 발생한 것이 아니라, 만성 질환이 재발된 것이다.

15 사랑은 눈이 멀지만, 결혼은 눈을 뜨게 해 준다.

16 이 무렵에, 나는 에너지 절약법에 관한 책을 한 권 손에 넣었는데, 그것은 정말로 내 눈을 뜨게 해주었다.

> 참고 여기 예문들이 쉽다고 슬슬 넘어가지 말고, 이런 표현을 배워서 앞으로 이런 식으로 문장을 만들 수 있도록 노력하세요.

17 자기 당의 열성당원에게만 주로 호소력을 갖는 대통령 후보는 누구든 1980년에 틀림없이 낙선될 것이다.

18 그녀는 50년의 생애 동안 사뭇 매우 정력적으로 삶과 사랑을 추구해왔다. 그녀는 독일의 가장 유명한 여배우 가운데 한 사람으로 54편의 영화에 출연했는데, 그녀가 출연한 영화에는 할리우드에서 제작된 〈실크 스타킹〉과 〈날이 밝기 전의 결정〉이 있다.

19 A: 이 처방전대로 다시 약을 지어주시겠어요?
B: 미안합니다. 그 처방으로는 다시 약을 지어 드릴 수 없습니다. 의사 선생님에게서 새 처방전을 받으셔야 됩니다.

20 나는 교환원에게 전화 한 통을 걸어달라고 부탁했다. 그녀는 딱딱하게 대답했다. "직접 다이얼을 돌리시면 시간과 돈을 절약하실 수 있습니다."
"알아요," 내가 말했다. "하지만 내게는 그런 시간이 있어서 쌓이기 전에 그 시간을 좀 쓰고 싶답니다." 그랬더니 그녀는 무엇인가 중얼거리더니 전화를 끊어버렸다.

21 경기가 지금은 절뚝거리는데[좋지 않은데], 겨울이 지나가고 봄이 옴에 따라서 좋아지기 시작할 테지만, 회복은 느리고 고통스러울 것이다. 개인의 저축과 소비자의 지출, 기업투자를 자극하기 위한 조세 인하가 금년이 끝나기 전에 이루어질 것이 거의 확실하다.

22 이상하게 보이지만, 불법적으로 주택에 침입하는 가장 흔한 방법은 잠겨져 있지 않은 문을 통해서 들어가는 것이다. 밤도둑들은 흔히 아파트 복도와 주택가를 거닐면서 손잡이를 들어서 열리는 문(잠겨 있지 않은 문)을 찾아본다. 심지어 집에 있을 경우에도, 문은, 차고 문을 포함해서, 언제나 잠가야 한다.

23 암스테르담 근처에 있는 한 도시에서는 네덜란드인들은 한번도 들어본 적이 없는 사람 — "피에터"를 위해서 동상을 세워야 했다. 그는 용감한 어린 네덜란드 소년으로 손가락을 제방에(나 있는 구멍에) 꽂아서 그 지역을 홍수로부터 구해주었다고 한다.
피에터의 이야기는 전적으로 미국인들이 만들어낸 것이지만, 너무도 많은 미국인 방문객들이 그에 관해서 묻기 때문에 네덜란드인들은 그를 기리기 위해 동상을 세우는 것이 지극히 합당한 일이라고 결정했던 것이다.

24 예술은 아름다운 것을 만들어내거나 이상을 구현하거나 표현하는 인간의 기술이라고 규정할 수 있다. 자연의 아름다움은 변하며 일시적이다. 그것은 왔다가는 사라진다. 폭풍우가 그것을 강타해서 빛을 잃게 하거나, 겨울의 거친 손

길이 그것을 파괴할 수도 있다. 예술은 아름다움을 포착해서 그것을 우리를 위해 영구적이며 이상적인 형태로 표현해 준다. 화가, 조각가, 건축가와 음악가 또는 주제가 작곡가는 아름다움의 천사들을 그들이 지나갈 때에 붙잡아서 그들이 우리에게 축복을 주도록 단단히 잡아준다.

25 빙 크로스비는 기차로 여러 해 전에 남서부 지방을 여행하는 동안에 겪은 한 가지 경험에 대해서 이렇게 글로 적고 있다.

우리가 탄 기차가 정지하고, 우리는 기다려야 한다는 얘기를 듣고, 나는 기차 뒤 철로를 따라 걸어서 왔다갔다 했다. 기차 뒤편에서 브레이크를 담당하는 사람 — 그는 거친, 체구가 작은 텍사스인이었다 — 역시 랜턴을 흔들면서 왔다갔다 하고 있었다. 그는 내게로 다가와서 말했다. "사람들 말을 들으니 빙 크로슬런드라는 작자가 탔다는군요. 그는 대단한 가수라고 하는데, 내가 아는 한, 래리 로스가 노래하는 걸 들으면 그 친구 쥐구멍에라도 들어가고 싶을 거요."

나는 나도 그렇게 생각한다고 말하고 거기에 대해서 더 이상 생각하지 않았다. 아침에 우리 문을 두드리는 소리가 났다. 바로 그 뒷브레이크 담당자였다. 그는 번뜩이는 눈빛으로 나를 바라보면서 말했다. "당신 날 속였죠, 안 그래요? 당신이 바로 빙 크로슬런드죠! 바로 그 이유로, 내 책에 서명을 해야 합니다."

그래서 나는 그렇게 서명했다. "빙 크로슬런드"라고.

26 얼마 전까지만 해도, 집에서 숨을 거두는 것은 머지않아 죽을 병에 걸려 있는 사람에게는 당연한 일이었다. 오늘날 사정은 더 이상 그렇지 않다. 의료기술의 엄청난 발전으로 질병과 맞서서 강력하게 투쟁하고 생명을 연장할 수 있게 되었지만, 그것이 가져온 한 가지 결과로 점점 더 많은 불치 환자들이 마지막 날들을 병원에서 보낸다.

27 펠리컨이 납작한 발을 모래 사장에 딛고 서 있는 모습을 보면, 이 새가 잘 날지 못한다고 생각할지 모른다. 그러나 이 새는 잘 난다. 이 새가 시속 약 26마일로, 거의 파도 윗부분에 닿을 듯 말듯 하면서 날아가는 모습을 보라. 흔히 펠리컨은 동료들과 함께 긴 줄을 이루면서 날아간다. 이들은 파도 위로, 파도를 넘어서 그리고 파도 아래로 서로를 따라가면서, 날개를 함께 움직이며 서로 같은 거리를 유지한다. 이것이야말로 완전한 단체비행쇼다.

EXERCISE 23

1 너는 그들을 도와야 한다, 그것도 지금 당장.

2 그들은 그가 수줍은 사람이라고 생각했는데, 사실 그랬다. 또 그들은 그가 둔한 사람이라고 생각했으나, 그렇지는 않았다.

3 분명히 히틀러는 천재였다. 비록 현대세계가 알아온〔보아온〕 가장 나쁜 천재이기는 했지만.

4 우리는 모두 이런 점에서 동등하다. 즉, 우리 모두 하루에 24시간이 있다는 점에서.

5 전통적인 기능 면에서 볼 때에, 예술은 존재이유를 상실해버렸다.

6 자신의 편견을 없애버리지 아니하고, 보통 사람은 그것의 결점을 숨겨서 원칙으로 통하게 하려고 애를 쓴다.

7 비록 주위에서 벌어지는 일에 초연하고 태도가 독립적이기는 하지만, 가축이 된 고양이는 인간에게 의존해서 먹이와 보호를 받아왔다.

8 어린이와 마찬가지로(그런데 어린이의 출생을 별이 상징해 주는데), 별은, 살다가 죽어감으로써, 완전한 새로운 세계가 태어나는 것을 가능하게 해준다.

주의 이 문장은 우리말로 옮기기가 어려우므로 주의하라!

9 두뇌가 더 뛰어나서가 아니라 연구 조건 때문에, 인류학자들은 인간 집단을 연구하는 방법들

을 개발해내었는데, 이러한 방법은 다른 분야 연구자들의 전형적인 방법보다 일정한 장점을 갖고 있는 것으로 밝혀졌다.

10 그것은 모든 것 중에서 가장 용감한 자질이다. 즉, 어두운 시대를 넘어서 밝은 시대를 내다보고, 질문에는 해답이 있고, 도전에는 대처할 수 있으며, 문제는 해결되리라고 믿을 수 있는 이런 능력 말이다.

11 나는 드물지 않게 스트릭트랜드를 만났고, 가끔 그와 체스를 했다. 그는 무뚝뚝한 성격이었다. 때때로 그는 말없이, 정신나간 것처럼 앉아 있곤 했으며, 주위에 있는 사람을 전혀 의식하지 못했다. 그리고 또 어떤 때, 기분이 좋을 때에는 자기 식대로 더듬으면서 말을 하곤 했다. 그는 한번도 현명한 말을 한 적은 없었으나, 언제나 자기가 생각하는 것을 정확하게 말했다.

12 때때로 나는 밤에 자신에게 물어본다. 내가 그 날 무엇을 했고, 어떤 새로운 생각을 했으며, 어떤 특별한 감정을 느꼈고, 그날을 다른 날들과 구분해 줄 어떤 일이 있었는지를. 그런데 흔히 그것은 하잘것없고 소용없어 보인다.

13 과학과 과학기술에 대한 깊은 불신을 오늘날 우리 사회의 많은 사람들이 나타내고 있다. 만일 이러한 불신이 널리 퍼진다면, 이러한 의혹과 좌절감 때문에 우리는 현재 우리의 위기 — 이 가운데 일부는 과거에 과학기술을 잘못 사용한 데서 빚어진 결과인데 — 를 해결할 수 없을 뿐만 아니라, 또한 장래에 현재로서는 예상조차 할 수 없는 문제들을 해결할 수 없게 되지도 모른다.

주의 이 구절의 두 번째 문장은 우리말로 옮기기가 쉽지 않으니 잘 연구해 보기 바랍니다.

14 그 시대의 가장 위대한 몇몇 작가들의 눈을 통해서 보면, 빅토리아 시대는 변화와 의혹의 시대로 볼 수 있다. 그러나 수많은 빅토리아 시대인들이 보기에 그것은 발전과 자신과 성취의 시대였다. 그리고 빅토리아 시대 직후의 사람들은 그 시대를 본질적으로 안정의 시대로 여겼다.

주의 이 구절의 다양한 문체에 주의를 기울여보세요.

15 전해내려오는 얘기에 의하면 존 F. 케네디는 어느 날 저녁 아버지와 오랫동안 얘기한 뒤에 정계에 들어가기로 결심했다고 한다. 조 1세(케네디 아버지)가 잭에게 이런 얘기를 한 것으로 생각된다. 즉 조 2세가 전쟁 때에 자신의 생명을 나라에 바쳤으므로 이제 잭이 정치적인 공직생활을 해온 가문의 전통을 지켜야 하고, 전 가족이 잭을 후원할 것이라고, 그의 아버지는 얘기했다. 그래서, 사람들 얘기에 의하면, 잭은 아버지의 역설에 귀를 기울여서, 즉석에서 정계에 들어가기로 결심했다고 한다.

그러나 사실은 이와는 다소 다르다. 확실히 케네디 가문에는 정치적인 전통이 있었다. 분명히, 조 1세는 그러한 전통이 이어져나가기를 원했고, 확실히 그는 그것이 조가 죽었으므로 잭에 의해서 이어져나가야 된다고 생각했다. 그러나 이것은 전적으로 너무 단순한 얘기다. 왜냐하면 이것은 모든 것을 고려하고는 있지만, 한 가지 가장 중요한 점 — 즉, 잭 케네디의 놀라운 인간성(이를테면, 정치가로서의 자질들)을 빼놓았기 때문이다.

주의 여러분, 마지막 문장의 번역이 근사하지 않습니까? 이 문장에서는 비중(또는 역점)이 "except" 이하에 있다는 데에 주의해야 합니다.

16 그것은 독특한 감정이다. 이러한 이중적인 의식, 언제나 자기 자신을 다른 사람들의 눈을 통해서 바라보고, 재미있다는 듯이 경멸과 동정 속에서 방관하는 세상의 줄자로 자신의 영혼을 재어보는 이런 느낌 말이다. 미국 흑인은 항상 이중성을 느낀다 — 미국인이자 흑인이라는 의식과 두 개의 영혼, 두 개의 생각, 두 개의 상반되는 투쟁을.

미국 흑인의 역사는 바로 이런 투쟁, 자신의 이중적인 자아를 더 낫고 진실한 자아로 통합하려는 이러한 갈망의 역사다. 이러한 통합에서 그는 과거의 자아들 가운데 그 어느 것도 상실하기를 바라지 않는다. 그는 미국을 아프리카화 하기를 바라지 않는다. 왜냐하면 미국은 세계와 아프리카에 가르쳐줄 수 있는 것을 너무도 많이 갖고 있기 때문이다. 또한 그는 자신의 흑인 영혼을 백인 미국문화의 홍수 속에 표백하고 싶지도 않다, 왜냐하면 흑인의 피가 세계에 가르쳐줄 것이 있다는 것을 그는 알고 있기 때문이다.

다만 그가 바라는 것은 흑인이면서 미국인이 될 수 있고, 동료인간들로부터 저주와 침뱉음을 당하지 않고, 기회의 문이 자신의 면전에서 난폭하게 닫히지 않는 것이다.

주의 여러분, 이 글은 보통 잘 쓰여진 글이 아닙니다. 왜냐하면 내용도 훌륭할 뿐만 아니라, 표현방식에서도 웬만한 시 이상으로 아름답고 운율도 뛰어나게 아름답기 때문입니다.

그리스 문명은 이 노인의 죽음으로부터 다시는 회복하지 못했다.

비교 이 글은 잘못 쓰여진 글의 대표적인 예이다. 왜냐하면, 마지막 문장의 내용이 나머지 부분과 '조화'를 이루지 못하므로 필자가 얘기하고자 하는 핵심이 무엇인지 뚜렷이 나타나 있지 않기 때문이다. 이런 글을 쓰는 것은 엄청난 죄악이다. 왜냐하면 자신의 인생뿐만 아니라 다른 사람들의 귀중한 인생의 일부를 낭비하는 것이니까.

EXERCISE 24

1 중학교 학생들을 위한 지질학 책의 저자인 골든씨는 현재 중학생들을 위한 천문학 책을 쓰고 있다.

2 나는, 비록 달라고 하더라도, 목숨을 빼앗는 약을 누구에게도 주지 않을 것이며, 그런 취지로 제의도 하지 않겠다.

3 이리를 가축으로 길들이는 것은 결코 일반적으로 생각하고 있는 것만큼 어렵지는 않다. 특히 미국종의 경우에는. 그러나 현대의 개와 그의 야생 사촌(이리) 사이에는 한 가지 두드러진 차이점이 있다.

4 우리는 모두 '문명'과 '문화'라는 단어가 나타내는 차이점을 잘 알고 있다. 문명은, 내가 이미 얘기했듯이, 주로 물질적으로 이루어놓은 것이고, 문화는 종교적인 것, 학문적인 것, 그리고 예술적인 것으로 생각되고 있다. 그러므로 두 현상 사이에는 비슷한 점뿐만 아니라 인과관계도 존재하는 것이라 생각된다.

5 〈변론〉이라는 책에서 얘기하듯이, 소크라테스는 당시에 전제정치와 민주정치에 모두 공공연히 반대했다. 그는 소수가 권력을 장악하고 있는 것도 다수가 권력을 갖고 있는 것에도 관심이 없었다. 비록 지금까지 그보다 더 웅변적으로 개인을 옹호한 사람은 없었지만, 그는 결코 자유롭고 안이한 뜻에서의 민주주의자는 아니었다. 바로 민주주의가 소크라테스를 죽였는데, 그것(민주주의)은 그러한 과정에서 사라졌다.

6 가끔 가다 동물원을 방문하는 사람들은, 동물 우리를 산책할 때에, 믿고 있다 — 그 우리에 갇혀있는 동물들의 우스운 행동이 오로지 자기들을 즐겁게 해주기 위해서 벌이는 행동 이상의 아무것도 아니라고. 그러나, 불행하게도, 우리에 갇혀 있는 동물들이 만족하고 있고 장난치기를 좋아한다고 보는 것보다 사실과 거리가 먼 것은 없을 것이다. 최근의 연구에서 충분히 밝혀졌듯이, 많은 우리에 갇혀 있는 동물들은 사실은 야생동물들의 생존문제만큼이나 심각한 생존문제에 부딪혀 있는데, 이것은, 간단히 말해서, 생활환경의 단조로움을 이겨내고 살아남으려는 투쟁이다. 비록 잘 먹여주고, 좋은 우리에 살게 해주고, 잘 보살펴주며, 천적으로부터 보호를 받고 있지만, 초복지국가에서와 같은 생활을 누리고 있는 동물원의 동물들은 따분하다, 때로는 그야말로 죽을 지경으로.

7 나는 결코 네루를 친밀하게 알지 못했다. 사실, 나는 그를 여러 번 만나지도 못했다. 그러나 그의 인간됨됨이는 처음 그를 만났을 때에 당장 인상을 주었으며 이러한 인상은 해가 지나도 바뀌지 않았다. 또한 그가 주는 영향은 단순히 인상이 아니었다. 인상이라는 단어는 약하고 너무 차다(감정이 없다). '매혹'이라는 말이 사실에 더 가깝다. 네루야말로 한 인간의 마음을 사로잡아서 그것을 유지해나갈 수 있는 사람이었다.(이 문장의 번역에 주의하라!)

이것은 어떤 사회적 지위에 있는 사람에게나 놀라운 일일 테지만, 지위가 낮고 이름이 세상에 알려져 있지 않은 사람의 경우보다는 세계적으로 유명한 정치가로 단지 자기 나라에서만이 아니라 전세계에 깊은 흔적을 남겨 놓은 사람일 경우에는 더욱 놀라운 일일 것이다. 이 위대한 정치가는 높은 공직에 있었지만 사람들로부터 사랑을 받을 수 있는 인간성을 잃지 않았고, 내 생각에 네루는 추호도 거만하거나, 잘난 체하거나, 자의식이 강하지 않았다. 그는 젊은 시절의 자연스러움과 명랑함을 지니고 있었다. 수년 동안 드물게 무거운 공직의 부담을 지니고온 뒤에도. 만년에 가서야 인도와 중국 사이에 예기치 않게 발생한 불화로 비로소 그는 굴복하기(일그러지기 — 다시 말해서, 과거의 인간성을 잃기) 시작했을 뿐이었다.

> 참고 이 글은 우리말로 옮기기가 상당히 어려우므로 번역에 관심이 있는 분들에게 좋은 참고자료가 될 것입니다.

8 우리 그레이스 아주머니는 버스를 타고 다니면서 대부분의 사람들이 지나쳐버리는 것을 눈여겨 보는 습관이 있다. 어느 토요일 오전에 144번 버스가 어느 번잡한 교차로를 지나갔는데, 이 교차로를 사람들은 흔히 다음 교차로와 혼동했다. 그레이스 아주머니가 창 밖을 내다보자, 두 젊은 여자들이 캠핑 갈 차림을 하고 있는 게 보였다. 그들은 안절부절 못하는 것 같았다. 아주머니가 탄 버스가 다음 교차로에 이르렀을 때에, 아주머니는 두 젊은 남자들이 같은 차림을 하고 승용차 곁에 서 있는 것을 보았다. 그들도 만나기로 약속한 사람들을 기다리고 있는 게 분명했다.

그레이스 아주머니는 버스에서 내려서(그런데 이것은 다음 버스를 타기 위해서 한 시간 정도 기다려야 한다는 것을 뜻했다), 그 젊은이들에게로 다가갔다. 그들은 아주머니에게 낯선 억양으로 말했다. 그레이스 아주머니가 자기가 본 여자들의 모습을 얘기해 주자, 그 젊은이들은 떠났다. 만나서 즐거워하는 네 젊은이들이 돌아와서 자기에게 고맙다는 인사를 하자, 아주머니가 생각했던 것이 확인된 셈이었다. 정말로 그 교차로에 대한 혼동이 있었던 것이다!

호의를 호의로 갚고 싶어서, 그 재잘거리는 젊은이들은 아주머니를 집까지 태워다 드리도록 허락해 달라고 고집했다. 그레이스 아주머니는 거절했다. 아주머니는 남의 신세를 지지 않는 사람이다. 그런데, 그 말(거절하는 말)을 차분하게 하는 것으로 보아 그것(남의 신세를 지지 않는 것)이 아주머니에게는 중요하다는 것을 알 수 있고, 그리고 어째서 그 젊은이들이 아주머니 의견에 동의했으며, 거리를 건너 선물가게로 가서 작은 코끼리 솜 인형을 사갖고 돌아왔는지 이해할 수 있을 것이다.

지금 그레이스 아주머니의 아파트에는 이 일을 기억나게 해주는 것[기념품]이 있고, 또한 거기에는 네 젊은이들에 대한 기억이 있는데, 이들이 어떤 행로를 택하든지 간에, 어떤 숙녀가 수고스럽게 자기들에게 친절을 베풀어준 한 낯선 도시를 틀림없이 기억하게 될 것이다.

9 우리 시대는 또한 '불안의 시대'로 널리 알려져 왔다. 특히 이런 제목의 W. H. 오든의 시가 1947년에 발행된 이래로. 이것은 이 시인이 그러한 감정을 불러일으켰다는 말이 아니다. 그는 단순히 그것을 포착해서 이름을 부여하고 우리로 하여금 그것이 널리 퍼져 있다는 것을 더 많이 의식하게 만들었을 뿐이다. 그로부터 32년이 지난 오늘날에도, 그러한 감정은 사라지지 않았고, 만일 그 동안에 어떤 차이가 있었다면 그것이 고조되었다는 점이다. 이 감정 가운데 얼마만큼이 과학지식의 가속화된 습득과 그것의 광범위한 응용에 그 원인이 있다고 할 수 있을까? 많다.

불안의 시대가 과학의 시대에 의해 초래되었다고 말한다면 그것은 지나친 말이 될 것이다. 우리의 불안 가운데 얼마가 직접적으로 과학과 관련되어 있고 또 얼마가 우리 생활의 다른 요인들과 관련되어 있는지를 정확하게 측정할 길은 없다. 그러나 과학이 불안을 가져다주는 주요한 원인이었다는 것은 거의 의심할 여지가 없는 것 같다.

10 1967년에 졸업할 하버드 대학교의 1,139명의 학생들 중에 90명은 자기 진로에 대한 계획에 대해서 "마음이 결정되어 있지 않다"고 선언했는데, 금년에 졸업할 1,000여 명의 학생들 가운데에는 적어도 250명이 그런 상태에 있다고 한다.

EXERCISE 25

1 나는 대학 졸업장이 사업에서 성공하는 데에 도움을 주지 않는다고 불평하는 대학 졸업자를 참을 수가 없다. 그리고 그것이 그렇게 해준다고 증명하려는 대학 졸업자는 더욱 더 참을 수가 없다.

2   어떤 젊은 회계원은 날마다 사무실에 늦게까지 남아 있었다. 마침내, 사장이 그를 불러들여서 해명을 요구했다.
    "저, 실은," 그는 더듬거리며 말했다. "제 아내도 직장에 나가는데, 만일 아내보다 먼저 집에 도착하면, 제가 저녁식사를 준비해야 합니다."

3   우리가 사려고 할 때가 아니라 팔려고 할 때에 부동산 중개인의 태도가 바뀌는 것을 보고 나는 언제나 놀란다. 나는 언젠가 집을 팔려고 중개업자를 불러들였다.
    "이건 큰 집이에요." 내가 말했다. "이 집에는 양쪽에 날개까지 달려 있답니다."
    "대부분 칠면조도 그렇죠!"라고 그가 말했다.

    주의 중개인의 말에는 깎아내리려는 뜻이 들어 있습니다.

4   나는 성공했다는 생각이 인생을 더 쉽게 즐길 수 있게 해준다는 사실을 부정하지 않는다. 예를 들어, 젊은 시절에 거의 이름이 알려져 있지 않던 화가가 자신의 재능을 인정받게 되면 그는 더 행복해질 가능성이 있다. 또한 나는 돈이, 어느 정도까지는, 행복을 증가시킬 가능성이 매우 크다는 것도 부정하지 않는다. 그러나 나는 그러한 정도를 넘으면, 그것이 그렇게 해준다고 생각하지 않는다. 내가 주장하는 것은 성공이란 행복의 한 요소에 불과하며, 따라서 그것을 얻기 위해 모든 다른 요소들이 희생되었다면 그것은 너무도 비싼 대가를 치른 것이라는 점이다.

5   대도시에서는 내부 교통에 드는 비용이 엄청나다. 해마다 사람을 운송하는 데에 소비되는 석유와 전기 비용이 누적되어 왔고, 생리적인[신체적인] 손상 면에서 인간이 치르는 대가 역시 마찬가지였다(누적되어 왔다).

    주의 이 구절은 우리말로 옮기기가 쉽지 않으니 주의하시기 바랍니다.

6   "예술"이라는 용어가 적용되는 영역이 너무도 방대하고 모호해서 문학, 음악과 무용, 연극과 영화, 시각 및 장식 예술과 그밖에 이와 마찬가지로 다양한 활동들을 포함하는 한, 이들의 분류 — 다시 말해서, 예술 하나하나를 독특하다거나 다른 것들과 비슷하다고 간주하는 방법 — 는 논쟁을 불러일으킬 수 있지만 필요한 과제로 남게 될 것이다. 분류는 어느 분야에서든지 지식을 조직하는 데에 유용한 접근방법이다(18세기에 있었던 식물과 동물의 분류가 19세기에 진화를 발견하게 이끌어주었다). 예술에서, 분류는 예술간의 상호관계를 이해하는 데에, 그리고 분류하지 않을 경우에 보지 못하고 지나칠 가능성이 있는 예술 하나하나의 특징에 주의를 환기시키는 데에 크게 도움이 될 수 있다.

    주의 끝에서 두 번째 문장에 나오는 colon 다음을 우리 말 번역에서는 괄호로 처리한 점에 주의하시기 바랍니다. 물론 다른 방법으로 처리할 수도 있습니다.

7   순회 도서실의 성장은 독서[문학]의 팽창에 도움을 주었다. 책 값이 대다수 사람들의 구매력에 비해서 매우 비쌀 때에, 순회 도서실은 중요한 사회적인 창안이었다. 그것은 독서가 취미인 사람들에게 그것이 없었더라면 손댈 수 없었을 책들에 접근할 수 있는 길을 제공해 주었고, 독서에 대한 관심과 구매력 사이의 간격을 좁히는 데에 도움을 주었다.
    최초의 순회 도서실은 1740년에 런던에서 문을 열었다. 경쟁이 되는 순회 도서실들이 곧 런던은 물론 지방에서도 생겨났다. 그 세기(18세기) 말에는, 약 1,000개의 도서실이 전국에 점점이 흩어져 있었다. 이들의 빠른 성장은 독서에 대한 관심의 증가를 증언해 준다.

8   현대 세계에서는 일이 빨리 움직이는 것이 중요하므로 우리는 돌아가는 일에 대해서 잘 알고 있어야 한다. 중요한 사회, 경제 및 정치적인 문제점들은 모두가 진지하고 허심탄회한 조사를 필요로 하며, 전보다 독자들이 그러한 문제들에 대해서 더 잘 알고 있어야 한다.
    지식에서 진보하기 위해서 우리는 언제나 더 많이 배우고, 더 많이 연구하고, 더 많이 생각해야 한다. 독서가 이것을 성취하는 데에 도움을 주는데, 대학에서는 모든 연구의 약 85%가 독서를 필요로 한다. 만일, 사실이 분명히 그러하듯이, 발전이 연구를 통해서 이루어진다면, 독서는 아마 학생이 학문에서 발전하기 위한 주된 수단일 것이다.

    주의 이 구절도 번역을 위한 좋은 참고자료가 될 수 있습니다. 우리말로 옮기기 어려운 부분을 어떻게 처리했는지 주의해 보시기 바랍니다.

EXERCISE 26

1 수많은 프랑스 가정들이 다른 산업경제국들에는 흔한 편의시설 없이 살고 있다. 프랑스 가정 셋 가운데 하나는 공식적으로 '좁은 공간에 지나치게 많은 사람들이 살고 있는' 것으로 간주되고 있고, 28%는 온수가 나오지 않으며, 55%는 욕실이 없고, 77%는 전화가 없다.

2 이론과 실제에 관해서 두 가지 견해가 있다. 어떤 사람들은 이론과 실제는 별개의 것이어서 양자가 반드시 일치하지는 않는다고 한다. 또 어떤 사람들은 바로 이론의 부정확성 때문에 그 둘이 일치하지 않는다고 한다.

> 참고 이 부분에서는 우리가 영어로 글을 쓸 때 어떻게 써야 하는지에 대해서 많은 것을 배울 수가 있습니다. 영어의 다양한 표현방식에 주의를 기울이기 바랍니다. 이해하는 데 그치지 말고, 주어진 구절들을 작문을 위한 자료로 이용하세요.

3 한국인들은 주로 시골에 많이 살고 있으나, 점차 도시화되고 있다. 1925년에는 인구의 5% 이하가 도시에 살았다. 1970년에 이르러서는, 남한 인구의 30% 이상이 그리고 거의 마찬가지 비율의 북한 사람들이 도시에 살고 있었다.

4 역사적인 변천에 관한 연구를 통해 맥루한은 다음과 같이 믿고 있다. 결정적으로 적절한 어떤 도구나 기계의 발명이 생활환경에 커다란 변화를 가져오는데, 이러한 변화는 또 인간의 사회적인 관계와 세계관에 모두 변화를 가져온다는 것이다.

> 여담 여러분, 이거 대단한 발견일까요? 필자는 그렇게 생각하지 않습니다. 과학적인 안목으로 보면, 지극히 초보적인 것이죠. 조건이 바뀌면 당연히 결과 또한 바뀌지 않겠어요?

5 노인들이 활동을 하지 않는다고 생각하는 것은 또 하나의 그릇된 생각이다. 여러 조사에 의하면, 60세 이상의 노인들이 20대보다 라디오를 듣고 텔레비전을 보면서 즐기는 데에 시간을 훨씬 더 적게 소비한다고 한다.

또 하나의 그릇된 생각은 노인들은 불평으로 가득차 있다는 것이다. 일부 조사에 의하면, 노인들은 젊은이들과 적어도 한 가지 공통점을 갖고 있다고 한다. 즉 이들은 중년층보다 일반적으로 더 행복하고 자기 자신과 자기 생활방식에 더 만족하고 있는 것 같다.

> 주의 진한 글자로 된 문장 덕분에 우리는 이 구절의 첫째 문장의 뜻을 구체적으로 파악할 수 있다.

6 우리는 셰익스피어에 대해서 아는 것이 거의 없는데, 그 이유는 당시 역사기록들은 왕들의 생활을 그려내는 데에 바쳐졌기 때문이었다. 평민인 배우가 후세에 사람들의 관심거리가 되리라고는 아무도 상상하지 못했다. 마찬가지로 스콧 조플린 시대에는, 후세 사람들이 작곡가 — 그것도 특히 흑인 작곡가 — 가 어떤 인물이었는지를 알고 싶어하리라고는 아무도 생각하지 못했다.

> 주의 이 글에서는 Similarly라는 단어가 문맥의 흐름을 보여준다.

7 니체는 생각하기를, 사람은 두 가지 상반되는 면을 갖고 있다. 그리스의 주신인 디오니시오스는 인간의 감정적인 면을 나타내는데, 이것은 활기 있고, 창의적이며 영감을 주지만, 지나치면 또한 탈선적(광적)이고 파괴적이다. 태양의 신인 아폴로는 인간의 이성적인 면을 나타내는데, 이것은 질서와 체계, 정의를 지향하지만, 물론, 감성을 마비시킬 정도로 지나치게 체계화할 위험성을 갖고 있다.

8 피의자가 체포되었을 경우에도, 그가 처벌받을 가능성은 매우 희박하다. 뉴욕 주에서는 해마다 중범죄로 약 13만 명이 체포되는데, 약 8,000명이 감옥에 간다. 뉴욕 시에서는 9만 4,000명이 중범죄로 체포되는데, 5,000 내지 6,000명이 복역한다. 컬럼비아 특별구에 대한 1974년의 조사는 비슷한 양상을 보여주었다. 무장강도로 체포된 사람들 중에서, 4분의 1 이하가 교도소에 갔다. 6,000건 이상의 가중폭행건이 보고되었으나, 투옥된 사람은 116명이었다. 디트로이트, 인디애나폴리스, 그리고 뉴올리언스와 같은 시에 대한 1977년의 조사에서는 이보다 약간 더 나은 통계숫자가 나왔지만, 뉴욕 경찰청장 로버트 맥과이어 씨의 다음과 같은 분노를 무마할 만한 것은 아무것도 없었다. "형사사법제도는 거리의 범죄자들을 부추기는 것이나 다름없습니다."

9 일부 사람들에게, 오토메이션이라는 말은 사람들이 일을 하지 않는 로봇의 세계를 생각나게 해준다. 또 어떤 사람들에게, 오토메이션은 자동조정장치의 복잡한 공학문제를 연상하게 해준다. 많은 사람들에게, 오토메이션은 실제로 산업에서 기계화와 동의어로 생각된다. 그러나, 대부분의 사람들에게 이 용어는 전자공학 및 자동생산과 다소 관계가 있는 모호한 것으로 간주된다. 보통 사람들에게 이것이 모두 무엇을 의미하는지는 별로 분명하지 않다.

> 해대 이 구절의 뼈대는 'A에게 X는 a를 뜻하고, B에게 X는 b를 뜻하며, C에게 X는 c를 뜻하지만, 그러나 D에게 X가 무엇을 뜻하는지는 분명하지 않다'는 것이다.

10 새 실업률은 8.9%다. 누구나 이 백분율을 들으면 그것이 골치아픈 전조로 가득차 있다는 것을 깨달을 것이다. 그러나 현대인들은 통계숫자를 현실로 착각하기 때문에 이 비율이 우리 사회가 소화할 수 없을 정도로 많은 950만 명의 실업자들을 나타낸다는 사실을 과과하기 쉽다. 실업률에서 숫자 1(다시 말해서 1%)은, 대통령이 지난 달에 설명했듯이, 약 190억 달러의 잠재적인 연방정부의 세입 손실에다가 연방정부가 실업자들에게 지급해 주는 약 60억 달러의 재정 원조를 나타낸다. 이러한 상세한 통계는 실업의 범위가 방대하다는 것과 잠재적인 부의 손실이 엄청나고 실업자들을 구제하는 데에 엄청난 비용이 든다는 것을 설명하는 데 유용하다. 그러나 통계숫자는 실업의 현실에 대해서는 전혀 아무것도 얘기해 주지 않는다는 점을 우리는 반드시 기억해야 한다.

그 현실은 언제나 개인적이며, 거의 언제나 여러 가지 어려운 감정들로 뒤범벅되어 있다. 정말이지, 실업이 심리적으로 주는 고통은 많은 희생자들(실업자들)에게는 수지를 맞추는 고통보다 더 크다. 소수의 사람들은, 정말이지, 너무도 이상한 성격을 갖고 있어서 낙관적으로 태연히 실업을 받아들이거나, 그것을 비웃어버리거나 그것을 기회로 삼아 직업을 바꾸기도 한다. 그렇지만, 미국인들은 보다 더 전형적으로 일자리를 잃게 되면(그 원인에는 상관없이) 심리적으로 심한 상처를 받는다. 그리고 만일 실업상태가 오랫동안 계속되면, 연령, 직업 및 경제적 계층을 불문하고 모든 사람들(남녀 다같이)이 급격한 자존심의 상실, 주체의식(자기가 누구라는 의식)의 감소, 목적의식의 혼란, 친구들로부터의 소외감 — 이것은 자기가 정말로 소속되어 있다고 생각하는 것이 어디이든지 간에 그곳으로부터의 일종의 추방당했다는 생각 — 을 겪곤 한다.

> 참고 여러분, 어렵습니까? 어려울수록 용기를 더 내어 머리를 쓰면 됩니다. 이 구절은 <TIME>의 essay란에서 뽑았습니다.

EXERCISE 27

1 요즘 젊은 남녀들은 과거보다 훨씬 더 쉽게 서로 만난다.

2 가이젤은 외모는 군인 같지만 생각은 민간인 같다. 메디치의 경우 사정은 이와 반대다. 가이젤이 더 똑똑하며, 그는 아무에게도 속해 있지 않은 것처럼 보인다. 그가 대통령 선거에서 이길 가능성이 더 많다.

3 어떤 역사가는 역사에 관해서 "그것은 현재를 집어삼킨다"고 말해왔다. 나는 그가 무엇을 의미하는지는 잘 이해되지 않지만, 과학의 경우는 분명히 사정은 반대다. 즉 현재가 과거를 집어삼킨다. 이것은 사상의 역사에 대한 과학자들의 잘못된 무관심을 용서해주는 데에 도움을 준다.

4 새는 날씨의 변화에 특히 민감한데, (유럽산) 땅까마귀는 특히 그렇다. 이들이 여느 때보다 더 높게 나무에 집을 지을 때에는 따뜻하고, 꽤 건조한 여름이 온다는 것을 우리는 흔히 보아왔다. 같은 얘기가 이들이 높이 날아다닐 때에도 적용되는데, 이들이 낮게 날아다니는 것이 보일 때에는 그 반대가 된다.

5 자동차에 대한 한 조사에 의하면, 1940년에는 도로에 다니는 승용차 한 대에 평균 3.2명이 탔다고 한다. 1950년에는 승용차 한 대당 탑승인원이 2.1인으로 떨어졌다. 1960년에는, 평균 승차인원이 1.4명으로 줄었다. 만일 이런 추세로 나간다면, 1980년에는 세 번째 차가 지나갈 때마다 아무도 타고 있지 않을 것이다(평균 승

차인원이 0.7명이 될 것이다).

6 무지했기 때문에, 인간은 자기 자신의 특별한 혹성이 우주의 중심이라고 믿었으나, 코페르니쿠스가 431년 전 이러한 믿음에 용감하게 도전했다. 지구가 태양의 주위를 돌지, 그 반대가 아니라고, 그는 주장했다. 그것은 깊고도 곤란한 생각이었다. 그러나 그것은 아직까지 완전한 진실과는 거리가 멀었다. 왜냐하면, 태양을 여전히 우주의 중심이라고 생각했기 때문이다. 그런데 그릇된 그 생각은 20세기의 사진술과 대형 망원경이 도래할 때까지 대부분의 사람들의 머릿속에 계속해서 남아 있었다.

7 처음에, 미국인들은 지방질과 콜레스테롤을 음식물로부터 줄이라는 말을 들었다. 그 다음에 그들은 설탕의 위험성에 대한 경고를 받았다. 최근에는 모든 조미료 가운데 가장 흔한 소금이 나쁘다는 말을 듣고 있다. 미국 학술원과 미국 식품 의약품국은 모든 사람들에게 고혈압을 예방하기 위해 소금의 섭취량을 줄이라고 충고해 왔다. 〈살인 소금〉과 같은 위협적인 책들이 후추 분쇄기 옆에 매복해 있는 위험(즉, 소금의 위험)을 떠들어대고 있고, 식품제조업자들도 나트륨 함량이 낮은 통조림 식품과 "노솔트"와 같은 소금 대체물을 제조해서 이 싸움에 가담해 왔다. 그러나 많은 고혈압 전문가들은 반격을 가하고 있다. 소금에 대항하는 이 광적인 운동은 소금을 더욱 많이 쳐서 받아들여야 한다(액면 그대로 받아들여서는 안 된다)고 이들은 지난 주에 경고했다.

   이들 전문가들은 미국의 4천만 내지 6천만의 고혈압 환자들 가운데 일부는 소금 섭취량을 줄여야 한다는 데에는 동의한다. 그러나 이것이 모든 사람들에게 어떤 이로움을 주리라는 점에 대해서는 강한 의혹을 품고 있다. "일반 사람들이 소금 섭취량이 적은 식사를 해야 한다고 권장할 과학상의 자료가 우리에게는 없다"고 뉴욕 병원 코넬 의료 센터의 존 H. 라라 박사는 말한다. 버지니아 주 알링턴에서 있었던 한 과학 심포지엄에서, 라라 박사와 그의 동료들의 지적에 의하면, 소금이 적게 든 식사는 따르기가 어렵고, 또 실제로 해로울지도 모른다고 한다.

8 당신이 콘택트 렌즈 한 쌍을 사는 데에 관심이 있다고 가정해 봅시다. 175달러 이상을 지불할 준비가 되어 있어야 합니다. 일반적으로 주로 세 가지 이유로 사람들은 콘택트 렌즈를 원합니다. 각막의 모양이 잘못 되어서 일반 안경은 만족스럽지 않기 때문에 콘택트 렌즈를 필요로 할 수도 있습니다. 만일 그렇다면, 당신은 콘택트 렌즈 사용자 가운데 1 내지 2%를 이루는 무리에 속하게 될 것입니다. 그러나 당신은 운동이나, 취미, 직업 때문에 콘택트 렌즈를 원할 수도 있습니다. 어쩌면 당신은 야구선수이거나, 권투선수, 수영선수, 비행사, 배우이거나, 또 어쩌면 날아다니는 입자가 당신의 눈을 위험하게 만들지도 모를 산업에 종사하고 있을지도 모릅니다. 만일 이들 이유 가운데 하나로 콘택트 렌즈를 산다면, 당신은 콘택트 렌즈 사용자의 약 20%에 해당하는 무리에 속해 있습니다. 그러나 만일, 어떤 이유로 안경을 쓰면 당신의 외모가 불리하게 보인다고 생각해서 눈에 보이지 않는 안경을 갖고 싶어한다면, 당신에게는 많은 동료가 있을 것입니다. 콘택트 렌즈 사용자 가운데 약 79%가 외모를 더 좋게 보이게 만들고 싶어합니다.

   주의 이 글은 친근감을 주는 문체로 쓰여 있습니다. 엄격한 논문을 이런 식으로 쓴다면 우스꽝스럽겠지만, 사람들에게 어떤 것을 말로 설명할 때에는 이런 방법이 가장 효과적일 것입니다. 필자가 강조해 왔듯이, 한국어와 다른 표현방식에 주의하시기 바랍니다.

9 아주 젊은 시절에 어딘가로 떠나고 싶은 충동이 나를 사로잡고 있을 때에 성숙한 사람들이 성숙함이 이러한 충동을 고쳐줄 거라고 나를 안심시켜 주었다. 내가 성숙해지자, 중년이 되면 그런 충동이 치유될 거라고 사람들은 얘기했다. 중년이 되자 나이가 더 들면 내 열병이 가라앉을 거라고 얘기했다. 이제 내 나이 58세니 어쩌면 노년이 그렇게 해줄지 모르겠다. 지금까지는 아무 것도 효력이 없었다. 뱃고동 소리가 네 번 거칠게 울리면 여전히 내 목덜미 위의 털은 쭝긋 일어서고 나는 발을 동동 구르게 된다. 제트기 소리, 시동을 걸고 있는 엔진 소리, 심지어 보도 위에서 딸각거리는 말발굽 소리에도 난 이 오래된 충동을 느끼게 되고, 입은 타고, 눈은 초점을 잃게 되며, 손바닥은 뜨거워지고, 아랫배는 흉곽 밑에서 꿈틀거리며 부풀어 오른다. 다시 말해서, 내 방랑벽은 나아지질 않는다. 다시 말하자면, 한번 방랑자가 되면 언제나 방랑자이게

마련이다. 이 질병은 고칠 수 없는 게 아닌가 생각된다.

> 참고 이 구절은 미국의 소설가 John Steinbeck이 쓴 Travels with Charley라는 책 첫머리에 나옵니다. 이 책은 조국을 더 잘 알아보려고 그가 사랑하는 개 Charley와 함께 camping truck을 몰고 미국 방방곡곡을 둘러본 뒤에 쓴 일종의 조국순례기입니다.

> 주의 Four hoarse blasts...under the rib cage 부분은 어딘지 가고픈 충동을 자극하는 일이 일어나면 떠나가고 싶어 못 견딘다는 필자의 상태를 묘사한 것이다.

10 시 감상을 통해서 내가 언제나 깨달아 온 것은 어떤 시인의 작품을 읽기 시작하기 전에 그 시인과 그의 작품에 관해서 내가 알고 있는 것이 적으면 적을수록 그만큼 더 좋다는 것이었다. 어떤 인용된 말이나 비판적인 얘기나 열광적인 논문이 계기가 되어 특정 작가를 읽게 될 가능성이 충분히 있으나, 어떤 작가의 시대적인 배경과 그의 생애에 관해서 애를 써 준비하는 것은 언제나 내게 주어진 작품을 이해하는 데에 장애가 되어 왔다. 이것이 내가 빈약한 지식을 옹호하려는 것이 아니다. 그리고 그런 나의 경험은, 만일 굳어져서 금언이 된다면, 로마와 그리스의 작가들에 대한 연구에는 적용하기가 매우 어려우리라는 것도 인정한다. 그러나 자신이 사용하는 언어로 작품을 쓴 작가들의 경우와 기타 현대어로 작품을 쓴 일부 작가들의 경우에도, 이 절차(어떤 작품을 읽을 때에 시대적인 배경이나 작가에 대해서 알아보지 않고 읽기 시작하는 것)는 가능하다. 적어도, 어떤 시를 좋아하기 때문에 자극을 받아서 그 시인의 시대적인 배경과 생애에 관한 지식을 얻게 되는 것이 그런 지식을 획득했기 때문에 그 시를 좋아한다고 생각하는 것보다 더 낫다. 나는 어떤 프랑스 시를 열렬히 좋아했다, 내가 그 시 가운데 두 편을 올바르게 번역할 수 있기 오래 전에. 단테의 경우에는 나의 즐거움과 이해 사이의 간격은 더욱 더 넓었다.

> 주의 끝에서 두 번째 문장 가운데 could have translated라는 가정법 시제는 필자가 실제로 번역을 해보지 않았다는 것을 암시해 줍니다.

> 참고 이 글의 내용을 이해하는 데에 T.S. Eliot의 다음 얘기가 도움이 될 것이다: Genuine poetry can communicate before it is understood.

EXERCISE 28

1 굴은 따뜻한 물을 좋아한다. 굴은 화씨 66도와 70도 사이 온도에서 가장 잘 자란다. 남쪽 바다에서 이들은 2년 내지 3년이면 완전히 성장한다. 북쪽에서는 이들이 성장하는 데에 약 4년이 걸린다.

* Topic sentence : 첫째 문장

2 야크(티베트산 들소)는, 크기가 대략 작은 황소만한 동물이다. 이것은 티베트에 사는데, 이곳은 중국의 한 고원지대에 있는 지방이다. 주민들은 야크를 교통수단으로 이용한다. 이들은 또한 야크의 젖을 마시고, 고기는 음식으로 먹으며, 털을 짜서 천을 만든다. 야크는 티베트에서 가장 유용한 동물이다.

* Topic sentence : 마지막 문장

> 주의 size, age 등으로 이루어진 형용사구에서는 흔히 전치사 of가 생략된다.

3 비록 아인슈타인은 종교 의식의 필요성을 느끼지 않았고 어떤 공식적인 종교단체에도 속하지 않았지만, 그는 내가 지금까지 알아온 가장 깊이 종교적인 사람이었다. 언젠가 그는 나에게 "아이디어는 하느님으로부터 나온다"고 말했는데, 그가 "하느님"이라는 단어를 발음하는 태도로 보아 그가 얼마나 하느님을 숭배하는지를 느낄 수 있었다. 프린스턴 대학교 수학관에 있는 대리석 벽난로 위에는, 본래의 독일어로 과학에 대한 그의 신조라고 볼 수 있는 다음과 같은 말이 새겨져 있다. "하느님은 이해하기는 어려우나 나쁜 뜻은 갖고 있지 않다." 이 말에서 아인슈타인이 의미했던 것은, 과학자들은 과제가 어렵기는 해도, 희망이 없지는 않다고 기대할 수 있다는 것이었다. 왜냐하면 우주는 법칙으로 이루어졌으며, 하느님이 일부러 역설과 모순으로 우리를 혼동하게 만드는 것은 아니기 때문이라는 것이다.

* Topic sentence : 첫째 문장

> 주의 이 구절의 마지막 문장에 나오는 colon은 "첫째 진술을 설명해 주는 제2의 진술을 도입할 때"(when introducing a second statement which explains the first)에 사용되는 것입니다. 다음 예문을 보세요.
> We know why he did it : he needed money.

4 대부분의 꿀벌은 부지런하지만, 일부는 사람과 비슷해서 일하는 것에 대해서 무성의한 태도를 취한다. 이들은 집을 늦게 떠나서 일찍 돌아오며, 될 수 있는 대로 나들이를 적게 한다. 어떤 꿀벌은 무척 애를 써서 일을 피하고 심지어 "강도"벌이 되어 범죄 생활을 영위하기까지 한다. 이들 꿀 강도들은 저 악명높은 블랙 바트라는 강도의 온갖 간교한 계략으로 다른 벌집의 꿀 저장고를 습격한다. 대개 이러한 습격은 풍부한 꿀 저장고를 보호하는 임무를 부여받고 정신을 바짝 차리고 있는 경비 꿀벌들에 의해 좌절된다. 그러나 성공을 거둔 강도들은 자기들의 집으로 돌아와서 자기들의 공적을 뽐낸다. 색다른 춤으로 이들은 벌집에 있는 다른 벌들에게 자기들이 "말랑말랑한 털 곳"(쉽게 털 수 있는 곳)을 찾았다고 알려준다. 다른 벌들도, 너무 게을러 일을 하기 싫어서, 이들에게 매료되어 벌집을 떠나 훔치는 데에 자기들의 운을 시험해 본다.

* Topic sentence : 첫째 문장

참고 이 구절을 읽을 때에 필자는 어떤 심리학자가 실시한 재미 있는 실험이 생각났습니다. 그 실험은 다음과 같습니다.

세 개의 우리에 각각 세 마리씩을 넣고 관찰했더니, 각 우리에 한 마리만 부지런히 일하고 나머지 두 마리는 게으름을 부렸다. 그런데 이들 세 우리로부터 부지런히 일하던 쥐를 골라서 한 우리에 넣었더니 똑같은 현상이 벌어졌다.

여기서 우리는 생물계의 개체 사이에 미묘한 '역학 관계'가 발생한다는 것을 알 수 있습니다. 앞으로 어떤 조직체를 만들어보려는 분들은 여기서 좋은 교훈을 얻을 수 있을 것 같습니다.

5 "왜 제가 영어를 공부해야 합니까?"라고 어떤 반항적인 젊은이가 반발했다. "저는 영어를 알고 있고, 또 저는 영국인인데요."

그러나 영어를 공부하고 있다고 누구나 정말로 영어를 알고 있는 것은 아니고, 또한 누구나 같은 종류의 영어를 모두 알고 있는 것도 아니다. 직업적인 야구선수는 커브 볼을 던지는 법을 알고 있을 수 있다. 어떤 물리학자도 같은 사실을 알고 있을 수 있으나, 그가 알고 있는 것은 전혀 다른 방법일 수 있다. 그가 알고 있는 방법은 더 나은 것일 수 있다. 왜냐하면 비록 그가 현재로서는 직업적인 야구선수만큼 커브 볼을 잘 던질 수 없을지라도, 다른 조건이 같고 그가 야구선수만큼 많은 시간을 연습한다면, 충분히, 그는 더 나은 커브 볼을 던질 수 있을 것이다. 다시 말해서(왜냐하면), 분석적인 지식(물리학자가 알고 있는 것과 같은 지식)은 경험적인 지식을 도와주며 떠받쳐준다(주기 때문이다).

* Topic sentence : 마지막 문장

여담 여러분, 잊지 말고 먼저 머리를 쓰세요!

6 어느 정도까지, 의심은 우리의 사고(thinking)에 이롭다. 의심하는 사람은 감정에 지배될 위험 속에 놓여 있지 않기 때문이다. 그러나 어떠한 긍정적인 믿음이 전혀 없는 사람은 흔히 쓸모없는 사람이며, 무엇인가 긍정적인 것에 대한 믿음이 없는 생활은 견딜 수 없다. 모든 것을 의심하지 말고, 충분한 증거가 있을 때에는 믿을 준비가 되어 있어야 하며, 증거가 없는 경우에는 판단을 내리려고 하지 말아야 한다. 바꾸어 말하면, 우리의 정신적인 태도는 "비판적"이어야지, "부정적"이어서는 안 된다.

* Topic sentence : 마지막 문장

주의 윗글에서는 주어진 문장이 주어진 구절에서 갖는 비중을 보여주는 말(예를 들어, To a certain extent라는 말은 이 문장의 비중이 크지 않다는 것을 보여준다)이나 문맥의 흐름을 보여주는 말(예를 들어, In other words라는 말은 뒤에 나오는 말이 바로 앞의 진술을 바꾸어 쓴 말이라는 것을 보여준다)에 주의하기 바란다.

7 몇 년 전에 나는 어떤 분을 만났는데, 이 분은 뉴욕 시내에 있는 어떤 사무실 건물에서 화물 엘리베이터를 운행하고 있었다. 알고 보니 그의 왼쪽 손은 손목에서 잘려 나가고 없었다. 나는 그에게 왼쪽 손이 없어서 불편하지 않느냐고 물어보았다. 그는 말했다. "아니, 그렇지 않습니다. 나는 거기에 대해서 거의 생각하지 않아요. 전 결혼을 하지 않았죠. 그런데 제가 거기에 대해서 생각하는 유일한 때는 바늘에 실을 꿰우려고 할 때랍니다." 참으로 놀라운 일은 너무도 빨리 우리는 거의 어떤 사태든지, 그것이 불가피한 경우에는, 그것을 받아들이고, 우리 자신을 그것에 적응시키고 그것에 대해서 잊어버릴 수 있다는 점이다.

* Topic sentence : 마지막 문장

8 너무 어린 취학 아동들을 연구한 사람들은 한결같이 한 가지 가공할 상황을 제시한다. 이 어린이는 늘상 불안스럽게 비틀거리면서 유치원과 초등학교 저학년을 거쳐 나간다. 반면에 일년쯤 늦게 학교에 들어온 그의 친구들은 재빨리 그를 따라와서 그를 능가하는데, 대개 이들은 매우

안정적이고 배우려는 의욕이 높아진다. 학습한 것을 기억하는 정도는 흔히 나중에 시작한 친구들보다 이 어린이가 더 낮다, 그의 영리한 정도와는 상관없이. 바꾸어 말해서, 조기 학교교육이 어린이를 거의 무능력하게 만드는 것이나 다름없다는 결론을 피하기 어렵다.

* Topic sentence: 마지막 문장

9 한 편의 문학작품에 대한 연구는 작가, 그 작품의 문화적인 배경, 그리고 작품 자체와 관련해서(중심으로 해서) 이루어질 수 있다. 우리는 한 작가의 작품을 그 작가의 개성이나 세계관에 대한 정보를 얻기 위해 연구할 수도 있다. 그러나 독자는 한 작가의 작품을 근거로 해서 그에 대한 판단을 내릴 때에는 주의해야 한다. 왜냐하면 어떤 소설의 주인공의 태도와 가치관이 반드시 작가 자신의 것을 반영해 주는 것은 아니기 때문이다. 문학작품은 한 시대의 산물이므로, 그 시대의 정치 및 경제적인 조건과 철학 및 종교적인 사상에 대한 지식은 유용하다. 그러나 아무리 흥미있고 유용하더라도, 작가나 그의 배경에 대한 관심은 본질적으로 이차적이다. 작품 자체에 대한 연구가 일차적인 것이다. 만일 우리가 한 편의 소설이나 희곡 또는 시의 핵심을 파악하려면, 우리는 그 작품의 내용과 구조에 관심을 집중해야 한다. (다시 말해서) 우리는 작가가 전달하는 경험과 그것을 전달하는 형식에 관심을 가져야 하는 것이다.

* Topic sentence: But however interesting and helpful, concern for the author or his background is essentially secondary. The study of the work itself is primary.

주의 이 구절의 첫 문장이나 끝에서 두 번째 문장을 주제문장으로 간주하고 싶은 분들도 있겠지만, 그것은 일반적인 견해가 아니라고 필자는 생각합니다. 왜냐하면 첫 문장은 얘기를 전개해나가기 위한 하나의 도입적인 문장(an introductory sentence)에 더 가깝고, 끝에서 두 번째 문장에는 물론 중요한 주장이 들어 있기는 하지만 그것은 바로 앞에 나오는 두 개의 문장의 내용을 '발전시킨 것'이라고 볼 수 있고, 다른 한편으로 그것은 이 구절의 결론이라고 보는 것이 더 타당하기 때문입니다.

Topic sentence에 대한 Webster's New World Dictionary (Second College Edition)의 다음 정의를 참조해 보세요.

the principal sentence, setting forth the main idea and coming usually at the beginning, in a paragraph or section of a discourse, esp. of an expository nature.

(논설문 — 특히 설명적인 성격의 — 의 한 문단이나 부분에서 주축을 이루는 문장으로, 주제를 제시해 주며 대개 첫머리에 온다)

10 개인으로서, 우리의 발전은 우리가 살아가는 과정에서 만나는 사람들에게 달려 있다.(이런 사람들 중에는 우리가 읽은 책의 저자와 소설과 역사적인 저술에 나오는 인물들이 포함된다.) 이러한 만남이 주는 혜택은 사람들 간의 비슷한 점에 못지 않게 차이점에서, 그리고 의견의 일치는 물론 의견의 차이에서 비롯된다. 적절한 순간에 적절한 친구를 만나는 사람은 운이 좋으며, 적절한 순간에 적절한 적을 만나는 사람 또한 운이 좋다. 나는 적을 완전히 제거하는 것에 찬성하지 않는다. 적을 완전히 제거하려는, 또는, 사람들이 야만스럽게 얘기하듯이, 싹 쓸어버리려는 정책은, 문화가 계속 존재하기를 바라는 사람들의 관점에서 볼 때에, 현대의 전쟁과 평화가 만들어낸 가장 무서운 사태 가운데 하나다. 우리에게는 적이 필요하다. 그러므로, 일정한 한도 내에서는 개인들 사이는 물론 집단 사이의 마찰은 내가 생각하기엔 문명을 위해 아주 필요한 것 같다. 어디서나 의견이 일치하지 않는다면 평화가 보장될 가능성은 가장 높다. 지나치게 분열되어 있는 나라는 그 나라 자체에 위험한 존재이며, 지나치게 잘 단결되어 있는 나라는 — 그것이 저절로 그렇게 되었든지 계획적으로 되었든지, 정직한 목적에 의해서든지 혹은 사기와 억압에 의해서든지 간에 — 다른 나라들에 위험이 된다. 이탈리아와 독일에서는 정치 · 경제적인 목표를 지닌 단결이 — 이것은 격렬하고 너무 급격히 부과되었다 — 양국에 불행한 영향을 미쳤다는 것을 우리는 보아왔다. 이들의 문화는 극단적이며 극단적으로 세분된 지역주의의 역사 과정에서 발전해왔는데, 독일인들에게 자기 자신을 먼저 독일인이라고 생각하도록 가르치려는 시도와, 이탈리아인들에게 먼저 이탈리아인으로 생각하도록 가르치려는 시도는 결국 미래 문화의 유일한 기반이 될 수 있는 전통적인 문화를 뒤흔들어놓는(파괴하는) 결과를 가져왔다.

* Topic sentence: So, within limits, the friction, not only between individuals but between groups, seems to me quite necessary for civilization.

주의 이 구절이 무척 어렵기는 하지만, 주제는 너무도 뚜렷이 나타나 있으므로 그것만 찾아내면 충분히 이해할 수 있을 것입니다. 참고로 이 구절의 key words를 추려보면 다음과 같습니다.

differences, conflict, enemy, friction, irritation, division, regionalism.

이 단어들이 모여서 주제를 이루므로, 이것들의 의미는 반드시 주제와의 관련 속에서 찾아야 합니다.

주의 Fortunate와 fortunate 바로 뒤에 동사 is를 생략한 것으로 생각하라.

주의 as much x as y나 x as well as y에서 x가 y보다 더 중시된다. 그러므로, 우리는 지문에서 resemblances, sympathy, friend, unity 따위의 말들보다 differences, conflict, enemy, friction 따위가 더 중시된다는 것을 알 수 있다.

EXERCISE 29

1 D (우리에게는 과거에 의하지 않고 미래를 판단할 방법이 없다. 미래에 대한 우리의 투시는 희미하지만 우리는 경험이라는 등불로부터 약간의 빛을 받고 있다.)

　* Key Words: the past → experience

2 B (보통 사람은 자신의 의사를 글로 나타낼 때와 말로 나타낼 때에 다르게 나타낸다. 바르게 연습하면 이런 차이는 극복될 수 있으므로, 자신이 쓰는 글이 말과 더욱 비슷하게 될 것이다.)

　* Key Words: differently → difference → like

3 C (베토벤은 음악은 작곡가의 생각을 표현하기 위한 매개체여야 하며, 모든 그밖의 요소는 이차적인 중요성을 갖는다고 믿었다. 그에게, 일차적인 강조점은 내용에 있었다.)

　* Key Words: ideas → content

4 B (공기는 그것을 통과하는 물체의 운동에 저항한다. 비행기와 자동차는 유선형으로 만드는데, 그것은 이들이 공기를 통과할 때에 저항을 더 적게 받도록 하기 위해서이다.)

　* Key Words: resists → resistance

5 A (사람들에게 일반적으로 받아들여지고 있는 것과 반대되는 새로운 생각을 가르치는 것은 언제나 위험한 일이었다. 처음으로 지구가 둥글다고 가르친 사람들은 박해를 당했다.)

　* Key Words: dangerous → persecuted

6 D (우리는 한 공동체 사회의 교육받은 사람들이 그 사회의 유일한 명석하게 사고하는 주민들이라고는 생각할 수 없다. 왜냐하면 훌륭한 판단이 반드시 교육과 비례하는 것은 아니라는 것이 밝혀져왔기 때문이다.)

　* Key Words: educated → education

7 B (벼는 자라기 위해 많은 물이 필요하다. 대부분의 벼를 재배하는 지역에서는 비가 벼에게 충분한 수분을 제공해 주지 못한다. 그래서 논에 물을 대주어야 한다.)

　* Key Words: water → moisture → irrigated

8 D (등산에는 많은 위험이 따른다. 그래서 등산하는 사람은 언제나 정신을 바짝 차려야 한다. 무모하게 산에 오르는 사람은 곧 사고를 당한다. 등산은 정말이지 신중한 사람을 위한 것이다.)

　* Key Words: risk → alert → reckless → prudent

9 C (책은 영화로 만들어지는 과정에서 거의 불가피하게 손실을 겪는다. 책에는 영화를 위해 만들어져있는 것 같아 보이는 장면들이 있을지 모르나, 그러한 장면들에게 의의를 부여하는 예비적인 서술은 쉽게 필름으로 옮겨 놓을 수가 없다.)

　* Key Words: movies → filming → celluloid

10 D (인간은 모든 동물 가운데에서 가장 무서운 것 가운데 하나며, 끊임없이 자기 자신의 종족을 공격하기를 좋아하는 유일한 동물이다. 역사를 통해서 줄곧, 짧은 기간을 제외하고, 한번도 치열한 전쟁이 없이 그가 살아온 적이 없었다.)

　* Key Words: formidable → attack → warfare

11 D (새로운 기술이나 보조학문을 배우기 위한 커다란 자극은 그것을 이용해야 할 긴급한 필요성이다. 이런 이유로 많은 과학자들이 새로운 기술을 배우거나 새로운 학문을 습득하게 되는 것은 그렇게 해야 할 압력을 받는 다음부터다.)

* Key Words: an urgent need → pressure

12 C (어떤 시대의 어떤 과학자나 중요한 발견을 하기 바란다면 중요한 문제를 연구해야 한다고 말할 수 있다. 재미없는 문제는 재미없는 해답을 낳는다. 문제가 재미있는 것으로 충분하지 않다. 문제는 마땅히 그 해답이 무엇이냐가 중요해야 한다 — 그것이 과학 전반에게 중요한 것이든 혹은 인류에게 중요한 것이든.)

* Key Words: important → matters

13 C (자연과학에 관한 지식이 "출세"의 수단으로서 가치가 있다는 것은 의심할 여지가 없다. 어떤 직업에 종사하는 사람이라도 과학에 관한 다소간의 지식이 유익하다는 것을 깨닫게 될 것이다.)

* Key Words: a means of 'getting on' → profitable

14 C (사람에게는 도전적인 일을 할 기회가 필요하다. 나는 이 범주 안에 단순히 반복적인 따분한 많은 일들은 포함시키지 않는다. 나는 단조로운 일에는 관심이 없다.)

* Key Words: repetitive drudgery → monotonous work

15 D (글을 쓰는 사람은 매우 주의해서 진실한 것만 얘기해야 한다. 그는 그릇된 진술이나 암시를 하지 말아야 한다. 그는 정확해야 한다.)

* Key Words: true → accurate

16 A ("문화 충격"이라는 용어를 만들어낸 것은 낯선 문화에 들어갔을 때에 그 문화를 모르는 방문객이 받는 영향을 설명하기 위해서였다. 이 현상이 발생하는 것은 한 개인으로 하여금 사회 안에서 기능을 발휘하는 데에 도움을 주는 그 개인에게 익숙한 심리적인 실마리들이 갑자기 낯설고 이해할 수 없는 새로운 실마리들로 대치될 때이다.)

* Key Words: strange → new → alien

17 A (진리에 대한 사랑이 이분의 철학의 핵심이다. 그는 자신의 견해가 타당하지 않다는 충분한 증거가 제시되면 언제나 자신의 견해를 바꿀 준비가 되어 있다.)

* Key Words: truth → validity

18 A (현대의 비평은, 문학 작품에 대한 세심한 연구를 통해서, 예술에서 아름다움과 진실은 분리될 수 없으며 하나라는 것을 결론적으로 보여주어 왔다.)

* Key Words: indivisible → one

19 D (자수성가한 사람은 물질적인 성공의 가치를 강조하고 겉으로 보기에 비생산적인 활동을 부정하려는 경향이 있다.)

* Key Words: emphasize → disapprove of

주의 nonproductive activities는 material success와 상반된다.

20 D (인디언 소녀들은 어머니로부터 요리하는 것과 옷 만드는 것을 배웠다. 소년들은 아버지로부터 고기를 잡고, 사냥하고, 싸우는 법을 배웠다. 그들에게는 읽기와 쓰기를 배우는 학교가 없었으나, 우리는 그들이 교육을 받지 않았다고 말할 수는 없다.)

* Key Words: learned → schools → education

....

1 B (조지 윌러드는 그 오하이오 주 마을 소년이었는데, 빠른 속도로 어른이 되어가고 있었고, 새로운 생각들이 그의 의식 속에 떠오르고 있었다. 그날 하루 종일, 시장에 많은 사람들이 빽빽히 몰려 있는 가운데, 그는 외로움을 느끼면서 돌아다녔다. 그는 와인즈버그를 떠나 어떤 도시로 가서 어떤 신문사에

일자리를 구하려던 참이었는데, 자신이 어른이 된 것 같은 기분이 들었다. 그를 사로잡은 기분은 어른들은 아는 것이었으나 아이들에게는 낯선 것이었다. 그는 나이가 들고 다소 피곤하다는 생각이 들었다. 여러 가지 기억들이 떠올랐다. 그가 생각하기에 자기가 성숙했다는 새로운 의식이 자기를 다른 사람들로부터 떼어놓고, 자기를 반쯤 비극적인 인물로 만드는 것 같았다.)

2 D (부모들로부터 사랑을 받는 어린이는 그들의 사랑을 당연한 것으로 받아들인다. 그는 거기에 대해서 별로 많이 생각하지 않는다. 비록 그것이 자신의 행복에 중요하지만. 그가 생각하는 것은 세상과 자기가 경험하게 될 신나는 일들과 자기가 어른이 되었을 때에 경험하게 될 더욱 신나는 일들이다. 그러나 이 모든 외적인 관심 뒤에는 자기가 부모의 사랑에 의해 재난으로부터 보호받으리라는 생각이 놓여 있다. 반면에, 어떤 이유로 부모의 사랑을 받지 못하는 어린이는 겁이 많고 모험을 하지 않게 되며, 두려움과 자신을 불쌍히 여기는 감정으로 가득차게 될 가능성이 있으며, 즐겁게 탐색하는 기분으로 더 이상 세상을 대할 수가 없다.)

EXERCISE 30

1 아이젠하워의 주요한 장점은 — 그런데 이 장점이 1962년에는 지금보다 덜 중요하게 보였다 — 비중에 대한 센스(판단력)였다. 다시 말해서, 그는 할 수 있는 일과, 더욱 중요한 것은, 할 수 없는 일이 무엇인지를 직감적으로 알고 있었다. 일찍이 1951년에 이미, 예를 들어, 프랑스가 베트남에서 전쟁을 하고 있을 때에, 그가 예견한 것은 늪뿐이었다(즉, 그는 프랑스가 결코 승리할 수 없을 것으로 내다보았다는 뜻임). "나는 그런 종류의 무대에서는 그 어떤 군사적인 승리도 불가능하다고 확신합니다"라고 그는 말했다. 1955년에 그의 내각 각료들이 대만 해협에서 중공과의 전쟁이 곧 일어날 것이라고 예언했다. 아이크는 그렇지 않으리라는 것을 알고 있었다. "나는 너무도 자주 이러한 긴장 시기를 거쳐 왔기 때문에 우리가 예상하는 재난들 가운데 대부분은 실제로 결코 일어나지 않는다는 사실에 익숙해지게 되었습니다."

* 예시: "As far back as 1951" 이하 전부

2 해군제독과 장군들이 전쟁을 승리로 이끄는 것이 아니다. 대통령이 그렇게 하는 것이다. 다음 대통령들을 생각해 보라. 워싱턴(그는 미국 독립 혁명 기간 중에 대통령에 가장 가까운 존재였다), 링컨, 윌슨, 그리고 프랭클린 루스벨트.

해군제독과 장군들이 전쟁에서 패하는 것이 아니다. 대통령이 그렇게 하거나, 적어도 대통령이 전쟁을 승리로 이끌지 못하는 것이다. 다음 대통령들을 생각해 보라. 한국전 때의 트루먼과 베트남전 때의 린든 잔슨.

전시에, 모든 것을 좌우하는 것은 위대한 전략, 다시 말해서 힘의 위협과 목적, 그리고 현실(즉, 주어진 전쟁의 여건들)을 어떻게 이용해야 하느냐에 대한 대통령의 구상이다. 구상이 없이 승리할 수 없다. 워싱턴은 젊은 미국의 유격전 기술 — 이것은 개척지와 미개척지 사이의 경계 지역에서 벌어진 싸움에서 연마된 것이었다 — 을 이용해서 대규모의 영국군을 물리쳤다. 링컨은, 자신의 일선 지휘관들이 남부동맹군의 야전 전략가들보다 실력이 모자랐지만, 많은 병력, 보다 나은 화력, 그리고 이것들을 이용할 줄 아는 그랜트와 같은 장군들에 의존했다. 윌슨과 루스벨트는 미국의 산업력을 이용해서 세계대전에서 승리했다. 잔슨과 트루먼은 자기가 원하는 것이 무엇인지 결코 이해하지 못했기에, 그들은 어떻게 싸워야 할지 한번도 마음을 결정하지 못했다.

* 예시: 첫째 문단 : "Consider" 이하
둘째 문단 : "Consider" 이하
셋째 문단 : "Washington wisely employed" 이하

참고 좀 어렵다고 쉽게 포기하지 마세요. 어려울수록 힘을 내고 머리를 더 쓰는 것이 현명한 사람의 태도입니다.

3 프랭클린의 미래에 대한 꿈은 또한 그의 성격의 모순되는 점들 가운데 많은 것의 근원이었다. 그는 여러 가지 운동에 깊이 관여했으나, 그러면서도 이상하게도 초연했다. 그는 혁명가였으나 유머에 대한 감각을 갖고 있었다. 그는 진지했다. 왜냐하면 우리가 실제로 우리 자신의 세계를 만

들기 때문에 우리는 그것을 우리가 만들 수 있는 최선의 세계로 만들어야 한다는 것을 그는 알고 있었기 때문이었다. 그러나 그는 회의적이었다. 왜냐하면 인간의 노력이 흔히 비참하고 우스꽝스러운 결과를 가져온다는 것을 그는 알고 있었기 때문이었다. 이러한 모순 가운데 일부는 프랭클린으로부터 나와서 미국인의 성격이 되었다 — 이를테면, 신념과 회의, 열성과 해학, 진보주의적인 사고방식과 보수주의적인 사고방식이 뒤섞여 있는 미국인의 성격 말이다.

* 예시 : He was deeply involved... a sorry and ludicrous botch.

4 진실한 사람들은 자기들의 인생이 가도록 의도된 방향을 깨닫는다. 저 위대한 선교사로 의사 노릇을 했던 앨버트 슈바이처가 소년이었을 때에, 한 친구가 산에 올라가서 새를 잡자고 제의했다. 앨버트는 마음이 내키지 않았으나, 조롱당할까 두려워서 따라갔다. 그들이 어떤 나무에 도착했을 때에 거기에서는 한 무리의 새들이 노래하고 있었다. 이 아이들은 고무줄이 달린 자기들의 새총에 돌을 집어넣었다. 그때 교회의 종소리가 울리기 시작해서, 음악과 새들의 노래를 뒤섞이게 했다. 앨버트에게, 그것은 하늘로부터 나오는 소리였다. 그는 쉿 하는 소리를 질러서 새들을 쫓아버리고 집으로 갔다. 그날부터, 생명에 대한 존중이 그에게는 조롱당하는데 대한 두려움보다 더 중요했다. 그가 중시해야 할 것들이 무엇인지는 분명했다.

* 예시 : 둘째 문장 이하 전부

EXERCISE 31

1 D 우리가 보겠듯이, 그 두 논제는 밀접하게 관련되어 있어서, 정말이지 단일한 논제의 다른 양상이라고 간주할 만하다.

2 C 개인으로 하여금 사회제도를 현재의 형태로 받아들이게 이끌어주는 사회화의 세력들은 쉽게 깨뜨려지고 변형되지 않는다.

요령 여기 and 앞과 뒤에는 비슷한 내용의 말이 와야 된다.

3 A 내용과 형식은 둘 다 훌륭한 시에 필요불가결하다. 좋은 소재가 좋은 시를 보장해 주지 않으며, 정교한 형식은 무엇인가 내용이 없는 경우에는 우스꽝스럽다.

4 B 생각은 때로는 말에 의해서보다는 몸짓에 의해서 더 잘 전달될 수 있다. 어떤 사람에게 방에서 나가 달라고 얘기하는 것은 문을 가리키는 것보다 훨씬 덜 효과적이다.

5 D 사람들은 아는 것이 힘이라고 얘기해 왔지만, 그러나 위대한 힘은 아는 것을 이용할 수 있는 능력에 달려 있다. 훈련된 강력한 두뇌에 무엇인가 들어 있는 것은 확실하지만, 그것의 주된 가치는 그것이 무엇을 할 수 있느냐에 달려 있다.

6 D 악이 존재한다는 것은 하느님이 존재한다는 증거다. 만일 세상이 전적으로 그리고 오로지 선과 정의로 이루어져 있다면, 하느님이 필요없을 것이다. 왜냐하면 그렇게 되면 세상 자체가 하느님일 테니까. 하느님이 존재하는 것은 악이 존재하기 때문이다.

7 C 흄과 같은 철학자나 기번과 같은 역사학자의 초연한 태도를 지니고 이성을 구사하기 위해서는, 지성 외에, 두 가지 — 즉, 자신을 아는 것과 유머 감각 — 가 필요하다. 다시 말해서, (그러기 위해서는) 자신을 속여도 안 되고, 자신을 너무 중요하게 생각해서도 안 된다.

참고 마지막 문장은 self-knowledge and a sense of humor에 대한 부연이다.

8 D 어떤 환자든지 의료상의 실험에 참가하게 되면 "자기가 내용을 알고 동의했다"는 서류에 서명해야 한다. 이 서류는 두 가지 목적을 갖고 있다. 한 가지 목적은 실험 대상인 사람들이 주어진 치료의 실험적인 성격을 완전히 이해하고 있다는 것을 확인하는 것이고, 또 하나는 그들의 결정이 압력을 받지 않고 이루어졌다는 것을 보증하는 것이다.

9 A 비록 소크라테스의 가르침들 가운데 많은 것들이 오늘날에는 일반적으로 받아들여지고 있지만, 그 당시에는 지배적인 사상과 일치하지 않았으며 매우 극단적인 것으로 생각되었다.

10 A 이성을 지닌 존재이기에, 우리는 어느 정도까지는 우리의 주위환경을 통제할 수 있다. 우리가 사회적인 혹은 경제적인 힘에 지배될지 모르나, 시민으로서 노력해서 우리 사회를 개조할 수 있다.

11 C 처음에는, 별 하나하나가 모든 다른 별들로부터 떨어져 있는 것처럼 보이나, 좀더 오랫동안 관찰해 보면 무리들이 나타나기 시작하고, 짝이 나타나며, 집단이 보이게 된다.

12 D 세상이 아주 명백하게 필요로 하는 것이 몇 가지 있는데, 그것은 우리가 독단적으로 생각하거나 주장하지 말고 확실한 증거가 있을 때까지 판단을 보류하는 것, 사회적인 관계에서 경쟁보다는 협조를 기대하는 것, 질투와 집단적인 증오심을 줄이는 것이다. 이러한 것들은 교육을 통해 큰 어려움 없이 만들어낼 수 있다.

13 C 과거와 과거의 저작물에 대한 연구를 경멸하는 사람들의 일반적인 생각은 과거는 현재와 전혀 다르며, 따라서 우리는 과거로부터 아무 것도 가치있는 것을 배울 수 없다는 것이다.

14 B 중세에, 가수들은 이곳저곳으로 떠돌아다녔는데, 가는 곳마다 환영받았다. 그들은 흔히 노래로 가까운 곳과 먼 곳에서 일어난 일들을 얘기했다. 그들은, 말하자면, 당대의 뉴스 논평가였다.

15 C 한 편의 글의 질을 더 좋게 고치려면, 우리는 단순한 비판 이상의 것을 해야 한다. 우리는 왜 그것을 비판하는지를 설명해야 한다. 질이 떨어지는 글은 왜 그것이 좋지 않은지를 우리가 알고 있을 때에 가장 효과적으로 고쳐진다.

16 A 바로 어떤 이유 때문에 잠이 필요한지를 아직도 학자들은 이해하지 못하고 있다. 그것은 건강에 필요불가결한 것 같지 않다. 장기간 잠을 자지 못하게 되면 일시적인 방향감각상의 혼란이 일어날 수 있으나, 그 영향은 영구적이 아니다.

17 C 남성의 자살률은 여성의 자살률의 무려 네 배쯤 된다. 그러나 여성들의 자살기도의 빈도수는 남자들 빈도수의 거의 세 배다. 그런데 여성들의 성공률이 더 낮은 것은 이들이 약을 먹는 것과 같이 덜 치명적인 방법을 사용하는 반면에, 남성들은 총을 좋아하는 경향이 있기 때문이다.

18 D 어떤 것을 철저히 이해하려면, 그것을 이루는 부분을 알아야 한다. 예를 들어, 우리가 어떤 집을 알고 있다는 것은 우리가 그 집의 방들과 그 집의 건축상의 여러 가지 세부사항들을 잘 알고 있을 때이다. 단어의 구성은 집과 아주 비슷하다. 그러므로 단어를 이루는 구성요소들을 익힘으로써 우리는 단어들을 더 잘 이해하게 될 것이다.

19 D DNA 재조합이 1973년에 유전혁명에 불을 붙이자, 과학자와 실업가들은 그것의 거의 기적에 가까운 의학적인 가능성에 매력을 느꼈다. 그러나 오늘날, 식량부족이 임박하고 경작가능한 땅이 점차 사라짐에 따라, 유전자 결합은 농업으로 옮겨가고 있다.

20 D 비록 과학의 목표는 지식의 획득이지만, 그 지식은 물론 믿을 만한 것이어야 한다. 그러므로 과학에는 지식을 모으는 체계적인 방법이 필요하다. 바로 이런 체계화가 과학과 기타 학문 사이의 본질적인 차이점이다.

21 A 현대 작곡가들은 이런 종류의 현실주의에 강한 반발을 보여왔다. 실제로, 이 반발은 일찍이 우리 세기 초에 시작되었다.

22 B 미국인들이 잘난 척하는 것으로 유명한 적은 한번도 없었다. 오히려 그들의 특징은 개인이 평등하다는 것을 믿고, 잘난 척하는 것을 참지 못하는 것인데, 이러한 특징은 개척시대에 모든 사람들을 좋은 이웃사람처럼 대하던 친절과 잘난 척하는 데 대한 의혹에서 생긴 것이다.

  주의 짧지만, 우리말로 옮기기가 쉽지 않은 구절이니 특별히 주의하시기 바랍니다.

23 B 귀양을 보내는 것은, 드 또끄빌의 얘기에 의하면, 모든 처벌 가운데에서 가장 잔인한 것이라고 한다. 왜냐하면 그것은 고통을 주는 반면에 아무 것도 가르쳐주지 않으니까. 그것은 귀양 가는 사람의 의식을 굳어지게 하고, 그들의 의식 속에 젊은 시절에 획득한 생각들을 고정시킨다.

24 B 일부 작가들은 역사적인 관심거리만 된다. 이들의 얘기가 당대 사람들을 감동시켰을지 모르나, 이들은 오늘날 우리를 감동시키지 않는다. 참으로 위대한 작가는 당대인들뿐만 아니라 후세 사람들도 감동시키는 사람이다.

  주의 우리말 번역에 주의하라.
  참고 두 번째 문장은 첫째 문장에 대한 부연이다.

25 B 좋은 추리소설의 특징은 하나의 결정적인 단서가 미궁에 빠진 사건에 대한 해결책을 드러내주지만, 그 단서와 그것의 중요성이 결코 명백하지 않아야 한다는 것이다.

26 D 서구문명의 두 가지 근본적이며 상호관련되어 있는 목표는 인간의 생명을 보존하는 것과 경제적인 안정을 제공하는 것이다. 서구문명은 건강과 부를 동시에 추구한다.

27 A 가치있는 운동을 보면, 손더스 부인은 아낌없이 자신의 시간과 재능을 바쳤지만, 그녀의 금전적인 기부는 어쩔 수 없이 제한되어 있었다.

28 C 어째서 인생은 살 가치가 있는가? 당신이 인생에서 가장 좋아하거나 인생에서 가장 원하는 것은 무엇인가? 무엇으로부터 당신은 가장 완전한 만족을 얻는가? 실질적으로 당신이 원하는 것은 다른 사람들이 원하는 것과 비슷한가, 그렇지 않으면 당신이 인생에서 바라는 것은 독특한가?

  주의 마지막 문장의 접속사 "or"에 주의하라.

29 D 그 인류학자는 서로 다른 종족의 사람들이 비슷한 상황 속에서 행동하는 다양한 방식에 너무도 익숙해져 있어서 가장 이상한 관습에도 놀라지 않는 경향이 있다.

30 C 우리는 자유를 갖고 있다고 생각하지만, 언제나 인과법칙에 묶여 있다. 우리는 고층건물로부터 뛰어내리거나 일주일 동안 먹지 않을 자유는 있을지 모르나, 그런 행동의 결과를 피할 자유는 없다.

31 D 대도시가 혼잡하다는 사실은 부정할 수가 없다. 그러한 사실은 대도시 생활의 모든 면에서 볼 수 있다. 끊임없는 교통 정체나 사람들이 훨씬 더 빽빽히 탄 전철 칸에서 대도시의 번잡을 볼 수 있다.

  참고 visible과 관련이 있는 단어를 찾아라.

32 A 내가 자라난 중산층의 중심적인 믿음은 도랑을 파는 노동자의 아들은 대학 총장이 될 수 있는 반면에, 시내 최고 가문의 몰지각한 아들은 만회하기 어려운 실수를 쉽게 저지를 수 있다는 것이었다. 이러한 두 가지 믿음은 전설적인 것이 아니었다. 해마다 그러한 믿음은 우리 지역사회의 특정한 사람들의 삶이 보여주었고, 지금도 보여주고 있다.

33 C 한 시대의 이단적인 견해가 흔히 다음 시대의 정통 견해가 된다. 기존 견해의 결함들은 지적되며, 마침내 이들 견해는 변경되거나 버려진다. 독단적인 견해는 오래가지 못한다.

34 A 처음 그 책을 읽을 때, 나는 그 책의 생각들을 다만 잠정적으로 받아들였다. 그러나 그 때 이후로 그 생각들은 내 철학 속에 너무도 단단히 뿌리박혀서 나는 더 이상 달리 생각할 수가 없다.

> 요령 어떤 사람의 철학 속에 단단히 뿌리박은 "ideas"(생각들)가 지배하는 것은 무엇이겠는가?

35 A 베이커 교수의 가장 최근의 책에 대해서 내가 할 수 있는 유일한 얘기는 그의 견해와 내 견해가 천지차이로 남아 있다는 것이다. 비록 나는 아무에게도 지지 않을 만큼 그의 유려한 문체를 찬양하지만, 이 책의 내용에 대한 내 의견은 전혀 다른 문제이다.

36 B 췌장암이 퍼지면서 사람들을 당황케 만들고 치명적인 결과를 가져왔다. 미국에서 이 병의 발생은 20년 동안에 두 배로 증가했고, 이 병으로 2만 명의 미국인들이 해마다 사망한다. 이것은 또한 치료하기 가장 어려운 암 가운데 하나인데, 이 병에 걸린 사람들 가운데 3년 이상 살아남은 사람이 거의 없다.

37 B 영어의 표준 방언들, 즉 영국 영어, 캐나다 영어, 미국 영어, 남아프리카 영어, 그리고 그밖의 영어 중 어느 방언의 특징도 이해하는 데 아무런 심각한 어려움을 빚어내지 않는다. 우리들 영어를 사용하는 사람들 사이에 완전한 동일성은 없으나, 다양성 속에 통일성은 있다.

> 주의 "Nothing...creates any serious difficulties in understanding"이라는 말로 보아 A는 정답이 될 수 없다.

38 D 비록 결함이 있는 가설도 때가 되면 받아들일 수 있는 가설로 대치되리라는 근거 위에서 용납될 수 있지만, 그것은 그것을 갖고 있는 사람들에게 심각한 해를 줄 수 있다. 왜냐하면 과학자가 자신의 가설을 깊이 사랑하게 되면 그만큼 그는 그 가설에 대한 부정을 하나의 실험적인 해답으로 받아들이려고 하지 않을 터이기 때문이다.

39 A 사고가 펜실베이니아에서 일어날 때까지, 원자로는 놀라운 안전기록을 보유하고 있었다. 그러나, 원자력에 대한 반대는 본질적으로 더 심각한 사고가 앞으로 언젠가 예측할 수 없는 때에 일어나리라는 예상에서 비롯된다.

40 D 발전하고 있는 과학에서의 변화는 새 건물의 터전을 마련하기 위해 낡은 건물을 허물어뜨리는 것이라기보다는 동물의 진화와 같은 유형의 점진적인 진화와 같다고 보아야 된다. 우리는 폐기된 이론이 무익하거나 헛된 것이었다고 생각해서는 안 된다.

41 B '진실'이라는 약의 기능은 개인으로 하여금 감정을 자유로이 나타내지 못하게 억제하는 것들을 허물어뜨리는 것이다. 주전자 주둥이를 마개로 막고 주전자에 든 물을 끓여보라. 그러면 증기가 그 마개를 밀어낼 것이다. 이와 마찬가지로, 감정을 억제하는 것은 병마개와 같은 구실을 하고, 이 약은 그런 억제를 제거해 주는 경향이 있다.

42 D 미국의 자연자원 덕분에, 미국인은 누구나, 아주 최근까지, 자기 아버지보다 더 많은 돈을 벌 수 있으리라고 마땅히 기대할 수 있었다. 그래서, 만일 자기가 그보다 더 적게 버는 경우에 그 잘못은 틀림없이 자신에게 있다, 즉 그런 사람은 게으르거나 무능한 사람이기 때문이다.

43 A 우유로 키우는 아이는 흔히 정해진 우유 분량의 마지막 한 방울까지 다 먹도록 어머니가 시킨다, 아이가 그것을 원하든지 않든지 간에. 우유로 아이를 키우는 어머니들은 또한 모유로 아이를 키우는 어머니들보다 더 일찍 아이들로 하여금 고체 음식물을 먹게 만드는데, 고체 음식물은 열량이 높다. 유년기의 이런 습관은 나중에 과식하는 습관을 길러줄지도 모른다.

> 참고 whether he wants it or not이란 말로 보아 indulgence(탐닉)는 정답이 될 수 없다.

44 B 연구팀 과학자는 이 세기의 산물이다. 그리고 한 나라의 모든 시민이 어떤 과학상의 연

47

구에 관여하는 것은 지난 몇 십 년 동안에 발생한 현상이다. 요즈음에는 모든 교육받은 사람은 과학의 업적과 특징의 일부에 대해서 잘 알고 있다.

> 참고 과학에 대한 시민들의 태도(그것이 우호적인지 아닌지)에 대해서는 아무런 언급이 없으므로 C는 정답이 될 수 없다.

45 B 전체주의 국가들의 경우 대부분의 역사는 민족주의적이고, 애국적이며, 감상적인 것이고, 민족의 자아와 자기 나라가 전적으로 우월하다는 착각에 사로잡혀 있다.

> 참고 전체주의 국가는 '평화'를 추구하지도 아니하고 다른 나라에 '의존'하려고도 하지 않는다.

46 C 한 조사연구에 의하면 사무직 노동자는 자신의 옷이 상관들에게 주는 인상에 대해서 지극히 관심을 갖고 있는 것으로 드러났다. 반면 육체 노동자들은 옷에 의해 자신이 판단받을지도 모른다는 사실에 대해서 사무직 노동자만큼 의식하지는 않았지만, 이들은 동료 노동자와 옷을 달리 입으면 그들로부터 비웃음을 받으리라는 것을 알고 있었다.

47 B 사람과 컴퓨터, 동물은 어떤 의미에서 생각한다고 볼 수 있을 것이다. 그러나 이들 하나하나의 사고과정은 다를 것이다. 이들은 각각 독특한 강점과 약점들을 갖고 있을 것이다. 이들 강점과 약점을 어떻게 결합하는 것이 효과적인지는 처리해야 할 일에 좌우될 것이다.

48 B 음악의 보편적인 호소력과 그 영향을 설명하려는 이론가들의 노력은, 19세기 이래로, 지금까지 다양하고, 모순되고, 그리고 지극히 논쟁적인 것이었다.

> 참고 예를 들어, harmonious라는 말은 본문에 주어져 있는 various, contradictory와 '조화'를 이루지 않는다.

49 A 과학자들은 원자력의 좋은 용도와 나쁜 용도를 둘 다 찾아냈다. 석유가 고갈되면 우리의 주요 동력원은 아마 원자력 발전소가 될 것이다. 반면에 핵무기가 거의 확실히 미래의 전쟁에서 사용될 위험성이 있다. 일부 사람들은 과학자들이 세계를 파괴할 가능성을 발견했다고 비난하며, 원자력의 발견은 도덕적으로 옳지 않은 것이었다고 생각하고 있다.

> 주의 마지막 문장에서 접속사 "and" 앞의 내용으로 보아, B, C, D는 정답이 될 수 없습니다.

50 B 법률은 자유라는 개념을 낳았다. 정말이지 주위에 있는 모든 사람과 모든 것이 변덕스럽거나 예측할 수 없게, 혹은 다시 말해서, 무법적으로 행동하는 상황 속에서는 안전을 누릴 수가 없다. 그러나 내가 주장하고 싶은 요지는 그러한 환경 속에서 우리는 안전을 누리지 못하겠지만, 더욱 중요한 것은 자유를 누리지 못하리라는 것이다. 그런 상황 속에서 자유를 누릴 수 없는 이유는 우리가 가고 싶은 곳에 갈 수가 없거나 우리가 하고 싶은 것을 성공적으로 할 수 없을 것이기 때문이다.

> 주의 이 구절에 나오는 것과 같은 대명사 you는 '일반적인 사람'을 가리키는데, 우리말로 옮길 때는 '우리'라고 하거나 아예 빼버리고 다른 것을 주어로 삼아서 옮기는 것이 좋다.

> 참고 Topic sentence를 생각하라.

EXERCISE 32

1 완전한 자유는, 물론 불가능하지만, 압력을 줄이는 것은 가능할지 모른다.

2 너는 언젠가 네가 타고난 작가가 아니라고 말했다. 맙소사! 너는 물론 글을 쓰는 기술을 습득했지만, 이런 것을 쓰려면 글쓰는 기술을 훨씬 능가하는 그 무엇(이를테면, 타고난 재능)이 필요했을 것이다.

3 문제는 이들 과학 기록들을 정확하게 읽는 법을 배우는 것이다. 그런 노력에는 어느 것이든지 함정이 있다. 주어진 문제에 대한 접근방법이 함정으로부터 해방될수록, 그러한 함정들이 극복되고 의의 있는 해결방법이 얻어질 가능성은

그만큼 더 크다.

> 요지 '무엇으로부터 독립된(벗어난)' 접근방법일지를 생각해 보라.

4 동정이라는 것은 흔히 다른 사람들의 불행 속에서 우리 자신의 불행을 감지하는 것이다. 그것은 우리가 빠질지도 모를 불행을 예리하게 미리 내다보는 것이다. 우리가 다른 사람들을 돕는 것은 우리가 비슷한 상황에 놓이게 될 때에 그들로 하여금 우리를 돕도록 하기 위해서다. 그리고 우리가 그들에게 베푸는 선은, 정확히 말하면, 앞일을 예상해서 우리가 자신에게 베푸는 선이라고 볼 수 있다.

> 주의 evils는 앞에 나온 misfortunes와 같은 뜻으로 쓰였습니다.

5 우리 모두가 마땅히 인정해야 하는 것은 우리에게는 충분한 양의 공기와 물과 땅이 있어야 생존을 유지할 수 있다는 것이다. 우리가 또한 인정해야 하는 것은 공기와 물과 땅은 유한한 자원이라는 것이다. 이것들은 고갈될 수 있다. 우리가 이것들을 다 소모하게 되면, 지구상에서 우리의 존재는 끝이다.

> 주의 이 구절은 인간의 생존조건에 관한 논의이므로, 마지막 문장의 뒷부분이 마치 지구라는 혹성이 우주에서 사라지는 것처럼 "지구는 끝장난다"는 식으로 옮겨서는 안 됩니다.

6 사실 자신의 땅을 경작하는 농부의 일은 다양하다. 즉 그는 땅을 갈고, 씨를 뿌리며, 재배한 농작물을 거두어들인다. 그러나 그는 자연의 지배를 받으며, 자기가 자연에 의존하고 있다는 것을 잘 알고 있다. 반면에 현대적인 기계를 조종하는 사람은 자기에게 힘이 있다고 생각하며, 사람은 자연의 지배자이지 노예가 아니라는 의식을 갖는다.

7 어떤 노스캐롤라이나 대학교 영어강사가 자기 반 학생들에게 자신이 생각하기에 "영어에서 가장 훌륭하고, 가장 우아한 시구 가운데 하나"를 소개했다. 그는 그것을 자신의 모든 노트에 올바르게 적어 놓았는데, 그것은 그것의 아름다움을 끊임없이 상기시켜 주도록 하기 위해서였다. "빛과 함께 걸어라!"라고 인용하고 나서, 그는 부드럽게 그리고 황홀하게 또다시 자신에게 말했다, "빛과 함께 걸어라… 음, 이거 누군가에게 얘기해줄 만한 멋진 것이 아닌가?" 학생들도, 물론, 그렇게 생각해서, 작자를 알고 싶었다.

"제 생각에 작자는 알려져 있지 않습니다"라고 강사가 말했다. "그건 프랭클린 가의 어느 교차로에 있는 표지판에 쓰여 있습니다."

> 주의 여러분, 이것은 고급 유머입니다. 교통과 관련해서 쓰일 때에 walk with light라는 말은 '신호를 따라서 건너가세요'라는 뜻을 갖습니다.

8 적어도 영국에서는, 이것은 빛이 전력 및 자력이 에테르를 통과하는 것임을 증명해 주는 것이라고 일반적으로 믿었다. 그러나 유럽대륙에서는 비교적 그렇게 믿지 않고 있었다. 1879년에 베를린 학술원에서는 "빛이란 무엇인가?"라는 질문에 관련이 있는 논문을 제출하면 상금을 주겠다고 제의했다.

9 소련의 강경한 발언은 폴란드 국내외에서의 광범위한 바르샤바 동맹군의 기동훈련이 뒷받침해주었다. 이 기동훈련은, 본래 지난 주에 끝날 예정이었는데, 무기한 연장되었다. 매일밤 장시간에 걸친 텔레비전 보도는 폴란드인들에게 수륙양용차의 상륙, 모의 탱크전 및 공습에 관한 소름끼치는 장면을 보여주었다. 1968년의 체코슬로바키아 침공 전에 바르샤바 동맹군의 기동훈련이 있었었다. 폴란드인들은 이 교훈을 놓치지 않았다(깨닫지 못한 게 아니었다).

> 주의 His message was lost on them.
> = They failed to understand his message.
> (그들은 그가 전하려는 말을 이해하지 못했다.)

10 모리아크는 죽기 20년 전에 자신이 죽은 뒤에 발표하라고 자기 자신의 추도사를 녹음해 놓았다. 거기에는 그가 일생동안 인간은 신의 은총을 받을 수 있다는 문제에 몰두해 있었다는 것이 반영되어 있었는데, 그는 이 문제를 자신의 수필에서 탐구했다. 다른 저술에서는 그렇게 하지 않았지만. 그는 말했다, "나는, 내가 어린 시절에 그랬듯이, 믿고 있습니다. 인생에는 의미와 방향과 가치가 있고, 그 어떤 고통도 무의미하지 않으며, 우리가 흘리는 눈물과 피 한방울이 중요하고, 이 세상의 비밀은 성 요한의 '하느님은 사랑이다'라는 말에서 찾을 수 있다고."

> 참고 여러분, 다같이 기도합시다. 참으로 경건한 종교인의 자세는 곧 참된 인간적 자세라고 믿고 있습니다. 한없는 우주의 신비와 조화 앞에 어떻게 인간이 다른 태도를 취할 수 있을까요?

11 심장마비는 해마다 약 55만 명의 인명을 앗아가는데, 심장근육에 피를 공급해 주는 관상동맥이 막힐 때에 발생한다. 피가 산소와 기타 영양분을 공급해 주지 않으면, 심장조직은 죽거나 손상된다. 만일 너무 많은 심장조직이 이런 영향을 받게 되면(죽거나 손상되면), 심장은 너무 약해져서 피를 내보낼 수 없다. 그러나 아무리 가벼운 손상이라도 심장의 규칙적인 박동을 조절하는 전기 자극을 붕괴시킴으로써 사람을 죽게 만들 수 있다. 뇌졸중 또한 17만 명의 인명을 앗아가는데, 이것 역시 피가 통하지 않을 때에 일어나며, 이것은 뇌로 피가 통하지 않을 경우이다.

> 요정 진한 글자로 된 부분에서 '문맥어'(문맥의 흐름을 보여주는 단어) another와 also에 주목하라.

12 과학적으로 설명할 수 있는 물리적인 현상들의 수는 10년 주기로 증가하지만(즉, 물리적인 현상에 관한 과학 지식은 놀라울 정도로 증가해 왔으나), 인간의 행동에 대한 우리의 과학상의 지식은 상대적으로 보잘것없는 상태이다. 천문학과 물리학에 관한 아리스토텔레스의 가르침은 이미 오래 전에 대치되었으나, 윤리학에 관한 그의 학설은 아직 다른 이론으로 대치되지 않았다.

> 요정 문맥어 whereas에 주의하라.

13 영국해협 건너, 프랑스 대통령 프랑소와 미떼랑은 대처의 정책과 정반대되는 정책을 추구하고 있다. 대처가 끈기있게 영국의 물가상승을 낮추려고 노력하는 데 비해, 그는 프랑스의 14.5%의 물가상승률을 증가시킬 위험을 무릅쓰고 총력을 기울여 새 일자리를 창출하기 위해 애쓰고 있다. 그녀가 정부의 지출을 억제해 온 데 비해, 그는 국고를 활짝 열어 놓았다. 그녀는 높은 이자율[금리]을 필요한 처방으로 받아들이고 있으나, 그는 그것을 잔인한 장애물로 저주하고 있다. 그녀는 영국 경제를 재팽창시키기를 거부하고 있으나, 그는 프랑스 경제를 팽창시킬 작정이다. 이 두 경제철학은 극히 상반되거나, 많은 사람들이 보기에, 성공할 가능성이 매우 비슷하다.

14 인생은 불충분한 증거를 가지고 결론을 내려야 하는 거의 끊임없는 경험이라고 한다. (그러므로) 다른 많은 결론을 내릴 수 있는 가능성이 다양하게 존재한다.

> 요정 진한 글자로 된 단어에 구체적인 뜻을 부여해주는 단어를 생각하라.

15 서유럽 전역에 걸쳐서, 베긴의 명성은 거의 땅바닥으로 떨어졌다. 영국 외무장관 캐링턴 경은 이스라엘 대사에게 경고하기를 선제공격은, "무서운 인명피해를 가져오므로, 평화라는 대의명분을 증진시킬 수 없다"고 했다. 파리와 본에서도, 고위 관리들이 비공식적으로 이스라엘의 선제공격에 대해서 마찬가지로 신랄하게 비난했다.

> 요정 문맥어 equally에 주의를 기울여라.

16 새로운 전쟁에 대한 두려움과 혼란에 빠져 있는 경제 난국 외에, 오래된 사회 문제와 새로운 사회 문제들이 이스라엘의 사회조직을 분열시키고 있다. 인종상의 차이는 사회적 불평등 때문에 악화되고 있으며, 북유럽 출신의 아슈케나지 유대인과 지중해 출신의 세파르디 유대인과 이슬람교계 사회의 관계를 긴장시키고 있다. 종교적인 논쟁이, 엄격하게 종교적 계율을 지키는 정통 유대인과 이들보다 신앙심이 부족한 이스라엘인들의 세속적인 가치를 대립시키고 있다. 전반적인 무법상태가 여기(무법상태)에 익숙해져 있지 않은 이스라엘에서 급격하게 증가했고, 규모가 작지만 번창하는 이스라엘 "마피아단"이 국제 조직 범죄계에 새로이 등장해서 사람들을 당황케 하고 있다. 안절부절 못하는 보다 젊은 세대는 고용 기회의 부족과 병역의 의무가 주는 파괴적인 영향, 주택 부족 및 정치적 절차에 대해서 점점 더 많은 불만을 보여왔다.

> 주의 우리말로 옮기기에 쉽지 않은 부분, 특히 명사 앞에 있는 형용사(예를 들어, "an embarrassing new entry"에서 embarrassing)에 주의해 보세요.

> 요정 진한 글자로 된 부분과 대조되는 어구를 생각해보라.

17 소설가 귄터 그라스는 이것을 이 시대의 현실에 가장 가까운 도시라고 부르고 있다. 186평방 마일의 서방측 주둔기지로 동독 내부 110마일 지점에 자리잡고 있는 서베를린은 서독의 11개 주 가운데 하나로 언제나 일종의 시대적 상징물로 여겨졌다. 냉전이 절정에 이르렀을 때, 명랑하고 해학적인 서베를린 시민들은 과거에 독일의 수도였던 이 도시를 소련의 침입에 대한 용감한 저항을 상징해 주는 존재로 바꾸어 놓았다. 20년 전 지난 주에 소련과 소련의 동독 앞잡이들이 갑자기 저 악명높은 길이 28마일의 장벽을 이 도시를 가로질러 세웠는데, 이것은 공산제국으로부터 사람들이 나가는 것을 막기 위해서였다. 그리하여 서베를린은 유럽 분단의 기념비적인 존재가 되었다. 동서간의 긴장완화로 이 도시의 영웅적인 역할은 퇴색했다. 이 변경지는 내면으로 관심을 돌리게 되었고, 오늘날 이 도시는 또 다른 종류의 현실, 즉 서독을 통해서 유입되는 사회적인 교류들을 적나라하게 보여주고 있다. 즉 서베를린에서 정치적인 항의의 소리가 가장 높고, 마약 문제가 최악의 상태에 놓여 있으며, 무단입주운동이 가장 극성스럽다.

18 또한 그녀답게 사우라는 젊은 여자로 자기 나라에서 혼자 살고 있는 나를 만났을 때에 나를 "양녀로 삼겠다"고 고집했다. 그녀에게는 내가 미국사람이라는 것이 문제가 되지 않았다. 그녀는 내게 말했다. "당신에게 필요한 것은 온전한 부모와 좋은 형제 자매들이 많은 거예요." 가족과 전통, 그리고 손님들에 대한 환대가 사우라의 인생에서는 가장 중요한 것들이고, 서구의 ─ 아니, 보다 정확히 말해서, 소련의 ─ 물질적인 혜택과 가치들은 아주 중요하기는 해도, 그녀의 인생관에서는 분명히 이차적인 것이다.

  사우라 압둘라에바와 3천만 명의 그밖의 중앙아시아의 이슬람교인들이 세계를 어떻게 바라보느냐는 것이 요사이 크렘린 통치자들을 사로잡고 있는 문제다. 근본적인 이유는 이러하다. 소련의 중앙아시아 이슬람교 인구가 소련의 러시아 민족 인구보다 다섯 배 빠르게 증가하고 있는데, 이것은 러시아 민족이 곧 소수가 될 것이고, 어쩌면 러시아 민족과 같은 수의 중앙아시아인들이 노동계와 군대에 들어가고 있을지도 모른다는 뜻이다.

> **주의** 이 구절에 나오는 a good set of parents에서 good이 의미하는 것은 '온전한'(complete)이지, '좋은'이 아닙니다.

19 여기 영국에 대한 두 가지 일반적인 얘기가 있는데, 이것은 영국을 관찰해 온 사람들이라면 거의 대부분 받아들일 것이다. 첫째는 영국인들은 예술적인 재능이 없다는 것이다. 이들은 독일인이나 이탈리아인만큼 음악적인 재능이 없고, 회화와 조각이 프랑스에서처럼 번창한 적이 한번도 없었다. 또 하나는 다른 유럽인들에 비해서, 영국인들은 지적이지 않다는 것이다. 이들은 추상적인 사고를 무척 싫어하고, 어떤 철학이나 체계적인 "세계관"에 대한 필요성을 느끼지 않는다. 또한 이것은 이들이 "실제적"이어서가 아니라, 자기들은 그렇게 주장하기를 무척 좋아하지만. 이들의 도시계획과 급수시설 방법, 오래되고 까다로운 모든 일을 끈질기게 고수하는 것, 분석할 수 없는 철자법, 산수 교과서 편찬자들만이 이해할 수 있는 무게와 측정의 체계만 보아도 이들이 단순한 효율성에 얼마나 마음을 쓰지 않는지를 알 수 있다. 그러나 이들은 생각하지 않고 행동하는 어떤 힘을 갖고 있다. 극도의 위기에 놓이게 될 때에는 전 국민이 갑자기 뭉쳐서 일종의 본능에 의해 행동하는데, 이것은 정말이지 거의 누구나가 이해하지만 한번도 공식적으로 정해진 적이 없는 행동규범이다. 히틀러가 독일인들을 위해서 만들어낸 "자면서 걷는 국민"이라는 말은 영국인들에게 적용하는 것이 더 좋았을 것이다.

20 공화국에 대한 플라톤의 구상은 시인들은 마땅히 추방되어 사람들을 잘못 인도하지 말도록 해야 한다는 것이었다. 그러나 플라톤은 또한 자신의 논거를 신화(이것은 인간의 시적인 사고를 보여주는데)로 보충하지 않았던가? 확실히 플라톤은 모순된 생각을 갖고 있는 사람이었다.

EXERCISE 33

1 그는 나를 속여서 내 유산을 빼앗을 작정이다.

2 나는 그에게 사리를 설명해서 그가 갖고 있는 불합리한 생각에서 벗어나게 하려고 시도했다.

> **표현** absurdities = absurd thoughts

3 대처의 주장의 요지는 영국 상품은 가격을 높게 매겨서[가격이 비싸서] 국제시장에서 팔리지 않게 되었다는 것이다.

표현 crux: the essential point

4 그러나 희망적인 견해를 취할 수 있는 근거들이 있다. 이들 근거 가운데에서 가장 중요한 것은 물가상승률이 1979년과 1980년의 무서운 절정으로부터 비록 불규칙적이기는 하지만 사뭇 꾸준히 떨어져왔다는 점이다. 1970년대에는 급격한 물가상승이 종국에 가서 모든 경기 상승을 저해하여 새로운 불황을 초래했는데, 이 불황은 일시적인 물가상승의 둔화를 가져오는 데 그쳤다. 그러나 많은 경제학자들은 현재의 경기 후퇴(불황)의 장기성과 깊이는 종래의 불황들보다 더 철저히 물가상승을 경제로부터 몰아냈다고 믿고 있다.

5 부드럽게, 그는 나를 밀어서 일어서게 했다.

6 그 책은 나를 싫증나게 해서 나의 주의력이 다른 곳으로 향하게 만들었다.

7 그녀는 남편을 설득해서 자기가 원하는 것을 그가 하도록 만들었다.

8 그가 뻔뻔스럽게 행동하자 그녀는 화가 나서 그의 얼굴을 찰싹 때렸다.

9 닉슨 행정부는, 물론, 동서간의 긴장완화에 지나친 우선권을 부여하고 대서양 동맹을 희생한 최초의 행정부는 아니다. 적어도 세 행정부가 잇따라, 핵전쟁의 위협에 질겁을 해서 소련과의 관계가 유럽과의 관계에 우선해야 한다는 결론을 내려왔다. 그러나 소련과 핵전쟁에 빠져들어가는 실수를 피하기 위한 최선의 길은 튼튼한 세력균형을 유지하는 것이다. 그런데 그러한 세력균형에서 불가결한 요인은 유럽의 힘과 단결이다. 그러므로 러시아가 아니라 유럽이 우리의 정책결정에서 우선권을 차지해야 한다.

10 그는 거울을 지나갈 때마다 걸음을 멈추고 머리를 다독거려서 제자리로 들어가게 만든다[머리를 가다듬는다].

문맥 = Whenever he passes a mirror, he stops to pat his hair into place.

주의 (a) be in place (제자리에 들어와 있다 — '상태' 표현)
(b) come in place (제자리에 들어오다 — 자동사 표현)
(c) put~into place (제자리에 들어가게 하다 — 타동사 표현)

11 방문객들이 보기에, 케네디가의 아이들이 유일하게 쉬는 것 같아 보이는 때는 이들이 잠자고 있을 때였다. 그런데 이들은 한번도 그런 모습을 보인 적이 없는 것 같다. 이들은 함께 모일 때마다, 놀이할 준비가 되어 있었다.

　케네디 가의 사람들은 터치 풋볼을 항상 좋아했다. 심지어는 나중에 결혼을 해서 이 가문에 들어온 사람들도 이 경기를 잘 해야 했다. 친구들은 바비 케네디가 경기 도중에 울타리에 부딪친 때를 기억하고 있다. 얼굴이 피로 덮여 있었지만, 그는 경기를 중단하지 않았다. 여러 해 뒤에 잭 케네디는 어떤 친구에게 바비의 새 아내인 에셀에 대해서 이렇게 얘기하곤 했다. "그녀는 정말 경기를 잘 해. 그녀가 달리거나 공 던지는 모습을 보아야 해."

12 어느 일요일 밤 7시 30분에, 데이비드 스톡먼은 크고 장식이 많은 관리예산청장 서재에 있는 회의용 탁자에 혼자 앉아서, 컴퓨터로 인쇄한 자료와 숫자도표를 열심히 연구하고 있다. 방문객이 저녁약속 시간에 맞춰 도착하자, 스톡먼은 낙담한 기색을 보인다. "벌써 시간이 그렇게 됐습니까? 5분만 기다려 주십시오." 이 말이 입밖으로 나오기도 전에, 그는 눈길을 서류로 돌렸다.

　드디어, 예산청장은 힘들여 웃옷과 오버코트를 입고 복도를 따라 내려가기 시작한다. "2주밖에 시간이 없어요"라고 그는 어깨 너머로 말한다. 그가 얘기하는 마감기일은 2월 18일인데, 이 날 로널드 레이건은 자신의 재정계획 — 연방정부의 예산에 대한 철저한 수술을 포함해서 — 의 세부사항을 발표할 계획이다.

13 a. 산이 먹어들어가서 그 금속을 관통했다.

b. 우리 휴일이 우리가 저축한 돈을 먹어들어갔다.(먹어들어가다=많이 축내다)

c. 대만과 한국이 다같이 부딪힌 것은 성장에는 한계가 있다는 가혹한 교훈이다. 심지어 호경기에도, 양국의 경제계획관들은 크게 도약해서 부국의 대열 속으로 들어가려면 자기 나라의 경제를 합리적으로 만들고 현대화해야 한다는 것을 인정했다. 그러나 심판의 날은 예상했던 것보다 더 일찍 찾아왔다. 보호무역정책이 — 이것의 원인은 세계적인 불황과 1979년의 석유위기였는데 — 양국의 수출을 감소시켰는데, 이것은 바로 중국과 필리핀 같은 이들보다 덜 개발되어 있는 다른 나라들이 훨씬 낮은 인건비로 자국의 생산품을 만들어서 수출하기 시작한 때였다. 한국의 경제학자 유영 씨는 이렇게 설명한다. "우리는 강대국들과 제3세계 저개발국들 사이에 샌드위치가 되어 있습니다."

14 여성들은 이제 새로운 육체(운동으로 단련된 건강한 육체를 말함)가 주는 안전 속으로 자랑스럽게 들어갈 수 있다 — 즉, 이들은 조깅을 해서 몸매를 날씬하게 가꿀 수 있고, 역기를 사용해서 신체를 단련할 수 있으며, 재저사이즈의 신나는 디스코 음악에 맞추어 춤을 춰서 살을 뺄 수 있다. 그러나 남성은 어떤가? "재저사이즈는 파티나 마찬가집니다"라고 한 애틀랜타의 여성이 얘기한다. "당신이 처음 간 무도회를 기억하시죠? 남자들이 춤을 추지 못하기 때문에 모든 여자들이 결국에 가서 다른 여자들과 춤을 추게 된 그런 무도회 말이에요. 재저사이즈는 저에게 춤출 수 있는 기회를 주지만, 남편은 우리가 결혼식을 올린 이후 춤을 추지 않았어요. 그런데 남편은 아직도 춤을 추려고 하지 않아요. 생각해 보니, 저는 다시 여자들과 춤을 추게 되었군요. 지난 25년 동안에 별로 발전이 없었어요. 안 그래요?" 올해 34세의 웬디 메이는 애틀랜타에서 에어로빅 댄스를 가르치는데, 발전이 우선이고 잘 호응하려 들지 않는 남성을 교육하는 것은 이차적인 일이라고 말하는 것 같다 (그녀는 이렇게 얘기하니 말이다). "우리가 깨달은 것은 건강함이 섹시하게 해주기보다는 기분을 좋게 한다는 것입니다. 제 생각에 대부분의 남자들은 여성의 근육을 보면, 아니 어쩌면 여성의 건강만 보고도, 무서워할 것 같아요. 그러나 지금 그들로서는 어쩔 도리가 없는 것 같아요. 남성들은 십중팔구 그것(여성의 건강한 육체)이 섹시하다는 결정을 내릴 거예요. 왜냐 하면 그것이 유행하고 있으니까요."

15 그 법률안들은 거의 다 국회의 승인을 받아야 할 것이다. 그리고 그것들이 국회에서 가결되어 법률이 된다고 하더라도, 대부분 1984년이 되어야 효력을 발휘하게 될 것이다.

16 일주일에 두 번 정도 저의 아내는 지겨울 정도로 술에 취합니다. 아내의 무절제한 행동에 저와 저의 십대 아들은 질겁을 합니다. 아내는 거칠어지고 구역질나는 말을 사용합니다. 유일하게 우리 자신을 보호하는 길은 우리 방문을 잠가서 아내가 들어오지 못하게 하는 것입니다.

몇 시간 동안 고함을 치다가 아내는 마루바닥 위에서 의식을 잃습니다. 나는 그녀가 거기에서 자게 내버려둡니다. 너무 무거워서 옮길 수가 없으니까요. 술에 취한 어머니가 네 활개를 쭉 뻗고 복도에 누워 있는 것을 아이가 아침에 학교에 갈 때에 보게 되는 것은 결코 유쾌한 광경이 아닙니다.

17 a. 귀하의 글은 기사가 넘쳐서 본지에 싣지 못했습니다.

b. 다채로운 책들이 서로를 서점에서 밀어내는 시대에 흑백으로 인쇄된 이 책은 참신한 것 이상이다. 이 책은 계시적인 책이다(많은 것을 보여준다).

요점 out 뒤에 생략된 말을 생각해보라.

18 친애하는 애비 씨 : 저는 이 문제 때문에 미칠 지경입니다. 저에게는 두 아이가 있는데, 한 아이는 일곱 살이고 또 한 아이는 한 살 반입니다. 둘 다 엄마 젖으로 키웠고 사랑도 많이 주었지만, 결국 이 두 아이는 엄지손가락을 빨게 되었습니다. 우리가 어떤 면에서 실패했을까요? 이것은 유전적인 것입니까, 그렇지 않으면 무엇 때문일까요? 큰 딸은 자라서 이 버릇을 그만두었지만, 아직도 잠잘 때에 엄지손가락을 입에 물고 있습니다. 제가 염려하는 것은 작은 녀석입니다.

이 사내 아이는 항상 엄지손가락을 입에 넣고 있습니다. 먹거나 울 때를 제외하고는 말입니다. 애가 언제나 엄지손가락을 입에 물고 있는 것을 보면 정말 미칠 지경입니다. 쓴 약을 그의 엄지손가락에 발라보았으나, 거기에 익숙해지게 되어 아무튼 엄지손가락을 빱니다. 심지어 장갑까지 만들어주어 보았지만, 손이 워낙 작고 유연해서 불과 얼마 안 가 엄지손가락을 빼내서 빱니다.

제가 꾸짖으면, 이 녀석은 가서 숨는답니다, 손가락을 빨려고 말입니다. 저는 이 녀석과의 이런 줄다리기가 지겹습니다. 소아과의사도 도움이 되지 않습니다. 이 분은 아이를 그대로 내버려두라고 하십니다. 도움을 청할 수 있는 분은 당신, 애비 씨 외에는 아무도 없습니다. 만일 당신이 해결책을 찾을 수 없는 경우에는 당신의 독자들에게 물어주십시오, 혹시 아이가 엄지손가락을 입에 물지 않도록 하는 아주 간단하고 안전한 병법을 알고 있는지 말이에요.

> 참고 어렵지는 않지만, 이 글은 우리말로 옮기는 방법을 연구하는 데 좋은 참고자료가 될 수 있을 것 같습니다. 제가 옮겨놓은 글을 원문과 주의 깊게 비교해 보세요.

19 "내 정책은 가끔 바뀐다, 때로는 근본적으로. 그런데 상황도 그렇게 된다. 나는 변화하는 상황에 자신을 적응시키고, 변화에 반응하며, 때로는 그러한 변화를 가져오는 데 도움을 주는 사람들 가운데 한 사람이라고 나 자신을 생각하고 싶다." — 모셰 다이언

전 세계 수많은 사람들이 보기에, 그는, 아주 간단히 말해서, 살아 있는 이스라엘의 상징이었다. 뚜렷이 눈에 띄는 검은 안대와 둥글고 소년 같은 얼굴〔동안〕때문에, 그는 어느 나라에 있든지, 어떤 제복을 입고 있든지, 심지어 위장하고 있어도 즉각 알아볼 수 있었다(그런데 그는 자기 나라 외교를 위하여 때때로 위장복을 입었다). 군인으로서, 정치가로서, 그리고 아랍 이웃 국들과 이스라엘 간의 전쟁의 야단스레 뿜내는 영웅으로서, 모셰 다이언은 이스라엘의 중앙무대를 30년 넘게 차지했다. 지난 주 심장마비로 66세에 사망했을 때, 다이언은 대체로 군인이라는 인상에서 벗어나서 열렬한 평화 옹호자가 되어 있었다.

20 그러나 만일 레이건이 공급에 중점을 두는 경제 정책이 현실에 맞지 않는다는 것을 깨달아서 거기에 대한 집착에서 벗어나고, 만일 그가 대통령으로서 나라를 이끌어간다는 것이 무엇을 의미하는지를 파악하며, 설교보다는 성취하는 데서 기쁨을 느낀다면, 그가 앞에 가로놓여 있는 어려운 과제들에서 성공할 가능성은 더 많다.

일부 레이건의 지지자들과 심지어 소수의 적들이 사려깊게 지니고 있는 또 하나의 희망이 있다. 그것은 그가 일관성이 있어야 한다는 집착으로부터 또한 벗어났다는 것이다. 레이건은 일관성 없는 행동이 지미 카터의 명성을 손상했다고 믿고 있다. 역사의 이 한 조각은 어느 정도 진실성을 갖고 있으나, 언제나 그렇듯이, 역사의 한 조각은 다른 시대에 대한 안내자로서는 불완전하다. 사람들은 카터가 입장을 바꾼 것(일관성 없는 정책수행)은 국가의 이익을 위해서가 아니라 자신의 개인적인 정치적 운명을 위해서라고 생각했다. 만일 로널드 레이건이 모든 미국인들을 위해서 행동하겠다고 지난 주에 한 얘기를 이해한다면, 그것은 그가 대통령으로서 발표한 가장 중요한 선언이 될 수 있을 것이다. 그것(모든 국민을 위해 행동하는 것)이 곧 진정한 일관성 있는 정책수행이니까 말이다.

> 참고 둘째 문단에 나오는 "he has also escaped his obsession with being consistent."라는 말이 첫째 문단의 "Reagan has grown bigger than supply-side economics"라는 말의 의미에 대한 안내자 구실을 합니다. 문맥의 흐름을 보여주는 also라는 단어로 보아서, 우리는 grown bigger than이라는 말이 escaped his obsession with와 같은 뜻으로 사용되었다는 것을 알 수 있습니다.

21 친애하는 애비 씨 : 저는 당신이 그 15세 소녀에게 자신의 종교를 버리고 다른 종교를 믿는 사람과 결혼할 의사가 없다면 다른 종교를 믿는 청년과 데이트하지 말라고 충고해 주어 기쁩니다.

저는 엄격한 침례교도 집안에서 자랐지만, 제가 알기에 저와 결혼할 수 없는 청년들과 데이트를 했습니다. 저는 유대인 청년과 깊은 사랑에 빠졌지만, 다른 사람과 결혼했습니다. 그게 30년 이상 전이었는데, 저는 아직도 저의 첫사랑에 대한 꿈을 꾼답니다. 지금 저는 그와 결혼했거나 아니면 제가 결혼할 수 없는 남자와 사랑에 빠지지 않았더라면 좋았으리라고 생각하고 있습니다.

22 a. 어떻게 하면 우리는 새로운 세금을 내지 않고 좀더 많은 돈을 가질 수 있을까?
b. 1966년 이후(그런데 그 해에 제미니 9호가

전기 기능장애로 지연되었다) 우주비행사가 이미 조종실에 탑승했을 때에 인공위성의 발사가 취소된 적은 없었다. 그러나 제미니 9호는 이틀 뒤에 의기양양하게 날아갔고 컬럼비아 호도 마찬가지였다. 철야작업으로 휴스턴에 있는 컴퓨터 전문가들은 전기 기능장애를 우회하는 작업을 해서 그 장애를 제거했다. 토요일에, 이들 전문가들은, 제2차 발사시도 몇 시간 전에, 일찍 컴퓨터에 스위치를 켰다. 이번에는 이들 기계(컴퓨터)가 완전히 순조롭게 작동했다. 그래서 통제관들은 그 전기 기능장애물들을 정복했다는 것을 알았다. 그리하여, 일요일 날이 샌 지 1시간 뒤에, 발사신호가 주어져서, 엔진들은 요란한 소리를 냈으며, 플로리다 해안의 목초지와 모래 덮인 해변이 떨면서, 컬럼비아 호는 마침내 비행길에 올랐다.

> **주의** "전기 기능장애를 우회하는 작업을 해서 그 장애를 제거했다"는 말은, 가령, 어떤 **컴퓨터**의 A라는 부분에 장애가 발생했을 경우에 다른 곳에 A의 기능을 떠맡을 장치를 해서 그 장애를 극복했다는 뜻입니다.

c. 그의 변호사들은 사유지에 묘소를 금지하는 캘리포니아 주의 법률을 피해 갈 수 있는 방도를 하나 찾아냈다.

EXERCISE 34

1 쇼팽의 연주자로서, 이 세기 후반에 아르투어 루빈슈타인과 맞먹는 사람은 블라디미르 호로비츠뿐이었다. 그는 또한 브람스, 슈만, 슈베르트, 베토벤, 리스트, 라벨, 드비시, 파야, 알베니스, 그리고 같은 폴란드인인 시마노프스키의 연주로 유명했다.

2 어려운 시절에는, 할로 씨의 관찰에 의하면, 문제에 대한 절대적으로 정확한 해답은 없고, 비슷한 해답이 있을 뿐이라고 한다. 그가 보기에, 국가를 지휘하는 대통령은 자신의 진로를 유지하고, 자기와 의견을 달리하는 사람들은 지옥에나 가라고 하고, 가능하면, 그들이 그 진로를 좋아하게 만들고, 적들에게는 다소 두려움을 불어넣어야 한다. "세계 평화와 경제적인 건강(안정)이라는 두 가지 문제가 지금 레이건 앞에 놓여 있다"라고 할로 씨는 말한다. "나머지 문제들은 이 두 문제에 비해 하찮은 것이다. 대통령은 고래와 같은 존재이므로, 송사리들에게 자신이 먹히도록 내버려 두어서는 안 된다."

3 확실히, 아르헨티나는 영국과 이스라엘에 없는 어떤 경제적인 이점들을 갖고 있다. 이 나라는 주요한 곡물과 소고기 수출국이고, 영국처럼 석유를 자급자족한다. 그럼에도 불구하고, 지난 수년에 걸쳐서 경제관리를 잘못함으로써 정기적으로 이러한 이점들을 낭비해왔고, 엄청난 피해를 가져오는 한 차례 인플레이션을 불러왔는데, 이것은 약한 정부들이 은행 융자를 쉽게 받을 수 있게 하고 노동자들에게 많은 임금을 제공함으로써 자기들의 인기를 유지하려고 해 왔기 때문이다. 포클랜드 전쟁에서 패배하게 되면 이런 일이 더 많이 일어날 수 있을 것이다. 부에노스아이레스에 있는 한 서방 외교관은 이렇게 요약해서 얘기한다. "새 정부는 임금을 25% 내지 30% 인상(공공부문에서)하지 않을 수 없는 입장에 놓여지게 될 테고, 뒤이어 엄청난 물가상승이 발생하고, 뒤이어 더 많은 경제적인 문제들이 따라오고, 뒤이어 은행파산과 기업체의 몰락이 따라오고, 뒤이어 외채상환문제들이 따라오고, 뒤이어 또다시 정부가 쓰러지는 일이 따라올 것입니다. 그 다음에는 이런 일이 다시 시작될 것입니다."

> **의** 참으로 안타까운 일이군요! 우리 인간 사회에서 정치의 중요성을 뼈저리게 느낄 수 있겠죠?

4 다행히, 힐러리가 그런 평가를 한 이후로 사정은 다소 좋아져 왔다. 비록 쿰부 계곡이 지금은 다소 이상향에 못 미치지만, 이곳은 저 희귀한 장소 가운데 하나로 남아 있다. 즉 현실을 우편엽서에 있는 그대로 담을 수가 없고, 자연이 아직도 사람을 압도할 수 있고, 이곳보다 더 세속적인 지역에서 도피해온 사람들이 매스너가 산에 오르는 그만의 이유를 이해하기 시작할 수 있는 그런 곳 말이다. 그는 글에서 이렇게 썼다. "높은 산 속에서는 삶의 순수한 기쁨이 살려는 필사적인 노력을 능가할 수 있다"(즉, 높은 산 속에서는 살려고 발버둥치는 것을 잊고 삶의 순수한 기쁨을 맛볼 수 있다는 뜻임).

5 그리하여 중국이 자주 되풀이하여 소련을 "세계 평화에 대해 가장 위협적인 초강대국"이라고 비난하던 말이 두 초강대국(미국과 소련)에 대한 비판으로 대치되었다. 중국의 대변인들은 최근에 중동과 포클랜드 제도에 이르는 국제적인 소요의 원인이 "초강대국간의 투쟁"에 있다고 주장하고 있다. 더구나, "미국 제국주의의 달리는 개들"이라든지, "미국은 종이 호랑이다"와 같은 과거의 반미적인 구호들은, 리처드 닉슨이 10년 전에 중국을 방문했을 때 매장되었다가, 또다시 중국의 정치용어 속으로 살금살금 기어 들어왔다.

6 엘살바도르는 분명히 또 하나의 베트남은 아니다. 피상적인 비슷한 점들보다는 몇 가지 매우 현실적인 차이점들이 더 중요하다. 이러한 차이점 가운데에는 다음과 같은 것들이 있다. 엘 살바도르는 미국 해안으로부터 8,000마일 떨어져 있는 마구 뻗어 있는 밀림이 아니라, 이 나라의 군사정권은 양심적으로 농토분배 개혁 사업을 실천하려고 노력하고 있으며, 4,000명의 이곳 좌익 유격대원들은 월맹군 규모의 군대로부터 지원을 받고 있지 않다는 점이다. 그럼에도 불구하고, 로널드 레이건 대통령과 알렉산더 헤이그 국무장관은 매사추세츠 주의 면적만한 이 공화국에서 벌어지는 유격전에 막대한 돈을 투입해 왔다. 엘살바도르의 좌익 유격대원들에게 몰래 무기를 공급하는 외국 공산주의자들의 "간접적인 무력침략"에 대항하는 운동을 전개함으로써, 레이건 행정부는 소련 세력의 팽창이 억제되고 있다는 것을 세계에 보여주고 있다. "이 폭력배들이 단지 엘살바도르만을 겨냥하고 있는 것은 아닙니다"라고 레이건은 백악관 기자회견에서 지난 주에 설명했다. "이들은 중미 전체를 겨냥하고 있고, 어쩌면 나중에는 남미를, 그리고, 확실히, 종국에 가서는 북미를 겨냥할 것입니다. 우리가 하고 있는 것은 안정을 무너뜨리는 이 유격전 세력과 혁명이 이곳으로 수출되는 것을 막으려는 것입니다."

7 a. 나는 네 얘기보다 훨씬 더 우스운 얘기를 할 수 있다.
   b. 그는 일자리를 잃었고, 게다가, 아내까지 그를 떠났다.
   c. 그의 집은 불타버렸고, 그의 승용차는 도난당했으며, 게다가, 그는 일자리를 잃었다.

d. **알렉산더는 주정뱅이였는가?**
   알렉산더 대왕은 또한 알렉산더 대주정뱅이였는가? 세계를 정복한 이 사람의 짧고 다난한 생애에 대해서 학자들은 오랫동안 의아해했다. 심지어 그리스 문명을 인도의 변경에까지 사뭇 밀고갈 때에, 그는 일시적인 의식의 상실과 폭음, 광적인 정신이상적인 행동, 그리고 나서는 후회하는 소용돌이 속으로 가라앉는 것 같아 보였다. 뉴욕에 있는 퀸즈 대학의 쟌 맥스웰 오브라이언 교수의 주장은 이 영웅의 수많은 지지자들을 격분케 하고 있다. 오브라이언의 주장에 의하면, 알렉산더는 만년에 심한 알코올 중독의 전형적인 증세들을 갖고 살았다고 한다.

   주연 : 오브라이언 교수의 연구는 얼마 전에 <Annals of Scholarship>에 실렸는데, 그는 술의 영향이 알렉산더의 생애 마지막 7년간의 결정적인 순간들 가운데 여러 차례 나타났던 것으로 보고 있다. 기원전 330년에, 술에 흠뻑 빠진 승전 주연 뒤에, 그는 무의미하게 페르시아의 옛 수도 페르세폴리스를 불태워버렸다. 2년 뒤에, 술에 취한 채 발광해서, 그는 자신의 오랜 친구 클레이투스를 죽이고, 그런 뒤에는 슬픔에 압도되어 자살을 시도했었다. 그러나 그가 분명히 사랑했고, 가장 신뢰하던 지휘관 헤파이스티온의 죽음은 알렉산더를 정신이상자로 만들었다. 이 32세의 정복자는 무시무시한 마지막 해의 대량살육과 숙청과 끝없는 폭음 속으로 빠져들어갔고, 종국에는 오브라이언 교수가 주장하는 치명적인 무기력증에다가 말라리아까지 걸리게 되었다.

   이런 주장은 예상할 수 있듯이 아테네에서나 또는 알렉산더의 생애를 연구해온 일부 다른 학자들에게는 잘 받아들여지지 않는다. "불과 10년 이내에 알렉산더는 정복과 문명의 전파 면에서 다른 어떤 사람보다 더 많은 것을 성취했다"고 그리스 문화부의 고적 감독관인 니코스 얄루리스가 말했다. "그가 알코올 중독자였는지에 대한 사소한 증거는, 비교적, 하찮은 것입니다." 전기작가 메리 리놀트는 알렉산더에 관한 여러 권의 책을 썼는데, 이 영웅의 이미지를 옹호하는 강력한 편지를 써서 이 싸움(논쟁)에 가담했다. 이 편지는 런던 〈더 타임스〉에 실렸고 — 그리고 발행부수가 많은 아테네의 신문에 특종으로 보도되었다. 오브라이언을 헐뜯는 사람들은 아무도 알렉산더가, 그 당시 모든 마케도니아 사람들처럼, 술을 많이 마셨다는 것을 부정하지 않는다. 그러나 이 위대한 정복자를 현대 유형의 불운하고 무기력한 주정뱅이와 동일하게 취급함으로써 그의 명성을 깎아내리려는 사람들은 거의 없다. 프랑스 학자 모리스 드뤼옹은 이렇게 얘기한다. "알코올 중독자라고요? 천만에요. 술을 잘 마시는 사람이었겠죠. 정말이지, 그토록 많은 승리를 거둔 뒤였으니 그에게는 한잔할 자격이 있었던 거죠."

참고 이 예문을 보고 고개를 갸우뚱하는 사람들(native speakers of English)이 더러 있습니다. 그것은 당연한 것 같습니다. 왜냐하면 주어진 문장의 의미가 애매하기 때문입니다. 주어져 있는 말만으로는 그들의 결혼생활이 얼마 동안이나 지속되었는지 정확하게 알 수 없습니다. 가령, "두 사람의 차이점들로 보아, 1년 안에 결혼생활이 깨어지는 것이 보통인데, 그 기간(1년)보다 더 오래 지속되었다"는 뜻으로는 주어진 문장이 사용될 수 있으나, "그들 두 사람 사이에는 여러 가지 차이점들이 있었지만 그들의 결혼생활은 깨어지지 않았다"는 뜻으로는 적합하지 않습니다. 후자의 의미는 다음과 같이 표현하는 것이 좋습니다.
→ Their marriage survived their differences.

8 볼셰비키들이 4월에 〈프라우다〉라는 신문을 내놓았는데, 이 신문의 발행부수는 멘셰비키들이 발행하는 신문을 능가했다.

9 그는 상상력이 풍부하고 발랄할 뿐 아니라 재주가 많고 창의적이어서 그들 모두를 경쟁에서 이겼다.

10 불행하게도, 그는 경쟁에서 이길 수 없는 상대를 만났다.

11 그는 결코 작은 인물은 아니었으나, 동료보다는 못했다.

12 비록 그가 입고 있는 옷은 다소 몸에 작았지만, 그 소년에게는 어떤 매력적인 데가 있었다.

13 하트 씨는 사업을 관리하는 장교가 아니라 전술과 혁신에 능한 장교들에게 보상을 주고 그들을 진급시킴으로써 군사적인 생각을 바꾸어놓으려고 한다. "우리는 적보다 머리를 더 써서 적을 물리쳐야 한다"고 이 상원의원은 주장하는데, 그는 사관학교들이 사실상 필수과목인 군사역사와 전술학을 빼고 사회과학 및 정치학을 가르치고 있다는 사실을 알고 충격을 받았다.

14 이것은 자기 꾀에 넘어가는 불리한 민중선동 술책이었다.

15 싱가포르의 조숙한 발전은 이토록 역사가 짧은 나라에서는 유례없는 일이다. 1960년에, 미국

EXERCISE 35

1 도시에서 사는 이점들은 단점들보다 더 크다.

2 사람은 아무리 나이가 들어도 사랑이 필요하다.
문맥 = No matter how old one may grow, one needs love.

3 그 아이는 자라자 그 전에 갖고 있던 관심사들을 버렸다.

4 나는 그보다 더 빨리 달릴 수 없었기 때문에, 그보다 머리를 더 써서 그를 물리쳐야 했다.
주의 outfox: to outwit; outsmart

5 그 미식축구 경기에는 다른 모든 대학 스포츠를 합친 것보다 더 많은 관중이 왔다.

6 그들은 아직도 미라처럼 되어버린 상당수의 관습을 고수하고 있는데, 이들 관습은 이미 오래 전에 무익하게 되었다.
주의 mummified: dead or withered

7 그들의 결혼생활은 그들 두 사람 사이의 여러 가지 차이점들에 비해 오래 지속되었다.

의 경제사가 월트 W. 로스토가 "경제성장의 단계"(이것은 국민경제에 대한 그의 표준적인 척도였다)를 펴냈을 때에, 싱가포르는 아직도 영국의 직할식민지로 리콴유의 지도 아래 국내문제에 대한 자치 정부가 갓 탄생되었고, 리콴유는 총리가 된 지 막 2년이 넘었을 때였다. 그 이후 이 나라는 빠른 속도로 로스토의 "도약" 단계를 거쳐, 전 국민이 단결해서 "성숙으로의 운동"을 거쳤고, 오늘날에는 "고도대량소비 시대"의 문턱에 서 있다. 로스토는 지금 오스틴에 있는 텍사스 대학교에서 가르치고 있는데, 싱가포르는 "이른바 제1세계 경제의 바로 가장자리에" 와 있다고 말한다. 그는 현재의 성장률로 나간다면, 이 나라는 틀림없이 앞으로 몇 년 이내에 이 대열로 올라가리라고 예언한다.

싱가포르는 아무튼 빠른 속도로 산업시장경제국이 되어가고 있다. 1981년의 최종통계에 의하면, 이 나라의 개인당 GNP는 5,000달러를 넘어서, 대부분의 라틴 아메리카, 아시아, 아프리카 및 동유럽을 능가하고, 아일랜드와 동등한 위치에 서는 한편 스페인을 능가할 준비가 되어 있을 것으로 보인다. 그러나 리콴유에게는 그것이 충분하지 않다. 1990년에 이르러 그는 자기 나라가 오늘의 일본의 수준에 도달하고, 고도기술로 상품을 제조하고 금융 및 통신과 같은 산업에서 컴퓨터화된 용역을 제공하는 나라가 되기를 바라고 있다. 리콴유는 1988년에 65세가 되는데 그 전에 총리직에서 물러날 것이라고 한다. 이를 위해서 그는 후계자들을 양성하려고 노력하고 있을 뿐만 아니라, 총리직을 넘겨주기 전에 자신의 목표를 될 수 있는대로 많이 성취하려고 자기 나라를 밀고 나가고 있다고 한다.

16 많은 사람들이 사랑의 필요성에 대해서 말해왔다. 그런데 사랑은 서로 다른 사람들에게 이들 각자의 생애에서 서로 다른 시기에 서로 다른 의미를 갖는다. 적절히 보살펴주고 이끌어주면, 사람은 체구와 몸무게가 자라는 것과 마찬가지로 사랑할 수 있는 능력도 자란다. 자신을 돌볼 능력이 없는 갓난아이에게, 사랑은 자신의 욕구를 즉각 보살펴주는 것을 의미한다. 이 아이는 자기를 안아주고 돌보아주는 방법을 통해 사랑을 감지한다. 아주 어린 아이까지도 사람들이 자기를 원하는 때를 알고 있다. 사랑을 통해서, 아이는 신뢰감을 갖게 된다. 친절하게 자기를 보살펴준다는 것은 자기가 가치 있는 존재라는 것을 아이에게 얘기해 준다. 그것은 아이가 사회적으로 성장하고 배워나가도록 준비하는 데에 도움을 준다. 사랑이 없다면, 인격의 기틀을 형성할 수가 없다. 어린이("baby"보다 더 큰 아이)에게도 사랑이 필요하다. 10대도 마찬가지다. 그리고 여러분들의 부모님들은 어떠하겠는가? (=여러분들의 부모님들도 마찬가지다.) 사람들이 사랑이 필요하지 않을 만큼 나이가 들까? (=사람은 아무리 나이가 들어도 사랑이 필요하다.)

> 주의 이 구절에 나오는 "the framework into which the pieces of his personality must fit"라는 말은, 줄여서 "the framework of his personality"로 나타낼 수 있습니다.

EXERCISE 36

1 above   배우고 싶다면, 질문하는 것을 부끄럽게 여기지 말아야 한다.

2 much   너의 발음은 완벽과는 거리가 멀다.

3 last   여기서 너를 만나다니 너무 뜻밖이다.

4 but   얼마간의 결점이 없는 사람은 있을 수 없다.

5 without   이 사진을 볼 때마다 어린 시절이 생각난다.

6 so, but   연습에 의해서 쉬워지지 않을 만큼 어려운 것은 아무것도 없다.

7 prevent   그는 아무리 바빠도 자기가 받은 편지에 답장을 보낸다.

8 Nothing, from   어떤 대가를 치르더라도 나는 가야 한다.

9 than   그는 수학을 제외한 과목들에 강하다.

10 less   나는 영어로도 내 의사를 잘 나타내지 못하고, 프랑스어로는 훨씬 더 잘 못한다.

11 too   업무용 서신은 분명할수록 좋다.

....

1 먼지로 덮인 작업복을 입고 있어서 그들은 결코 부유한 사람들처럼 보이지 않았다.

2 그는 볼일 보러 밖에 나가 있으나, 곧 돌아올 것이다.

3 a. 건강에 대해서는 아무리 조심해도 지나치다고 할 수 없다.

b. 정확할수록 좋다.

c. 비타민 결핍의 위험은 아무리 강조해도 지나치다고 할 수 없다.

d. 어린이는 아무리 잘 대해주어도 지나치다고 할 수 없다. 어린이를 망쳐놓는 것은 지나치게 무시하거나 거칠게 다루는 것이지, 친절이 아니다. 부유한 집의 어린이를 흔히 망쳐 놓는 것은 이들의 장난감과 자동차가 아니라 너무 바빠서 많은 관심을 줄 수 없는 부모들이다.

4 a. 우리가 어떤 감정을 한번도 경험한 적이 없는 사람에게 설명해 줄 수 없는 것은 빛을 장님에게 설명해 줄 수 없는 것이나 마찬가지다.

b. 약 40년 전까지만 해도 유행을 따르는 숙녀들은 햇빛에 자신의 몸을 노출시키려 하지 않았는데, 오늘날 여성들이 비를 맞으려고 하지 않으려는 것이나 마찬가지다. 왜냐하면 피부가 하얀 것이 그 당시에는 사회적으로 뛰어난 신분의 징표였기 때문이었다.

5 a. 지구상에 존재하는 것으로 태양의 영향을 받지 않는 것은 아무것도 없다.

b. 나는 누구하고든 한 시간을 함께 보내면 그에 관해서 적어도 한 편의 읽을 만한 이야기를 쓸 수 있는 자료를 얻을 수 있었다.

문제 = When I spent an hour in anyone's company, I could get the material to write at least a readable story about him.

c. 사람은 누구나 아무리 자기 직업상의 일에 바쁠지라도 신문을 읽을 시간은 있다.

d. 아무리 현명한 사람이라도 때로는 어리석은 짓을 하는 법이다.

6 a. 때때로 사람들은 "건강이 곧 재산이다"라고 주장하지만, 사실은 그렇지 않다.

b. 많은 사람들의 생각과는 달리, 그는 그 살인에 대해 죄가 없었다.

c. 미국에서 공공기금의 지원을 받는 고등교육기관은, 초등학교와 중등학교와는 달리, 완전히 무료는 아니다.

d. 공상은 창작을 위한 상상의 기반인데, 예술가의 특전은 그것(공상)이, 다른 사람에게서와는 달리, 현실로부터의 도피가 아니라 현실로 이르는 수단이라는 점이다.

예문 여러분 이것이 무슨 뜻인지 아시겠어요? 예술가는 엉뚱한 생각을 해서(다시 말해서, 보통 사람들과는 다른 각도에서 현실을 바라보아서), 새롭게 현실을 파악하는 특전을 누린다는 얘깁니다.

e. 성경을 쓴 사람들은 오늘날 우리가 사용하는 그런 의미에서 유식한 사람들은 아니었다. 그러나 이들의 위대한 저술은 다른 저술들과는 달리 오랫동안 생명을 유지해왔고 또 널리 읽혀져왔다.

f. 비록 그의 책은 새로운 분야에 대해서 다룬 게 거의 없지만(다시 말해서, 내용상으로 새로운 점은 거의 없지만), 그가 히틀러에 관한 얘기를 다루는 방법은 독일인이 아닌 사람으로서는 아무도 할 수 없는 방법이다. 다시 말해서, 그는 감정에 흔들리지 않으나, 내막을 잘 아는 사람의 입장에서 얘기를 하고 있다. 그러므로, 그가 히틀러를 만들어냈다고 독일인을 비난할 때에(사실 그는 그렇게 하고 있다), 그의 비난은 옳게 들린다.

참고 여러분, 이거 우리말로 옮기기가 보통 어려운 게 아닙니다. 며칠 후에 여러분이 번역을 해서 제가 한 것과 비교해 보세요. 많은 것을 배우게 될 것입니다.

7 a. 너는 그를 다시는 보지 않을 거라고 기대할 수 없다. 그는 악화처럼 다시 나타날 테니까.

    b. 수출의 감소는 아마 한국경제가(한국경제는 이미 무거운 외채 부담 때문에 신음하고 있다) 결코 감당할 수 없는 일일 것이다.

> **표현** about: all but; almost

8 야세르 아라파트는 지극히 실제적인 사람이다. 그러므로 그는 지금 서방에서 팔레스타인들에 대해 증가하고 있는 동정심(또는 이해)을 저해할 일은 하지 않을 것이다.

9 어머니가 재워서 기쁘지 않을 만큼 사랑스런 아이는 아무도 없었다(다시 말해서, 아무리 사랑스런 아이라도 어머니는 기꺼이 그를 재우려 하는 법이다).

> **예문** 아이는 어머니를 너무도 고달프게 한다는 뜻입니다.

10 석유는 요즈음 구매자가 지배하는 시장으로, 가격은 생산이 저조한 데도 불구하고 떨어지고 있다. 석유계약고가 로테르담 현물시장에서 지난 주에 배럴당 30달러 아래로 떨어졌는데, 이것은 표준 오페크 가격보다 2달러가 적은 가격이다. 또한, 많은 양의 원유를 그토록 엄청난 할인가로 구할 수 있기 때문에 세계의 큰 석유회사들은 일부 생산지(공장) 가격을 종전의 수준으로 내리라는 강한 압력을 받고 있다. 이미, 독립해서 영업하는 정유회사와 판매회사들은 영국과 일부 유럽 국가에서 가솔린 가격을 과감하게 내리기 시작했으며 — 그리고 더 많은 가격인하가 곧 있을 전망이다.

    석유생산도 줄어들고 있다. 세계의 원유 생산이 1980년 상반기 6개월 동안에 떨어졌다. 5년간 꾸준히 증가해온 뒤에. 오페크의 생산이 가장 심하게 떨어졌으며(5% 이상), 반면에 북해의 생산자들은 이러한 추세에 끈질기게 저항해서 13%의 증가를 기록했다.

    미국에서의 저조한 소비자 수요가 석유공급 초과 뒤에 놓여 있는 주요 원인이다. 8월 15일에 끝나는 주에 미국의 석유수입은 하루 평균 420만 배럴이었는데, 이것은 1979년보다 거의 40% 떨어진 분량이었다. 그러나, 구매자가 지배하는 현재의 석유시장이 오래 지속되리라고 생각하는 전문가는 거의 없다. 석유회사들은 기록적인 금액을 석유탐사에 소비하고 싶어하는 것 같아 보이며, 원유가격이 떨어지는 데도 불구하고 연안개발 작업이 늘어남에 따라 석유채굴장비에 대한 수요가 강하다. 지난 주 한 노르웨이의 회사는 7년 된 석유채굴장비 한 대를 하루에 8만 4천 달러라는 기록적인 돈을 주고 전세로 얻었는데, 이것은 석유가격이, 종국에 가서는, 틀림없이 오르리라는 증거나 다름없다.

> **주의** 마지막 문장에서 'hardly 이하'를 한국어의 구조에 가깝게 고쳐보면 다음과 같습니다.
> →almost an indication that the price of oil, in the long run, is going nowhere but up.

EXERCISE 37

1 그녀는 담배를 한모금 빨아들이고 나서 굵은 연기를 내 얼굴 쪽으로 내뿜었다.

2 그는 담배를 피우지 않으며, 가끔 스카치를 마시고, 허리가 너무 굵어질까봐 염려하고 또 자기 부하들에 대해서 염려하는데, 그들에게 그는 아버지와 같은 존재이다.

3 근처의 섬들이 물 속에 비쳤는데, 우리는 거기서 가끔 사람들이 돌아다니는 것을 볼 수 있었다.

4 최근의 한 여론조사에 의하면, 놀랍게도 프랑스 사람들 가운데 69%가 "사정이 더욱 악화되고 있다"고 염려하고 있는 것으로 밝혀졌다.

5 대부분의 노동자들은 그다니스크 협정이 자유 노조와 기타 정치적인 양보를 약속해 주자 일터로 돌아갔으나, 지난 주에 파업이 여기저기서 산발적으로 발생했다.

6 어쩌면 그녀의 활기찬 변론 때문에 궁지에 몰려서, 법정은 아무런 설명 없이 휴정에 들어갔는지 모른다. 심의과정은 나중에(아마 다음 주) 완료되도록 내버려두고.

7 미국인들은 포크와 칼을 사용해서 빵을 먹지 않는다. 그들은 손가락으로 집고, 대개 먼저 그것을 찢는다. 다음과 같이 하면 이상한 사람으로 간주된다 — 즉, 빵조각을 포크로 접시에 단단히 고정시키고, 칼로 빵 전체에 버터를 바르고 나서 그것을 자른 다음에 칼과 포크를 사용해서 먹음으로써 손에 기름이 묻는 것을 피하는 행위 말이다.

8 비록 의도적으로 경박하게 씌어 있지만, 이 소설이 다루는 소재는 매우 흥미롭다. 사실, 독자는 이 책의 반을 읽으면서 많은 즐거움과 다소 짜증스러움을 맛보다가 이것이 분명해지는데, 정확하게 158페이지에서 작가는 오랫동안 유지해온 아리송한 암시들을 던져버리고, 명백하게, 독자에게 자신의 주재가 돈이라는 것을 얘기해 준다.

> 참고 여러분, 잊지 않으셨죠? 영어를 우리말로 옮길 때에 될 수 있는 대로 앞에서 뒤로 내려가면서 옮기도록 노력하라는 저의 간곡한 충고 말입니다. 그렇게 하는 것은 영어를 올바르게 대하는 태도이기도 하지만, 시간도 절약됩니다. 제가 옮겨놓은 것을 주의깊게 연구해 보시면, 제 얘기가 옳다는 것을 틀림없이 깨달으실 것입니다.

9 이 삼두마차 내부에서의 의견 차이는, 또한, 레이건 행정부를 마비시킬 수 있다. 왜냐하면 이들 세 사람의 고위층 밑에는, 불안할 정도로 인재가 희박하기 때문이다. 비록 겉으로 보기에는 사실과 달리 직원이 많아 보이지만. 백악관 직원으로 약 350명이 있는데, 약 40명은 디버에게 보고하고 25명은 미즈에게 보고한다. 나머지 직원들이 대부분 베이커 밑에 있다고 해서 그것이 그의 영향력을 정확하게 보여주는 것은 아니다.

> 주의 다음 영어 표현을 정확하게 우리말로 옮겨 보세요 :
> deceptively simple
> 이것은 이렇게 바꾸어 표현할 수가 있습니다 :
> deceptively simple but actually complicated
> (겉으로 보기에는 단순해 보이지만 실제로는 복잡한)
> 이와 같이, 한국어의 표현과 다른 영어 표현에 늘 주의하세요.

10 대통령이 시작한 운동이 수많은 시민들의 참상(곤경)을 드러내주었는데, 이들은 유례없는 번영의 시기에 재정적 재난의 수면 위로 머리를 쳐들고 있을 능력이 없다(영어에서는 재정적인 어려움에 놓여 있는 것을 흔히 물 속에 빠져 있는 것으로 비유함). 금년 봄에 국민들은 또다시 충격을 받을 것이다, 군인들의 봉급 인상 문제가 의회에 상정될 때에 말이다. 미국 국민들은 그때에 가면 가장 가죽이 두꺼운 사람들을 제외한 모든 사람들을 틀림없이 수치심으로 채워줄 사태를 괴롭지만 자세히 보게 될 텐데, 그 사태란 곧 우리나라를 지키고 있는 사람들의 재정적인 참상을 말한다.

> 표현 get a good hard look at: (보기에 괴로운 것을) 자세히 보다

11 국회가 판사들의 봉급을 올리기 위한 1년 동안의 투쟁에 주요 장애물 구실을 해왔다. 국회의원들은 자기들의 봉급을 인상해 주지 않는 한 판사들의 봉급을 인상해 주려고 하지 않는다. 국회는 사법부에 대해서 인색하게 대해왔다. 국회는 연방정부의 봉급 규모를 사기업의 봉급 규모와 동일하게 만들려는 법률 아래서 봉급을 인상해 주려는 대통령의 건의안을 거듭해서 봉쇄해왔다.

12 a. 자기 자신을 가장 잘 비판할 수 있는 작가는 드물다.

b. 우리는 우리의 삶을 자동차 안에서 보내지만, 우리들 가운데 대부분은 모터가 작동하지 않을 때에 연료 탱크를 들여다 볼 정도로 자동차에 대해서 아는 것이 없다. 오늘날 우리들의 생활은 전기가 없다면 순조롭게 움직이지 않겠지만, 전기가 나갈 때에 타버린 퓨즈를 찾아서 대체할 줄 아는 사람은 드물다.

13 바르샤바를 떠나기 전에, 교황은 자기 모국이 제2차 세계대전 중에 겪은 비극적인 시련을 기리는 기념비들을 예고 없이 방문했다.

EXERCISE 38

1 출입구에서는 일손이 부족하다.

> 주의 하이픈은 같은 내용을 보다 더 경제적으로 나타낼 수 있다는 점에 주의하라.

2 그녀는 길다란 거울에 비친 자신의 모습을 바라보며, 감탄에 빠져 있었다.

3 그는 철학자였다가 시인으로 전향한 사람이다.
   > 참고 대부분의 사람들은 여기 "turned" 앞에 하이픈을 사용하지 않으나, 구조로 보아 하이픈을 사용하는 것이 바람직하다고 필자는 믿는다.

4 많은 성취지향적인 사람들은 남들보다 뒤떨어질까봐 걱정한다.

5 그 한국 태생의 미국 소설가는 작가로서 30대 초기에 인정을 받았다.

6 한국인들의 손님에 대한 환대는 세계적으로 유명하다.

7 그러나 일부 흑인들은 새 행정부에 대해서 기다려 보자는 태도를 취하고 있다.
   > 참고 여러분, 우리는 이제 종착역 가까이에 와 있습니다. 마지막 역을 떠날 때까지, 그리고 이 역을 떠난 뒤에도 여러분의 영어실력 배양을 위한 영양분 섭취를 게을리하지 마세요. 예를 들어, 바로 위의 예문을 충분히 소화했다면, 다음에 주어진 내용을 영어로 나타낼 수 있어야 합니다.
   > "그 나라는 미국에 대해서 마치 하인처럼 굽신거리는 태도를 취해 왔다."
   > → That country has taken a servile attitude toward the United States of America.
   > 이렇게 하는 것이 가장 빠른 시일 안에 영어를 정복할 수 있는 길이라는 것을 언제나 명심하세요.

8 그것은 잭 케네디와 같은 정치학도에게는 일생에 한 번 있는 귀중한 기회였다.

9 어떤 사람 왈 추수감사절을 넓은 가슴을 가진 칠면조와 좁은 마음을 가진 친척들과 지낼 작정이라는구먼.(여러분, 웃으세요!)

10 지지자들은 신속배치군을 창설하려는 카터 행정부의 노력을, 쇠퇴했다고 생각되는 미국의 군사력에 대한 늦었지만 없는 것보다는 더 나은 처방으로 보고 있다.

11 1920년대 초기 이래로 사뭇, 연방정부의 예산청장들은 "사용하지 않으면 잃는다"는 신드롬에 대해서 불평을 해왔는데, 이것은 신기한 질병으로서 정부 관청들로 하여금 — 연말에 예산이 남았을 때에 그것이 초래할 일을 염려해서 — 무척 애를 쓰고 머리를 짜서 받은 예산을 확실하게 한푼도 남김없이 쓰도록 노력하게 만들고 있다.
   > 주의 인용부호도 하이픈처럼 형용사를 만드는 구실을 한다는 점에 주의하라.

12 그녀는 직업학교에서 용접을 공부했는데, 알루미늄 회사에 일자리를 얻으려고 지원했을 때에 예상대로 "당신 그게 정말이요?" 하는 눈초리로 사람들은 그녀를 맞이했다. 그녀는 설득을 통해서 일자리를 하나 얻었는데, 하루에 110마일을 통근해야 했다. 그것 때문에 그녀는 할 수 없이 1년 뒤에 그 직장을 그만두어야 했으나, 자랑스럽게 그 때 일을 회상한다. "제가 떠날 때에 그 회사 부사장님께서 말씀하셨습니다, 제가 어쩌면 그분이 그때까지 고용한 가장 훌륭한 알루미늄 용접공이었다고 말이에요."

13 고장을 막는 장치를 갖추고 있고, 잘못을 점검하는 그 컴퓨터는 자체의 고장까지도 찾아내어 수리를 지시했다. 어떤 것이 잘못되면, 그것은 자체를 점검해서 메시지를 내보내 조작하는 사람에게 무엇이 잘못되었는지와 그것을 수리하는 방법을 일러주었다.

EXERCISE 39

1 그녀는 식사를 조절해서 몸무게를 20파운드 줄였다.

2 그는 대개 잠을 자서 피로를 떨쳐버린다.

3 그가 나를 화나게 하면, 나는 계단을 내려가 내 우편함으로 갔는데, 이것은 단순히 걸어서 화를 떨쳐버리기 위해서였다. 우편물을 보고 싶은 마음은 별로 없었다.

4   웃어 넘길 수 있는 능력은 사회생활에서 많은 난처한 입장을 면하게 해줄 것이다.

5   38세에, 20년 동안 폭음한 뒤에, 오늘은 맹세하고 술을 끊었다. 가끔 이 맹세를 어긴 것을 제외하고, 그는 남은 29년 동안 술을 마시지 않았다.

6   그녀는 자기 리무진 안에서, 두 여자와 함께 바보스러운 머리가 떨어져 나가라 지껄여대고 있었다.

7   남자 아이들은 15세나 16세에 이르면, 머리가 떨어져 나가라 먹어댄다.

8   안내원은 우리가 흥미있는 모든 것을 보기를 무척이나 원해서 우리를 많이 걷게 해서 녹초가 되게 했다.

9   발을 딛고 설 공간이 거의 없는 곳에서 위엄을 딛고 선다는 것은 어리석은 일일 것이다.

10 학기 중 휴가 기간에 우리 이웃집 딸이 자기 남자친구를 집에서 요리한 식사에 초대했는데, 이 초대를 그는 열광적으로 받아들였다. 저녁식사 때에 그는 곧 세 번째 많은 음식을 먹고 있었는데, 이 때 모두가 놀라서 지켜보고 있었다.

    네 번째 접시 가득 음식을 먹은 뒤에 그는 주인 여자에게 요리를 잘 했다고 칭찬해 주었다. 그러고 나서, 자기 접시 곁에 있는 디저트용 포크를 보고, 그는 물었다, "이 포크 어디에 쓸 거죠?"

    주저하지 않고 그의 여자친구는 대답했다, "그건 첫 번째 포크가 닿아서 못 쓰는 경우에 대비하기 위한 거야."

EXERCISE 40

1   a. smiled

    b. nodded

2   a. 나는 병으로 말미암아 한 달을 놀면서 보냈다.

    b. 그들은 하루가 끝나면 노래를 불러서 피로를 쫓아버렸다.

    c. 그는 언젠가 하룻밤을 꼬박 어니스트 헤밍웨이와 함께 술을 마시고 얘기하면서 보냈다.

    d. 한두 시간 정도 재미있는 이야기(소설)를 읽으면서 보내는 것보다 더 즐거운 방법은 없다.

    e. 넉 달에 세 번째 나의 남편은 도박을 해서 자신의 2주치 봉급을 몽땅 날려버렸다. 나는 그를 떠나고 싶지 않다. 우리에게는 아주 훌륭한 아이 셋이 있다. 내가 미치기 전에 어떻게 했으면 좋겠는지 얘기해 달라.

3   a. 아무도 그 논쟁이 빨리 끝나리라 기대하지 않는다.

    = No one expects that the controversy will come to an early end.

    이 표현보다 처음에 주어진 표현이 훨씬 더 경제적이라는 점에 주의하세요.

    b. 대부분의 경제학자들은 물가상승의 압력이 빨리 끝나지 않을 것으로 보고 있다.

    c. 매우 화가 난 의장은 의사봉을 쳐서 회의를 잠시 정지시켰다.

    d. 호메이니는 2월 이래로 인질문제에 대한 논평을 회피해 왔는데, 2월에는 그 문제를 의회로 넘겼다. 그가 어쩌면 또다시 이 문제에 개입하기로 작정했는지도 모르는데, 이것은 이란의 비종교적인 온건파 — 이들은 이 위기(인질문제)를 빨리 끝내는 것을 찬성한다 — 와 신앙심이 깊은 강경파 사이에 이란인을 분열시키고 이란의 국정을 마비시키는 문제를 제거하기 위해서인 것 같다.

    e. 지난 주 어느 날, 정확하게 오전 11시에, 공습 사이렌이 이스라엘 전역에 걸쳐서 단 한 번 높은 음조로 '완전 해제' 신호를 2분간 울렸다. 그러자 전국이 잠잠해졌다. 예루살렘의 심장부에 있는 야파 가에서는, 보행인들이 가던 길에서 얼어붙은 듯이 멈춰섰다.

한가로이 어정거리던 국경지방의 군인들은 재깍 차렷자세를 취했다. 자동차들은 교차로 중간에서 브레이크를 밟아 정지했다. 버스 승객들은 자리에서 일어섰다. 사람들이 전국에 걸쳐서 모두 그랬듯이. 상점과 식당, 사무실에서는 대화가 중지되고, 포크가 내려졌으며, 타자기와 사무기계가 잠잠해졌다. 이 날은 이스라엘의 현충일이었다. 조용히 행동을 삼가하는 가운데, 이스라엘인들은 1948년에 이스라엘 국가가 탄생된 이래 치러 온 다섯 차례의 전쟁에서 사망한 사람들을 추모했다.

그 다음, 해가 지자, 다음 날의 행사가 시작되었는데, 이것은 슬픔이 아니라 기쁨 속에서였다. 추도일 다음에는 축제분위기의 독립일이 뒤따라왔는데, 금년은 이스라엘이 국가로서 탄생한 지 33년이 되는 해였다. 예루살렘의 킹 조지 가는 교통이 차단되었다. 젊은이들이 팔을 끼고 호라춤(이스라엘의 민속춤)을 추고 축제를 시작함에 따라서. 어떤 축제는 봄철의 자유분방한 분위기에서 밤새도록 계속되었다.

4   a. 언제나 짝수로 양말을 내놓는 세탁기를 발명했으면 좋겠다.

   주의 wish 뒤에 절이 오면 그 절에서는 가정법 과거 또는 과거완료 시제가 사용된다.

   b. 인도는 세계에서 가장 큰 영화산업 가운데 하나를 보유하고 있다. 이 나라의 제작자들은 해마다 400편 이상의 장편 특작 영화를 만들어낸다. 수요가 끝이 없어서 이 산업은 교대근무제로 운영되며, 단 하루도 완전히 문을 닫는 날이 없다. 영화관은 심지어 오전 9시라는 이른 시각에 문을 연다.

   c. 칩을 사용하려는 저돌적인 움직임 때문에 이 나라의 자동차 제작업자들은 칩을 응용한 새로운 부품을 만들어내기 위한 걷잡을 수 없는 경쟁에 들어가게 되었다. 도요타가 작년에 세계 최초로 칩에 의해 작동되는 음성 합성기 — 이것은 운전자에게 연료와 유동액이 부족하다는 것을 경고해 준다 — 를 도입하자, 닛산 자동차도 수주일 이내에 이와 경쟁적인 제품을 만들어냈다.

   d. 젊은 치버는 가문의 전통을 따라 세이어 아카데미에 다녔으나, 그 후 17세에 담배를 피우고 게으름을 부려서 퇴학당하는 데에 성공했다. 일 년이 안 되어, 그의 단편 소설 〈퇴학당한〉이 〈뉴 리퍼블릭〉에 실렸다. 그는 얼마 동안 보스턴에서 형 프레드와 지내다가, 맨해튼에 값싼 방을 하나 구해서 방세를 내기 위해 단편소설을 타자기로 두들겨 냈다. 22세에, 그는 한 편을 〈뉴 요커〉지에 팔았는데, 그와 이 잡지가 함께 성장했다.

   e. 한 코미디언이 바르샤바 라디오 방송에서 어떤 선생이 유리는 모래로 만들어진다는 것을 설명하려고 했다는 얘기를 했다. 그러자 아이들은 유리가 모래로 만들어진다는 것은 터무니없는 생각이라고 웃음을 터뜨렸다. 어째서 깔깔대느냐는 질문을 받자, 한 아이는 이렇게 대답했다. "아, 저희는 저희들에게 그렇게 가르치도록 당국에서 선생님에게 강요하고 있다는 걸 알고 있습니다."

   폴란드 당국은 선생님들이 많은 것을 학생들에게 가르치도록 강요해 왔는데, 이제 폴란드인들은 일을 바로잡기를 원한다. 수개월 동안의 협상 끝에, 독립(자유)교사 노조는 역사 교과서의 내용 — 소련과 관련된 내용을 포함해서 — 을 대대적으로 고치도록 관리들을 설득했다. 이제부터는, "교과내용을 사실에 바탕을 두어야 한다"고 선생님들은 주장하고 있다.

   작업은 이미 시작되었다. 일부 교과서들은 '계몽 위원회'의 지도 아래 개정 중에 있는데, 이 위원회의 위원장은 마리안 마렉 드로조프스키로, 그는 폴란드에서 가장 존경받는 역사학자 가운데 한 사람이다. 저자들도 새로운 교재를 만들어내고 있고, 출판업자들은 보다 더 크고, 더 현대적인 교과서들을 내놓을 계획이다. 특히, 이 개정작업에서 현행 교육과정의 지나친 해석이 일부 삭제될 것이다. 해석 대신에, 아이들에게 사실을 제시해서 스스로 결론에 도달하도록 고무시킬 것이다. "진실은 누구에게나 어려운 것이다"라고 한 전문가가 말하고 있다. "그러나 그것은 우리 아이들을 교육하는 유일한 방법이다."

   여러분, 얼마나 처절한 해학입니까? 사람들이 — 그것도 천진난만해야 할 어린이들이 — 진실을 진실로 받아들이려고 하지 않을 만큼 속아 온 사회! 이런 질식할 듯한 사회에 잠시나마 숨을 돌려서 웃을 수 있는 여유가 없다면 제정신을 갖고 있는 사람들은 모두 제정신이 아닌 사람이 되거나 질식당하는 수밖에 없겠죠. 폴란드인들은 유럽에서 가장 유머 감각이 발달된 사람들로 알려져 있습니다. 이것은 이들의 처절한 역사 속에서 얻어진 자신을 온전하게 보존하기 위한 일종의 보호막이었다고 볼 수 있지 않을까요?

5 방대한 옥스퍼드 영어사전에는 영국영어의 41만 4,825단어가 수록되어 있다. 13권으로 된 이 책은 1884년과 1928년 사이에 드문드문 나왔는데, 1957년에 로버트 버치필드가 첫 최신 증보판을 편집해달라는 제의를 받았다. 지금까지, 그의 노력으로 단 두 권이 나왔는데, 제3권은 현재 작업중에 있고, 마지막 제4권은 1985년까지는 판매될 것으로 그는 희망하고 있다. 그는 이미 자신의 "단어와의 피비린내나는 전쟁"을 끝마치고 벌써 은퇴할 것을 고대하고 있다.

41만 4,825단어 가운데 버치필드가 가장 좋아하는 것은 무엇일까? "Finished"라고 그는 미소를 지으면서 힘주어 말한다. "예를 들어 다음 문장에서와 같은 뜻으로 쓰인 것 말입니다. '난 그 사전을 끝냈다.'"

6 현재 거의 2백만 대의 개인 및 가정용 컴퓨터가 미국에 있는데, 컴퓨터 제작회사들이 대략 2백만 대를 금년에 더 내보낼 예정이다. 타이멕스라는 한 회사에서만 99달러 95센트짜리 컴퓨터를 10초마다 한 대 비율로 만들어내고 있다. 주먹구구식으로, 칼럼니스트인 아트 북월드는 이렇게 말했다. "미국에서 가정용 컴퓨터 한 대가 판매될 때마다, 어딘가에 컴퓨터 과부 한 사람이 생긴다."

"운동 과부, 컴퓨터 과부, 뭐든지 대보세요, 그게 바로 저랍니다"라고 여배우 일레인 그랜트(25세)가 말한다. 석 달 전에, 그녀 남편이 250달러짜리 커모더 VIC 20 한 대를 집에 가져왔다. "저는 가끔 웃지 않을 수가 없어요"라고 그녀가 말한다. "친구들이 오면, 남편은 당장 그들을 끌고 가서 컴퓨터를 보여줍니다. 그들 가운데 일부는 실제로 컴퓨터에 관해서 이해하고 있을지 모르나, 대부분은 단지 거기 서서 미소를 지으며 어서 그 자리를 벗어나고 싶어 못 견딘답니다." 그녀의 남편 제리(42세)는 보스턴 교향악단의 바이얼리니스트인데, 아홉 살인 아들 데이비드와 지금 한가한 시간에 컴퓨터로 게임을 즐기고, 작곡하며, 복잡한 프로그램을 해독하면서 지낸다. "남편은 저에게 관심을 좀 보여달라고 간청해 왔지만, 전 그럴 수가 없어요"라고 일레인이 고백한다. "그건 보기 흉측해요. 불쾌한 소리를 내고요. 화면 뒤에는 수많은 것들이 붙어 있죠. 헤어 드라이어도 내가 손을 대면 저절로 망가지는데, 어째서 제가 컴퓨터에 손을 대야 하나요?"

많은 여성들은 컴퓨터 혁명에 가담하지 않고, 무척 애를 써서 남편들과 평화 협정을 마련해냈다. 캘리포니아 주 팰러앨토에서, 한 여성은 아타리 상사의 프로그래머와 5년을 지냈는데, 그가 자신의 일에 대해서 마음대로 얘기할 수 있는 시간을 15분으로 제한했다. 애틀랜타에서 과거에 카메라광이었다가 가정용 컴퓨터로 전환한 어떤 사람의 아내는 여행을 이용해서 자기들의 관계를 보호한다. 그녀는 이렇게 얘기한다. "저는 그이를 컴퓨터에서 떼어놓기 위해서 주말마다 호숫가의 우리만의 장소로 가야 한다고 우긴답니다."

7 a. 본지 〈타임지〉 특파원 베리 캘브가 이탈리아에서의 테러에 관한 글을 읽고 있을 때 공교롭게도 로마 지국에 있던 그에게 소식이 왔다. 교황 요한 바오로 II세가 성 베드로 광장에서 저격을 당했다고. 그는 그동안 벌어진 이 무서운 사건에 대해서 자기에게 입수된 자료를 모아서 기사를 작성한(작성해서 본사로 보낸) 뒤에 교황의 상태에 대해서 알아보려고 게멜리 병원으로 달려갔다.

b. 신임 총리는 초기에 전임자의 국내 사업들 가운데 많은 것 — 예를 들어, 문맹자를 위한 읽기와 쓰기 교육과 실업 구제 따위 — 을 계속해 나가기로 결정했다. 그 결과로 그는 앞으로 3년간에 걸쳐서 적어도 25억 달러가 소요될 사업에 자신이 묶여 있다는 사실을 알게 되었다. 그러한 비용을 부담하고 자메이카의 수지적자(작년에 7억 달러)를 점차 줄이기 위해서, 신임 총리 — 그는 하버드 대학에서 교육받은 사회학자에서 정치가로 전향했다 — 은 복잡한 재정 방안을 마련했다.

c. 그런데 워싱턴 시에 대한 사람들의 사랑은 아직도 더 간접적인 상황 속에서 나타난다 — 즉 조용히 그리고 허심탄회하게 이 도시를 방문하는 사람들과 이곳 주민들이 한결같이 권력에 대한 배경이라든지 권력 따위의 얘기를 집어치우고 자기도 모르게 애국자가 되어 이 도시의 기념비 사이를 한가로이 거니는 순간에 말이다. 어린이들은 더욱

노골적이다. 이들은 링컨의 커다란 귀를 보고 고함을 치거나, 국회의사당 계단을 한꺼번에 세 개씩 뛰면서, 마치 이곳을 소유한 것처럼 행동한다.

어린이들이 요즈음에는 의사당 계단에서 그렇게 뛰어다닐 수가 없다. 계단에 목재를 쌓아놓고, 인부들이 대통령 취임식을 위한 관람대를 만들고 있기 때문이다.

참고 이 구절은 영어를 우리말로 옮기는 데 관심이 있는 분들에게는 좋은 참고자료가 될 수 있으리라 생각됩니다.

d. 팔레스타인 해방기구의 레바논 철수에 관한 협정 — 이것은 세심한 외교활동의 개가(승리)였다 — 을 마련해낸 사람은 너무도 사람들 모르게 그리고 대중에게 알려지는 것을 싫어하면서 일을 했기 때문에 중동에 있는 그의 고위 동료들 가운데 많은 사람들도 그야말로 그가 어떻게 해나가고 있는지 몰랐다.

11주 이상 동안, 필립 찰스 하비브는 중동을 왕래했는데, 그의 여행일정은 젊은이에게도 힘겨울 정도였을 것이다. 네 차례 심장마비를 겪었고 혈관우회수술을 받은 62세의 관리에게는 더 말할 나위도 없다. 하비브는 약은 물론 자신의 모든 치료기록을 갖고 다녔다. 그는 오후에 잠시 동안 쉬는 것을 좋아하지만, 회담기간 중에는 그럴 시간이 거의 없었다.

8 a. 주요 산업경제국가들은 수출을 통해서 현재의 경기하락추세(불황)에서 벗어날 수 있는 전망이 거의 없다고 보고 있다. 미국 또한 불황 속에 놓여 있는 한.

b. 가난한 사람들은 더 이상 꾸준히 일함으로써 더 나은 삶을 누리리라 기대할 수 없다. 그리고 더 이상 미국인들은 과거의 세대들이 갖고 있었던 커다란 기대를 갖고 있지 않다. 처음으로, 여론조사에 의하면, 보통 미국 시민은 자식들의 생활이 자신의 생활보다 더 좋거나, 아니 심지어 자신의 생활만큼 좋으리라고도 전혀 확신하지 못하고 있다고 한다.

c. 코가 우리의 언어에 얼마나 밀고 들어와 있는지 아세요? 화가 나 있으면, 코가 빠져 있다고 하고, 남의 일에 호기심이 많으면 남의 일에 코를 들이밀기 좋아한다고 하고, 상대를 코 하나 높이 만큼만(약간만) 물리치면, 이겼다고 하고, 코를 맷돌에 처박고 있으면 근면하다고 하고, 코로 이끌려 갈 수 있는 사람은 고분고분하다고 하고, 코를 쳐들고 있으면 거만하다고 합니다.

d. 케네디가 백악관에 들어가서(대통령이 된 뒤에) 첫 번째 한 행동들 가운데 하나는 대통령직에 관한 200권의 책을 주문해서 자기가 쉽게 볼 수 있도록 서가에 꽂아놓게 지시한 것이었다. "루스벨트는 자기 생각의 대부분을 사람들과 얘기하는 데서 얻었습니다"라고 케네디는 역사학자인 제임스 맥그래거 번스에게 말했다. "저는 제 아이디어의 대부분을 독서로부터 얻습니다."

케네디가 가장 좋아하는 책 열 권 가운데 여덟 권은 역사와 전기였다. 그는 407페이지에 이르는 〈로버트 월폴 경 : 정치가의 형성〉이라는 책을 하루 저녁에 다 읽어 치웠다. 중국을 주의깊게 관찰하면서, J. F. K.는 모택동의 책 두 권을 구해달라고 했다. 세계의 문제지역들을 꿰뚫어보려고, 그는 유격전에 관한 체 게바라의 얘기를 탐독했다.

이러한 모든 것이 요사이 강력하게 암시해 주는 바가 있다. 왜냐하면 지미 카터와 로널드 레이건은 둘 다 지금 세계가 자기들이 태어난 시기에 형성된 것으로 보고 있는 것 같았기 때문이다. 카터가 거듭해서 소련을 이해하지 못하고 소련의 조처에 대비하지 못한 원인은 적어도 부분적으로는 그가 미소관계의 역사에 대해서 몰랐다는 데에 있었다고 볼 수 있다. 그가 이룬 대대적인 성공인 캠프 데이비드 평화협정은 분명히 그가 중동분쟁의 역사에 관해서 열심히 연구한 밑바탕 위에서 이루어졌다. 레이건이 국내에서와 국제적으로 취하는 세상을 뒤흔드는 조처는 너무도 흔히 다름아닌 이데올로기로 말미암은 편견에서 나온다. 레이건과 그의 보좌관들은 어떻게 해서 젊은 케네디가 독서와 사고를 통해서 위험으로 가득 찬 한 시대를 안전하게 헤쳐나갔는지를 고려해 보는 것이 좋을 것이다.

e. 산림원 로버트 퍼셸이 요사이 코네티컷의 숲 속을 거닐 때에, 나뭇잎들은 마치 사격수가 그것을 과녁연습으로 사용한 것 같아 보인다. 그리고 딱다구리들이 스타카토식 대위법 멜로디를 딱딱 찍어낼 적에 퍼셸은 산림에 해를 끼치는 동물들의 불길한 소리를 듣는다. "곤충들이 산림을 잡아먹는 소리를

실제로 듣게 되면 무시무시하다"고 그는 말한다.

짚시나방이 북동부 지방에 돌아왔다. 2년 동안 계속해서, 수많은 애벌레들이 떡갈나무를 솜털 같은 갈색의 얇은 막으로 덮고 있고, 장식해 놓은 것처럼 아름다운 자작나무와 산사나무의 봄철의 모습을 앙상한 가지만 남아 있는 겨울철의 모습으로 바꾸어놓고 있다. 1980년에 이 곤충은 메인 주로부터 메릴랜드에 이르기까지 12개 주에서 510만 에이커의 산림을 갉아먹었다. 많은 주에서는 기록적인 피해를 입었는데 ─ 뉴욕 주에서는 250만 에이커가 잎을 잃었는데 이것은 종전 기록의 다섯 배였다 ─ 그런데 금년에는 피해가 훨씬 더 심한 것 같다. 매사추세츠 주의 곤충학자들은 일부 지역에서는 10배 이상으로 잎을 갉아먹을 수 있는 이 곤충의 알 덩어리(이것이 애벌레가 된다)가 있는 것으로 보고 있다. 작년의 곤충으로 말미암은 피해와 계속되는 가뭄으로 약화되어, 많은 나무들이 죽게 될 것이다. 이것은 애벌레들에게 먹힌 잎을 대치할 힘이 이들 나무에게 없기 때문이다. "뉴 잉글랜드 지방 모두가 심각한 문제를 갖게 될 것이다"라고 찰스 슈월브가 경고하는데, 이 분은 케이프 코드에 있는 농무부의 짚시나방 실험실에서 근무한다. "일부 주에서는, 유례없는 피해가 예상됩니다."

우리는 짚시나방과 싸울 때 자연으로부터 도움을 많이 얻지 못한다. 왜냐하면 이 곤충은, 유럽에서 이주해온 것이기 때문에, 미국에 효과적인 천적이 거의 없기 때문이다. 이 해충이 태어난 것은 1869년 어느 프랑스 동물학자가 매사추세츠에서 누에와 짚시나방을 교배시키려다가 10여 마리를 세차게 부는 바람에 날려버렸을 때였다. 이 나방은 미풍과 사람에 편승해서 1905년에는 코네티컷 주에, 1922년에는 뉴욕 주에, 1934년에는 펜실베이니아 주에, 그리고 1954년에는 미시건 주에 이르렀다. 연구원들은 말벌과 파리 같은 수입 기생충으로 이 나방을 억제하려고 시도해왔으나 ─ 지금까지 주목할 만한 성공을 거두지 못했고 ─ 늘 살충제 사용에 다시 의존한다.

짚시나방은 증권시장과 마찬가지로 불황과 호황이 불안정한 주기를 보인다. "만일 우리가 가만히 내버려두면 이 나방은 멸망할 것입니다"라고 매사추세츠 주 곤충피해 통제국의 책임자 찰스 후드가 말한다. "전에는 늘 그랬습니다." 그것이 언제 일어날지는 별도의 문제지만, 궁극적으로 자연은 언제나 포식자와 피식자의 균형을 유지함으로써 자신을 괴롭히는 것들을 억제한다. 과학자들은 대부분의 산림은 최악의 피해로부터도 회복할 수 있다고 확신하고 있다. 이것은 물론, 곤충들이 자기 정원에 있는 단풍나무의 파란 잎들을 가난뱅이의 누더기처럼 만들어 놓는 것을 지켜보는 사람들에게는 거의 위안이 되지 않는다.

9 전쟁이 끝난 뒤에 맥아더는 웨스트포인트로 돌아와서 이 학교의 가장 혁신적인 교장 가운데 한 사람이 되었다. 42세에 그는 결혼을 했는데, 7년 뒤에 이혼했다. 필리핀에 가서 복무한 뒤, 1930년에 워싱턴으로 돌아와서 육군 참모총장이 되었다. 이것은 그의 아버지가 추구했으나 이르지 못한 직책이었다. 2년 뒤에, 맥아더는 "보너스 행군자"라고 불리던 굶주린 재향군인들을 워싱턴에 있는 이들의 캠프로부터 강제 추방하라는 명령을 내렸는데, 이것은 전적으로 불필요했던 조처로 분노와 분개만 남겨주었다. 그는 또한 자기 자신에 대해서 다음과 같이 3인칭을 사용해서 거창하게 얘기하기 시작했다. "맥아더는 야전 사령관이 되겠다고 결심했습니다. 초기단계의 혁명이 진행 중에 있습니다."

사실, 유일한 혁명은 뉴딜 정책으로 판명되었는데, 루스벨트의 행정고문들은 맥아더가 자기들을 의심하는 만큼 마찬가지로 의혹의 눈으로 맥아더를 바라보았다. 1935년에 참모총장직을 떠난 뒤에, 그는 미국 육군에서 물러나, 필리핀에서 거의 존재하지 않는 거나 다름없는 군대를 조직하는 일을 떠맡았는데, 필리핀은 미국으로부터 독립할 준비 중에 있었다. 누가 ─ 맥아더 자신을 포함해서 ─ 보더라도, 이 일은 막다른 골목이었다.

10 또 하나의 방법은 어떤 정부의 규제들을 없애는 것이 될 것이다. 오늘날, 예를 들어, 새로운 약이나 살충제 또는 제초제를 생산하는 회사들은 무려 13년 동안이나 발버둥치면서 미로처럼 복잡한 여러 가지 규제를 거쳐서 절차를 밟아야만 제품을 시장에 내놓을 수가 있다.

11 스위스 사람들의 농담에 의하면, 스위스의 전투기에는 좋은 브레이크가 필요하다고 한다 — 왜냐하면 마하 2 제트 전투기가 정확하게 4.73분에 스위스를 쏜살같이 가로질러 지나갈 수 있기 때문이다. 지구상의 가장 작은 나라 가운데 하나로, 이 나라는 웨스트 버지니아보다 더 작다. 그러나 유럽에서 가장 오래된 공화국으로 이 나라는 면적을 훨씬 초월하는 힘과 영향력을 행사한다. 엄격하게 말해서 자연자원이라고는 아무 것도 없는 나라로 — 석유, 석탄, 금, 우라늄이 없음 — 스위스는 그럼에도 불구하고 1978년에 지구상에서 가장 부유한 국가가 되었다. 이 나라의 개인당 국민소득은 급격하게 증가해서 1년에 1만 3,853달러라는 비길 데 없는 수준에 도달함으로써, 온통 석유로 배가 가득 채워져 있는 쿠웨이트를 2위로($1만 3,000), 그리고 미국을 초라한 8위로($9,646) 밀어냈다.

12 수술 후 회복 중에 있을 때에, 우리 이웃사람은 성질이 고약해져서 10분간 하루에 세 차례 산책하라는 의사의 지시를 따르기를 거부했다. 그의 아내가 달래기도 하고, 아첨을 떨면서 꾀어도 보고, 잔소리도 해보았지만, 아무것도 그를 움직이지 못했다.
　　절망적인 상황에서 그녀에게 번쩍 해결책이 떠올랐다. 하루에 세 차례 그녀는 집안에 있는 모든 전등을 켰다. 그녀의 남편은 이런 낭비에 벌벌 떨었고, 그가 걸어다니면서 전등을 끄는 데에 하루에 세 차례 10분씩 걸렸다.(참 어지간 하군요!)

EXERCISE 41

1　"내가 알기로 그 은행은 출납계원을 찾고 있다지."
　　"난 한 달 전에 한 사람을 채용한 걸로 생각하고 있었다네."
　　"바로 그 사람을 찾고 있다는 말일세."
　　주의 look for 1) 구하다 2) 찾다

2　남편과 아내가 벽난로 앞에 앉아 있었다. 아내가 물었다. "당신 저 불 속에서 모습들을 볼 수 있으세요?"
　　"그래, 여보"라고 남편이 대답했다.
　　"어떤 종류의 모습들이죠?" 아내가 계속해서 물었다.
　　"나무 1코드에 40달러라는 숫자의 모습 말이야"라고 그는 한숨을 쉬면서 말했다.
　　어답 Humor에는 이런 잔인한 면이 있습니다. 아름다운 벽난로의 불꽃 속에서 아름다운 모습을 생각해 내려는 아내의 낭만적인 세계와 그것과는 너무도 동떨어져 있는 남편의 현실세계가 '잔인한 조화'를 이루고 있군요. 허나 웃을 수 있는 마음의 여유마저 없다면 인생은 얼마나 더 잔인하게 느껴질까요!

3　어떤 국회의원의 아내가 한밤중에 그를 힘차게 뒤흔들었다.
　　"일어나요, 여보!" 그녀가 작은 소리로 미친 듯이 말했다. "'집'에 도둑이 있어요."
　　"그럴 리 없어"라고 그는 졸리는 목소리로 대답했다. "상원이라면 몰라. 하원에는 천만에."
　　참고 이 유머는 언어상의 차이 때문에 한국어로는 영어에서 얻는 웃음을 얻어내지 못합니다. 불행하게도, 이것은 어쩔 수 없는 일인 것 같군요. 궁여지책으로 '집'이란 단어에 작은 따옴표를 붙여보았지만, 별 효과가 없군요. 번역을 하다보면 가끔 이런 고충에 부딪히게 됩니다. 유명한 얘기가 있죠. 어떤 외국인이 연설을 하던 중에 재미있는 농담을 하나 했는데, 그의 얘기를 통역하던 사람이 바로 이런 고충에 놓이게 되었습니다. 그 연사의 얘기를 문자 그대로 옮겼다가는 아무도 웃지 않을 테니까, 그는 궁여지책으로 이렇게 말했다고 합니다. "여러분, 지금 이분이 재미있는 농담을 했습니다. 웃어주시기 바랍니다."

4　세 사람이 시끄러운 낡은 차를 몰고 런던으로 가고 있었는데, 말을 알아듣기가 어려웠다. 이 도시에 가까이 다가가고 있을 때에, 한 사람이 물었다. "여기가 웸블리인가?"
　　"아냐, 목요일이야."
　　"나도 그래. 멈춰서 한잔 하세."
　　주의 Wembley → Wednesday
　　　　Thursday → thirsty

5　우리 남편은 영업시간에 돌보는 사람이 없이 자기가 경영하는 레코드 가게를 떠나야 하는 경우에는, 문에 쪽지를 붙여놓는다. 내가 어느 날 이 가게를 찾아갔더니 기다리는 고객 두 사람이 다음 쪽지를 보고 껄껄 웃고 있었다. "다섯 개의 미누에트 속의 바흐"(5분 뒤에 돌아옴).
　　주의 Bach는 Back 대신에, minutes는 minutes 대신에 사용되었음.

6 전형적인 가족의 저녁이었다 — 아버지는 자기가 좋아하는 의자에 앉아서 신문을 읽고 있었고, 아기는 아버지 발 밑에서 장난감을 갖고 놀고 있었으며, 어머니는 자기가 좋아하는 의자에 앉아서 뜨개질을 하고 있었다. 아버지가 우연히 아기를 내려다 보았다. "아기가 콧물을 흘리고 있네"라고 그가 말했다.

어머니는 넌더리가 나서 뜨개질하던 것을 무릎 위에 내려놓았다. "도대체 당신은 경마밖에 생각하지 않나요?"

7 어린시절부터 안경을 끼어온 친구 한 사람이 콘택트 렌즈 한 쌍을 사기로 결정했다. 그녀는 안경 때문에 인기가 없어서 남들이 춤을 출 때 "벽쪽에 앉아서 구경만 하던" 시절을 이것이 끝내 주기를 바랐다.

그 다음 주, 우리는 우리가 사는 지역에서 베풀어지는 무도회에 갔는데, 거기서 새로운 외모 때문에 그녀에게 춤을 청하는 사람들이 많았다. 집으로 돌아오는 길에, 그녀는 신이 나서 말했다. "이제 어째서 이것을 '콘택트'(접촉) 렌즈라고 부르는지 알겠어."

8 어린 자니의 아버지가 보니까 그가 애완용 토끼를 잡고 물었다. "5+5, 그게 얼마지?"

"너 뭘 하는 거니?" 자니의 아버지가 어리둥절해서 물었다.

"저희 선생님께서 말씀하시기를 토끼는 빠르게 multiply한대요." 자니는 화가 나서 대답했다.

"그런데 이 멍청이 토끼는 더하기조차 못해요."

주의 선생은 multiply를 "번식하다"라는 뜻으로 사용했으나, 자니는 그것을 "곱하다"라는 뜻으로 이해했다.

9 한 시장 후보자가 지난번 선거 기간중 어느 날 아침 8시에 샌디에이고의 한 사무실 건물 앞에 서서, 한 예쁜 여자가 입구쪽으로 달려갈 때에 자기 손을 내밀었다. "안녕하세요"라고 그가 말했다. "전 리 허바드입니다. 전 시장이 되려고 뛰고 있는 중입니다."

그녀는 미소를 지었지만 달리는 속도를 늦추지 않았다. "안녕하세요"라고 그녀가 말했다. "전 태니어 스미스인데요, 전 직장으로 뛰고 있는 중입니다."

10 내가 근무하는 병원 응급실이 빌리 캐시라는 이름의 아이가 어머니와 함께 병원으로 오고 있는 중이라는 연락을 받았다. 새로 들어온 직원이 이들이 도착하는지 보라는 지시를 받았다.

이 직원은 마치 군인처럼 입구에서 자기 자리를 잡고 서 있었다. 마침내 문이 열리고, 한 어린이와 여자가 보이자, 이 종업원은 쏜살같이 앞으로 나가서 소리쳤다. "애가 캐시입니까?"

다소 놀라서 어리둥절했지만, 그 여자는 침착하게 대답했다. "아, 저는 보험에 들어 있죠. 그거면 됩니까?"

11 어떤 스포츠 만찬장에서 많은 연사들이 따분하고 장황한 얘기를 한 뒤에, 한 유명한 운동선수는, 일부 손님들이 잠이 든 것을 보고, 자기 연설을 이렇게 시작했다. "친구 여러분 그리고 목례지기 여러분."

12 작년에, 젊은 첼리스트로서, 나는 Bowdoin 대학 여름 음악제에서 열심히 일하고 있었다. 자신의 편지에, 우리 어머니께서는 가끔 내가 관심을 갖고 있는 소재에 관한 기사를 잘라서 함께 보내주셨다. 그런 동봉한 기사 하나는 금년 23세의 인도네시아 태생 미국 첼리스트인 요 요 마에 관한 고무적인 기사였다. 이 기사의 위쪽 가장자리에 어머니께서 다음과 같이 써놓으셨다. "요 요 마에 관한 이 기사를 재미있게 읽어라…너의 마마(Your Mama)로부터!"

13 군관련 라디오 방송국을 이 방송국에 속해 있는 민간인 및 군 라디오 방송 담당자들은 흔히 MARS라고 부른다. 이들이 하는 일의 일부는 라디오를 통해서 전화 "통신"을 보내서 해외에서 근무하는 군인들로 하여금 고국에 있는 가족들 및 친구들과 얘기를 할 수 있도록 해주는 것이다. 최근에, 한 방송국 직원이 한 여자에게 전화를 걸어서 이렇게 자신의 신분을 밝혔다. "안녕하세요, 여기는 MARS 라디오 방송국입니다." 잠시 침묵이 흘렀다. 그러다가 그녀가 흥분한 목소리로 대답했다. "안녕하세요, 화성. 안녕하세요, 화성. 여기는 지구입니다."

14 어떤 말 사육가가 자신이 갖고 있는 가장 훌륭한 성숙한 암말 가운데 한 마리를 우리에게 보

여주고 나서 그 말의 새끼를 가리켰다. "이 귀여운 새끼 암말은 4월 첫째 날에 태어났습니다"라고 그가 말했다. "우리는 이 말을 에이프릴 포울이라고 이름지었습니다."

15 어느 백화점의 몸에 꼭 끼는 기성복 청바지 계산대에서 엿들은 이야기. "이걸 넓적다리에 맞는지 입어 봐도 괜찮습니까?"

> 여담 이런 얘기를 듣고 웃을 수 있어야 영어의 유머 감각이 제대로 발달되어 있다고 볼 수 있습니다.

16 어떤 남자가 이웃사람에게 얘기하고 있었다. "저 있잖아! 난 근사한 새 캐딜락 한 대를 아내에게 사주었다네."
상대방 남자는 친구의 어깨를 두드리면서 말했다. "어, 자네 거래를 꽤 잘 한 것 같네."

> 주의 이 얘기의 유머는 'B에게 A를 사주다'는 뜻으로 상대방이 한 얘기를 'B를 A와 바꾸다'는 뜻으로 졸지에 전락시켜 놓은 데서 발생합니다.

17 여러 해 동안 나는 어떤 대학교에서 극장장으로 있었다. 내 아내가 언젠가 고객 한 사람에게서 다가오는 주말 계획에 관한 질문을 받은 적이 있었다. "저는 'husband's play' (남편의 연극) — 듣는 사람은 이것을 'husbands play' (남편들이 놀다)로 둔갑시켰음 — 를 구경할까 생각 중이에요"라고 아내가 대답했다. "아," 고객은 말했다. "당신은 남편을 몇이나 갖고 있는 거예요?"

18 어떤 선원이 파선을 당해서 어떤 작은 섬에서 수개월 동안 열두 명의 남자 선원들과 한 명의 여자 선원과 함께 지냈다. 그가 마침내 구조되어 집에 돌아오자, 중년을 넘은 그의 숙모 한 사람이 그토록 많은 남자들과 여자 혼자만 무인고도에 놓여진 상황에 매우 관심이 있었다. "그 여자에 대해선데", 숙모가 말했다, "그 여자는 '정숙했느냐 (chaste)?'" — 듣는 사람은 이것을 '추격당했느냐 (chased)로 둔갑시켰음.
그 선원은 대답했다. "아, 예, 숙모님 — 온통 섬 전체에 걸쳐서 말이에요!"

여담 뜻풀이

p22 가게들의 장사가 금년에는 워낙 나쁜지라 어제 보니까 어떤 들치기가 살금살금 어느 카운터에 다가가더니 뭔가를 남겨놓고 가더라.

p23 때때로 아이가 시험을 잘 못 보는 것은 시험에 대한 불안 때문이다. 불안하고, 억지로 기억하려고 애쓰다 보니 결국은 시험 시간 중에 아무것도 기억할 수 없게 된다.

p30 어느 날 아침 남편이 통근 기차를 놓칠 것 같아서 우리 가족 모두는 어떻게든 도우려고 옷을 꺼내주고 가방을 챙겨주고 하면서 정신없이 이리저리 뛰어 다녔어요. 두 살짜리 빌리도 뭔가 하고 싶었지만 계속 방해만 되었지요. 그러다 이 꼬마가 마침내 한 가지 남은 일을 찾긴 했는데요. 그건 얼른 앉아 아빠의 아침식사를 먹어 치우는 일이었어요.

p33 열성적이고 싶으면, 열성적으로 행동하라.

p36 우리는 언제나 살려는 준비만 하나 한번도 살지는 않는다. —랠프 월도 에머슨
인간이 태어나는 것은 살기 위해서지, 사는 것을 준비하기 위해서가 아니다.
—보리스 파스테르나크
인생은 우리가 다른 계획들을 세우고 있는 동안 벌어지는 것이다. —쟌 레논

p39 내가 좋아하는 대학 교수님 한 분은 익살스런 유머로 유명했다. 어느 1학년 반 학생들에게 자신의 강의의 기본 지침에 대해 설명하면서 이렇게 말씀하셨다. "자, 내 강의가 종종 딱딱하고 지루해질 수 있다는 것을 나는 압니다. 그래서 강의 시간에 여러분이 시계를 보는 것은 상관하지 않습니다. 그러나 시계가 아직 가고있는지 확인해 보려고 책상에다 두드려 보는 것은 반대합니다."

> 문맥 object to = mind

p47 어떤 선교사가 밀림에서 으르렁거리는 사자

와 마주치게 되었다. "널 잡아먹겠다."고 사자가 으르렁거렸다.
"죽을 준비를 하라."
그러자, 선교사는 무릎을 꿇고, 전에 했던 것보다 더 열렬히 기도했다. 그러다가 조심스럽게 손가락 사이로 빠끔 내다 보았더니, 사자도 무릎을 꿇고, 앞발로 얼굴을 가리고 있었다. 하늘을 바라보며 선교사가 외쳤다.
"놀라워라, 내 말이 맹수의 마음을 누그러지게 할 수 있다니."
그러자 사자가 발을 내리고 으르렁거렸다.
"조용히 해! 식사 전에 감사기도하고 있는 거니까."

p51 한 승객이 LA발 뉴욕행 비행기에 탑승할 때, 자기를 깨워서 달라스에서 꼭 내리게 해달라고 승무원에게 말했다. 그 승객이 잠에서 깼을 때 비행기는 막 뉴욕에 착륙하고 있었다. 화가 나서, 그 승객은 승무원을 불러서 해명하라고 요구했다. 승무원이 중얼중얼 사과하자, 화가 난 그 승객은 쿵쿵 울리는 걸음으로 비행기에서 내렸다.
"야, 그 양반 화 한번 되게 났구만!" 다른 승무원이 그 잘못한 동료에게 말했다.
"저 분이 화났다고 생각하면," 그 승무원이 대답했다.
"내가 달라스에서 내려 준 사람을 봤어야 하는 건데!"

p58 몇년 전 어느 일요일 아침이었다. 아빠와 나는 늪이 있는 목장에서 소 몇 마리를 옮기려고 갔다. 우리가 개들을 그 주위로 보내자 모든 소들이 출구 쪽으로 향했다―한 마리를 제외하고.
검은 소 한 마리가 늪지 건너편에 남아있었다. 그 암소는 우리를 응시하면서 끊임없이 움매움매 소리를 내며 전혀 움직이지 않았다. 개들이 그 소에게 달려가서 짖어대고, 펄쩍펄쩍 뛰었지만, 그 소는 여전히 꼼작하지 않았다. 마침내 아빠는 참을 수가 없게 되어 우리는 차를 몰고 늪을 돌아서 그 소에게로 갔다.
우리는 소에게 이르렀다, 왜 그 소가 움직이지 않았는지 궁금하게 여기면서. 그 소는 다시 움매움매 소리를 냈는데, 놀랍게도, 늪 안에 있는 어떤 것에게로 머리를 기울이고 있었다. 늪 쪽을 보자, 양 한 마리가 진흙 속

에 목까지 갇혀있는 것이 보였다. 우리는 땅을 파고 열심히 그 양을 잡아 당기기 시작했다. 잠시 뒤에 그 양은 거기서 빠져나왔다. 그제서야 그 소는 움매 소리를 멈추고 타닥타닥 걸어서 그 늪의 측면을 돌아서 출구로 나가기 시작했다. 나는 그 목장에 들어갈 때마다 번쩍 그 날이 다시 떠오르고 그 소가 보여준 용기와 지혜(모두 한 농장 친구를 돕기 위한)가 생각난다.

p60 (생략)

p62 (생략)

p71 한번은, 영화 줄거리에 대해 협의하고 있던 중에, 예측불허의 괴짜 찰리 채플린이 머리 위로 왱왱거리며 날아다니는 파리를 잡으려고 계속해서 손바닥으로 쳤다. 파리채를 가져오라고 해서 여러차례 휘둘렀으나 놓쳤다. 마침내 그 파리가 자기 앞으로 내려 앉자, 채플린은 파리채를 들어 치명타를 가하려했다. 그는 멈추고, 주의깊게 그 파리를 보더니 파리채를 내렸다. "왜 치지 않았소?" 라는 질문을 받자, 늘 하듯이 어깨를 으쓱하며 말했다.
"아까 그 파리가 아니었소."

p73 사람들은 노상 자신들의 환경 때문에 지금과 같은 사람이 되었다고 한다. 나는 환경이 그렇게 한다고 생각하지 않는다. 이 세상에서 출세하는 사람들은 일어나서 자기들이 바라는 환경을 찾아보고, 찾지 못할 때에는 그런 환경을 만드는 사람들이다. ―버나드 쇼

p74 어떤 여자가 옷을 벗은채로 집안일을 하고있을 때에 초인종이 울렸다.
"누구세요?" 그녀가 물었다. '블라인드 맨' 이라는 대답이 들렸다.
여자가 문을 열자, 남자가 말했다.
"이 블라인드 어디다 걸까요, 부인?"

p78 찰리, 당신의 시간에 대해 경고하겠어요.
그저께 밤에, 당신은 어제 귀가했어요.
지난 밤에, 당신은 오늘 아침에 귀가했어요.
오늘 저녁에, 만일 당신이 내일 귀가하면, 난 여기 없을거예요.

p82 하루는 나폴레옹이 서재에서 책을 찾고 있었다. 마침내 찾긴 했는데, 하필이면 손이 닿지 않는 높은 선반에 있는 것이었다. 직원들 중에서 가장 키가 큰 사람이 앞으로 나서며 말했다.
"제가 하도록 해주십시오. 제가 각하보다 높습니다."
"자네가 더 긴 거지." 황제는 찡그리며 말했다.

주의 high는 지위가 높다는 것을 떠올리게 하는 말이므로 long으로 바꾼 것

p83 약한 심장
아일랜드에서 큰 재산을 상속받게 된 심장 약한 젊은이에 대한 이야기다. 변호사는 많은 재산을 상속받게 되었다는 말을 할 사람으로 교회 신부님이 가장 적격이라고 생각했다. 신부는 "아무 걱정 마세요. 제가 가서 그 젊은이에게 알려 줄게요"라고 말했다.
젊은이가 사는 작은 집에서 신부는 이런저런 얘기를 하다가 물었다. "이보게. 자네가 만약에 돈을, 그것도 아주 많은 돈을 상속받게 된다면 그 돈 대부분으로 뭘 할 텐가?"
"신부님, 참 말하기 쉽지 않네요. 아마도 거의 전부 교회에 쓰시라고 신부님께 드릴 것 같아요." 이 말을 듣자마자 신부는 고꾸라져 죽었다.

p85 내가 아는 사람이 직장에서 승진하게 되자 집에서도 새로운 지위를 누리게 되었어요. 힘든 하루 일을 끝내고 전처럼 녹초가 되어 집에 오지만, 가족들은 더 이상 그를 '투덜이'라고 부르지 않는데요. 그가 이렇게 전하더군요 "이제 가족들은 내가 '간부의 스트레스'를 받고 있다고 한다니까."

p86 사인과 코사인
매일 대낮에 난 오락실에서 비디오 게임을 해요. 하루는 이런 표지가 기계 위에 붙어 있었어요. "바보는 돈을 쉽게 잃는다." 그걸 보고 자존심이 상해서 그 기분 나쁜 종이를 찢어 버렸지요. 그러자 바로 아래에 표지가 하나 더 붙어 있더군요. "진실은 마음을 상하게 하죠, 안 그래요?"

주의 표지와 또 하나의 표지라는 뜻이지만 수학의 sine, cosine과 발음이 같아 더 재미있다.

p89 마이애미에서는 사정이 너무도 어려워서 강도들이 차용증을 받는다.

p94 "갖고 있는 돈을 전부 내게 주시오, 그렇지 않으면 지리가 될거요!"라고 무장 강도가 출납계원에게 말했다.
"'그렇지 않으면 당신은 역사가 될거요(＝죽었소)'라는 뜻 아니에요?'
"과목/화제 바꾸지 마시오!"라고 강도가 쏘아 붙였다.

p104 "당신 제복 위에 붙어있는 인식표가 무슨 뜻입니까?"라고 호기심이 많은 여자가 물었다.
"전 해군/배꼽 외과의사입니다."라고 그가 대답했다.
"맙소사," 그녀가 감탄하며 말했다. "당신들 의사들은 요사이 별걸 다 전문으로 하는군요!"

p109 내가 아내에게 누빈 겉옷을 세탁해달라고 했더니 아내는 세탁 안내 꼬리표를 보고 말했다.
"단독 세탁하라고 되어 있어요. 전기와 물을 절약하기 위해, 단독 세탁해야 할 다른 빨래감이 나올 때까지 기다렸다가 둘을 함께 빨아야겠어요."

p110 어느 성대한 크리스마스 파티에서, 젊은 남자가 매력적인 중년 여인에게 춤을 청했다.
"미안하지만, 전 어린애하고는 춤추지 않아요."라고 여인이 거절했다. 그러자 젊은 남자가 받아쳤다. "미안합니다. 임신중인걸 몰랐군요."

주의 거절하는 이유로 내세운 '어린애하고는'(with a baby)이라는 말을 졸지에 '어린애를 가진/임신한'(pregnant)이란 뜻으로 바꿈으로서 pun이 만들어졌습니다.

p114 정신 나간 교수 세 사람이 기차를 기다리며 기차역에 앉아 있었다. 그 교수들은 생각에 너무 빠져 있어서 기차가 도착하는 것도 모르고 있었다. 그러다 갑자기 그중 한 명이 기차가 막 출발하려고 할 때 알아채서 모두 급히 뛰어갔다. 두 명은 기차를 탔다. 그 모습을 구경하고 있던 사람이 기차를 놓친 세 번째 남자를 위로했다.
"너무 속상해 말아요. 그래도 둘은 탔잖아요." 교수가 대답했다. "알아요. 하지만 그 두 사람은 저를 배웅하러 나온 거예요."

p117 훌륭한 번역은 여인과 비슷하다. 즉, 충실하면 예쁘지 아니하고, 예쁘면 충실하지 아니하다.

  * 그렇다면 여러분은 어떤 '여인'을 택하시렵니까? 그야 물론, 아름다우면서도 충실한 여인이겠죠!

p121 짐 부튼은 스포츠 중계자이자 「볼넷」의 저자인데 그의 책에 대한 반응에 대해 이렇게 말한다.
"피트 로즈는 덕아웃에서 나에게 소리를 질러대곤 했죠, 내가 경기에 대해 너무 많이 드러냈다고. 그러면서 지금 그는 속옷 바람으로 잡지 광고에 나와 자기 자신을 드러내고 있군요."

p126 고인이 된 여배우 Madge Kendal은 세월이 많이 흘렀는데도 어떻게 그렇게 아름다움을 유지하느냐는 질문을 받자, 이렇게 대답했다. "저는 저의 주름살을 지성으로 채우려고 노력해요."

p130 영국 사람들은 특히 자기들 자신을 대상으로 농담하는 것, 자기들 자신을 조롱하는 것을 좋아한다. 내가 생각하기에 이런 것을 할 수 있는 것은 완전히 자신감이 있고 정신적으로 건강한 국민뿐이다. 여기 영국인들이 자신을 비웃는 하나의 방법이 있다.
한 영국 사업가가 은행에 대출을 받으러 갔다. 일부 영국의 업체들이 그러하듯, 그의 사업도 잘 되지 않기 때문이었다.
그 사람의 자격 요건을 검토해 보더니 은행 담당자가 말했다. 사실 손님의 요청을 거절해야 하지만, 제가 승률이 50%인 기회를 드리겠습니다. 자, 제 눈 중에 하나가 의안입니다. 만일 손님께서 어느 쪽이 유리눈인지 맞히면 대출해 드리겠습니다.
고객이 잠깐 담당자의 눈을 주의깊게 살피더니 말했다. "왼쪽 눈이군요."
"맞습니다." 담당자가 말했다.
"대출을 받으시게 됐습니다. 그런데 어느 쪽이 유리눈인지 어떻게 짐작하셨죠?"
"글쎄요." 고객이 말했다. "유리눈이 진짜 눈보다 절 더 동정하는 것 같더라고요."

p131 정확하게
작가 James Thurber는 말을 이용하여 사람들을 즐겁게 했다. 그는 자기가 병원에 머무르고 있을 때에 어떤 간호사에게 써먹은 말장난에 대해 나에게 언젠가 얘기해 주었다. 그는 그녀에게 물었다, 어떤 일곱 글자로 된 단어에 'U'가 세 개 들어있느냐고. 그녀는 생각해 보더니 말했다. "전 모르겠는데요, 그렇지만 그건 틀림없이 예사롭지 않은 것이겠네요."

주의 자기도 모르게 답을 제시하게 하는 고도의 재주! 이것은 최고급 말장난입니다.

p142 크리스마스가 가까왔다. 92세 노인이 세 아들 볼 날을 고대하고 있었다.
첫째가 도착해서 말했다. "성탄 축하해요, 아빠. 죄송해요, 선물을 못 샀어요. 제가 얼마 전에 스노우모빌을 샀거든요."
아버지는 괜찮다고 말했다.
둘째 아들이 몇 분 뒤에 들어와서 말했다.
"성탄 축하해요, 아빠. 선물을 못 사와서 죄송해요. 얼마 전에 새 차를 샀거든요."
아버지는 이해한다고 말했다.
셋째 아들이 걸어 들어와서 말했다.
"성탄 축하해요, 아빠. 선물을 못 사와서 죄송해요. 제가 도박판에서 돈을 많이 잃었거든요."
아버지는 고개를 끄덕였다. "얘들아" 하고 그가 마침내 말했다.
"내가 이 세상을 떠나기 전에 너희들에게 알려주고 싶은 것이 있다. 니들 엄마와 나는 결혼한 적이 없단다."
그럼, 우리는…" 아이들이 일제히 질겁하면서 말했다.
"그럼, 그렇구 말고, 그것도 아주 값싼(=존중받을 가치가 없는 또는 인색한) 것들이기도 하지"라고 노인이 말했다.

p147 재치

어떤 여자가 구두 가게에 들어가서 수십 켤레를 신어 봤으나 제대로 맞는 것이 없었다. 마침내 지루해진 점원이 그녀에게 말했다.
"손님, 한쪽 발이 다른 쪽보다 더 커서 맞는 신발이 없군요."
그 여자는 아무것도 사지 않고 그 가게에서 나갔다. 다음 가게에서 역시 맞는 신발을 찾기가 어려웠다. 마침내 미소를 지으면서 점원이 설명했다.

"손님, 한쪽 발이 다른 쪽보다 더 작다는 거 아세요?"
그 여자는 새 신발 두 켤레를 사 갖고 기뻐하며 그 가게를 떠났다.

p152 　두 런던 토박이가 차를 마시고 있었다. 그들 중 하나가 말했다. "Alfie, 내가 자네를 안 지 지금 55년이 되었지. 이런 말 하기 싫지만, 자넨 잘난 척해. 자네가 아침에 일어나서 밤에 잠자리에 들 때까지 자네가 하는 것은 모두 잘난 척하는 거야."
Alfie는 다소 기분이 상한 것 같았다. 그러더니 친구를 보고 말했다.
"잘난 척한다….(이 유식한) 내가?"

　　주의　마지막엔 불어 moi(영어의 me)까지 동원해서 잘난 척한다.

p157 　정말 놀라운 일을 요사이 해변에서 볼 수 있다. 나이가 30세나 되는 여자가 아직도 몸이 자라서 자기 수영복을 입을 수가 없다니 말이다!

　　주의　이것은 여성들의 비만에 대한 풍자입니다.

p159 **좋은 예**
　마사추세츠 주 Fall River에 있는 Bristol 지역 대학 게시판에 붙어있는 강좌 안내: "결정, 결정, 결정 —이 강좌는 날마다 결정을 내리는 데에 어려움을 겪는 사람들을 위한 강좌입니다. 이것은 지루하고 답답한 문제 해결 방식이 아닙니다.
그러니 자기가 모든 해결책을 갖고 있다고 생각하는 분들은 등록하지 마세요. 만일 당신이 이 강좌에 등록을 하고 싶어하는지 아닌지 모른다면, 당신은 이 강좌를 들을 자격이 있습니다."

p160 　어떤 고용주가 지원자를 면담하면서 말했다. "당신은 높은 임금을 요구하는군요. 경험이 전혀 없는 사람치고는 말이예요."
"글쎄요, 전혀 모르는 일은 하기가 훨씬 더 힘들잖아요."라고 지원자가 대답했다.

p166 　"여러분에게 정확하게 두 시간을 드립니다." 라고 교수가 말했다. 강의실에 가득 찬 학생들에게 시험지를 나눠 주면서.
"어떤 상황에서도 시간이 지난 뒤에는 답안지를 받지 않겠습니다."
두 시간 뒤에 교수가 침묵을 깨고, "시간이 다 됐습니다"라고 말했다. 그러나 한 학생이 계속해서 열심히 답안지를 작성했다. 교수가 시험지 더미 뒤에서 노려보고 있었는데, 그 늦은 학생이 그에게 다가왔다. 거의 15분이나 늦게, 시험지를 등 뒤에 움켜쥐고. 교수가 받기를 거부하자, 그 학생은 몸을 똑바로 세우면서 물었다.
"교수님, 제가 누군지 아세요?"
"아니."라고 교수가 말했다.
"잘 됐군요."라고 말하면서 그는 자기 시험지를 시험지 더미 중간에 쑤셔 넣었다.

p180 **연회장의 대화**
　사람들의 얘기에 의하면 어떤 칵테일 파티에서 T. E. Lawrence에게 나이가 불확실한 어떤 여자가 접근했는데, 그녀는 자기가 사교적으로 아는 사람들의 명단에 유명한 인사들을 보태려고 애쓰는 사람으로 평판이 나 있었다. 파티의 열기를 이용하여 그를 대화에 끌어들이고는 그녀는 이렇게 Lawrence를 공격했다.
"아흔 둘이에요, Lawrence 대령님! 생각해 보세요! 아흔 둘이라니까요!"
"생일 축하합니다, 부인."이라고 그가 대꾸했다.

　　주의　Lawrence 대령의 반격이 기가 막히군요.

p182 　"어쩔 줄 몰라"라는 자신의 신문 칼럼에서 Erma Bombeck은 어떤 California 단체로부터의 초대에 다음과 같은 답장을 썼다.
"어제 귀하의 다채로운 안내책자와 귀하의 나체 목장에 손님으로 와 달라는 초대장을 받았습니다. 저에게는 안 입을 옷이 아무것도 없어서 초대를 거절할 수 밖에 없다고 말씀드리게 된 것을 양해하시기 바랍니다."

　　주의　그녀(Erma Bombeck)가 제시하는 더할 나위없이 훌륭한 변명이 '어쩔 줄 몰라'라는 말과 어울려 아름다움의 극치를 만들어 냅니다.
　　　　　오, 그대들이 이런 아름다움을 즐길 수 있기를!

p183 　75세 신랑이 신혼여행의 밤을 너무 열정적으로 만드는 바람에 젊은 신부는 지쳐버렸다. 신랑이 면도하러 가서 잠깐 쉬는 동안, 신부는 지쳐서 아래층 커피숍으로 내려갔다.
"무슨 일 있으세요, 손님?" 종업원이 물었다.

"손님은, 젊은 신부고 남편 분이 늙으셨는데, 지친 건 손님이시네요."
신부는 이렇게 답했다. "남편이 절 속였어요. 60년 동안 저축해 놓았다고 해서 전 돈 얘긴 줄 알았거든요."

p192 **아버지의 충고**
"성실과 지혜, 이것이 사업에서 성공하는 열쇠란다." 노인이 아들에게 말했다. "내가 말하는 성실은 네가 언제까지 물품을 보내주겠다고 약속을 했으면 파산하는 한이 있더라도 그 약속을 지키는 것을 뜻하는 거야."
"그럼, 지혜는 뭐예요?" 아들이 물었다.
"그런 약속을 하지 않는 것이지."

p204 **환자가 의사에게**
"한번 검진 후에 선생님은 제가 담배를 끊게 하셨어요. 제가 너무 많이 피운다고요. 다음 검진 때는 술을 너무 많이 마신다고 금주하게 하셨고요. 지금 저는 신혼여행에서 막 돌아왔는데요, 이번 검진은 정말 엄청나게 두렵네요!"

주의 금욕하라는 결과가 나올까봐 걱정하는 남자의 마음을 읽을 수 있다.

p205 몽유병 환자를 깨우려고 하지 마라. 부드럽게 유도하여 다시 자도록 하는 편이 더 낫다. 몽유병에 관해 가장 희망적인 점은 아이들 대부분이 자라면서 지도 그리는 것과 악몽 꾸는 것이 없어지듯이 몽유병도 자라면 없어진다는 것이다.

p208 교회협의회 만찬에서 우리 부모님이 목사님과 같은 테이블에 앉게 되었다. 회의가 끝날 때쯤 목사님께서 일어나 마무리 인사말을 하시는데 그것이 꽤 길어졌다. 두서없이 길어지더니 메모의 어느 부분인지 헤매게 되었다. 그게 벌써 세 번째였다. "지금 제가 어디까지 했죠?"라고 그는 멋쩍어서 머리를 긁적거리며 물었다.
청중과 연사 모두가 기뻐하는 일이 다음에 일어났다. 우리 어머니가 큰 소리로 "결론적으로요!"라고 말했던 것이다.

p215 **성공 이야기**
나는 하위 판매부장에 지원한 후보자들을 면접하고 있었고 네 명으로 후보자 리스트를 좁혔다. 마지막 테스트로 지원자들에게 기압계를 주고 그걸 이용해서 특정 건물의 높이를 측정하라는 과제를 내주었다. 가장 독창적인 방법을 쓴 사람을 뽑을 생각이었다.
두어 시간이 지나자 그 사람들이 돌아와 각자 어떻게 했는지 발표했다. 네 번째 지원자가 이렇게 말했다. "면접관님이 찾는 사람은 수학자가 아니라 사람을 다룰 줄 아는 인재라고 생각했습니다. 그래서 건물 관리인에게 제 소개를 하고 이 건물 높이를 말해주면 기압계를 주겠다고 했습니다."
그가 뽑혔다.

p218 내 차가 수리 중이어서 버스를 타고 슈퍼마켓에 갔어요. 쇼핑을 한참 하는데 임신 8개월 반인 지금의 내 상황이 불현듯 떠오르는 거예요. 식료품을 들고 집까지 갈 수가 없잖아요. 그래서 젊은 가게 직원에게 배달해줄 수 있겠냐고 물었더니 이 남자가 한참동안 나를 살펴보더니 이렇게 말하더군요. "식료품만이에요, 아주머니."

주의 deliver에는 '출산을 돕다'는 뜻도 있다.

p221 **그래도**
사람들은 불합리하고, 비논리적이며 자기 중심적이다.
그래도 그들을 사랑하라.
만일 당신이 좋은 일을 하면, 사람들은 이기적인 딴 속셈이 있다고 비난할 것이다.
그래도 좋은 일을 하라.
만일 당신이 성공하면, 당신에게 거짓 친구와 진짜 적들이 생길 것이다.
그래도 성공하라.
만일 당신이 정직하고 솔직하면, 당신은 해를 입을 가능성이 있을 것이다.
그래도 정직하고 솔직하라.
당신이 오늘 하는 선행이 내일이면 잊혀질 것이다.
그래도 선행하라.
가장 큰 생각을 갖고 있는 가장 큰 사람들도 가장 작은 마음(=생각)을 가진 사람들의 총탄에 쓰러질 수 있다.
그래도 크게 생각하라.
사람들은 경쟁에서 불리한 사람들을 지지하

지만 추종하는 것은 유리한 사람들뿐이다.
그래도 일부 불리한 사람들을 위해 싸워라.
당신이 수년을 걸려 건설해 놓은 것들이 하룻밤 사이에 파괴될 수 있다.
그래도 건설하라.
세상 사람들에게 당신이 갖고 있는 가장 좋은 것을 주어도 당신은 그들에게 얼굴을 차일 것이다.
그래도 세상 사람들에게 당신이 갖고 있는 가장 좋은 것을 주어라.

p223 저항의 말

어느 일요일 아침, 미사가 끝나고 제 남편이 신부님에게 성도들 사이에 친밀감이 부족하고 교회에서 서로 인사하기를 꺼려하는 것 같다고 말했어요. 이 말에 동의하며 신부님은 변화를 일으킬 계획을 생각해냈다고 했어요.
　그 다음 주일 미사 중에 신부님은 신도들에게 상황을 설명하고 다음 일요일에는 뒤에 앉은 신도와 다정한 인사를 나누는 시간을 잠깐 갖겠다고 말씀하셨어요. 미사가 끝나고 제 남편이 뒤에 앉아 있던 여자를 보고 "안녕하세요"라고 인사했는데요. 그 여자는 놀라 분개한 표정으로 쳐다보더니, "다음 일요일에 시작하는 거잖아요!"라고 소리치더군요.

p225 대부분의 사람들은 자신이 부과한 한계 속에 너무 많이 갇혀 산다.

p228 미 내무부는 미국 철새들에게 "Wash. Biol. Surv."라고 쓴 금속 조각을 매달아 놓았는데 이것은 워싱턴 생물학 조사부(Washington Biological Survey)를 뜻했다. 그 표시가 바뀌게 된 사연은 아칸소 주의 한 농부가 내무부로 보낸 편지 때문이라고 한다.
"선생님들께, 제가 거기 까마귀를 하나 잡았거든요. 집사람이 거기 붙어있는 대로 요리를 했는데 말이죠. 그러니까 씻고(wash), 끓이고(boil), 내왔죠(serve). 그런데 맛이 최악이더라고요."

p230 내가 일하는 보석 상점의 계산대 위에 어떤 여자가 지친 듯이 손가방을 내려놓았어요. 나는 뭘 도와드릴지를 물었죠. "됐어요, 아가씨." 하고 여자는 말하더니 이러더군요. "난 그냥 정신과 의사랑 상담하는 내내 너무 화가 나서 마음 좀 진정시키려고 온 거예요. 그 의사는 어찌나 고집이 센지 내가 생각하는 방식으로 좀처럼 따라오질 않는 거예요."

p232 남편이 부인에게 이렇게 털어놨다.
"오늘 우리 상사가 갑자기 화를 내더니 나보고 지옥에나 가라고 말을 하는 거야."
"그래서 어떻게 했어?" 부인이 물었다.
"바로 집에 왔지." 남편은 온순하게 대답했다.

p242 동음이의어는 재밌다!

윌톤 래케이는 시카고 모임에서 연설을 하기로 되어 있었다. 늦은 저녁이었고 청중은 다른 연사들 때문에 이미 지루해져 있었다.
사회자가 이렇게 소개했다. "유명 배우, 윌톤 래케이 씨가 다음 연설을 해주시겠습니다."
래케이는 일어나 말했다. "사회자분과 청중 여러분, 제 주소는 뉴욕시티 램즈 클럽입니다." 그가 자리에 앉을 때 우레와 같은 박수갈채가 나왔다.

　주의 address 연설; 주소

p246 아버지: 거짓말쟁이들이 죽으면 어떻게 되는지 아니?
아들: 여전히 거짓말하죠. (가만히 누워 있죠.)

　주의 lie 누워 있다; 거짓말하다.　still 가만히 있는; 여전히